MW01067801

Guatemala in the Spanish Colonial Period

Guatemala in the
Spanish Colonial Period

By Oakah L. Jones, Jr.

UNIVERSITY OF OKLAHOMA PRESS

NORMAN AND LONDON

BY OAKAH L. JONES, JR.

Pueblo Warriors and Spanish Conquest (Norman, 1966)
Santa Anna (New York, 1968)
(ed.) *Federal Control of the Western Apaches, 1848–1886,* by Ralph Ogle (Albuquerque, 1970)
(ed.) *My Adventures in Zuñi,* by Frank Cushing (Palmer Lake, Colo., and Palo Alto, Calif., 1970)
(ed.) *The Spanish Borderlands: A First Reader* (Los Angeles, 1974)
Los Paisanos: Spanish Settlers on the Northern Frontier of New Spain (Norman, 1979)
Nueva Vizcaya: Heartland of the Spanish Frontier (Albuquerque, 1988)
Guatemala in the Spanish Colonial Period (Norman, 1994)

Library of Congress Cataloging-in-Publication Data

Jones, Oakah L.
    Guatemala in the Spanish colonial period / by Oakah L. Jones, Jr.
        p.   cm.
    Includes bibliographical references and index.
    ISBN 0–8061–2603–5 (alk. paper)
    1. Guatemala—History—To 1821.   I. Title.
F1466.4.J66 1994
972.81'03—dc20   93-37914
                                                          CIP

The paper in this book meets the guidelines for permanence and durability of the Committee on Production Guidelines for Book Longevity of the Council on Library Resources, Inc. ∞

1   2   3   4   5   6   7   8   9   10

For my son, Chris, and daughter, Kathy,
in remembrance of our adventures across
and within Guatemala, both known and unknown

Contents

Illustrations

Maps and Plans

ix

Tables

Preface

THE REPUBLIC OF GUATEMALA has been, is, and always will be a focal point of my interest in Latin America. Since my first visit there in the late 1940s, I have been attracted to Guatemala personally and professionally. Its spectacular scenery, diversity of climate, interesting people, colorful and diverse flora and fauna, and importance in all periods of history from the pre-Columbian to the present have all served as a magnet for me and whetted my appetite to learn more about the country and its people each time I have had the opportunity to visit or read about it in published and manuscript sources.

Two factors are chiefly responsible for my continuous interest in Guatemala. First, there are the people, the Guatemaltecos, who are of European, Amerindian (Indian), African, and ladino (mixed) descent. That Guatemalans represent principally the Spanish and Indian heritages of Central America originally led me over forty years ago to study the Spanish borderlands and the northern frontier of New Spain. Their demography has naturally piqued and continued to feed my interests. Second, the vitality, the friendliness, and warm receptions of Guatemalans have constantly encouraged me in the pursuit of my research specialties, which are primarily in the colonial period of Spain in America, and in my teaching, which concentrates on the histories of Central America and Mexico. I have always found enjoyment and learning from serious investigation of Guatemala's rich, challenging, and rewarding history. With an abundance of resources to pursue, Guatemala and Guatemalans have been the principal reasons for this study.

When Doris Morris, of the University of Oklahoma Press, suggested in 1983 that I produce a study of Spanish colonial Guatemala, I was intrigued by the topic and well aware of the country's general historical development, sources for research, and the problems in writing such a work. She was conscious that, in its Civilization of the American Indian Series and its publication of national Guatemalan history, the Press had left a large gap in the nearly three centuries of Spanish presence in and administration of Guatemala—as had other scholarly presses, societies, and commercial publishers. Although some Guatemalan historians had written concerning the Kingdom of Guatemala, no extant studies of colonial Guatemala covered the entire Spanish period, in English or Spanish. I was researching and writing *Nueva Vizcaya: Heartland of the Spanish Frontier* (Albuquerque, 1988), but I decided to use my sabbatical leave in Spain during 1983 and 1984 to investigate manuscripts and published sources pertaining to Guatemala as well as Nueva Vizcaya. Once *Nueva Vizcaya* was published, I concentrated on Guatemala, including a research trip in the summer of 1988 to Guatemala City and reading of monographs pertinent to phases and topics in Guatemala's colonial history. Thus this book is the result of more than eight years of investigation, organization, reorganization, and writing, supplemented by my personal observations during my visits to the country and my teaching over the past thirty years or so.

The purpose of this study is to examine and relate the Spanish colonial experience of Guatemala from conquest and settlement to the establishment of its independence from Spain. If I have a thesis it is that Guatemala was the most important political, economic, social, religious, and cultural region of colonial Latin America between New Spain (Mexico) and Nueva Granada (of which today's Colombia was the central region). Furthermore, colonial Guatemala was not a static entity, but one undergoing constant change and significant development. I have endeavored to show how Guatemala related to the rest of Central America, Latin America as a whole, and Europe in the same period.

I have tried to concentrate on what is today's republic of Guatemala during the Spanish colonial period; however, it is difficult, if not impossible, to separate what was once the province of Guatemala from the Kingdom of Guatemala, which extended from the modern Panama–Costa Rica border to the present state of Chiapas in Mexico. Therefore, from time to time I have included information about both province and kingdom, fully realizing that Guatemala's experience and development were as but a portion of the larger region and that this work is not a comprehensive history of the entire Kingdom of Guatemala. Also, as a result of my earlier works on the Spanish frontiers in northern New Spain, I have been interested in Spanish civil and ecclesiastical officials who served in both northern New Spain and Guatemala during the Spanish period, as well as similarities and differences in institutions, practices, and problems in the two regions. For example, Pedro de Rivera conducted his extensive visit to and investigation of the frontiers of New Spain from 1724 to 1728 and subsequently served as governor, captain general, and president of the audiencia of the Kingdom of Guatemala from 1733 to 1742.

Basically, I have pursued both a chronological and topical approach in relating the narrative of Spain's colonial experience in Guatemala. Chapter 1 provides an introduction to the physical features, topography, regions, climate, flora, fauna, and pre-Columbian Indians before Spanish contact. Chapters 2 and 9 pertain to the conquest, colonization, and independence periods. The remaining chapters cover specific topics ranging over government, the church, Spanish-Indian relations, labor practices, land distribution, the founding of towns, population, society, culture, disasters, and defense against internal and external threats. Throughout I have referred to Guatemala's natives as "Indians" or "Amerindians," knowing full well that anthropologists and other social scientists prefer "Amerindians" or, in the United States, "Native Americans." Yet historians and Spaniards writing in the colonial period referred (and Guatemalans today refer) to these people as "Indios" (Indians).

The archival research was conducted in Spain, Guatemala, Mexico, and some repositories in the United States. In Spain most of my investigation took place in Seville's Archivo General de Indias, especially in the *ramo,* or branch, of "Guatemala," and in Madrid's Archivo Histórico Nacional. I also consulted materials in the Biblioteca Nacional, in Madrid, and in the Archivo General de Simancas and the Escuela de Estudios Hispano-Americanos, in Seville. In Guatemala I consulted the extensive collection in the Archivo General de Centro América in Guatemala City, the best single collection of manuscripts on colonial Central America in the entire region. My research also

took me to the Academia de Geografía e Historia de Guatemala, especially for published works on colonial Guatemala. In Mexico, I
examined materials on specific subjects in the Archivo General de la
Nación, in Mexico City. Finally, in the United States, I consulted
materials in the Edward E. Ayer Collection of the Newberry Library,
Chicago; the Lilly Library of Indiana University, Bloomington; and
the Nettie Lee Benson Latin American Library, Special Collections
Room, of the University of Texas at Austin.

Without others' encouragement and help, this project would have
been infinitely more difficult. I especially want to thank Ralph Lee
Woodward, of Tulane University; William L. Sherman, of the University of Nebraska; and Christopher H. Lutz, director of the Centro
de Investigaciones Regionales de Mesoamerica (CIRMA) in Antigua,
Guatemala, and South Woodstock, Vermont. Frequently cited (with the
works of Murdo J. MacLeod and Miles Wortman) in this study, these
specialists in Central American history not only shared with me their
expertise, published works, and unpublished papers, but also made
suggestions concerning additional resources and methods of approaching
and conducting research in archival collections, especially in Guatemala. Their contributions have been invaluable to me and have greatly
facilitated my own investigations and writing.

In Spain, I am indebted to the staff of the Archivo General de
Indias; its director, Señora Rosario Parra Cala; and especially Srta.
Gloria Muñiz, Don Pedro Romero, and Srta. María Antonia Columar,
who all warmly welcomed me to the archives, taught me the proper
procedures, and continually encouraged and assisted me in locating
legajos (bundles), finding appropriate maps and drawings, and resolv-
ing problems during my eight months in Seville.

At the Archivo General de Centro América in Guatemala City, my
thanks go to its director, Licenciado Guillermo Díaz Romeu, for his
personal reception, encouragement of my project, and introductions
both to his staff members and to finding aids in the archive. In the
research reading room of the repository, Señora Violeta Reyes de
Cerón and Señora Violeta Reyes Rubio helped me with my requests for
legajos and documents, ensuring that I never lacked materials to con-
sult. I especially want to thank Señor Gregorio Concoha Chet, a Cakchiquel Indian from the village of San Juan Suchitepéques, whose

thirty-five years of service in the archive, along with his friendliness and constant willingness to provide assistance, were very valuable to me as I delved into manuscripts there. Licenciado Manuel Rubio Sánchez of the Academia de Geografía e Historia de Guatemala (known as the Sociedad de Geografía e Historia de Guatemala before 7 August 1979) welcomed me to the resources of that important facility and its collections, instructed me about the collections and the publications of the Academia, and kindly arranged for me to purchase some of his and the Academia's published works.

Finally, to the staffs of the Mendel Collection of the Lilly Library at Indiana University, the Edward E. Ayer Collection of the Newberry Library in Chicago, and the Special Collections Room of the Nettie Lee Benson Latin American Library at the University of Texas in Austin, I extend my sincere thanks for their helpfulness both in my research and in obtaining photocopies of such manuscripts as Felipe Cádena's report on the destruction of Santiago de Guatemala (Antigua) in 1773.

As I have pursued this lengthy research project, I have been fortunate to have had the patience and encouragement of John N. Drayton, Editor-in-Chief of the University of Oklahoma Press. He has listened to my changing plans, offered suggestions, and urged me to proceed, for all of which I extend to him my sincere appreciation.

While I have been conducting research, organizing materials, and especially during the writing of this manuscript, my thoughts have continuously wandered to and concentrated on a visit to Guatemala I made with my daughter, Kathleen Ann Jones (now deceased), and my son, Christopher André Jones, in the summer of 1977. We visited and explored the temples and archaeological complex at Tikal; stood on the banks of the Río Dulce; entered the fortress of San Felipe near Lake Izabal; examined the archaeological site of Quirigua and the principal plaza and colonial buildings surrounding it in Guatemala City; spent time seeing the communities of Ciudad Vieja, Antigua, Sololá, and Panajachel; visited the site of the great church at Esquipulas; and in the dark of night, driving in our four-wheel-drive vehicle toward the Mexico border, got lost on the slopes of rugged mountains in northern Guatemala that I have since suspected were the Cuchumatanes range north of Totonicapán. With fond memories of our adventures, with smiles and occasionally with moisture in my eyes, I have had a focus for this study, and now I dedicate it to my travel companions, Kathy and Chris.

This work also recognizes the Columbian quincentenary of 1992, the commemoration of Columbus's discovery of America. Written as the international event approached, it emphasizes the theme of the anniversary as an "encounter of the two worlds" and the continuity of the Spanish exploration, settlement, and development set in motion by the discoveries of Columbus. Colonial Guatemala was one result of that momentous event in world history, and the long Spanish presence and administration in what is today's Guatemala was a significant phase of that nation's history, as well as an important part of the rich heritage of Spain in colonial Latin America.

OAKAH L. JONES

Chronology

800 B.C.–A.D. 900	Site of Kaminaljuyu occupied by Mayans.
A.D. 150–850/900	Tikal rises to prominence as a center of Mayan civilization.
1519–1521	Epidemic among Cakchiqueles and Tzutujiles, believed to be smallpox but possibly measles.
1523 (6 December)	Pedro de Alvarado and his army depart from Mexico City.
1524 (25 July)	Alvarado formally founds town of Santiago de los Caballeros de Guatemala at Iximché. First cabildo appointed.
1525 (May)	Alvarado founds town of San Salvador.
1526 (26 August)	Alvarado departs for Spain.
1527 (20 March)	Jorge de Alvarado and Dominican priests arrive at Santiago de Guatemala.
1527 (October–November)	Jorge de Alvarado moves capital from Iximché to Almolonga in valley of Panchoy.
1527 (23 November)	Formal dedication of new capital at Almolonga.
1528–30	War with Cakchiqueles.
1530 (April)	Pedro de Alvarado returns to Guatemala after his visit to Spain. Father Francisco de Marroquín arrives with him and in the mid-1530s becomes first bishop of Guatemala until his death in 1563.
1530–40	Franciscans, Dominicans, Augustinians, and Mercedarians begin religious work in Guatemala.
1532 (28 July)	King Carlos I grants Santiago de Guatemala the title and status of a *ciudad* (city).
1534 (23 January)	Pedro de Alvarado departs for South America, returning to Guatemala in April 1535.
1536 (August)–1539 (September)	Alvarado's second visit to Spain, where he marries Beatriz de la Cueva.

1537 (8 April)	Diocese of Guatemala (authorized by Pope Paul III on 18 December 1534) is officially consecrated and dedicated when Francisco de Marroquín is consecrated as bishop in Mexico City.
1540 (4 June)	Pedro de Alvarado sails for New Spain.
1540 (10 June)	*Congregación* policy for Indians begun (suggested by Bishop Marroquín in 1537?).
1541 (4 July)	Pedro de Alvarado dies in Nueva Galicia after being crushed beneath the falling horse of one of his followers during the Mixtón War.
1541 (10–11 September)	Ciudad Vieja at Almolonga destroyed by two days of heavy rain, floods, and mud slides. Beatriz de la Cueva dies during the disaster.
1542	Santiago de Guatemala reestablished as capital of the province in Panchoy valley.
1542 (20 November)	King Carlos I authorizes establishment of the Audiencia de los Confines.
1542–43	New Laws passed in Spain.
1543 (13 September)	First meeting of the Audiencia de los Confines in Comayagua.
1544	Audiencia de los Confines moved to Gracias a Dios.
1548	Audiencia de los Confines transferred to Santiago de Guatemala. Franciscan school for Indian youths founded by Bishop Marroquín at Santiago de Guatemala.
1549–55	Reforms of Alonso López de Cerrato.
1562 (9 March)	Colegio de Santo Tomás Aquinas established (refounded in 1620).
1563	Parts of Central America attached to the Audiencia de Panamá.
1566 (10 March)	King Felipe II grants title "la muy noble y muy leal Ciudad de Santiago de los Caballeros de Guatemala."
1570	Audiencia de Guatemala officially established as authorized in preceding year, with the capital of the audiencia at Santiago de Guatemala.
1582	Jesuits arrive in Guatemala.

1596	Fuerte de Bustamante established on Río Dulce near Lake Izabal.
1645–55	Fortress of San Felipe de Lara constructed on Río Dulce near Lake Izabal.
1660	First printing press arrives in Guatemala and is established in Santiago de Guatemala.
1676 (31 January)	King Carlos II officially authorizes founding of the university of San Carlos de Guatemala.
1680	Cathedral dedicated at Santiago de Guatemala (built from 1669 to 1679).
1681 (7–8 January)	Classes begin at University of San Carlos.
1683 (October)	First graduates from University of San Carlos.
1687 (10 January)	Official dedication of the University of San Carlos.
1701–1713	War of the Spanish Succession, which ended in 1713 with the Treaty of Utrecht.
1712–13	Tzeltzales Indian rebellion in Chiapas.
1717 (27–29 August and 29 September)	Earthquakes and volcanic eruptions (Earthquake of San Miguel) cause great damage to Santiago de Guatemala.
1733	Royal mint, authorized in 1731 for the Kingdom of Guatemala, is established at Santiago de Guatemala, and first coins are minted.
1733–42	Brigadier Pedro de Rivera governs the Kingdom of Guatemala.
1742	Archdiocese of Guatemala created by Pope Benedict XIV, and Father Pedro Pardo de Figueroa becomes first archbishop in 1743.
1743	Reconstruction of Fort San Felipe begun by engineer Luis Díez de Navarro.
1751 (4 March)	Earthquake of San Casimiro at Santiago de Guatemala.
1752 (27 March)	King orders construction of fortress of San Fernando de Omoa.
1756–63	Seven Years War, ending with the Treaty of Paris, 1763.
1758	Church of Esquipulas is completed, housing the image of the Black Christ completed by Quirio Cataño in 1594–95.

1767 (26 June– 26 July)	Expulsion of Jesuits from Guatemala by order of King Carlos III.
1768–70	Archbishop Pedro Cortés y Larraz visits within the diocese and reports to the king (archbishop until 1779).
1773 (29 July)	Catastrophic earthquake (Santa Marta) at Santiago de Guatemala and in highland region.
1773 (3–5 December)	Second major earthquake causes great destruction at Santiago de Guatemala.
1775 (21 July)	King Carlos III issues order for transfer of the capital to Nueva Guatemala de la Asunción in valley of La Hermita (or valley of the Virgin), where some officials and settlers had already relocated as early as January 1774.
1779–83	Matías de Gálvez governs Kingdom of Guatemala.
1779 (28 November)	Gálvez retakes fortress of Omoa from British.
1780 (22 February)	Gálvez begins defense of Nicaragua from British invasion.
1782 (10–17 March)	Successful assault by Matías de Gálvez on British garrison located on Roatán Island.
1785–87	Intendancy system established for Central America, but no intendancy created for the province of Guatemala.
1794	Consulado de Guatemala authorized by the king. *Gazeta de Guatemala* begins publication (suspended in 1795, resumed in 1797, renamed *Gazeta del Gobierno de Guatemala* in 1812).
1794–95	Sociedad Económica de Amigos del País chartered and founded at the capital (suppressed 14 July 1800, restored in 1811).
1801–1811	Lieutenant General Antonio González Mollinedo y Saravia and interim rulers govern the kingdom.
1804 (May)	Beginning of cowpox vaccination for smallpox in Guatemala.
1807–1808	Napoleon Bonaparte invades Spain, installing Joseph Bonaparte as king and capturing the Spanish Bourbon family.
1808–1810	Juntas formed to govern in Spain in absence of monarch.

1810 (24 July)	Antonio Larrazábal selected by Guatemala as delegate to the Spanish Cortes.
1811–18	General José de Bustamante y Guerra governs the Kingdom of Guatemala.
1812 (March)	Constitution of 1812 proclaimed in Spain.
1812 (24 September)	Bustamante swears allegiance to the Constitution of 1812.
1813 (December)	Conspiracy of Belén and arrest of the alleged conspirators.
1818 (28 March)	Lieutenant General Carlos Urrutia y Montoya takes possession of the government.
1820 (1 January)	Revolt of Colonel Rafael Riego and troops at Cádiz, Spain.
1820 (6 October)	José Cecilio del Valle begins publishing *El Amigo de la Patria.*
1821 (10 March)	Subinspector of Militias Gabino Gaínza placed in charge of the government; Urrutia's resignation forced by Guatemala's Provincial Deputation.
1821 (31 August)	Ayuntamiento of Guatemala discusses possibility of declaring independence.
1821 (15 September)	Junta Consultativa meets and votes to declare independence which is proclaimed to the public.
1821 (16 September)	Document declaring independence is signed.

Guatemala in the Spanish Colonial Period

CHAPTER 1

Catastrophe, Land, Amerindians

[The earthquake] was so quick, so violent, so fierce that from the first swaying it began to have its deplorable effect in the horrendous destruction of buildings; before it was half over, between the first impulse and the destruction of buildings, because at the same time that the movement of the earth was felt, it [also] began to divide into parts [causing the buildings] to collapse. All the various and ruinous movements, some moving horizontally, some vertically, were in the way that waves move on the sea, pressing and raising the ground while ruinously moving and shaking so violently that [the earth] would leap when pressed by the gravity of its weight so that no one could maintain himself on foot, not even on his knees. At times [the quake] moderated; at others, it seemed, it boiled, and because of the violence of its thrusts, cracks opened; and many of those who perished trying to retreat, fleeing along the precipice that supported them (it seemed as though the axis of the earth had finally weakened, or that the poles of the globe had detached and deflected from the central point on which the Creator had placed them on a solid foundation), lost their balance and fell headlong into the depths of a cavern. Those persons who did not fall, at full speed took the position of lying down prostrate on the ground; the animals did the same—four feet not being sufficient to support them. The trees, those that did not fall, leaned one way or the other with their branches on the ground. The bricks, so bound and tightly joined with cement on the houses, and the stones in the streets broke [from] their fittings and cracked.[1]

SO WROTE Father Felipe Cádena, lecturer on theology and doctor on the faculty in the Royal University of San Carlos, describing as an eyewitness the destruction of Guatemala's colonial capital, Santiago de los Caballeros de Guatemala (now known as Antigua) at 3:25 P.M. on

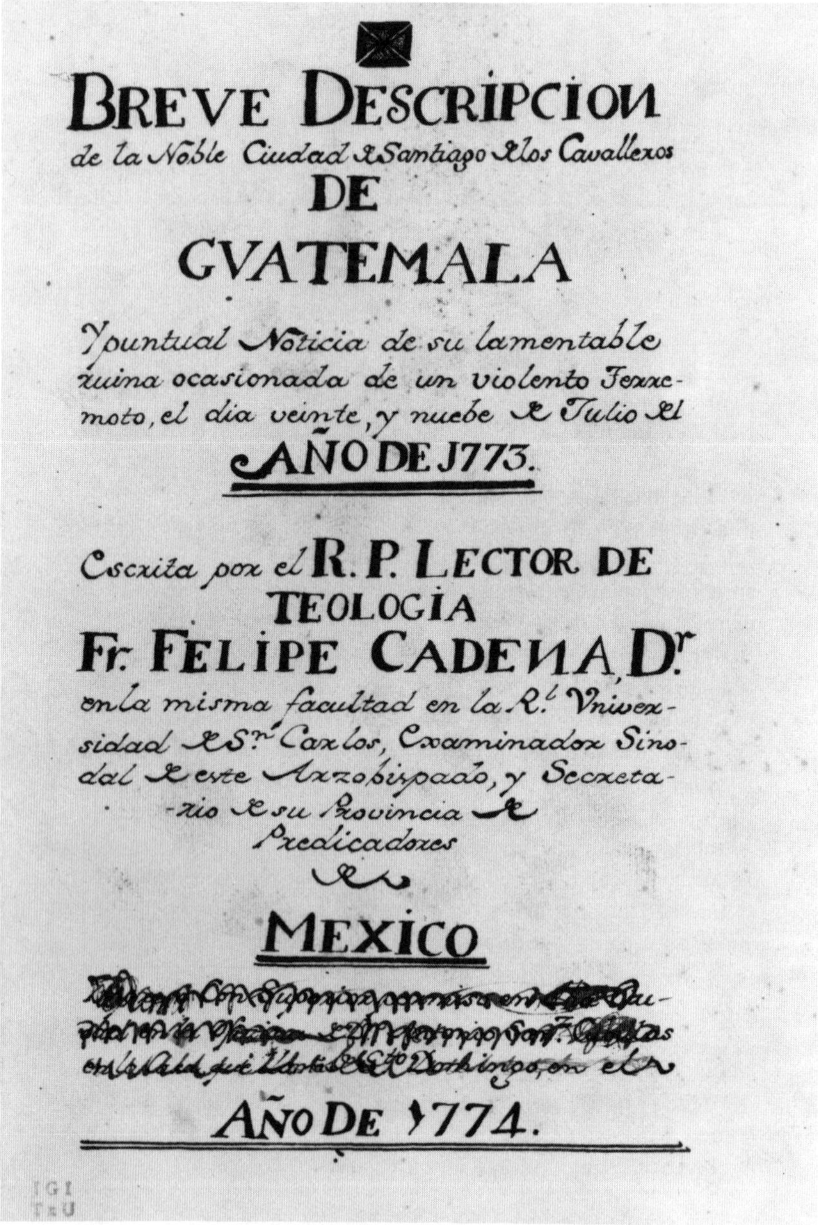

BREVE DESCRIPCION
de la Noble Ciudad de Santiago de los Cavalleros
DE
GVATEMALA
Y puntual Noticia de su lamentable
ruina ocasionada de un violento Terre-
moto, el dia veinte, y nuebe de Julio del
AÑO DE J773.
Escrita por el R. P. LECTOR DE
TEOLOGIA
Fr. FELIPE CADENA, Dr.
en la misma facultad en la R.l Vniver-
sidad de Sr. Carlos, Examinador Sino-
dal de este Arzobispado, y Secreta-
-rio de su Provincia de
Predicadores
MEXICO
[illegible]
AÑO DE 1774.

Cover of Father Felipe Cádena's "Breve descripción de la Noble Ciudad de Santiago de los Caballeros de Guatemala," 1774 (Special Collections, Nettie Lee Benson Latin American Library, University of Texas at Austin)

29 July 1773. Father Cádena wrote his comprehensive report on 10 March 1774 at La Hermita on the outskirts of the new capital, Asunción de Guatemala (present-day Guatemala City). He intended to relate and publicize the condition of the city before the earthquake, as well as what he had witnessed during the disaster, and to explain the succession of events and decisions that followed it.[2]

At the time of the earthquake Santiago de Guatemala was the capital of the Kingdom of Guatemala, a region embracing all of present Central America from Chiapas, in today's southern Mexico, to the Costa Rica border with Panama. Dominated by the three towering volcanoes of Agua, Acatenango, and Fuego, it was the political, economic, and cultural center of the Spanish kingdom and, as Father Cádena noted, was "one of the most famous cities that our Spanish Catholic Monarch Señor Don Carlos III ruled in this northern America."[3] The city had a "magnificent" *plaza mayor* (main public square), markets, and such public and ecclesiastical buildings as the *casa real,* or royal palace; the *casa de moneda,* or royal mint; and the *cabildo,* or meeting place of the town council. Also notable were its *portales,* or arcades; its well-built houses, with doors of fine wood, carved windows, and enclosed balconies; the University of San Carlos; two hospitals; two jails (one for men, another for women); the archbishop's palace; the cathedral and twenty-six churches; three seminaries (two for boys and one for girls); eight monasteries for priests; five convents for nuns; and three *beaterios,* or houses inhabited by pious women. Santiago de Guatemala was the seat of the Royal Audiencia of Guatemala and of the president, captain general, and governor (the one officer of royal authority), who was also governor of the province of Guatemala.[4]

The opulence of the city and its beautiful setting belied its location in a geologically unstable region that had been subject to volcanic eruptions, earthquakes, and floods ever since the arrival of the first Spaniards in the valley and the designation of the city as the capital in the early 1540s. Father Cádena recognized the instability, pointing out that there had been fourteen earthquakes the site between 1530 and 1765.[5] Furthermore, according to his account, the great quake of 29 July 1773 had been preceded by a lesser one on 11 June that damaged many houses as well as the roofs and churches of the Carmelite nuns, the Dominicans, and the Royal Hospital of San Juan de Dios.[6] Ten minutes before the catastrophic earthquake itself, the ground shook for "a moment," serving as a warning of what would follow, and allowing many of the city's sixty thousand residents (according to Father Cádena) to prepare themselves or flee before the disaster struck, thereby saving many lives.[7]

Yet, the cost in human suffering and material damage to the city was extensive as, panic-stricken, the people of the city tried to save their lives. Father Cádena related how fathers forgot their children and husbands abandoned their wives in the confusion and terror that reigned. Many suffocated in the huge dust cloud that blanketed the city; others died or were buried when the walls collapsed upon them. Although he reported that he could not estimate the total number who had died, Father Cádena noted that there were "many" and that 123 bodies had been located. Often buried by the dust and the ruins, the remains of some of the city's residents were not found until later, badly decomposed and contagious to the living.[8]

A storm of heavy rain, mixed with the dust, descended upon the city all during the night following the earthquake. It intensified the suffering of those whose houses had been ruined and who were without coats, food, and water. Likewise, it contributed to the material damages wrought by the earthquake. Buildings that had not completely collapsed became so weakened and badly damaged that they were judged useless, unsafe to occupy and impossible to repair. The rain mixed with dust destroyed valuable merchandise, costly furniture, beautiful paintings, books, archives, and public records, while holy images in the churches became buried in the dust and rubble.[9] As if the initial damages and loss of life were not enough, lesser earthquakes struck the city four months later between noon and one o'clock during the afternoon on 3 December and again at 3:30 A.M. on the night of 4 December, destroying buildings that had been left standing after the 29 July disaster.[10]

Faced with the destruction of the city and the continuing suffering of its people, the governor and captain general, Martín de Mayorga; the town council; the alcalde mayor of San Salvador, Don Francisco Antonio de Aldama y Guerra; the archbishop, Pedro Cortés y Larraz; and other ecclesiastics acted quickly to bring relief to the survivors. Governor Mayorga issued orders for Indians to bring food from the mountains and their villages to the city. He also sent a regidor, Don Nicolás de Obregón, to bring grain from the Sierra de Canales and other places. Furthermore, the governor ordered the district officials, or *corregidores,* of Sololá and Quezaltenango to bring wheat and flour, and he instructed Don Juan de Carrascosa to bring maize. He ordered the militia companies of the valley to come to the city and supplement its dragoon squadron in maintaining order. Since "some individuals" among the populace had dedicated themselves to robbery and pillage, Mayorga issued a *bando* (decree) providing severe punishments for the guilty—two hundred lashes for stealing property valued at more than ten pesos and ten days in jail for those who robbed a lesser amount. As a further deterrent, he had a gallows erected in the plaza mayor. Aldama y Guerra, as alcalde mayor of San Salvador, sent a portion of the cattle from his jurisdiction to the archbishop for distribution to the residents of the city. Thus the archbishop, provided corporal as well as spiritual aid to the suffering survivors of the earthquake, as did other members of the clergy and the Royal Hospital of San Juan de Dios.[11]

Plans to move the capital of the kingdom resulted in a meeting on 14 January 1774 in which sixty-one persons voted in a "loud voice" to do so, while only four wished to rebuild the ruined city on its present site.[12] The actual transfer of the capital took place over a period of years and is more appropriately discussed later in chapter 6.

THE LAND, CLIMATE, FLORA, AND FAUNA

Father Felipe Cádena's description of the destruction of Santiago de los Caballeros is valuable not only because he was an eyewitness at a spectacular event in the history of Spanish colonial Guatemala, but also because it introduces the reader to the interrelationship of guatemaltecos (Guatemalans) with their geography and environment. The physical features and climate of Guatemala have been factors in human occupancy throughout the nation's history. Also, the priest and university professor's account of perhaps the worst single catastrophe that Guatemalans have experienced, in the nearly three hundred years of the Spanish presence and afterward, illustrates a fact of life to which all Guatemalans have had to adapt: the imminent danger of destruction and death from natural catastrophe. Eric Wolf described the people of Mexico and Guatemala as "Sons of the Shaking Earth," who "live in

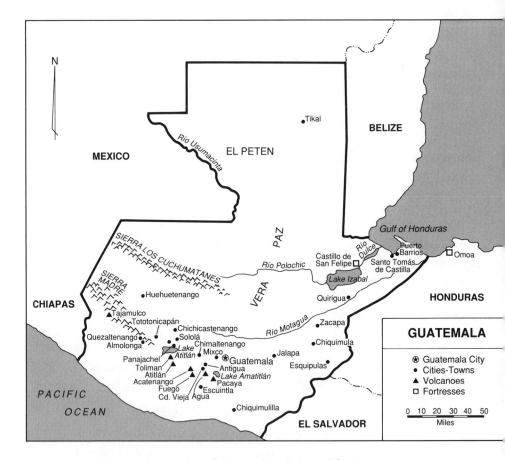

Map of Guatemalan places and features

the mouth of the volcano"[13] and have faced disaster from volcanic eruptions, earthquakes, floods, epidemics, and violence throughout the Spanish colonial era and since the establishment of Guatemala's independence from Spain in 1821.

Guatemala's geographical diversity illustrates clearly the terms that Wolf applied to all of Middle America, of which Guatemala is a major part: "astonishing" and a "mosaic of geographical environments and of human physical types . . . as well as human languages."[14] Because of the diversity of the topography, climate, soils, vegetation, and animal life, human habitation is conditioned by altitude in addition to latitude and surface-environment conditions. Ranging from sea level to nearly 14,000 feet, Guatemala's topography can be categorized in three geographical zones: the *tierra caliente,* or hot lands, from sea level to about 2,500 feet; the *tierra templada,* or temperate region, between 2,500 and 5,500 feet; and the *tierra fría,* or cold lands, above 5,500 feet. Guatemala City, the capital since the late 1770s, is in the valley of La Hermita (or the valley of La Virgen, as it is also called) at an altitude of almost 5,000 feet.[15]

Approximately 42,000 square miles in surface area, the present republic is smaller than it was in the Spanish period, when as the Kingdom of Guatemala it embraced Chiapas (now part of Mexico), San Salvador, Honduras, Nicaragua, Costa Rica, and part of Yucatán, as a subsidiary of the Kingdom and Viceroyalty of New Spain, which had its capital in Mexico City. There are three major geographical areas within today's Guatemala: the coastal plains or lowlands; the piedmont, a transitional zone; and the highlands and mountains that cover almost two-thirds of the country.[16]

Rugged mountains are the dominant feature of the Guatemalan landscape. Two ranges extend east to west across Guatemala from Mexico: the Sierra Madre and the Sierra de Cuchumatanes. Both are extremely rugged because erosion has exposed granite beneath their original limestone surface.[17] While the Cuchumatanes rise to altitudes of 9,000 to 11,000 feet and are characterized by very rough topography, the Sierra Madre is the highest range. It contains thirty-three volcanoes, many of which are still active; and the highest peaks in Los Altos reach an altitude of 10,000 to nearly 14,000 feet. Tajamulco Volcano at 13,809 feet, north of Quezaltenango, is the highest point in the nation, but other volcanoes are impressive in the southern range: Tacaná, 13,300 feet; Acatenango, 13,000 feet; Fuego, 12,600 feet; Agua, 12,300 feet; and Atitlán, 11,600 feet. Although it is not one of the highest volcanoes in Guatemala, Pacaya, south of Guatemala City, has been one of the most active, having erupted in 1775 and as recently as 1964.[18]

Between the Sierra Madre and the Sierra de Cuchumatanes lies the valley of the Motagua River, which rises near Chichicastenango in the Sierra Madre, flows east and northeast some 250 miles, and empties into the Bahía de Omoa near the border with Honduras on the shores of the Caribbean Sea. Highland lakes, most notably Lake Atitlán (about 150 square miles, and 1,000 feet deep in some places) and Lake Amatitlán (just south of Guatemala City), also add to the beauty and majesty of this geographical region. Fault zones just off the Pacific coast contribute to the frequency and destructiveness of the earthquakes, which have been more widespread and serious than the volcanic eruptions.[19]

Guatemala's two other regions are in marked contrast to the mountainous highlands. The Caribbean coastal area, which includes a narrow opening on the Gulf of Honduras, extends west and north to Verapaz and El Petén (a limestone plateau about 500 to 700 feet in altitude, which alone comprises about one-third of Guatemala's total land surface). This lowland region contains four rivers: the Usumacinta, which forms the boundary with Mexico; the lower reaches of the Motagua River; the Polochic, which rises in Alta Verapaz and flows westward, emptying into Lake Izabal; and the Río Dulce, which connects Lake Izabal with the Gulf of Honduras, a distance of only about thirty miles, or fifty kilometers. A prominent feature of this region is Lake Izabal itself, about twenty-seven miles long and twelve miles wide, one of the largest lakes in all of Central America. It and the Río Dulce occupied a position of strategic importance in the defense of the province and Kingdom of Guatemala during the Spanish colonial period.[20]

The Pacific coastal plain and the *boca costa,* or piedmont, are located along a narrow band between the highlands and the Pacific Ocean that runs generally northwest to southeast for a distance of approximately 225 miles, or about three times the length of the Caribbean coastal region. The plain is covered with grass and forests, with scattered lagoons and short rivers coursing downward from the highlands to the sea. One of the principal drawbacks of this region is the absence of any deep-water harbors, inhibiting the growth of maritime commerce. Another limiting factor is the presence nearby of the earthquake-producing fault line just off the coast.[21]

Corresponding to the different geographical features are climate zones that vary widely with the latitude, the complicated terrain, the altitude, the proximity of the Caribbean Sea and the Pacific Ocean, dominant pressure areas, and different wind systems. The mountainous region enjoys a more temperate climate, with warm days and cool evenings; the Caribbean coastal area is generally hot, humid, and tropical; and the Pacific coastal plain is hot and drier. Rainfall occurs annually in the months from May to October, which are called the *invierno,* meaning the winter rainy season. The season from October to May 15 known as the *verano,* meaning the dry season or summer. Approximately 75 to 80 percent of the annual rainfall occurs in the wet months, often in sudden thunderstorms. The heavy annual rainfall in El Petén ranges from 80 inches in the north to 150 inches in the south. In contrast, Guatemala City receives 40 to 60 inches of precipitation yearly. Tropical hurricanes occur on both the Caribbean and Pacific sides of the country between July and October, and winds called *nortes* (northers) blow across the Guatemalan highlands occasionally. No snow is present except on the higher peaks of the volcanoes, but frost is common at altitudes above 4,800 feet.[22]

The wide range of wild flora and fauna and agricultural products throughout the nation also depends on climate, soils, rainfall, vegetation, and altitude. Tropical rain forests abound in the Caribbean coastal region, as they do on the limestone plateau of El Petén and in Verapaz. In the tropical forests are found mahogany, tropical cedar, ceiba, and chicozapote trees (the last are the source of the chicle latex used in chewing gum). Among the rain-forest fauna are parrots and macaws of many varieties, monkeys, poisonous snakes, ducks, wild pigs, armadillos, crocodiles, jaguars, caymans, water rats, leaf-cutter ants, squirrels, frogs, bobcats, iguanas, opossums, tropical birds in profusion, parakeets, butterflies, gnats, locusts, mosquitoes, and other insects. The *monja blanca* (white nun) grows only in Alta Verapaz and has been adopted as Guatemala's national flower. While this abundant and diverse wild life and flora are less evident in the mountain and Pacific regions, deer and other animals are present in both. Of special note in the wildlife of Guatemala is the colorful quetzal bird, which lives only in the highland region in the tallest of trees, usually the pine and oak forests above 5,000 feet. Distinctive to Guatemala, although it is also found elsewhere in Central America and in the mountains of western Panamá, the quetzal has become the national bird and is depicted on the nation's currency, coat of arms, and flag. With its brilliant red and green coloring and long trailing feathers, it was once sought by the Aztecs of Mexico for the headdresses of their principal priests and warrior leaders.[23]

The agricultural products of Guatemala are also many and diverse. Bananas, tropical fruits, maize, beans, rice, and yuca (a potato substitute) are all grown in the Caribbean region. Bananas are produced in the Pacific coastal area. The principal crop of the nation is coffee, grown in the piedmont at altitudes ranging from 2,000 to 5,000 feet. Cotton also has become an important crop there during the past fifty years or so. In the highlands potatoes, maize, and wheat constitute the major crops, although some coffee also is grown there. Livestock raising has been important in both the Pacific coastal region and the mountains, especially in the semiarid corridor along the middle Motagua River, where short grass provides good grazing.[24]

PRE-COLUMBIAN INDIANS

Guatemala today is principally a land of *indios* (Indians) and *ladinos* (persons of mixed racial descent, or Westernized, acculturated people) with others of European origins or descent. While eastern Guatemala is largely ladino with a few pockets of Indians, western Guatemala is the opposite, mostly Indians with ladinos in the towns and villages as well as the major cities.[25] Both groups of people will be considered in Chapter 7, "Population, Society, and Culture," but here it is appropriate to describe the origins and development of Indian civilizations in pre-Columbian Guatemala before the coming of the Spaniards.

Before the arrival of the Spaniards, present-day Guatemala was an integral part of what archaeologists and anthropologists have termed Middle America, an area encompassing today's central and southern Mexico as well as Central America.[26] While archaeological research within the region has revealed many sites of pre-Columbian habitation from Panama to Guatemala, the early cultures before 500 B.C. were primarily tribal groups that practiced a hunting, gathering, and fishing economy. By approximately the sixth century before the birth of Christ, some groups in the Guatemalan highlands had begun to develop agricultural communities based on the cultivation of maize, beans, and squash. The ruins of Kaminaljuyú, on the outskirts of today's Guatemala City, date from the early Mayan civilization in the Preclassic period (from about 2000 B.C. to A.D. 300), when the community was prospering and the population increased. About one hundred years later, those early Mayans were invaded by Nahua-speaking people from Teotihuacán in central Mexico, and the site was dominated by a ceremonial, nucleated center, ball courts, and an acropolis arrangement of impressive buildings resembling those on the Mayan lowlands in northern Guatemala and Yucatán. Archaeologists believe that Kaminaljuyú then became a center controlling trade in northern Central America and that its Nahua-influenced Mayan culture continued to exist until about A.D. 900, when the site was abandoned because of military pressures.[27]

Thus Mayan and Nahuatl linguistic groups contributed to the rise of one of the Americas' most highly developed Amerindian civilizations before the coming of any Europeans to the western hemisphere. This occurred not overnight or in a generation, but over hundreds of years. Mayan civilization has been classified into three cultural periods: the early, formative Preclassic era from about 2000 B.C. to approximately A.D. 300; the Classical period from A.D. 300 to 900, when Maya civilization reached its height; and the historical, or Postclassical, period from A.D. 900 to about 1500, when Mayans, especially on the Yucatán peninsula, were invaded by warlike Nahuatl-speaking people from the north and west (perhaps Toltecs from Tula in central Mexico) and Mayan administration and culture became greatly influenced by these newcomers. It was in the last few decades of the Postclassical period that Spaniards arrived on the coasts of Central America and initiated the first European contacts with the natives, who at the time were experiencing separatism, civil wars, and cultural decline.[28]

Unquestionably, the Mayans, during their Classical period and the early centuries of the Postclassical period, achieved greatly in many areas. Numerous ceremonial centers with impressive architecture can still be seen in southern Mexico and the Yucatán peninsula and south to Copan in Honduras. Such sites abound in Guatemala: Tikal, Piedras Negras, Quirigua, and Kaminaljuyú, for example. While Quirigua is noted for its many stone stelae and its acropolis, Tikal is perhaps the most extensive and spectacular conglomeration of Maya buildings in Guatemala, extending two to three miles in all directions from the mile-square core formed by six temples (one reaching a height of 229 feet) and surrounding buildings, all built of stone.

Yet the temples, or stepped pyramids, were not the only achieve-ments of the Mayans. Whether they developed independently or were influenced by other Amerindian cultures, the Mayans made remarkable advances in mathematics, science, astronomy, architecture, sculpture, painting, and hieroglyphic writing, developing an accurate calendar, trade, farming techniques, polychrome ceramics, and textile produc-tion, and establishing a formal religion. For example, in addition to the pyramidlike temples, they constructed massive acropolislike struc-tures, palaces, ball courts, and stone stelae that were monuments to their principal rulers—all adorned by detailed sculptures and ornate decoration. They employed the corbeled arch over entryways with stone lintels at the top, the whole being carefully integrated into stone walls. Their study of the sciences is exemplified by their establishment of observatories and their knowledge of heavenly bodies such as the sun, moon, and stars, as well as their understanding of mathematics. These advances enabled them to develop two remarkably accurate calendars (which perhaps were originated by the Olmec people of southern Veracruz and Tehuantepec in Mexico): a ritual or religious one of 260 days and a solar one of 365 days divided into eighteen months of twenty days each with a year-end period of five days. The two calendars coincided every fifty-two years. Mayans also developed a system of writing wherein symbols stood for numbers and pictures for ideas, events, or personalities. The system was used not only in sculptural carvings but also in the books of folded bark or skin that provided historical annals, maps, and drawings.[29]

Mayan society was basically a theocracy of separate city states during the Classical period, although a confederation was established under Mexican influence after A.D. 1000. The government never achieved the centralization it did in central Mexico under the Aztecs or in Peru under the Quechuas (Incas). Each community of Mayans had a feudalistic social structure with priests and nobles at the apex, lesser caciques, everyday people organized into patrilineal clans, and families under a *señorio,* or territorial leader. At the bottom of the social structure were slaves, who usually were captives taken in war. Most people farmed, raising maize, beans, squash, cotton, vegetables, chiles, herbs, plants, and cacao. They practiced advanced methods of agriculture, by em-ploying irrigation canals and terracing while continuing the slash-and-burn methods that were typical of the rest of Central America then as well as now.

In the Classic period, and more commonly in the Postclassical era, the Mayans usually waged war to obtain sacrificial victims or establish control over a neighboring city state. In combat they used obsidian-edged swords and clubs along with two-handled shields, and they generally wore cotton tunics as a kind of armor. Especially during the Postclassic period, when warfare was endemic, human sacrifice was common. Burning people alive, dancing in the flayed skins of victims, throwing maidens into cenotes as at Chichen Itzá, decapitation, and sacrifices of palpitating human hearts torn from the breasts of unfortunate captives and offered to such gods as Tlaloc and Kukulcán (Quetzalcoatl), all were methods of human sacrifice.[30]

There were perhaps over one million natives inhabiting Guatemala at the time of the first Spanish contact in the early sixteenth century, including other groups besides the Mayans.[31] For example, the Pipiles of southeastern Guatemala, a Nahuatl-speaking people, and the Chortis east of today's Chiquimula constituted important groups in the region's pre-Columbian population. Yet, the majority of Indians were Mayans, divided into various territorial groupings or nations. The principal ones at the time of the arrival of the Spaniards in 1524 were the Quichés, the Cakchiqueles, the Tzutujiles, the Mames, and the Kekchis, each occupying a particular region of what is today Guatemala.[32] The Quichés dwelled largely in the area north and northeast of Lake Atitlán, extending east into Alta Verapaz, and they also lived as far west of the lake as the Pacific coast. Heavily influenced by the Toltec people, they displayed customs typical of Mexican Indians, and they rose to dominance between the thirteenth and fifteenth centuries, establishing their capital at Utatlán. South of them and below the Río Motagua were the Cakchiqueles, who, originally allied with the Quichés, had separated from them in the midfifteenth century, had become their enemies, and had founded their capital at Iximché, ostensibly in 1463. South of Lake Atitlán, on its southern shores, lived the Tzutujil Mayas, while the Mames occupied northwestern Guatemala near Tajamulco Volcano and today's city of Huehuetenango. The Kekchis lived in northeastern Guatemala, Verapaz, and southern El Petén.[33]

By the late fifteenth century and the beginning of the sixteenth, the

Quiché, Cakchiquel, and Tzutujil Mayas were disunited kingdoms, each endeavoring to expand its power and territory. Hostilities had become constant by the time Pedro de Alvarado and his army arrived from New Spain in 1524. He and other conquistadores took advantage of this disunity and civil warfare to accomplish the conquest and colonization of Guatemala.[34]

CHAPTER 2

Contact, Conquest, and Colonization

THE COLUMBIAN QUINCENTENARY celebrated the anniversary of the first voyage of Cristóbal Colón (Christopher Columbus) from Palos de la Frontera in Spain to the Bahama Islands and the Greater Antilles in the Caribbean Sea. This momentous exploration brought Spaniards into their initial contacts with the *indios* of the Americas, beginning what became the theme of the Columbian quincentenary, *el encuentro de dos mundos.* Thus with the first voyage of Columbus began an "encounter, or meeting, of two worlds," the "old" and the "new" worlds of Europe and America. It also began the explorations, conquests, colonization, and administration by Spain in the Americas that continued for more than three centuries. Europe and America were brought into a close relationship, and the prolonged contacts of different, previously isolated peoples resulted in conflicts and accommodations on the part of each.

That was precisely what happened in the region known today as Central America and Panama, and specifically in the area of present-day Guatemala. Maritime explorations took place from the time of Rodrigo de Bastidas's voyage along the Panamanian coast in 1501 and Columbus's fourth voyage along the northern coast of Central America between 1502 and 1504, although the first meaningful exploration of Guatemala did not occur until the conquest of the Quiché Mayas by Pedro de Alvarado began in 1523–24. Alvarado's invasion of what today constitutes Guatemala brought Indians and Spaniards into violent confrontation, taking advantage of the Quichés' decimation by the smallpox, which evidently spread from Mexico or Yucatán, and Alvarado's alliance with the Cakchiqueles against their enemies. This invasion, which led to the prolonged conquest and pacification of Guatemala, opened the era of the Spanish presence there. It brought warfare, Indian uprisings, unstable personalistic Spanish governments, and great problems of adjustment between Spaniards and Indians.

During, this period of initial colonization of Guatemala its first two Spanish capitals, Iximché and Ciudad Vieja (both known as Santiago de los Caballeros de Guatemala), were founded by the invaders. The migration of conquistadores, and others who followed them over the next two decades, peopled the first communities and rural areas of Guatemala and extended into neighboring regions of today's El Salvador (called Salvador throughout the colonial period) and Honduras. In the latter region during the mid-1520s violent clashes of competing Spanish armies from New Spain and Panama and Nicaragua made Honduras a battleground of warring Spanish armies with Indian auxiliaries. Pedro de Alvarado also became involved in the struggle, bringing Guatemala into a drawn-out conflict.

The death of Alvarado in 1541, while he was fighting in New Spain during the Mixtón War, and the destruction of the capital at Ciudad Vieja on 10 September 1541 ended seventeen years that were marked by violence, *personalismo,* initial contacts between Spaniards and Indians, and the establishment of Spanish institutions. This brief transition phase constituted the beginning of the Spanish colonial era in Guatemala, which lasted nearly three centuries until Guatemala proclaimed its independence from the mother country in September 1821.

THE GUATEMALAN CONQUEST, 1524–1530

Responding to a request by a Cakchiquel emissary who visited Mexico City, Hernán Cortés dispatched two Spaniards to Guatemala to report on conditions there, especially the nature of the civil war between the Quichés and the Cakchiqueles.[1] After the return of those agents, Cortés determined to send an expedition, commanded by his captain Pedro de Alvarado, to form an alliance with the Cakchiqueles, subdue the Quichés, establish Spanish settlements, and control the Indians and require them to accept Christianity.[2]

Pedro de Alvarado was already an experienced conquistador in 1523. Thirty-eight years old, he had been a resident of Spanish colonies in the western hemisphere since 1519. Born in Badajoz, Extremadura, in 1485, he had emigrated from Spain to Santo Domingo in 1510, accompanied by his four brothers, Jorge, Gonzalo, Gómez, and Juan.

He had been in Santo Domingo by 1510; therefore, that date is more accurate than 1519. He had tried farming, not very successfully, on the island of Española, and his adventurous, restless nature led him to seek pursuits more in keeping with his temperament. In 1518, while he was temporarily in Santiago de Cuba, Alvarado joined the expedition of Juan de Grijalva, participating as a captain in its exploration of Yucatán and the Mexican coastline from April to November. The next year he became one of eleven captains in Cortés's expedition that departed from Santiago de Cuba. Throughout the conquest of Mexico from 1519 to 1521, Alvarado was one of Cortés's most loyal and trusted captains. He and his brothers participated in almost every engagement with the Tenochas (Aztecs), from the landing at Veracruz to the final assault at Tenochtitlán. While it is not relevant here to examine in detail his roles in the conquest of Mexico, it should be noted that Alvarado, left in charge of Spanish forces in the Aztec capital, precipitated the attack on the great temple during an Aztec ceremony while Cortés was absent to meet the forces of Panfilo de Narváez near Veracruz. Later in the same year, 1520, he participated in the retreat from Mexico City on "la noche triste" (the Sad Night), reportedly surviving because of his "salto de Alvarado," a pole vault with a lance across a break in the causeway. After the reduction of the Aztecs in the following year, Cortés sent Alvarado with 180 soldiers (including 35 cavalrymen) and some Indian auxiliaries to pacify Oaxaca early in 1522. Later Alvarado participated in the campaign against Francisco de Garay in the Pánuco region, near today's Tampico.[3]

Thus Alvarado had gained considerable military experience by the time he was appointed to command the conquering expedition in Guatemala. His impetuous nature, restlessness, fiery temper, and ruthlessness in campaigns against the Indians of New Spain had already distinguished him as a forceful and courageous leader. He also had learned by experience with Cortés which military, diplomatic, and psychological techniques worked, and which did not, in combatting hostile Indians in New Spain.

Alvarado led his expeditionary force from Mexico City on 6 December 1523.[4] His army consisted of 120 cavalry with forty extra horses, 300 foot soldiers (130 crossbowmen and musketeers and 170 with shields and swords), and about 300 Indian auxiliaries—Cholultecans, Tlaxcaltecans, and "Mexicans" (Aztecs). Among the personnel were Alvarado's four brothers and two chaplains, the Franciscan friars Juan Godinez and Juan Díaz. There were four small cannon as pieces of artillery. The force, evidently marched to Tehuantepec and then to Soconusco, where Alvarado was received peacefully by the natives, and by 24 February 1524 he had entered Quiché territory.[5]

With this total force of 420 Spaniards and 300 Indian auxiliaries, Alvarado first encountered Quiché resistance late in February near today's Retalhuleu, and soon again at Quezaltenango. Within the next one hundred days, his invading force carried out the initial conquest of Guatemala and began a period of pacification that would last nearly six years. Thousands of Quichés, commanded by Tecúm-Umán, resisted Alvarado's army in a pitched battle during the last week of February 1524, but the Spanish cavalry surprised and frightened the Indians, winning the engagement. During the battle Tecúm-Umán, clad in jaguar skins over his military uniform and adorned with feathers and precious stones, was allegedly slain in personal combat by Alvarado, who is said to have run his adversary through with a lance,[6] causing the other Indians to flee. Later, in April near Quezaltenango, after another battle with a large force of Quichés, Alvarado occupied the town and accepted his enemies' invitation to visit them at their capital, Utatlán. Learning through his Cakchiquel allies of a plot by the Quichés to burn the city while he was there and annihilate the Spaniards, Alvarado moved his army outside the capital onto the nearby plain, where he again defeated the Quichés, succeeding in capturing the Quiché caciques.[7] After holding a war council with his principal officers, Alvarado reported in his letter of 11 April 1524 to Cortés, "I burnt them and sent [others?] to burn the town and to destroy it." The Quiché prisoners were "branded and made slaves"; one-fifth of them were given to the king's treasurer to be "sold at public auction," according to Alvarado.[8] Thus ended the Quiché resistance, the first part of the conquest of Guatemala.

From Utatlán, Alvarado's army moved to the Cakchiquel capital of Iximché, where he and his allies organized an expedition against the Tzutujiles on the southern shore of Lake Atitlán. With five or six thousand Cakchiqueles accompanying his army, Alvarado's force defeated the Tzutujiles, forcing many of them to flee to the nearby mountains. He burned their principal city of Panatacat; demanded tributes of blankets, turkeys, honey, and maize; and sent messengers into the mountains to tell the refugee Tzutujiles that he would burn their maize crops if they did not surrender. These enemies of the Cakchiqueles and Spaniards thereupon agreed to surrender and accept the sovereignty of the king of Spain.[9]

Having now subjugated or allied with the three principal Indian nations of Guatemala—Quiché, Cakchiquel, and Tzutujil—Alvarado next turned to the Pipiles of southwestern Guatemala, whom he could not conquer there or on his expedition to Cuscatlán in present-day El Salvador. In one of his engagements with the Pipiles, Alvarado was wounded by an arrow in the leg, an incident that lamed him for the rest of his life.[10]

After a forty-five day absence on this campaign to Salvador, Alvarado and his army returned to Iximché (named by the Cakchiquel word for corn or maize).[11] Near that Cakchiquel city, on 25 July 1524, the conquistador formally founded the first Spanish capital, named Santiago de los Caballeros de Guatemala in honor of Saint James, whose day it was in the Spanish calendar. Domingo Juarros, in his early nineteenth-century history of Guatemala, reported that Chaplain Juan Godinez said Mass on the occasion of the town's establishment and that celebrations continued for three days afterward. Alvarado appointed Diego de Rojas and Baltasar de Mendoza as the first alcaldes of the town, and named four regidores to the cabildo. They were Pedro Portocarrero, Hernán Carrillo, Juan Pérez Dardon, and Domingo Zubiarreta. In addition, Gonzalo de Alvarado was named *alguacil mayor,* or chief constable. This first cabildo, or *ayuntamiento,* as it was often called, met on 27 July, and at its second session two days later it used the name Santiago de los Caballeros for the settlement.[12] Thus, as in other areas occupied by Spain, legal government of Spanish municipalities began with the early conquests and simultaneous establishment of towns.

Yet, the conquest of Guatemala had really just begun. Conflict erupted when Pedro de Alvarado imposed a heavy tribute, payable in gold, on his allies, the Cakchiqueles, and it intensified because of the brutalities of Gonzalo de Alvarado, who later served as lieutenant governor during the absence of his brother.[13] Six years of almost continuous, bloody warfare followed. Spurning an offer by the Cakchiqueles to unite against the Spaniards, the Quichés and the Tzutujiles now allied themselves with the Europeans against the rebellious Cakchiqueles and the Cakchiquel allies, the Pokomanes of the Motagua river valley. Having fled to the mountains, the Cakchiqueles initiated a general insurrection under the leadership of their chieftain Sinacam. Alvarado retaliated against the rebels in a war of extermination. Threatened by the presence of the Cakchiqueles and wishing to deny them access to their capital, Pedro de Alvarado burned the capital Iximché, and took to the fields and mountains to campaign against his new enemies. By 1525 he had succeeded in defeating the Cakchiqueles in a series of bloody battles, but he did not subjugate them or capture Sinacam. Over the objections of his followers, Alvarado then decided to depart from Guatemala and join Cortés in Honduras, leaving the administration and fighting in Guatemala to his brother Gonzalo, who enriched himself by imposing further heavy tributes on the Indians and by requiring young boys to work the gold deposits found near Iximché.[14] Pedro de Alvarado meanwhile reached Honduras, but found that Cortés had already returned to Mexico. While Gonzalo de Alvarado conquered the Pokomanes, Pedro returned to Guatemala via Salvador to complete the conquest there, and in May 1525 he founded the *villa* (chartered town) of San Salvador.[15]

On his return to Guatemala, believing that the Cakchiquel uprising had been largely subdued by his brother, Pedro de Alvarado decided to depart for Spain to seek confirmation from the king as governor of the territories he had conquered and colonized. On 26 August 1526 he left Santiago de Guatemala for New Spain, leaving Pedro de Portocarrero and Hernán Carrillo to govern in his absence. From Mexico City, he appointed his brother Jorge de Alvarado as lieutenant general and acting governor of Guatemala. While Pedro de Alvarado sailed early in 1527 from Veracruz, Jorge and several Dominican priests proceeded overland, arriving at the Spanish capital of Guatemala on 20 March 1527.[16]

During his eighteen months in Spain, Pedro de Alvarado acquired a wife and an official decree granting him the government of the "kingdom of Guatemala."[17] He married Doña Francisca de la Cueva, the niece of the duke of Albuquerque, and on 18 December 1527, Emperor

Charles V of the Holy Roman Empire (who was Carlos I of Spain) granted him the title of *adelantado,* governor, and captain general of the kingdom that later embraced not only today's Guatemala but also Costa Rica, Nicaragua, Salvador, Honduras, Belize, and Chiapas in present-day Mexico. The royal decree, issued at Burgos, also established Alvarado's annual salary at 572,500 maravedis, which, according to John E. Kelly in his 1932 biography of Alvarado, amounted to 2,068 Guatemalan pesos or approximately $1,000 in 1930s U.S. currency.[18]

When Alvarado returned to Veracruz in October 1528, his wife became seriously ill and died with a high fever. This tragic loss and an investigation of his conduct by the Audiencia of Mexico delayed the conquistador's return to Guatemala. In a lengthy defense against his detractors, Alvarado succeeded in exonerating himself of wrongdoing. He reached Santiago de Guatemala early in April 1530.[19]

During the three years and eight months of his absence, much had happened in Guatemala, but the war against the Cakchiqueles, now allied with the Quichés, had resumed and raged on. In fact, it intensified in the period from 1528 to 1530. Captain Pedro de Portocarrero, who had been left in charge of military operations when Alvarado left for Spain in 1526, pursued the war with a force of 60 cavalry, 80 foot soldiers armed with arquebuses, 550 Tlaxcaltecan and Mexican Indian allies, and 100 Zacatepecs. He first defeated the enemy forces of Panagual and later conducted a two-month siege of Sinacam's stone fortress in the Comalape mountains. Panagual was publicly executed after his capture following a three-day battle in which he and other caciques were made prisoners. Sinacam and many of his followers were captured on 22 November 1526.[20]

When warfare threatened to break out anew the next year, this time with Quichés joining the Cakchiqueles as enemies, interim governor Jorge de Alvarado decided to move the Spanish capital from its site near Iximché to the valley of Panchoy. The site had been visited by Pedro de Alvarado in July 1524 while returning from his first expedition to Salvador, and it had seemed to him a good place for future settlement. His Mexican Indian allies had called it Almolonga, which in their language meant a spring of water. It was located at the base of a mountain that the Spaniards called Volcán de Agua (Water Volcano) and near another, at a distance of about one and one-half leagues (about four miles), from whose summit came smoke and flames, which they named Volcán de Fuego (Fire Volcano). During the months of October and November 1527, Jorge de Alvarado moved the Spanish capital of the Kingdom of Guatemala to the new site at Almolonga. This new villa located on the lower slopes of the Volcán de Agua became known as Ciudad Vieja, although this second location of the capital still officially bore the title of Santiago de los Caballeros de Guatemala.[21]

In the following year another general uprising of the Cakchiqueles and the Quichés more seriously imperiled the Spaniards than had earlier ones. It lasted until Pedro de Alvarado's return to Guatemala in April 1530. At that time the remaining Cakchiquel rebels came down from the mountains to surrender to the governor and captain general. Although skirmishes and outbreaks occurred sporadically for the next ten years, the first, aggressive phase of Spanish-Indian contact had passed, and as Salvador Rodríguez Becerra has noted, the area of Guatemala by 1530 could be considered conquered.[22]

AFTERMATH, 1530–1541

Pedro de Alvarado returned to a Guatemala different from that he had left in the hands of his brothers Gonzalo and Jorge nearly four years earlier. Santiago de Guatemala was still the capital, but it was now on a new site in the valley of Panchoy at Almolonga, or Ciudad Vieja, at the foot of the Volcán de Agua. Originally enrolling twenty-four *vecinos* (recognized heads of households, or citizens) at the end of 1527, Almolonga contained a total of forty-one vecinos by September of the following year. When Alvarado arrived in 1530, its population had risen to 150 vecinos, and the cabildo had eight regidores instead of the original four.[23] One of the residents of this town was Juan Rodríguez Cabrillo, the future explorer and discoverer of California in 1542. Rodríguez had served in Alvarado's army as a captain and on 12 August 1524 had been one of the first citizens of Santiago de los Caballeros at Iximché. Four days after the establishment of Almolonga on 22 November 1527, Rodríguez and twenty other men were made original citizens of the new town. He received town lots, farmlands, and several encomiendas (grants of Indians), including one at Cobán, where gold placers were worked. Married in Spain in late 1532 or early 1533, Rodríguez and his wife, Beatriz, returned to Santiago de los Caballeros at Almolonga, where they were evidently respected as persons of honor. Rodríguez derived wealth from his encomiendas, invested in Peruvian trading ventures, and built a ship, *Santiago,* for Pacific Ocean trading enterprises. He did not accompany Alvarado to Peru in the mid-1530s, but did go with him on an expedition to Honduras before Alvarado's departure for Spain. Rodríguez built many of the ships at Iztapa that comprised Alvarado's new fleet in 1540, and he and Bishop Francisco Marroquín accompanied Alvarado on the expedition to New Spain. After the conquistador's death Rodríguez returned to Guatemala, arriving after the disaster of 11 September 1541, when he moved to the new capital site at Antigua. In the spring of 1542 he departed for his California exploration.[24]

Father Francisco Marroquín, another newcomer at Almolonga, had traveled from Spain through New Spain with Alvarado. In June 1530 he replaced Father Juan Godinez as chaplain of the army and the colony,[25] and in the middle of the decade he became the first royally appointed bishop of the diocese of Guatemala. A staunch supporter of Alvarado (to whom he owed his appointment), Marroquín possessed a strong will, and after the conquistador's death he served temporarily, although not immediately, as interim governor of Guatemala. His long period of residence in the kingdom, spanning thirty-three years, had much to do with the firm establishment of the Catholic Church and the growth of the regular and secular clergy. In fact, during the decade of the 1530s such religious orders as the Franciscans, the Dominicans, the Augustinians, and the Mercedarians began their work in the spread of Christianity to the Amerindians, as well as the day-to-day administration of the religious needs of the Spanish settlers.[26]

Land allocations and Amerindian labor arrangements for the conquering and settling Spaniards were also consummated during this period. Beginning in 1528, lands were subdivided among those who had participated in the conquest and settlement of Guatemala. Each of the horsemen received a *caballería* of land (about 105 acres), while each foot soldier was granted half of a caballería (a *peonía*) as his own property.[27] Only enrolled citizens could own land, and each of them was restricted to two caballerías or less.[28] At the same time those who had participated in the conquest, especially Alvarado, were rewarded with *encomiendas,* wherein pacified natives were entrusted or assigned to *encomenderos* (the holders of encomiendas) to pay tribute and contribute their labor in return for protection, religious instruction, and food and shelter. As historian William L. Sherman has noted, Alvarado accumulated impressive wealth before his death in 1541 because of the various assets he held. In all, he possessed at least nineteen encomiendas—seven in Guatemala (including the villages of Quezaltenango and Atitlán), nine in Honduras, and three in New Spain. His tributaries in Guatemala alone may be conservatively estimated at three thousand persons in addition to the Indian and Negro slaves (an undetermined number of the former, plus at least fifteen of the latter, who engaged in the work on his ships). Most of the tribute he collected annually was in the form of goods and a variety of personal services performed by the Indians. In 1538 an inventory of Alvarado's personal belongings and holdings, not counting encomiendas, stores, plots of land, household furnishings, jewelry, and business enterprises, showed that he possessed two silver mines (one owned outright, the other in partnership), unspecified lands, 125 mares, 635 head of cattle, 1,100 sheep, 47 goats, two ships, one small brigantine, two galleons at his shipyard, and the fifteen black slaves. Although his annual income generally exceeded the equivalent of $100,000 for many of his years in Guatemala, his lavish spending on the conquest, travels, expeditions, and his life-style contributed to his being in debt when he died, even though at that time he still had 700 head of cattle and 4,000 sheep.[29]

As one would expect, there were complaints that Alvarado's holdings were excessive—and they probably were. Furthermore, it is evident that Spanish settlers clashed with one another about overlapping and insufficient allotments of land, conflicting assignments of encomiendas and Indian villages to administer, and some land and labor allocations in unconquered territories.[30] That some encomenderos mistreated their Indians is apparent. Alvarado, to counteract such transgressions, began issuing ordinances for "good government" after his return in 1530. Designed to protect the Indians from mistreatment by Spanish residents, these ordinances, although well intentioned, were frequently violated. Among them were laws prohibiting the employment of Indians in mines or anywhere else during the months of July, August, and September, so that they could plant their own crops and take advantage of the abundant rains; laws imposing forfeiture of Indians entrusted to those who did not comply with the previous law, or fines on those who used them for work as human carriers or to construct vessels without paying them laws prohibiting taking by force articles being sold by Indians at markets, or other abuses of natives in the marketplace, punishing Spaniards who did not obey with fifteen days in jail and Negroes with one hundred lashes; laws that forbade taking Indians out of Guatemala and selling them as slaves, punishing violators with the death penalty; and laws ordering those who held encomiendas to reside in them for more than four days each year "to avoid injustices and abuses" that they would otherwise commit.[31] Yet, encomenderos did commit abuses, circumventing the laws. Some evidently mistreated Indian women, and in an effort to treat this last problem, the Crown issued a decree in 1538 ordering encomenderos to marry within three years or forfeit their Indians to married persons.[32]

Most likely one of the main reasons for the lax enforcement of laws regulating the encomenderos was that Alvarado was frequently engaged on expeditions outside of Guatemala or was traveling to and from Spain once again. The boredom of administering the kingdom with its many details and quarrels soon overcame the governor's restless, adventurous spirit. Likewise, his lust for power, prestige, and wealth led him to become involved in the civil wars in Peru after the initial conquest there by Francisco Pizarro. Seeking an opportunity to carve out a kingdom of his own and greater wealth, Alvarado left Guatemala with an army of five hundred Spaniards, after naming his brother Jorge once again as lieutenant governor to rule over the kingdom in his absence. His force sailed on 23 January 1534 from Iztapa on the Pacific coast, where Alvarado had supported the building of ships. Subsequent events in Ecuador and Peru were a disaster, ending with an agreement between Diego de Almagro and Alvarado, and the latter's frustrated withdrawal and return to Guatemala in April 1535.[33]

In the early days of August 1536, Alvarado began another absence from Guatemala of two years and nine months when he made his second visit to Spain. Instead of going through New Spain as he had the previous time, he sailed from Puerto Caballos (now Puerto Cortés), Honduras, and returned there on 4 April 1539. While in his homeland, he married Doña Beatriz de la Cueva, the sister of his first wife, and learned of the discoveries of Alvar Núñez Cabeza de Vaca, including the reports of rich, village-dwelling Indians in the far northern reaches of New Spain. Intrigued by this possibility for future exploration, Alvarado reached Santiago de Guatemala on 15 September 1539, accompanied by his wife, twenty unmarried women, and three hundred soldiers.[34]

Having received from the king, while he was in Spain, the authorization to build a fleet to sail to the Spice Islands, Alvarado concentrated his energies and finances for this new venture. This fleet of thirteen vessels sailed from the port of Acajutla in Salvador on 4 June 1540 with Alvarado in command of 850 Spanish soldiers and some Indian allies, including caciques of the Quiché and Cakchiquel nations. When this formidable force arrived on the western coast of Jalisco, in New Spain, its leader became involved in a plan of Viceroy Antonio de Mendoza to locate the Seven Cities of Cíbola associated with the reports of Fray Marcos de Niza about the far north of New Spain. After reaching an agreement with the viceroy on 29 November 1540, Alvarado remained in Mexico City until the end of May 1541. Then, when he returned to his ships on the Jaliscan coast early in June, he was informed of the serious Indian rebellion in Nueva Galicia that began the Mixtón War. Responding to Governor Cristóbal de Oñate's requests for military help, Alvarado marched with most of his personal army to Nochistlán, north of Guadalajara, through rugged mountains and deep ravines. After launching an immediate attack on 24 June, he was forced to retreat from the rebels, who were entrenched high above his position. Alvarado, who was now on foot, was crushed by the rearing horse of one of his followers. He died ten days later and was buried beneath the altar of a nearby village church. His remains were later moved twice in New Spain, and in 1570, by order of his daughter, Doña Leonor, they were brought back to Guatemala and interred at the cathedral in Santiago de Guatemala (Antigua).[35]

The news of Alvarado's death was communicated by Viceroy Mendoza to the acting governor of the Kingdom of Guatemala, Francisco de la Cueva, reaching the capital on 29 August. A mourning period of nine days was proclaimed. Doña Beatriz, understandably grief-stricken, wept and screamed, beat herself, and ordered all the walls of the governor's palace painted black, along with the roof and the stone courtyard. On 8 September she initiated a request to be named by the town officials to fill the vacant position created by the death of her husband. The members of the cabildo formally elected her as interim governor and captain general of the Kingdom of Guatemala of 9 September, when she took the oath and named her brother, Francisco de la Cueva, as lieutenant governor, signing the scribe's minutes as the "Unfortunate One."[36] Thus Doña Beatriz became the first and only woman to hold the highest office in colonial Guatemala during the entire period of the kingdom's existence.

DISASTER AND THE END OF AN ERA

Three days of continual heavy rain ended in a downpour from eight to ten o'clock on the night of 10 September 1541, bringing the water level in the streets of Almolonga to knee depth. Then, a couple of hours after dark on the same night, an earthquake struck. While the populace fled in terror to escape falling roofs and walls, the most damaging blow was on the eastern side of the Volcán de Agua, where the walls of the volcano broke down and released water from inside. A wall of water poured down an arroyo into the city, sweeping trees and boulders into the streets. The flood swept through the ground floor of Alvarado's palace, drowning many Indian servants and carrying others down the side of the mountain. Doña Beatriz took refuge on the chapel roof, but the walls collapsed and she was crushed beneath the rubble. One historian reported that six hundred Spaniards and a larger number of Indians died that night. The city was in ruins, with only a few houses and the cathedral left standing.[37]

Six days later, in the immediate aftermath of the disaster, the ayuntamiento elected Francisco de la Cueva and Bishop Marroquín as joint interim governors of the kingdom, and the aldermen decided to accept the recommendation of the royal engineer, Juan Bautista Antonelli (who fortunately was in Guatemala at the time) that the capital be moved to a site about two miles from Ciudad Vieja in the valley of Panchoy. On 22 October 1541 the town council resolved to move to the new location, and the capital reestablished there became the city now known as Antigua, although it still officially bore the name Santiago de Guatemala.[38]

In 1541, Alvarado's death, the destruction of Ciudad Vieja, and the death of Doña Beatriz essentially ended the period of conquest, initial settlements, first contacts between Spaniards and Indians, and personalismo in the administration of Guatemala that had begun with the Spanish invasion in 1524. Murdo J. MacLeod observed that "Central America was not conquered by men with the imperial imagination of Hernán Cortés, and the conquest was a difficult, destructive, bloody, and piecemeal task."[39] Indeed, it was not just a single confrontation of Spaniards and Indians. Salvador Rodríguez Becerra regarded that view as "overly simplistic and consequently false," and emphasized that the "participation of Indians in the conquest was of decisive importance as much as that of the Mexican and Tlaxcaltecan allies and that of the Guatemalans themselves."[40] At first, Indian resistance had as its purpose to repel the invaders, but when social disorganization resulted after the Spaniards remained in Guatemala, resistance took the form of uprisings and rebellions, confederations and alliances against the invaders, messianic movements, flight to regions inaccessible to the Christians, total abandonment of villages and regions, and sometimes suicide.[41] Ralph Lee Woodward stated accurately that the Indians had been defeated by 1541.[42] Although the period of the conquest and initial colonization was complicated, often confusing, and unstable, in the years that followed, royal government became organized and firmly planted in colonial Guatemala, replacing the earlier epoch of personalistic administration and instability.

CHAPTER 3

Government

SPAIN'S GOVERNMENT of colonial Guatemala was ever changing, more dynamic than static.[1] In the beginning it was personalist, as was the government in the parent country, since Guatemala, like other parts of colonial Spanish America, was essentially a kingdom under the personal rule of the monarch of Castile. No such entity as a unified Spain existed until the eighteenth century. In Guatemala, as the Spanish population grew and socioeconomic development occurred, the government passed from its early personalism into an increasingly complex bureaucratic phase. Finally, the reforms of the Bourbon dynasty and the Napoleonic invasion of Spain during the last half century of Spanish control brought increased royalization and a highly complex administration. During those three periods of Spanish government, colonial Guatemala was indistinguishable from the Kingdom of Guatemala. What is today the Guatemalan nation was in the Spanish period only a province, or *gobernación* (governance), of the kingdom, as were El Salvador, Nicaragua, Honduras, Costa Rica, and today's Mexican state of Chiapas.

This chapter examines the three phases of Spanish government, concentrating on what is today's Guatemala, but recognizing its relationship to the overall Kingdom of Guatemala.

THE ERA OF PERSONALISMO

For almost the first two decades (1524–42) of Spain's presence, modern Guatemala and the rest of Central America were governed in a haphazard, personalist, and tumultuous manner. The early government during the conquest period was unstable and dominated by the adelantado, Pedro de Alvarado, or in his absence, his brothers or other relatives. Central America, along with Peru, remained one of the most

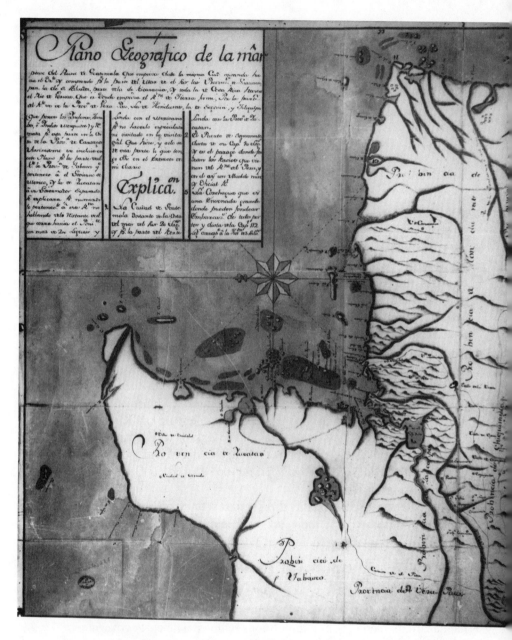

"Plano Geográfico de la mayor parte del Reino de Guatemala" (geographical plan of the greater part of the Kingdom of Guatemala), by Luis Díez Navarro, 1 August 1776 (AGI, Sevilla, Mapas y Planos, Guatemala, 225[1])

tumultuous of Spain's kingdoms in the Americas. Personal rivalries and the absence of royal institutions resulted in widespread violence among Spaniards in addition to the Indian resistance and revolts against Spanish administration. When the latter subsided after 1530, the former continued until after the destruction of Ciudad Vieja in 1541.

Pedro de Alvarado initially served as adelantado of Guatemala during the early conquest years. His role as a conquistador changed only when the king appointed him governor and captain general by a royal decree of 18 December 1527.[2] Yet, he governed directly for only brief periods (1524–26, 1530–34, eleven months in 1535 and 1536, and finally nine months in 1539 and 1540) because of his journeys to Mexico and Spain and his foray into Ecuador. Thus, in the eighteen years from 1524 to 1542, Guatemala's first governor and captain general administered the jurisdiction for approximately eight years. In his absence he appointed interim or lieutenant governors such as his brothers Gonzalo (twice) and Jorge (also twice, 1526–30 and 1534–36) and Licenciados Alonso de Maldonado and Francisco de la Cueva, the brother of Alvarado's second wife, Beatriz de la Cueva. Counting Alvarado's comings and goings, there were nineteen changes of government during this period.[3]

Nevertheless, while present in Guatemala, Alvarado succeeded in establishing its first cabildo and issued laws for the government of the jurisdiction. When he founded the settlement of Santiago de los Caballeros de Guatemala at Iximché in 1524, Alvarado established the cabildo and named Diego de Rojas and Baltasar Mendoza as the first *alcaldes mayores* (municipal officials) of the villa, or chartered town. The cabildo then consisted of four *regidores* (aldermen) and an alguacil mayor, his brother Gonzalo de Alvarado.[4] Likewise, after the capital was moved to Almolonga in 1527, the acting governor, Jorge de Alvarado, recognized and established the cabildo there in his Act of Foundation on 22 November. In it Jorge de Alvarado specifically named Gonzalo Dovalle as alcalde and four regidores—Pedro and Eugenio de Moscoso, Jorge de Acuña, and Pedro de Cuato—and he outlined the physical layout of the town and named its first twenty-two vecinos.[5]

On Pedro de Alvarado's return in 1530 from his first visit to Spain, he issued a set of regulations or ordinances for "good government" mostly concerning the treatment of Indians in Guatemala. In these he emphasized that while he had strongly opposed the Indians in warfare, he would now protect them and help them in peace. These ordinances, as well as imposing fines and punishments on those who mistreated Indians, set fees for judges, scribes, constables, and others of the cabildo; established tributes ("tasa en los trabajos") for tailors, blacksmiths, carpenters, munitions manufacturers, and others; fixed prices for medicines; prohibited Spaniards from traveling more than two leagues (about five or six miles) from the capital; and ordered those who had *pueblos* (towns) and encomiendas assigned to them to reside in these communities for more than four days each year to prevent abuses and injustices that would otherwise be committed.[6] Although the ordinances were issued by Alvarado with good intent, it is evident that Spaniards, the governor among them, continued to exploit, cheat, and mistreat the Indians in the decade that followed.

When the news arrived in Guatemala of Alvarado's death in the Mixtón War of Nueva Galicia, the cabildo met on 8 and 9 September 1541 to determine who should then be the governor. At her insistence, Alvarado's wife, Beatriz de la Cueva, was elected by the regidores. Her rule lasted two days, until her death in the disastrous destruction of Almolonga. Thereafter the cabildo met again, and on 16 and 17 September they selected her brother Francisco de la Cueva and Bishop Francisco Marroquín as joint interim governors. They continued to govern until replaced by Licenciado Alonso de Maldonado and the king's royal officials in 1542–43.[7]

Although this first period of Spanish government was an era of *personalismo* (personalist administration) by Alvarado and his relatives, decentralized authority, and instability,[8] one institution of Spanish government, the cabildo of the town of Santiago de Guatemala, was permanently established. It would endure and continue during the remaining two periods of Spanish administration, its powers waxing and waning with the imposition or lack of royal controls. In the final years of its existence during the independence era (1810–21), the cabildo once again became a powerful counterforce to royal authorities.

THE ERA OF HABSBURG BUREAUCRACY

To organize and establish more direct royal control over the Kingdom of Guatemala,[9] King Carlos I of Spain created, by a royal *cédula* (decree) of 20 November 1542, the Audiencia de los Confines ("of the boundaries") with three *oidores* (judges) and Maldonado as its first president *(presidente)*. It was one of two such bodies established by the New Laws of 1542–43 and was ordered to sit at Comayagua in today's Honduras on 13 September 1543.[10] With this act began a century and a half of increased royal administration resulting in the establishment of a royally appointed bureaucracy that extended from the top to the bottom of colonial government. At the apex of this system was the king, to whom the Kingdom of Guatemala and all other territories in the Americas were personal possessions. Indeed, as Lyle McAlister, among many others, has observed, "The Indies belonged exclusively to the Crown of Castile," and the separate kingdoms there were united to Spain only by their allegiance to the common crown.[11] Using the regular Habsburg practice of "divide and rule," the monarch created a system of checks and balances with purposely overlapping functions, proliferating the number of offices, raising revenue by heavy and sustained selling of offices, and preventing the exercise of absolute authority in any region or governmental office. The results were a cumbersome bureaucracy, long delays in administration, frequent neglect of royal directions by officials in America, and often vacillations by the Crown itself in the application of royal policies and directives. The system was decentralized and inefficient; the only centralization was in the king himself and the Council of the Indies (established in 1524). In Guatemala and other provinces in the Americas it led to jurisdictional disputes among officials and agencies of government, both civil and religious.[12] At the head of the bureaucracy government in Guatemala was the *audiencia,* which had various names until 1570, when it became the Audiencia de Guatemala. The functions of a royal audiencia were primarily judicial, but it also had governmental authority to curb the uncontrolled adelantados and end the turmoil of the conquest era, as in Guatemala. Also, audiencias distant from Mexico City and Lima enjoyed "virtual autonomy in all functions of government, reporting directly to the Council of the Indies."[13] Thus the audiencia was an excellent example of the clouded division of powers over judicial and administrative functions.

Usually audiencia members were headed by a president who was appointed from Spain by the king or the Council of the Indies, and who possessed status and a degree in law from a university such as that of Salamanca. In an outlying audiencia like that of Guatemala, the president also held the offices of governor, captain general, and superintendent of the royal treasury. He presided over meetings of the audiencia, which usually was composed of at least four oidores, or judges, all appointed by the Crown; a *fiscal,* or Crown attorney; an alguacil mayor; a chaplain; a solicitor for the poor; and assistant attorneys, notaries, and scribes.[14]

From its beginnings in 1543, as the Audiencia de los Confines, Guatemalan administration experienced changes in its seat and its jurisdictional responsibilities that did not stabilize until 1570. Originally located at Comayagua, in today's Honduras, it moved in 1544 to Gracias a Dios, also in modern Honduras; both sites were opposed by the residents of Santiago de Guatemala. Its initial jurisdiction extended from Tabasco and Yucatán (in modern Mexico) to Panama. In 1548 the king ordered the transfer of the audiencia to Santiago de Guatemala, where it remained until 1563.[15] The king reorganized the audiencia and changed its jurisdiction when the provinces of Chiapas, Soconusco, Guatemala, Verapaz, and Yucatán were placed under the control of the Audiencia de México, while those of Honduras, Nicaragua, and Costa Rica were attached to the Audiencia de Panamá.[16] With the dissolution of the Audiencia of Panama in 1568 and Panama's attachment to Peru, the Audiencia of Central America, or Guatemala as it was known then, was reconstituted with its seat at Santiago de Guatemala and jurisdiction extending from Chiapas in today's Mexico to Costa Rica. King Felipe II made it a "pretorial court independent of the viceroy of Mexico" and established its composition to consist of a president, governor, and captain general (all offices occupied by one individual), five magistrates, a Crown attorney, and a chief constable. The audiencia began its functions in Guatemala in 1570 and remained there until the end of the Spanish colonial period.[17]

Nominally subordinate to the viceroy of New Spain, the Audiencia de Guatemala operated as a virtually autonomous Spanish dominion throughout the remainder of Spain's control over Central America. Also under its authority were the present-day nations of Costa Rica, Nicaragua, Honduras, El Salvador, and Guatemala (including today's Belize), along with the modern Mexican state Chiapas; however, Guatemala emerged as the most important province and was also the social and economic center of the kingdom. For the entire period from 1570 to 1821 the president of the audiencia also headed the province of Guatemala, occupying the offices and carrying the titles of governor and captain general of Guatemala as well as president of the Audiencia de Guatemala.[18] In some capacities he reported directly to the king and the Council of the Indies; in others he reported to the viceroy of New Spain in Mexico City. He not only possessed jurisdiction as the chief executive of the Kingdom of Guatemala, governing the provinces within it, but also served as a legislator issuing decrees and promulgating laws and orders from the king.

Initially, while the Audiencia de Guatemala was still in Honduras, it consisted of three oidores and Alonso de Maldonado as president,[19] but of course it had a multitude of officials in its long tenure. Among them was the learned judge Alonso de Zorita, who served on it from 1552 to 1556. After arriving in Santiago de Guatemala, he was recognized officially by the audiencia on 20 September 1553 and served for a total of thirty-one months before his appointment to a similar position in the Audiencia de México, to which he departed on 25 April 1556. During his residency in Guatemala, Zorita made three visits within the kingdom, supporting the reforms of Alonso López de Cerrato (who died in 1555), correcting abuses, making head counts, moderating tributes, and helping to gather Indians into towns. He and López de Cerrato encountered resistance to their policies to reform the treatment of Indians from the cabildo of Santiago de Guatemala and settler encomenderos, who sent Bernal Díaz del Castillo (a soldier of Cortés's army of conquest in New Spain who then resided in Guatemala) to Spain to petition the king for a continuation of the encomienda and Indian slavery. King Carlos I denied their request. Bishop Marroquín and the secular clergy also opposed the reform efforts of López de Cerrato and Zorita, largely because they supported the Spanish settlers and because the Franciscans viewed Zorita as a creature of the rival Dominicans.[20]

Audiencia judges periodically made visits within the kingdom and rendered reports on conditions to the monarch in Spain. Licenciado Palacios, one of the magistrates of the audiencia, provided one of the earliest such reports to the king in 1576, describing the "province of

Guatemala," although actually he wrote an account of the kingdom rather than just the province. Since the king's royal orders had charged viceroys, presidents, and governors to make truthful reports concerning the lands, Indians, languages, customs, rivers, mountains, and "unusual things," Palacios pointed out that the Audiencia of Guatemala had appointed him to carry out the *visita* (tour of inspection), assigning him certain provinces to investigate. He then noted that the kingdom embraced a territory from the Isthmus of Tehuantepec to Costa Rica, covering three hundred leagues (about 780 miles) from northwest to southeast. In this vast area were thirteen principal provinces: Chiapas, Soconusco, Suchitepéques and "Cuahuatemala" (both in today's Guatemala), Verapaz, Icalcos, San Salvador, San Miguel, Honduras, Cholulteca, Nicaragua, Taguzgalpa (Tegucigalpa), and Costa Rica. Judge Palacios observed that the Indians spoke a different language in each one, "which made it seem as though . . . the Devil took in all these parts to plant discord and confusion with so many and so different languages." He then specified the Indian languages spoken in each of the thirteen provinces, noting for Soconusco and Guatemala mostly Mayan dialects except for the Pipil in Icalcos and along the Pacific coastal region. In what is present-day Guatemala, he visited the towns of Chiquimula de la Sierra and many other settlements inhabited by Spaniards and Indians. His descriptions of the Indians, products, insects, and strange creatures followed. Indians, he observed, paid tribute each year to their encomenderos. The land had valleys and abundant mountains, and it was well watered, producing cacao, fish, many fruits, very good oranges, and some figs and melons. However, the land was a "sick" one because of its heat and humidity. Mosquitoes of four kinds existed in great number. Together with flies and wasps, they made sleep at night impossible. In addition, Palacios noted the presence of caymans along the coast, scorpions, "some hairy caterpillars, some centipedes ["de ciento pies tan malos y tan venessos," or "of one hundred feet, so bad and so poisonous"], large snakes, and very bad vipers."[21] Palacios's description was only one of many rendered by magistrates of the audiencia. Other such reports were made by religious officials and will be discussed in chapter 4.

During the period between 1542 and 1700 forty-three persons occupied the position of president, captain general, and governor of the

Kingdom of Guatemala. On the death of an incumbent, his removal from office, or some other sudden change in the person occupying this position as the head of both the kingdom and the province of Guatemala, judges of the audiencia served as interim governors. Most of these officials were *licenciados* (most were lawyers holding a master's degree); others possessed doctoral degrees, were titled civilians, or occasionally, were bishops.[22] Although one authority notes that most of the governors between 1611 and 1657 were members of military orders,[23] a close examination of those occupying the office in that period reveals that only one (General Martín Carlos de Mencos y Arbizu, 1659–67) bore a military title in or near the period, and none of those in the office was recorded as a member of a military order such as that of Calatrava, Alcantara, or Santiago. In the 158 years between 1542 and 1700 only three governors had military titles, although it is possible some of the others may have had military experience.[24]

The president, captain general, and governor of the Kingdom of Guatemala also held administrative and legislative jurisdiction over the province of Guatemala,[25] as did the governors, of the other provinces, Honduras, Nicaragua, and Costa Rica, over their regions. Although Salvador was usually a part of Guatemala, it also had a separate governor responsible to the Kingdom of Guatemala.

While it would be tedious and impractical here to discuss all the presidents and governors of the kingdom over a century and a half, perhaps a few examples are worth noting. Licenciado Alonso de Maldonado, originally an oidor of the Audiencia de México and later interim governor of the Kingdom of Guatemala, occupied the position as the first president, captain general, and governor of the Audiencia de los Confines after receiving a royal appointment. He served from 20 November 1542 to 26 May 1548, having been officially installed in the office by the cabildo in Honduras.[26] At no time did he reside in Santiago de Guatemala, but only in Honduras, first at Comayagua and later at Gracias a Dios. During his presidency he had to deal with unrest created by the imposition of the New Laws in 1542–43. The judges of the audiencia failed to enforce those laws, which included the abolition of the encomienda, a restriction that was rescinded by the king in 1543. In fact, as one historian has noted, the judges were allied with the encomenderos and had encomiendas of their own, often renting Indians to others as human carriers.[27]

Alonso López de Cerrato became the second president and governor of the kingdom in 1548, serving until his death in 1555. López de Cerrato moved the audiencia, in accordance with the king's authorization, to Santiago de Guatemala in 1549. He is best known for the reforms he initiated to implement the New Laws and protect the Indians from mistreatment by the Spaniards. While those will be discussed more fully in chapter 5, "Spanish-Indian Relations and Labor Practices," it is appropriate to note here that López de Cerrato freed Indian slaves from Spaniards who could not show a title to them, ended the slave traffic in the province of Guatemala, moderated Indian tributes, and limited the use of Indians as human carriers. Of course, those reforms led to controversy with encomenderos, but surprisingly there also was opposition from Bishop Marroquín and the secular clergy.[28]

Among those who served as president, captain general, and governor in the seventeenth century was Licenciado Lope de Sierra Osorio (1678–81). Having served as governor of the Kingdom of Nueva Vizcaya, in what is today northern Mexico, he also had been an oidor of the Audiencia de México. The king appointed him to the Guatemalan post on 5 November 1677 to replace Fernando Francisco Escobedo. Sierra Osorio took possession of his office on 22 December 1678 and served exactly three years. During his term the cathedral of Santiago de Guatemala was dedicated on 26 November 1680, and he authorized the payment of a royal pension to the granddaughter of Pedro de Alvarado and her descendants, a practice that the king approved on 22 March 1691 and that continued at least until 1766, when King Carlos III approved payment of it to Doña Rosa María de Alvarado.[29] Unfortunately, Sierra Osorio's administration appears to have ended in controversy when the Crown ordered a *residencia* (end-of-term inspection). Evidently Sierra Osorio assigned an encomienda yielding five hundred pesos to his nephew Diego de Sierra Osorio, which the Crown declared null and void.[30]

Beneath the president, captain general, and governor and the Audiencia de Guatemala existed a host of subordinate royal officials in the period from 1542 to 1700. Generally known as alcaldes mayores or

TABLE 1. **Spanish Offices in the Kingdom of Guatemala**

	Year									
Office	1548	1550	1570	1600	1650	1700	1785	1787	1800	1821
Corregimientos	29	27	22	19	20	8	5	2	3	4
Alcaldías mayores	2	1	4	7	7	9	12	8	6	7
Gobernaciones	1	1	4	4	4	4	4	1	1	1
Gobernaciones-intendencias	0	0	0	0	0	0	0	4	3	3
Corregimientos-intendencias	0	0	0	0	0	0	0	0	1	1

corregidores, they were administrators of districts organized around important Spanish towns and Indian communities, of which there were many by the end of the seventeenth century. In addition to their responsibilities at the district level within the kingdom, the alcaldes mayores enforced the king's and the president's orders, collected revenues, and heard appeals from municipal justices.[31] Often underpaid and poorly supervised, they frequently exploited the residents of their jurisdictions, especially their Indian charges.

Carlos Molina Arguello, in his 1960 study of governors, alcaldes mayores, and corregidores during during the entire Spanish colonial period, observed that both district offices had been instituted in the kingdom and the province of Guatemala by the late 1540s. He also compiled a useful table showing the evolution of their numbers, reprinted as table 1.[32]

In addition to the royal officials at the kingdom, provincial, and district levels, the cabildos continued to function at the municipal level of principal urban settlements. The first one, as seen earlier in this chapter, was founded in 1524 in Iximché for the villa of Santiago de los Caballeros de Guatemala, and it was reestablished at the new capital of Almolonga (Ciudad Vieja) in 1527. Both were monopolized by the first settlers of Guatemala, originally consisting of four regidores, who were increased to eight in 1528.[33] That the cabildo continued at Almolonga is evident by its deliberations and selection of interim governors in 1542–43 after the death of Pedro de Alvarado and the destruction of the city. It continued at the new site of Antigua until the destruction of the city in the earthquake of July 1773 and the relocation to Nueva Guatemala by the end of that decade. There the cabildo continued to the end of the Spanish period. Its members were not appointed by the Crown, but they were dominated by the Creole elite of the city of Santiago de Guatemala.[34]

The cabildo of Santiago de Guatemala and others at principal towns, such as Gracias a Dios and San Salvador, represented the Castilian *municipio* and was a major institution of European colonization, as were cabildos all over Spanish America. Although the adelantado Pedro de Alvarado, like conquistadores elsewhere, appointed the first *alcaldes ordinarios* (municipal magistrates) and regidores, it was later common practice for the principal residents of the towns to elect the regidores, who in turn elected the alcaldes ordinarios from within the body. The cabildo was a tightly controlled institution charged with municipal functions, but it often became a focal point for resistance to and controversy with the audiencia. In later years the office of regidor often became hereditary and was occupied for life. In addition, other local officials had a place on the cabildo, such as the *alférez royal* (royal herald or standard bearer), the alguacil mayor, the *fiel ejecutor* (inspector of weights, measures, and prices), the *síndico* or *procurador* (attorney), and the *escribano* (scribe).[35]

Thus Spanish government of the kingdom and province of Guatemala grew and developed into a complex bureaucracy during the Habsburg monarchy in Spain. Replacing the earlier personalismo it became institutionalized as an administrative system of coordinate and overlapping functions and offices with a host of officials extending from the president and the audiencia down to district and municipal levels. With the advent of a new dynasty in Spain, the Bourbons, this system became increasingly complex and bureaucratic in the eighteenth century, producing controversy among office holders and whole institutions of government.

THE ERA OF GOVERNMENTAL REFORMS

With the death of the last Habsburg king, Carlos II, in 1700, a new line of monarchs began with the first Bourbon king, Felipe V. His successors reigned throughout the eighteenth century and during the first two decades of the nineteenth century before Guatemala declared its independence from Spain in September 1821. While all of the Spanish Bourbons made some reforms in the Americas, these changes reached their peak in the era of Carlos III (1759–88). As such changes do even now, the reforms instituted by the Bourbons, reflecting the ideas of the Enlightenment (reason, natural laws, progress, sciences, and intellectual awakening), introduced controversy and opposition among the inhabitants of the Americas. They have also been praised and criticized by historians of the twentieth century who regarded them as either Bourbon achievements or failures.[36] It is evident that the five Spanish kings between 1700 and 1821 introduced changes into the Americas that were both favorable and unfavorable.

Centralization and efficiency were the key characteristics of the Bourbon reforms, both in Spain and Spanish America. Miles Wortman has emphasized that the result in Central America was that more centralized government replaced local control. According to Wortman, the Bourbon strategy had six aims: to stimulate communications and trade, to limit ecclesiastical power by attacking the power and prestige of the Roman Catholic Church, to support interior producers of goods in opposition to the control and power of the Cádiz-Guatemala merchant class, to reform the tax structure, to introduce the system of intendencies, and to increase military activity in defense of the kingdom.[37] Historian Ralph Lee Woodward simplified those goals into four basic policies: anticlerical measures to reduce the temporal power of the clergy, commercial measures to increase production and trade between Spain and the Indies, administrative reforms to provide more responsive government and make tax collection more efficient, and military and naval measures to improve Spain's defensive posture and protect her commerce.[38]

While some of those aims will be discussed in later chapters, it is appropriate here to explain the administrative reforms as they pertain to the Kingdom of Guatemala and its provinces. In general, the quality of the Spanish officials improved notably under the Bourbons, and their salaries increased in proportion to their responsibilities, which they continued to exercise from Chiapas and Belize to Costa Rica.[39] By the time Alonso de Arcos y Moreno served as governor and captain general (1754–60) the annual salary of the position had been increased to 10,000 pesos.[40] During the 1770s the Crown also created the office of regent to act as president of the audiencia in the absence of the governor and captain general. The regent's annual salary was established at 6,600 pesos. Between 1759 and 1776 the audiencia's four alderman, each with a salary of 2,750 pesos, were increased to five with annual salaries in the latter year of 3,300 pesos each.[41]

Throughout the last 120 years of Spanish jurisdiction, an increased tendency to appoint military officers to the presidency and governorship was evident. Of the sixty persons who occupied the supreme position of authority in this period, at least thirty-one were senior military officers. All the governors between 1804 and 1821, with one exception, were military persons—an indication of the importance of their role as captains general in the defense of the kingdom.[42]

Royal control in the period from 1700 to 1800 increased the powers and responsibilities of the governor and the audiencia, while those of the cabildos diminished considerably. By 1720 the Crown had reduced the number of aldermen serving in the cabildo of Santiago de Guatemala from nineteen to five.[43] Although that cabildo remained important at the municipal level, between 1759 and 1788 (when it frequently was called the ayuntamiento) it consisted of eight regidores, who still elected their customary two alcaldes ordinarios. Each regidor had to pay 3,000 pesos to the Crown to obtain his position.[44] Thus the cabildo had become controlled by the king and royal government, and only wealthy persons could serve on it. When Napoleon Bonaparte invaded Spain in 1808, he forced the renunciation of King Carlos IV, captured the new king, Fernando VII, and installed Joseph Bonaparte as the unpopular monarch. In response, the Junta Central, on 22 January 1809, set a precedent for government in the absence of the legal Bourbon. Subsequently, the cabildo of Santiago de Guatemala—or as it was commonly known by then, the ayuntamiento—became an important center of opposition to Crown-appointed authorities, that is, to the governor and the audiencia, which consisted of the president, the regent, four oidores, and two Crown attorneys.[45] Consequently, during the independence era from 1811 to 1821, the ayuntamiento carried on a serious running opposition to the audiencia and the governor of the kingdom.[46]

One major governmental reform in the Kingdom of Guatemala and its component provinces was the establishment of the intendency system between 1785 and 1787. With judicial, fiscal, military, and administrative responsibilities, the office of the *intendente* (intendant) was at the district level in Central America. It was designed to improve local administration, establish more efficient royal control, and eliminate many alcaldes mayores and corregidores. Intendencies were created for Honduras, El Salvador, Nicaragua, and Chiapas, but not for the province of Guatemala, since it already was under the direct control and administration of the governor and captain general. El Salvador became the first intendency in September 1785, when the three alcaldías mayores of San Salvador, San Miguel, and San Vicente were consolidated. Chiapas became the last intendency in 1787. In all, throughout the kingdom, the new office reduced the number of gobernaciones from four to one, the number of corregimientos (districts ruled by corregidores) from five to two, and the total of alcaldías mayores from twelve to eight.[47] Yet, while consolidation occurred, it should be noted that some corregidores and alcaldes mayores continued to exist until the end of the Spanish period. Thus, the bureaucracy increased, especially since *subdelegados* (supervisors of areas within intendancies) were created within each district. Thus intendents, corregidores, and alcaldes mayores existed at the same time. Their overlapping functions caused confusion among governmental authorities over their jurisdictions and responsibilities. Of utmost importance, however, that the establishment of these intendencies encouraged regionalism and feelings of autonomy outside the province of Guatemala. During the last thirty-five years of Spanish administration the intendencies, that were separate from Guatemala evolved into centers of separatism and local identity. This was especially true in Salvador, which became a hotbed of opposition to the rule from Guatemala during the independence period. Likewise, the intendencies became a "major factor in the definition of areas that became independent nations" after 1830 and in the failure of the United Provinces of Central America.[48]

As in the earlier examination of the sixteenth and seventeenth centuries, it will be helpful to discuss some of the presidents of the kingdom during the eighteenth century. Certainly, the century began inauspiciously during the administration of General Gabriel Sánchez de Berrospe when he and the *visitador* (royal visitor or inspector), Fran-

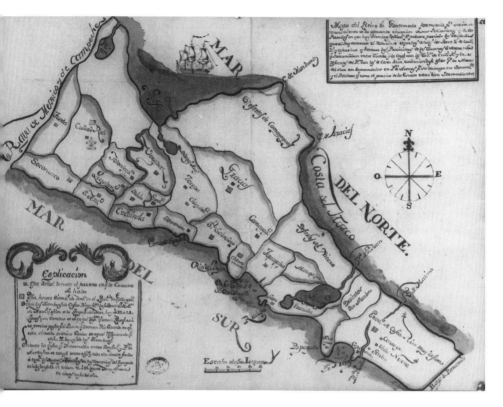

"Mapa del Reino de Guatemala," 1787 (AGI, Sevilla)

cisco Gómez de la Madriz, engaged in open warfare over the governor's poor conduct and administration, until the viceroy of New Spain intervened.[49] Conditions improved, and better administrators served as governor thereafter. One of them was Don Francisco Rodríguez de Rivas (1716–24). After the devastating earthquake and eruption of the Volcán de Agua on 29 September 1717, he planned and rebuilt the city of Santiago de Guatemala over the opposition of the bishop, who wanted to transfer it to another location. Rodríguez also took an active role in defending the Indians against mistreatment by the Spaniards.[50]

The king appointed Brigadier Pedro de Rivera y Villalón as president, of the Kingdom of Guatemala on 22 December 1729 to succeed

Antonio Pedro de Echevers y Subiza,[51] but Rivera did not actually take possession of the office until 12 July 1733.[52] For the next nine years, the longest term of any ruler in Guatemala during the eighteenth century, Rivera, who also bore the title of "Mariscal del Campo" (field marshal), occupied the highest governmental position in Central America. This native of Antequera in Málaga, Spain, already had already had experienced a distinguished military career of fifty-four years in service to the king in Europe, New Spain, and Yucatán before he arrived at Santiago de Guatemala. He had been captain of the presidio of Veracruz as early as 1711, had helped suppress a revolt in Tabasco, had expelled English corsairs from the island of Carmen, had served as "gobernador de armas" (chief military governor) of Yucatán, and by 30 December 1723 had been a corregidor, governor, and lieutenant captain general of Veracruz, as well as governor of Tlaxcala and its jurisdiction in central New Spain. He was most well known for his royal inspection of the northern frontier of New Spain, where he went as far as the province of New Mexico between 1724 and 1728. During that period of three years and seven months he personally conducted an extended investigation of frontier New Spain in which he and his followers traveled over 8,500 miles, visiting presidios and towns in today's Durango, Chihuahua, Coahuila, Sonora, Sinaloa, Nayarit, New Mexico, and Texas. His detailed report and his recommendations for the military defenses of New Spain's northern frontier became the basis for the Reglamento de 1729 (Regulation of 1729) establishing uniform practices and defenses there.[53] While serving afterwards as governor and captain general of the Kingdom of Guatemala in 1736, he forwarded a copy of his published *Diario y derrotero* ("diary and route") to an official in New Spain.[54]

Rivera seems to have performed very well in his various roles as chief executive of the kingdom. As captain general he expelled foreigners who did not possess royal licenses to reside and trade with the Indians in the kingdom, suppressed hostilities by the Mosquito Indians and their English allies on the Caribbean coast of Honduras and Costa Rica, and improved the forts and defenses of eastern ports (including the *castillo,* or fortress, of Petén and that of San Felipe del Río Dulce in eastern Guatemala). He also recommended increases of cavalry and infantry soldiers to protect the royal treasury, armory, archives, and newly established mint (dedicated in 1733) in Santiago de Guatemala. Although the king approved the increase of forty-five to fifty soldiers, at an increased cost of 1,718 pesos yearly, he denied troop increases suggested by Rivera for other posts.[55] As governor, Rivera took measures to prohibit illicit commerce; made detailed reports on the expenses of government and defenses of the kingdom; reconnoitered the mining establishments in Honduras; reported an abundance of metals produced, of "differing quality," in the jurisdiction of Chiquimula in mines "that had been retarded until the present time"; encouraged commerce and agricultural production throughout the kingdom; and established peaceful relations with ecclesiastical authorities. He also reported on the status of the missions in the Petén region, where he said seventeen Indian towns were administered by six ministers who were "good shepherds" for those in their charge. He had sent a squadron of loyal Indians with their bows and arrows, and "also with guns and munitions," into the mountains to attack the hostile Indians who had fled from the missions, thereby gaining some men and women of all ages to be baptized and converted to the Christian religion.[56]

Of special note were two of Rivera's reports concerning the administration and defenses of the kingdom. In his report of 23 November 1737 he observed that the Kingdom of Guatemala consisted of nineteen "gobiernos" (governmental jurisdictions) distributed in nine provinces and ten partidos (subdivisions). They were as indicated in table 2.[57]

Rivera's list of administrative districts showed four *gobernadores* (governancies) at a total annual salary of 6,774 pesos, or an average of 1,694 pesos yearly. It also indicates eleven alcaldias mayores at a total of 8,879 pesos, or an average of 807 pesos yearly, and four corregidores at a total of 1,337 pesos, or an average of 334 pesos yearly. It illustrates that total annual salaries for officials of the nineteen districts within the kingdom amounted to 16,990 pesos. In addition to showing the different annual salaries for royal officials at different levels of administration, it reveals wide variations between different geographical regions and the principal products within each jurisdiction.

Rivera's second detailed report, on 15 September 1740, examined the kingdom's defenses against the English, with whom Spain was at war. Although the presidency, according to Rivera, covered 650

TABLE 2. **Administrative jurisdictions of the Kingdom of Guatemala, 1737**

Province or Partido	Head Official and Sources of Income
Provinces	
Costa Rica	A governor and captain general with a salary of 2,750 pesos yearly.
Comayagua	Governor and captain general with annual salary of 1,654 pesos.
Nicaragua	Governor with 1,378 pesos yearly.
Soconusco	Governor with 992 pesos yearly supplemented by income from cacao production.
San Antonio Suchitepéques	Alcalde mayor with 1,158 pesos yearly supplemented by income from cacao contract.
San Salvador and San Miguel	Alcalde mayor with 827 pesos yearly supplemented by income from indigo-dye contract.
Chiapa	Alcalde mayor with 1,315 pesos yearly supplemented by income from wild grain and cotton.
Sonsonate	Alcalde mayor with 1,000 pesos yearly. Produced some fruits.
Verapaz	Alcalde mayor with 1,275 pesos yearly. Produced cotton and achiote (red or yellow vegetable dye).
Partidos	
Huehuetenango and Totonicapán	Alcalde mayor with salary of 330 pesos yearly. Cotton produced.
Atitlán and Tepanatitlán	Alcalde mayor with 661 pesos yearly.
Quezaltenango	Alcalde mayor with 330 pesos yearly. Wheat and weaving of wool.
Chiquimula de la Sierra, Sacapa, and Acuaguátlan	Alcalde mayor with 661 pesos yearly. Cacao and cotton spinning.
Esquintla Guasacapán	Alcalde mayor with 661 pesos yearly. Some cacao, fish in the rivers and creeks, and some grain crops.
Tegucigalpa	Alcalde mayor with 661 pesos yearly. Sales from silver mines.
Sutiaba	Corregidor with 250 pesos yearly. Indians in repartimiento for the benefit of haciendas, producing 9,000 pesos total annual benefit.
Realejo	Corregidor with 537 pesos yearly. Port of the South Sea.
Nicoya, or Nuevo Gobernado	Corregidor with 275 pesos yearly. Produced fodder taken to Panamá, thread and string from seashells; pearl fishing; abundant oysters.
Sebaco and Chontales	Corregidor with 275 pesos yearly.

leagues (about 1,700 miles), only nine of its provinces were "Mediterranean" (meaning on the Caribbean coast), while the rest were on the South Sea or Pacific Ocean. Only three "castles"—the fortresses on the Río San Juan de Nicaragua, San Felipe del Golfo de Honduras, and Petén de Itzá—existed on the Caribbean coast to defend the kingdom against English threats. Rivera pointed out that engineers were needed to correct the defects of each fortress, and he suggested that two new ones be constructed on the Río Matina in Costa Rica (where the port of Esparza, thirty leagues [about eighty miles] from the capital at Cartago, had been destroyed three times by the English) and at the port of Trujillo in Comayagua in Honduras. For each of the new garrisons Rivera suggested a complement of one hundred men and their officers.[58]

Rivera remained in Guatemala until 1743, evidently discharging his duties as president of the audiencia, as well as those of captain general and governor, to the satisfaction of the cabildo of Santiago de Guatemala. Its members informed the king in 1738 of the "common benefits, peace, and public tranquillity" that it enjoyed with the help of Pedro de Rivera, who dedicated himself "entirely to the good and conservation of the public."[59] On 16 October 1742, Don Tomás de Rivera y Santa Cruz (no relation to Pedro de Rivera) took possession of the office of president, captain general, and governor of the kingdom of Guatemala, replacing Pedro de Rivera, who departed for Mexico City.[60] Before his death there on 24 November 1744, the king granted him an annual pension of three thousand escudos, beginning from the day he ceased holding office in Guatemala.[61]

After another disastrous earthquake on 4 March 1751, the government of the kingdom entered a period of frequent changes until the decade between 1773 and 1783, when it stabilized under Martín de Mayorga (1773–79) and Colonel Matías de Gálvez (1779–83). Mayorga had scarcely arrived at the fortress of Omoa on the Honduran coast in May 1773 and proceeded to Santiago de Guatemala when the earthquake of 29 July 1773 struck the capital. Most of his administration was devoted to the needs of the populace in the heavily damaged capital city, today's Antigua, and the founding of and transfer to the new capital city in the valley of La Hermita, a city known officially as Nueva Guatemala de la Asunción, on the site of today's Guatemala City.[62] This transfer of the capital will be discussed more fully in a chapter 8.

With his promotion to the position of viceroy of New Spain in 1779, Mayorga departed for Mexico City. He turned over his office to Colonel Matías de Gálvez, the older brother of José de Gálvez, Minister of the Indies to King Carlos III in Spain and father of Bernardo de Gálvez, governor of Spanish Louisiana from 1776 to 1783 and later viceroy of New Spain after his father's death. The king appointed Matías de Gálvez as governor, captain general, and president of the audiencia on 22 January 1779. He took possession of the office on 15 May, but he had actually become head of the government earlier, on 4 April, when his predecessor, Mayorga, had departed for New Spain.[63] Gálvez was already present in Guatemala, having served as *comandante inspector* (commandant inspector) of troops and defenses after his arrival at the fortress of San Fernando de Omoa on 29 June 1778, and after taking residence at Nueva Guatemala on 17 July. In that capacity he had found the garrison at Omoa in a "deplorable state," and he took immediate action to rectify the poor condition of the company there, believing that Omoa was the "llave y antemural de todo el reyno" (the key and outer wall of the kingdom).[64]

Sixty-two years old when he took over the government of the kingdom, this former farmer from the province of Málaga in Spain faced numerous challenges during his administration and took vigorous actions to resolve them.[65] Gálvez, inheriting the problem of the uncompleted transfer of civil and religious agencies from Antigua to Nueva Guatemala, immediately directed the move of the audiencia into the new royal palace and the relocation of the offices of the royal treasury and customs. Then, on 6 June 1779, he ordered that all governmental officials move within fifteen days to the new capital, enforcing the order by sending a detachment of infantry and another of cavalry to ensure compliance with the king's earlier decree. He also sought and received King Carlos's permission to transfer all religious offices and institutions to the new capital.[66]

Of utmost importance to Spain and the Kingdom of Guatemala during the almost four years of his administration was Gálvez's role as captain general in the defense of the kingdom against the English, with whom Spain was at war as an ally of France and, indirectly, in support of the patriots during the American Revolution. Gálvez planned and personally conducted campaigns against British land and naval forces on the northern and eastern coasts of Central America and on islands in the Gulf of Honduras. His first objective was to recover the fortress of Omoa, which the British had seized. After spending the summer of 1779 coordinating and preparing plans, filling vacancies in military ranks, organizing and training regular and militia units, arranging for supplies and munitions, and requisitioning ships and financial support from other Spanish dependencies, Gálvez personally led a force of one thousand men overland from Nueva Guatemala to San Pedro Sula and then Omoa, where after a three-day siege the British defenders surrendered on 29 November. Promoted by the king to brigadier, Gálvez then countered British invasions of Nicaragua in 1780–81 by establishing a new fort and naval patrols on Lake Nicaragua to prevent the British from taking Granada and León. After the success of these ventures his forces proceeded up the Río San Juan, culminating their offensive with the capture of the fortress at San Juan del Río on 4 January 1781. Meanwhile Gálvez had already begun preparations for a land and water offensive against British posts in Honduras and against their Mosquito Indian allies by first cutting off their supply line from Roatán Island. After careful preparations, in March 1782, Gálvez (now promoted to field marshal) embarked six hundred troops and supplies on twenty-eight vessels for Roatán, where after a bombardment of New Port Royal his forces, led personally by their captain general, took the fort and received the surrender of the British garrison on 17 March.[67]

By late April 1782, Gálvez had returned to Nueva Guatemala to resume his governmental duties. In March 1783 the king promoted him to lieutenant general and appointed him viceroy of New Spain, a position he held until his death on 3 November 1784. That his administration of the Kingdom of Guatemala had been more than satisfactory is revealed in a report of the cabildo of Nueva Guatemala on 9 July 1782. Its members enthusiastically praised Gálvez for his defense of the kingdom from the British and their Indian allies, his efficient transfer of the capital, his promotion of agriculture and commerce, his control of prices and the abundance of provisions, his diligent and compassionate response to a smallpox epidemic in 1780, his appointments to public offices, his measures to eliminate loafers and vagabonds, and his construction and improvement of buildings in Nueva Guatemala. The nine members of the cabildo wrote their "most reverent thanks" to the king for having sent Gálvez to govern with fairness and public happiness the people of the kingdom. They emphasized that they "did not have a single complaint" against their governor and captain general.[68] The report on Gálvez's administration by José Pablo Valiente, an oidor of the Audiencia de Guatemala, on 3 December 1783, revealed that there had been no complaints registered against the outgoing governor. Therefore King Carlos III approved the recommendations of the Consejo Real de Indias (Royal Council of the Indies) and his attorney, expressing "my royal gratitude" for the general's services and dispensing with any penalties, fines, or reimbursements from Gálvez.[69] For his reforms and administration historians have observed that Gálvez became known as the "primero padre de la patria" (first father of the country).[70]

One may gain some insight into the size of the Spanish bureaucracy, the individuals occupying royal governmental positions, and their salaries from a report of the *contador mayor de cuentas* (chief accountant or auditor), Juan Manuel Ramírez, on 14 February 1783, near the end of Gálvez's administration. This detailed listing of royal offices throughout the kingdom and their incumbents, was headed by the lieutenant general, president, governor, and captain general, Matías de Gálvez, whose annual salary was 10,000 pesos. In addition Gálvez received 6,000 pesos for occupying the position of inspector general simultaneously. The report then listed the members of the audiencia—four oidores at a salary of 3,300 pesos each yearly, two fiscales with the same salaries, and an alguacil mayor with an annual salary of 2,775 pesos. It then listed subalterns of the audiencia, fourteen in all, including a counsellor, two attorneys for civil and criminal law, an official in charge of the jail, as well as other officials who supported the audiencia. Altogether, for twenty-two people, the total salaries for the audiencia amounted to 43,575 pesos annually. Members of the governor's staff were also listed, including a royal architect at 3,000 pesos and a surgeon at 1,200 pesos. The report also mentioned a variety of other royal offices, both within the capital and throughout the kingdom. These included the royal mint, the royal office of *alcabalas* (sales taxes), the director general of the royal tobacco office, the administrator general of gunpowder and playing cards, royal treasury officials, the commandant of the fortress of Omoa, and a host of corregidores and alcaldes mayores. Among the last were the district officials of Chimaltenango, Quezaltenango, Sololá, Amatitanes and Suchitepéques (one district), and Totonicapán, all within the province of Guatemala. All in all there were 152 royal positions listed in this report, and the total of the annual salaries amounted to 161,962 pesos and 6 reales, not including the infantry battalion, the officers and troops of the dragoons, and the militia assistants.[71]

By 1800 the captaincy general and kingdom of Guatemala comprised fifteen provinces with four intendencies, twenty-nine *subdelegaciones* (sub districts within the intendencies), four politico-military districts, three corregimientos, and seven alcaldias mayores. The salary plus emoluments of the president and captain general, amounted to 10,000 pesos annually. Four oidores and the fiscal were each paid a salary of 750,000 maravedis, or about 3,000 pesos, annually. The ayuntamiento of the capital had two alcaldes ordinarios elected by members of the ayuntamiento (an annual event that caused disputes between the *peninsulares,* or Spaniards born in the mother country, and the *criollos,* or American-born Spaniards), eight aldermen, a royal herald, a chief constable, an *alcalde provincial* (provincial magistrate), and one *síndico procurador* (lawyer or attorney). The regidores, or aldermen, held their offices in perpetuity and were generally members of old families whose fathers had purchased the offices that their sons inherited.[72]

During the last twenty years of Spanish administration the captaincy general of Guatemala (as it was by then known) was dominated by two officials: Brigadier Antonio González Mollinedo y Saravía (1801–1811, with some interim officials for brief periods) and Lieutenant General José de Bustamante y Guerra (1811–18, also with brief interim replacements).[73] These were years of turmoil, internal dissent between criollos and peninsulares and between the ayuntamiento, representing the new merchant elite, and the audiencia and captain general, representing the interests of the king and the conservative old guard. Of course, this was the era of the Napoleonic wars in Europe, the French invasion of Spain, unstable governments in the mother country, and independence movements in Latin America, including those of Guatemala and the rest of Central America, all of which will be treated more fully in chapter 9, "Instability and Independence." In 1821 the captaincy general of Guatemala consisted of fifteen provinces, of which

Map of the Kingdom of Guatemala, circa 1808 (from Domingo Juarros, *A Statistical and Commercial History of Guatemala*)

eight were alcaldias mayores, two, corregimientos; four, intendencies (León, Ciudad Real, Comayagua, and San Salvador); and one was the gobierno of Costa Rica.[74]

In the 297 years of Spanish government over the kingdom and province of Guatemala, its administration progressed from the haphazard, personalist rule of the Alvarado family and its friends to an increasingly royal-controlled, bureaucratic system consisting of numerous offices and officials, frequently with overlapping jurisdictions and responsibilities. The cabildo or ayuntamiento was the oldest, continuous body at the municipal level. Next came the office of president, captain general, and governor, together with the audiencia, both exercising royal authority at the top level of government. Beneath those offices, or institutions, a host of subordinate officials existed at the regional and district levels, a situation that was made more complicated by the reforms of the Bourbon kings. While this system of civil administration was increasingly complex, it was made more so by the development and administration of ecclesiastical institutions represented by the Roman Catholic Church.

CHAPTER 4

The Church

THE ROMAN CATHOLIC CHURCH in Guatemala, as in most other parts of colonial Spanish America, was a prestigious and powerful institution brought from Spain and adapted to the peoples and conditions of the Americas. Its primary purpose was religious: to convert the Indians to the Catholic faith and to administer to the spiritual needs of the Spanish populace. Yet, the church had an important secondary role among the hundreds of thousands of Indians in Guatemala: to acculturate, or Westernize, them by teaching European methods of agriculture and animal husbandry, trade skills, the Castilian language, and Spanish customs. In addition, clergymen and women taught the Indians European manners and what the churchmen determined was a civilized life. Thus the clergy in Guatemala, as elsewhere throughout the Americas, were both religious agents and in the forefront of what Spaniards viewed as their civilizing mission among the Indians of the Americas, whom they often referred to as *indios bárbaros*.

Friars and priests of the Catholic Church accompanied the conquest expedition to Guatemala in 1524 and were among the first permanent residents of that province as well as others within the Kingdom of Guatemala. Thirteen years later the king and pope established the diocese of Guatemala with Father Francisco de Marroquín as the first bishop. Mendicant orders of the Catholic Church reached all areas of Central America over the course of the next three centuries, but they concentrated especially on the province of Guatemala, which was densely-populated by Indians, establishing missions, churches, schools, convents, and hospitals in Santiago de los Caballeros de Guatemala (at Almolonga until 1541; then, until the mid-1770s, today's Antigua; and finally in Nueva Guatemala de la Asunción, today's Guatemala City), as well as in numerous villages in the countryside surrounding the capital and other regions of the province. As the church grew and spread in the first century and a half of Spanish occupation, it increased its power and took on many different roles, such as instruction of both Indians and Spaniards, mortgaging and financing landholdings, maintaining hospitals, becoming a major source of landholding and wealth in its own right, and reporting on conditions in both the province and the kingdom of Guatemala, which embraced all the area from southern Mexico to Costa Rica. During the last century and a half of Spanish rule the church experienced great changes and diminished authority when the Bourbon kings curtailed ecclesiastical privileges and powers and regulated the church and its clergy in the interests of greater royal control.

Church and state were closely related in Guatemala, and in all of colonial Latin America, from the outset of the conquest and colonization to the end of Spanish control with the independence of the Central American nations. Indeed, in addition to its religious functions, the church served as an arm of the state and its sovereigns. It had administrative functions in that it conveyed the king's will as supreme head of the temporal church to the communities and rural inhabitants—both Spaniards and Indians—of the province of Guatemala as well as other regions of the kingdom. Thus church and state were united in a governmental system that might be described as a theocracy. At all times this was in accordance with the *patronato real,* or royal patronage, granted by the popes to the monarchs of Castile, beginning with Queen Isabella in 1493.

THE ROYAL PATRONAGE

In 1493, Pope Alexander VI gave Queen Isabella of Castile and King Ferdinand of Aragon the title of "los Reyes Católicos," or "the Catholic Kings." After the discovery of America he and later popes issued papal bulls assigning to the Crown of Castile dominion over all islands and mainlands west and south of a line in the Atlantic Ocean from the North Pole to the South Pole that was one hundred leagues (about 270 miles) west and south of the Azores and the Cape Verde Islands. In 1494 the Treaty of Tordesillas between Spain and Portugal moved the line 270 leagues farther west, eventually giving Spain the majority of the territories in the Americas, and Portugal only a small claim to coastal Brazil. With those boundaries, Pope Alexander and his successors until 1508 granted Castile its title because of the church's obligation to evangelize the Indians.[1] Papal bulls of donation granted the monarch of Castile, beginning with Queen Isabella and continuing with her successors, the right and royal duty of patronage over all lands and peoples in the Americas. The temporal church in Spain and America was thereby subordinated to the Crown of Castile, while the spiritual function, dogma, and maintenance of religious discipline remained the responsibility of the pope. After the papal bull of 1501 the monarch of Castile had the specific duty of supporting the church in America. This responsibility meant that Queen Isabella and her successors administered the temporal or worldly affairs of the church—appointing and removing men and women of the clergy, requiring them to obtain licenses to go to or leave their jurisdictions, paying them an annual *sínodo* (financial remuneration), requiring oaths of loyalty from them, collecting revenues from settlers and Indians in the form of yearly tributes and fees, meeting the expenses of the church, and maintaining religious orthodoxy among the inhabitants of the Indies, as Spanish possessions in the Americas were called. The patronato real gave Castilian monarchs exclusive control of religious and administrative affairs of the church throughout the Americas, while spiritual matters remained the preserve of the pope. Lyle McAlister has noted that "the church became an arm and a shield of royal authority,"[2] an observation that accurately depicts the relationship of church and state in Guatemala.

Before her death in 1504, Queen Isabella as a devout Catholic, declared that Indians who accepted the Catholic religion and her dominion over them would become her free vassals with the same rights as Europeans. As a sign of their fidelity and homage to the Crown of Castile, Indians were required to pay tribute annually to her and her successors.[3] Possessing the right and the duty of royal patronage, the monarchs delegated *vicepatronato* (civil authority over the church's temporal affairs) to royal agencies and officials in the Americas, while the secular clergy, from archbishops and bishops to parish priests and members of religious orders, administered the spiritual affairs of the church. This system, or institution, was extended to Guatemala immediately after its conquest and settlement, and continued until the end of the Spanish colonial rule there.[4]

THE CHURCH IN GUATEMALA BEFORE 1700

The first Catholic clergymen recorded in Guatemala were with the expedition of Pedro de Alvarado, although it is possible that they were preceded by Fathers Bartolomé de Olmedo and Juan Díaz, who went in 1522–23 as "emissaries of Cortés" to the Tzutujil Mayas near Lake Atitlán.[5] Franciscan friars Juan Godinez and Juan Díaz accompanied Alvarado, serving as chaplains to the expeditionary force and conducting the first masses within Guatemala during the early months of the conquest in 1524.[6] Evidently they remained in Guatemala, establishing the Franciscans as the first order in the province and kingdom, and illustrating that most of the early clerics migrated to Guatemala from New Spain.

Members of the mendicant orders of the Catholic Church who belonged to the regular clergy (those who lived according to a rule) were in the forefront as missionaries during the first fifteen years or so of Spanish occupation in Guatemala. After the Franciscans came the Dominicans, who arrived in 1529 and founded a convent at Santiago de los Caballeros (Almolonga) in that year to serve as headquarters for their evangelization of the Indians.[7] Dominican friars Luis Cancer (who later was martyred in Florida), Rodrigo de Ladrada, and Father Bartolomé de las Casas (the famous "Protector of the Indians," later bishop of Chiapas) reached Guatemala in the 1530s. Fathers Cancer and Ladrada concentrated their missionary work among the Tzutujil Mayas near Lake Atitlán, while Las Casas had turned to the region known as Verapaz by 1537.[8] Mercedarian friars arrived in 1537, when they also established a *convento* in Santiago de Guatemala;[9] and Jesuits first came to Guatemala in 1582.[10] Those four orders remained paramount in the province throughout the sixteenth century, although other orders also established a presence there. In general, the Dominicans were responsible for Indian pueblos north of Santiago de Guatemala, the Franciscans were in towns south of the capital, and the Mercedarians on the west; but there were exceptions, and rivalries existed among those orders for control over the Indians in those jurisdictions as well as the rest of Central America.[11] By 1600 there were twenty-two Franciscan, fourteen Dominican, and six Mercedarian convents within the province of Guatemala.[12]

After the turn of the sixteenth century other regular orders established themselves in Guatemala. First came the Augustinians in 1610 with the arrival of friar Francisco de Ibarra and the foundation of their initial convent in Santiago during the following year.[13] In 1668 the Bethlehemite order was organized in Guatemala to maintain a hospital in the capital. It was the only male religious order to originate in Guatemala during the colonial era.[14] Toward the end of the seventeenth century four religious of the Recolete order (Cristo Crucificado ó Recolección) established themselves in Santiago de Guatemala and built a convent and an adjacent church on the west side of the city in 1700. Fray Antonio Margil de Jesús, later a leader in the foundation of the Catholic Church in eastern Texas, was among these *recoletos*.[15] Thus by 1700 the city of Santiago de Guatemala alone had a magnificent cathedral, twenty-four churches, eight *hermitas* (hermitages or small chapels), and fifteen convents. By then the Dominicans were the most influential, numerous, and wealthy of the religious orders.[16]

Yet, the establishment of the mendicant orders and their missionary work among the Indians were not the only or even the principal developments of the Catholic Church in Guatemala between 1524 and 1700. Missionary efforts and the policy of *congregaciones* (congregating Indians into towns), which began in 1537,[17] were only parts of the overall presence and activities of the church. Far more important was the early establishment of the secular church, whose clergymen and women were organizing and administering the church for both Spaniards and Indians by the mid-1530s. The secular clergy—archbishops, bishops, parish priests *(curas),* and a host of other ecclesiastics—constituted a bureaucracy within the province of Guatemala that extended to the other territories of the kingdom.

Pope Paul III, by a papal bull of 18 December 1534, authorized the establishment of the diocese, or bishopric, of Guatemala and appointed Francisco de Marroquín as the first bishop of the kingdom with a jurisdiction extending from Chiapas and Yucatán to today's Costa Rica.[18] Bishop Marroquín had the support of Bishop Juan de Zumárraga in Mexico City, who had sent him to Guatemala with Pedro de Alvarado when the conquistador returned there from Spain in 1530. Bishop Zumárraga appointed Marroquín initially as vicar-general, and Alvarado nominated him as parish priest to the cabildo of Santiago de Guatemala on 3 June 1530. Selected as the best candidate for the position, Marroquín was consecrated as bishop of Guatemala by Bishop

Zumárraga in Mexico City on 8 April 1537.[19] He served as bishop continuously until his death on Good Friday, 18 April 1563. Devoted to his priestly duties, he was responsible for beginning the construction of the first cathedral at Santiago de Guatemala in Almolonga, at his own expense of five thousand pesos. It withstood the flood of 11 September 1541, but a new cathedral was subsequently built in the new city of Santiago (Antigua), which lasted until 1669. In addition, Marroquín—who served as Protector de Indios (Protector of the Indians)—founded a hospital for their care in 1553, freed Alvarado's enslaved Indians after the conquistador's death, founded a school to teach youths in 1548, and established a college of arts and theology, which he hoped would grow into a university. Unsuccessful in this last endeavor, he bequeathed much of his property to a future university in his last will and testament.[20] It should also be noted that he and Father Bartolomé de las Casas had differences of opinion over who should administer the Indians of Verapaz, and Marroquín generally supported the town council of Santiago de Guatemala and the encomenderos in their resistance to the New Laws of 1542–43 and the reform efforts of Alonso López de Cerrato and Judge Alonso de Zorita in the 1550s.[21]

Although a succession of bishops followed Marroquín, Chiapas was erected as a separate see in 1542, and other dioceses were established in outlying provinces beyond Guatemala. An archbishopric was not established with its seat in Santiago de Guatemala until Pope Benedict XIV did so in 1742.[22] Between 1573 and 1578, there were five bishoprics in Central America: Guatemala, Chiapas, Honduras, Verapaz, and Nicaragua. Within the bishopric of Guatemala there were five pueblos of Spaniards—Santiago de Guatemala, Sonsonate, San Salvador, San Miguel, and Xeres de la Frontera—with 508 vecinos (227 in Santiago and 130 in San Salvador, for example), of whom 170 were encomenderos. In the bishopric of Chiapas there was one Spanish town, Ciudad Real, with 75 vecinos (47 of them encomenderos), and forty Indian towns. The bishopric of Verapaz had no Spanish towns and fifteen Indian towns. The bishopric of Nicaragua contained six Spanish towns (including León, Granada, Segovia, Realejo, and Gracias a Dios), and the bishopric of Honduras had five Spanish towns (including the communities of Trujillo and Comayagua, along with three villas).[23]

Beneath the bishop in the organization of the church, the diocese of Guatemala was divided into *doctrinas,* or parishes, each under the administration of a cura, who also was responsible for visitas in outlying smaller communities where no cleric resided.[24] Each town was responsible for maintaining its parish priest through payments of goods, services, and sometimes currency. In the Indian towns, as well as those of the Spaniards, all church rituals were paid for by the inhabitants.[25] Usually a *cofradía* (lay brotherhood) existed within each Spanish on Indian community to help implement the Catholic faith. Indians evidently showed great enthusiasm for them, and cofradias proliferated throughout Guatemala. The first one, Santa Veracruz, was founded for Spaniards in Santiago de Guatemala by Marroquín in 1533, and by 1559 another, known as Nuestra Señora del Rosario (Our Lady of the Rosary), had been established in the capital. Their main function was to celebrate the fiesta of the community's patron saint and provide support for religious ceremonies throughout the year, yet their members also visited the sick and celebrated monthly masses for the living and the dead; and the women assistants of the cofradia prepared food for celebrations as well as maintained the clothing and physical condition of the holy images. Each cofradia was headed by a mayordomo (manager or headman) and a scribe who kept the books. Membership dues, contributions, and fees financed their activities. A *caja de comunidad* (general community fund) was administered by the town officials—the alcalde mayor and the cabildo—with funds contributed from the cofradias as well as the land and labor from the community members. Indeed, as Sandra Orellana has noted for the Tzutujil Mayas, the cofradia "became a focal point of Indian life."[26] While not officially sanctioned by the church, cofradias were tolerated by priests because they provided local support for the conduct of religious ceremonies and extra income for the poorly paid local clergy.[27] Furthermore, as Lyle McAlister has observed, religion was thus "linked intimately with the community," and it provided a measure of unity, not only in Guatemala but throughout Spanish America.[28]

The church organization paralleled the governmental system, and its finances depended heavily upon the collection of the annual *diezmo,* or tithe. At the top of the ecclesiastical administration, along with the bishops and responsible to them, was the Cabildo Eclesiástico (church council). It consisted of the dean of the cathedral in Santiago de Guatemala, an archdeacon, a *chantre* (precentor, choir director, and schoolmaster); and a treasurer.[29] While it acted as an advisory body to the bishop, the cabildo also administered the affairs of the cathedral and collected yearly tithes from the citizenry. At the lower levels parish priests were assisted in their community churches by Indian church officials, two or three *cantores* (singers or musicians), a *sacristán* (sexton), and a *fiscal,* who assisted the priest and called the people to mass.[30] As we have seen, these religious also received considerable assistance from the cofradias of the parish.

Three sources of funds supported the church: (1) the state, through its royal sinódos; (2) the tithe; and (3) the contributions or donations collected at masses, as fees for religious services, and in dowries provided for nuns and priests. By far the most important source of revenue was the diezmo. Miles Wortman has observed that the tithe contributed at least 80 percent of all church income under the Habsburgs and during most of the Bourbon period, but it declined so that after 1763 it represented less than 50 percent, and by the early 1770s less than 40 percent, of the total income of the church.[31] This tribute of approximately 10 percent was paid by both Spaniards and Indians. It was collected by officials in each town and was usually paid in kind by Indians and in cash by ladinos.[32] The total funds received annually were divided into nine parts, called *novenas.* Two-ninths were sent to the king, and seven-ninths were dispensed at the cathedral level for the ecclesiastical chapter (Cabildo Eclesiástico), church construction and maintenance, sustenance of the hospital, social services provided by the church, and the bishop's use.[33]

Although the Holy Office of the Inquisition established tribunals in Lima (1570), Mexico City (1571), and Cartagena (1620),[34] it never held court in Guatemala during the colonial period, and its role there was relatively inconspicuous. Since Indians were specifically excluded from the jurisdiction of the Inquisition, and Guatemala had hundreds of thousands of them, the need for a separate tribunal was not great. Instead the jurisdiction of the tribunal in Mexico City was extended in 1572 to cover the Spaniards and *castas* (mixed-race citizens) in Guatemala. The members of the cabildo in that year received the first commissary of the Holy Office, Don Diego de Carbajal, and Guatemalans seem to have welcomed the institution. While there was occasional inquisitorial activity in Guatemala, it did not restrict academic life at the university after its founding in 1676, and did not convey the horrors felt elsewhere. Nor did it prosecute those who questioned religious doctrine. Instead its agents focused on domestic matters in maintaining the purity of the faith (such as) blasphemy, witchcraft, bigamy, adultery, Judaism, sacrilege, solicitation during the confession, and superstition. Seldom did it concern itself with the morals of the clergy except in rare cases of solicitation. During the first 110 years of the Inquisition's presence in Santiago de Guatemala, its commissary heard a total of 195 cases, fewer than 2 per year, and most of them were the common offenses heard everywhere in the Spanish dominions. In 1813 the Inquisition's authority was suppressed in accordance with the liberal Spanish Constitution of 1812, but King Fernando VII restored its jurisdiction in 1817, only four years before Guatemala established its independence.[35]

Colonial Guatemalans seem not only to have practiced religious orthodoxy but to have created and adapted new Americanized forms of ceremonies and worship. Tales of Tecum Umán, the Quiché Indian leader who reportedly perished in hand-to-hand combat with Pedro de Alvarado, became commonplace; and the cult of Nuestra Señora de Guadalupe (Our Lady of Guadalupe), an Americanization of the Virgin Mary originating in New Spain after 1531, spread to Guatemala during the sixteenth and seventeenth centuries.[36]

Of special note concerning religious veneration was the establishment and development of worship of Nuestro Señor de Esquipulas, commonly called the Cristo Negro (Black Christ). The town of Esquipulas, named for a Chorti Indian chieftain, was in the department of Chiquimula in southeastern Guatemala. It was founded for Chorti Indians between 1560 and 1570 on a site near an Indian shrine noted for its health-giving earth and sulphurous springs. When the Catholic Church outlawed the cult or adoration of Indian idols in 1578, the townspeople erected a small Christian chapel there. Sometime later the Chorti inhabitants raised one hundred *tostones* (the equivalent of about fifty ounces of silver), from the sale of cotton grown by their communal labor, to purchase a sacred image. In 1594 they commissioned Quirio Cataño, a noted sculptor of Antigua, to carve the image. Com-

Basilica of Esquipulas (INGUAT, Guatemalan Tourist Commission)

pleted the following year, this image of Christ, about four and one-half feet tall, is made of balsam and orangewood. Christ's body is dark brown in color, perhaps darkened by the smoke of the many candles and the incense burned nearby over the course of nearly four centuries. Since 1595 the Cristo Negro has been the focal point of worship by the townspeople and pilgrims from all over Central America seeking miraculous cures from illnesses and economic distress. Among those recorded cured in the seventeenth century were a poor laborer from Havana, named Juan García; a Spaniard from Nueva Granada (today's Colombia), named Pedro Ruiz, cured of ulcers on his legs; an Indian, named Juan Andrés; and in 1680, a blind Indian, Juan Ventura, who was completely paralyzed before his cure. The Catholic Church officially recognized the curative power of the Cristo Negro in 1737 when Bishop Fray Pedro Pardo de Figueroa (later archbishop) was cured there of a contagious disease. Later, as a sign of his gratitude and devotion, Archbishop Figueroa ordered the construction of the majestic white church in the baroque style (completed in 1758) that now is the home of the Cristo Negro. Although pilgrims come throughout the year, the townspeople of Esquipulas have three special celebrations: the titular festival of Santiago on 25 July, the great fairs around 15 January (the day of Esquipulas), and during Holy Week.[37]

THE BOURBONS AND THE CHURCH

After 1700 the Bourbon kings in Spain brought changes in church policies and practices because of reforms affecting the civil administration of Guatemala and other American possessions. Under Felipe V and through the reign of Fernando VII, the ideas of the Enlightenment increasingly were applied in the Americas, including Guatemala, especially centralization of administration under the direct control of the monarch and assumption by the Crown of some functions formerly exercised by regional or local authorities. Ecclesiastical reforms accompanied the administrative changes. They were anticlerical in nature, designed to reduce and limit the temporal powers, property, and prestige of the clergy.[38] Reform reached a peak during the reign of Carlos III (1759–88) with the expulsion of the Jesuits in Spain and all over the Spanish kingdoms in the Americas. However, they never were intended to separate church and state, establish religious freedom, or eliminate Catholicism as the one true religion. Instead, they were to enhance the power of the king and eliminate or control older Habsburg institutions such as the encomienda and the powers and privileges of ecclesiastical officials in the Americas. The Bourbon anticlerical reforms, while successful in establishing the king's authority and control over the church, also introduced conflict and controversy, and had unintended consequences in Guatemala and the rest of Spanish America.

What then were some of the reforms applied to Guatemala and the other provinces of the kingdom? Since Santiago de Guatemala (Antigua) and its successor Nueva Guatemala de la Asunción (Guatemala City) were strongholds of clerical wealth and prestige, and Dominicans, Franciscans, and other mendicant orders had powers that the monarchs viewed as too great, the Crown limited the construction of new monasteries and the religious acceptance of novices in those orders before they had reached adulthood. Reforms also decreased or abolished some taxes levied to support the church, especially the tribute from Indian parishes after the 1760s. As a general practice the Crown favored secularization of the church and more control by the secular instead of the regular clergy.[39] In 1742, Felipe V elevated the Guatemalan church to archdiocese status, thereby establishing centralized control over the various bishoprics that had existed previously. Father Pedro Pardo de Figueroa became the first archbishop in 1743, with the bishops of Chiapas, Comayagua, and León under his jurisdiction.[40] In 1751 a royal cedula prohibited tribute collection by ecclesiastics and ordered that civil authorities collect tribute and administer community funds. This was done to eliminate reported contraband trading by clerics, as well as to establish civil control of funds.[41] Two years later, in 1753 and again in 1757, the king ordered that curacies occupied by regular orders, on becoming vacant, be passed to the secular clergy after approval by the archbishop.[42]

While the expulsion of the Jesuits in 1767 was (and still is) the most controversial and sweeping reform by the Bourbons, it was not so important in Guatemala as it was in New Spain and South America, because the Jesuits were not the paramount religious order in the Kingdom of Guatemala. On the morning of 26 June 1767 the twenty Jesuits in the province of Guatemala were assembled in the Sala Capítular (capitular parlor) in Santiago de Guatemala after being rounded up in accordance with the king's order. With a small military escort, they departed on horseback for the Atlantic coast on 1 July, eventually arriving at the fortress of Omoa, from which they sailed for Spain on the frigate *Thetis* on 26 July. Because their numbers were small, and because they had administered relatively few Indian towns, in contrast to the Dominicans, Franciscans, and Mercedarians, the Jesuits' expulsion had only a minor effect on Central America. However, the later influence of the exiles in Europe on behalf of their "homeland" in Guatemala contributed to a growing sense of Guatemalan nationalism in the late eighteenth and early nineteenth centuries. For example, Father Rafael Landívar, in his writings between 1775 and 1780, reminisced about Guatemala City as the "fuente de mi vida" (fountain of my life).[43]

The reforms also increased the trend toward secularization of the church and more centralized control under the king and civil authorities in Guatemala. Likewise, they reduced the economic base of the church, replaced religious in outlying communities, and contributed to the growing scarcity of the clergy that was so evident by 1800. Finally, the reforms contributed to controversies and conflicts between clerics and civil authorities, thereby weakening the church's position and prestige in the last two decades of Spanish control before independence in 1821.

The changes began as early as the 1730s and continued at least until Archbishop Pedro Cortés y Larraz (1768–79) resisted the king's and the president and governor's orders to transfer the capital from Antigua to Nueva Guatemala in the late 1770s. As early as the administration of Pedro de Rivera, the president and governor had reported that he had difficulty with Bishop Pedro Pardo de Figueroa (before he became archbishop) over what Rivera termed the "trivial question" of precedence between members of the Audiencia de Guatemala and the Cabildo Eclesiástico.[44] Conflicts also developed over who should control Indian funds[45] and over reported abuses by regular clergy of Indians in their doctrinas. In such a complaint in 1726 to the Council of the Indies, it was explained that some clerics made the Indians pay one real for each confession, two reals for each communion, or half a fanega of maize, or other fruits of the soil, to hear Mass; and they prohibited those who could not so contribute from receiving the sacraments. Furthermore, this report stated, the mayordomos in those doctrinas beat the Indians, incarcerated them, and inflicted other "bad treatments" on them. The report also criticized clerics for absences from their curacies without permission from the bishop, for monetary charges for the election of Indian officials, and for enriching themselves at the "cost of the Indians' blood."[46] The king thereupon ordered all bishops and archbishops to comply with the papal bulls and the king's directives, and if viceroys, presidents, audiencias, and governors did not assist the secular clergy in correcting the abuses, he threatened to replace them.[47]

It is evident that Archbishop Pedro Cortés y Larraz failed to follow the king's orders of 1753 and 1757 to secularize doctrinas when regular clergy positions became vacant, and he protested and defied both the king's and the president-governor's orders to move the capital after the destruction of Santiago de Guatemala (Antigua) in the earthquake of 29 July 1773. That Cortés y Larraz and his clergy impeded secularization of doctrinas was reported by the *vicario provincial* (vicar of the province) late in 1803. He related that when a vacancy occurred in a doctrina during Cortés y Larraz's time and a letter had been addressed to the archbishop to see if he wanted to secularize the position, his answer was always no, so that the vacancy would be open not to a secular cleric.[48] On 1 December 1773, about four months after the disaster in Santiago de Guatemala, the archbishop wrote to the king, explaining his opposition to abandoning Antigua in favor of the proposed new site for the capital in the valley of La Hermita. He told him that it was "inconvenient" to move to the new city; that there was no other suitable site in Guatemala without tremors or earthquakes from which visits could be made to Indian towns; that it was a needless waste to lay out another site; that the churches, convents, schools, and university could not make such a transfer "without great loss"; and that the supervision and conduct of teaching would suffer for "many years."[49]

The archbishop and secular clergy continued to oppose the audiencia's and governor's desire to relocate the capital even after the king's order and after the governor's directive of 22 March 1777 that the final transfer be accomplished within one year and that the ruins of the buildings at Antigua be demolished. Included in Governor Martín de

Mayorga's order of 28 July 1777 were the Cabildo Eclesiástico, the university, and the prelates; all religious orders and their authorities were to make the transfer within two months without any delay or excuse whatsoever.[50] Yet, two months later Governor Mayorga wrote to José de Gálvez, minister of the Indies in Spain, that Archbishop Cortés y Larraz would not make the transfer of the cathedral or his offices until a license *(licencia)* was obtained from the pope, and that the Cabildo Eclesiástico still opposed the move. Criticizing the inflexibility of the archbishop and how he manipulated and attracted people to his views in "resistance to the expressed orders of Your Majesty," Governor Mayorga explained that the public had suffered for four years from the disharmony created by Cortés y Larraz, and he recommended that the four members of the cabildo who had voted for the archbishop be replaced and that Cortés y Larraz perhaps be given a new see in Spain.[51] The king accepted the governor's recommendation, transferring the archbishop to Spain and replacing him with Don Cayetano Monroy in 1779.[52]

While that episode illustrates the triumph of the king and the state over the church, it should not detract from the positive achievements of Archbishop Cortés y Larraz during his eleven years in office. He took seriously his responsibilities as shepherd of his Guatemalan flock, making personal visits to curacies and towns throughout the diocese. He compiled population statistics and observations about Indians, Spaniards, and ladinos, which are the best sources of such information ever assembled in the eighteenth century. He was also an intense reformer and humanist, revealing problems within the Catholic Church, especially among the clergy, and suggesting solutions to the abuses of Indians and other weaknesses and difficulties of ecclesiastical administration, particularly at the local, parish-priest level.

Archbishop Cortés y Larraz's population figures and observations about ladinos will be discussed in chapter 7, "Population, Society, and Culture," but it is appropriate here to examine his comments on the diocese of Guatemala. Soon after he took possession of his episcopal see, he made three extended visits throughout the countryside— between 3 November 1768 and 1 July 1769, from 22 November 1769 to 9 February 1770, and from 6 June to 29 August 1770. In all he visited 123 parishes in twelve alcaldías mayores in Guatemala, San Salvador,

"Mapa de los curatos de San Pedro [de la Laguna], Sololá, Panahachel, Atitlán,"
1768–1770 (Sevilla, AGI)

and Verapaz. Before undertaking the visits, he sent a letter on 23
September 1768 to all parish priests, advising them of his plans and
sending each of them ten questions that they were to address so that
they would have their responses ready when he arrived.[53]

In all those curacies, the archbishop noted a total of 289 parish
priests (123 in charge, 166 assistants), including 34 *religiosos,* or regular clerics. Thus 255 of the priests were secular clergy, revealing the
preponderance of seculars over regulars. Nearly all of the priests,
according to Cortés y Larraz, had been born in America, mostly within
the diocese. Only four were of foreign origin—two Spaniards, one
Mexican, and one Panamanian.[54] He noted the following statistics
pertaining to the parishes: the capital city of Santiago de Guatemala
had five parishes, with eighteen clergy; Chimaltenango had eleven
parishes, with nineteen clergy; Sololá had eleven parishes, with seventeen clergy; Chiquimula de la Sierra had ten parishes, with forty-three

"Mapa del Curato de La Hermita," 1768–1770 (Sevilla, AGI)

clergy; San Salvador had twenty-six parishes, with seventy-five clergy; and the thirty-four *religiosos* were all in the districts of Verapaz, Sololá, Totonicapán, and Quezaltenango.[55] Within the capital there were an additional fifty-eight *religiosos* of specified orders: twenty-five Dominicans, twenty-three Franciscans, nine Mercedarians, one of San Juan de Dios, and unspecified numbers of Recoletos, Augustinians, Bethlemites, and other orders. They resided primarily in convents, of which six were Franciscan, five Dominican, and four Mercedarian.[56]

But statistics concerning parishes and clergy were not Cortés y Larraz's only contributions. He made important observations on parish priests' qualifications, annual tribute, cofradias, Indian schools, and the geography and distribution of towns, in his detailed report of 1774 to the king.[57] From the 122 censused parishes (one was not available) the total annual tribute in 1768–69 was 192,835 pesos, an average of 1,580 pesos per parish;[58] however, some richer parishes gave 3,000 pesos, while poorer ones contributed only 600 to 900 pesos. To the total, the archbishop added 265,088 pesos and 4,149 reales as the capital income of the cofradias, noting also that the parishes had a total of 45,693 head of cattle and other livestock in their possession.[59] He believed that the annual salary of the parish priests was inadequate, although the king's annual sinódo of about 200 pesos was increased to 532 pesos by *limosnas* (alms) and "voluntary collections" from the Indians, who supplied parish priests with chickens, fish, milk, wool, water, and fodder for their mules.[60]

Turning to an evaluation of the clergy, the work of the cofradias, and the Indian schools, Cortés y Larraz not only explained their problems but also made suggestions for reform. He thought that only eighty of the parish priests were qualified for pastoral service. He judged seventy-six totally incompetent to be church ministers because they were not spiritually zealous toward their charges. They failed to require Indians in their parish to attend at Sunday Mass and festival days, and did not enforce participation in confessions and communions; they allowed such idolatry and superstition as the continued worship of a sacred hill, a large ceiba tree, tigers, or other animals; and they permitted "witchcraft" associated with belief in birds and sacrifices of chickens. In only seventy-seven parishes (62 percent) had the priests reported that the Indians understood the sacraments and were of "good faith," while in 15 percent of the parishes they were not.[61] Among the sins committed by the Indians the following were reported in the parishes: intoxication (seventy parishes); sexual excesses (thirty-six); theft (fifteen); gambling (seven); *amanecebamiento,* or living with unmarried partners (thirteen); homicide (four); plus fifty-one other offenses. The archbishop observed that drunkenness, lust, teaching women to live as concubines, incest, and *juego de cacao* (gambling using cacao beans) were common, and that all "these abuses and vices were present among not only Indians but also ladinos and Spaniards."[62] On that account, Cortés y Larraz expressed serious doubts about the Christianity of the Indians.[63]

He considered the cofradias in the diocese highly important because of their numbers, their organizations, and their impressive financial holdings and livestock. The brotherhoods bore various titles: 192 were named for the Santísimo Sacramento; 173, de Animas; 131, for the Concepción de Nuestra Señora de Rosario/Remedios, or another incarnation of the Virgin Mary; 128 for the Santa Cruz; 448 more, for the Virgin Mary; 42, for Jesús Nazareno; and others, for San Nicolás and San Antonio de Padua.[64] While the primary function of these sodalities was to support the life of the parish, they also provided sustenance to the parish priests and nearly one-third of the total funds received by the church, without which it could not subsist. Furthermore, they served important social functions. Their *santos* (religious images), for example, were an "obra maestra" (teaching work) of popular religion. However, the archbishop believed that cofradias also contributed to the disorder of the Indians, encouraging them to drunkenness through the widespread drinking of *chicha* (a corn liquor with a strong odor) and *aguardiente* (brandy), and using music and dancing to excess. In addition, he thought the *principales,* or headmen, perpetuated their power over their charges, enabling the Indians to conserve the past and their religious culture in opposition to Christianization. Although he opposed the institution of the cofradias, Cortés y Larraz did not feel that they could be abolished because of their important religious, economic, and social contributions. Instead he tolerated them while thinking they should be controlled better.[65]

The archbishop, also concerned about the schools for Indians, described their numbers, curricula, and problems. There were 103 such schools (each in a town) with an estimated total of nearly four thousand students, both boys and girls. In them parish priests taught the Castilian language and Christian doctrine, but Cortés y Larraz observed that instruction was reduced to "singing by memory the prayers and the doctrine." He believed that 76 of the schools had good teachers, and only 2 had poor ones. The salary of the teacher was provided by the community, but the archbishop did not specify the remuneration. Attendance of students he reported as poor, since Indian parents strongly resisted sending their children to school; and he believed that instruction should begin when the child was five years old.[66]

Cortés y Larraz's numbers and his observations concerning the church and its clergy illustrate the importance the church had achieved in colonial Guatemala by the 1770s. He described the conditions and the problems, especially at the local level, as well as the size and scope of the diocese of Guatemala. With his statistical data and observations on other societal groups and the abuses of the alcaldes mayores in the treatment of Indians, discussed in later chapters, he provides a good overview of colonial Guatemala in the late eighteenth century. In general, he found serious deficiencies among parish priests, had grave doubts about the Indians' acceptance and understanding of Christianity, and expressed opposition to the exploitation of Indians by Spanish and ladino residents as well as civil officials. He also objected to those who lived outside of towns, claiming that they were "a congregation of persons without subjection to God, the Church, or the King," and he urged that all should be congregated in communities.[67]

The city of Santiago de Guatemala and its successor, Nueva Guatemala de la Asunción, were the centers of religious administration, and they contained numerous church buildings, schools, convents, and hospitals operated by the various religious orders. The most prominent structure was the cathedral. Built between 1669 and 1679, and dedicated in 1680 at a cost of more than 200,000 pesos, the cathedral at Santiago de Guatemala (Antigua) was over 300 feet long, 120 feet wide, and 70 feet high, with fifty windows, three aisles in the nave, and eight side chapels. Beneath a cupola supported by sixteen columns was the grand altar, where the ashes of Pedro de Alvarado, Bishop Marroquín, and eight other bishops were buried.[68] The cathedral and many of the thirty-seven other religious buildings were severely damaged by the earthquake of July 1773. Engineer Don Antonio Marín observed that the cathedral's arches had been completely ruined, its walls were cracked or split, and it threatened to be a "total ruin."[69] After the civil-religious controversy between Governor Mayorga and Archbishop Cortés y Larraz, a new cathedral was constructed on the main plaza at Nueva Guatemala with two principal entrances, an altar beneath a cupola supported by four marble columns, and many side chapels.[70]

The reforms of the Bourbons resulted in more direct royal control and increased secularization of the church in Guatemala, but in the late eighteenth century the Catholic Church was still a significant institution. While secularization lessened the influence of the regular clergy, it did not decrease the strength of the secular church. In 1778 there were four bishoprics under the archbishop's jurisdiction: Guatemala, with 108 secular curacies and 23 administered by the regular clergy; León, for Nicaragua and Costa Rica; Chiapas; and Comayagua. By that time there were 424 churches for 539,765 inhabitants, and since the foundation of the bishopric in the 1530s, Guatemala had sixteen bishops and, since 1743, seven archbishops.[71] Until 1808, Bishop Juan Bautista Alvarez de Toledo (1713–23) was the only native of the Americas to occupy this highest position in the religious hierarchy.[72]

At the beginning of the nineteenth century the church in Guatemala and throughout Central America experienced a scarcity and aging of the clergy while undergoing uncertainties and changes resulting from the Napoleonic wars in Europe, Napoleon's invasion of Spain in 1807–1808, and the liberal-conservative clash in Guatemala during the independence period before 1821. The reforms, the expulsion of the Jesuits, the increased secularization, the population growth, and the aging of the clergy, all contributed to a scarcity of priests in the last thirty years of the Spanish colonial era. For example, Father Francisco Viteri, who was sent to Spain in 1800 to solicit religious for the convent of San Francisco de Guatemala, was able to recruit and bring back with him only twenty-nine priests and three lay brothers to meet a requirement for sixty priests and six lay brothers in Franciscan posts. In his detailed report of 1800 he listed seventy priests by name with their ages, some of whom were seventy to eighty-eight years of age. He listed Franciscan convents and vicarages throughout the kingdom, of which twelve were in the province of Guatemala: seven convents, three vicarages, and an orphanage in Antigua, and a convent for nuns in Nueva Guatemala. Eighty-nine priests were authorized for those posts, but only forty-two were actually present, and at least ten of them were ill. Similarly Viteri noted shortages of choristers and lay brothers in Nueva Guatemala, Quezaltenango, Totonicapán, Panajachel, Antigua Guatemala, and elsewhere.[73] Of the ninety-three Franciscan priests, choristers, and lay brothers for the entire diocese in 1801, seventy-three were priests, including twenty-seven "Europeos" (European-born) and forty-six "Americanos" (American-born), indicating a growing tendency to recruit priests whose origins were in the Americas.[74]

During the tumultuous years of the independence period after 1808, Archbishop Ramón Casaus y Torres arrived in Guatemala in 1811, but did not take possession of his diocese until four years later. He served as the last archbishop under Spanish jurisdiction and the first in the newly independent Guatemala after September 1821. A great orator who had lived previously in New Spain for twenty-three years, he denounced the rebellion of Father Miguel Hidalgo y Costilla and opposed insurrectionists there. He wrote denunciations of heretics and of the ideas of the philosophes of the Enlightenment, and he denounced Napoleon Bonaparte for his invasion of Spain and imprisonment of the royal family. In Guatemala he energetically opposed the emancipation of Guatemala from Spain and again denounced Napoleon from the pulpit of Santo Domingo church in Nueva Guatemala on 2 May 1812. Nine years later, after walking out of the patriotic gathering at the governmental palace and shutting himself up in the archbishop's palace to await developments, he reluctantly subscribed to the act of independence of the United Provinces of Guatemala on 16 September 1821.[75]

During the last decade of the Spanish era, after the passage of the Spanish Constitution of 1812, liberals in Guatemala endeavored to promote Catholic evangelization and instruction among the "negros caribes" (black Caribs) on the northern coast of Central America, especially in the vicinity of Trujillo in present-day Honduras. Guatemalan Creole José de Aycinena, one of the province's most vociferous liberals, wrote a letter to Don José Limonta on 2 November 1813 addressing the problem of the English and French black Caribs living in the community and environs of Trujillo. These people had migrated from Roatán Island in the Gulf of Honduras and from Haiti, settling as "negros emigrados" (black immigrants) in barrios separate from Spaniards, Gallegans, Asturians, Canary Islanders, and Comayaguans already residing there. Aycinena said that he could not look on with indifference when article 12 of the Constitution of 1812 protected the Catholic religion and prohibited the establishment of any other. He emphasized that these black Caribs practiced polygamy and had multiplied rapidly. Although they were adept fishermen, and 160 of them had served as soldiers in helping to suppress a revolt at Granada during the previous year, their men and women went about "nearly nude" or indecently dressed, but not for lack of clothes, which they did wear for special occasions. Aycinena urged the Regency in Spain to direct the government and archbishop of Guatemala to catechize and convert these black Caribs "for the advantage that would result to religion and the political state." He believed them to be a growing threat to the population because they might initiate a general uprising, uniting with the "sambos gentiles" (free un-Christianized blacks) living on the coasts and in the mountains, and with the nearby English in the Caribbean and on the coast of Central America, thereby bringing about a British reconquest of the region. Because there was a scarcity of religious in Honduras, Aycinena requested that a mission consisting of only four Franciscans from the Colegio de Cristo de Misioneros Apostólicos of Guatemala be established to administer the black Caribs at a cost of 332 pesos per missionary, or a total of 1,328 pesos annually. He believed that in four or five years all of them would be baptized and the costs would cease when a secular parish priest was assigned. Evidently his request was approved, and three religious for the mission were provided from among the thirty at the colegio in Santiago de Guatemala.[76]

In 1818, only three years before independence was proclaimed, the diocese of Guatemala had 131 parishes, 17 vicarages, 424 churches, and 1,720 cofradias administering to 540,508 Christians. Also, the church owned and operated 914 haciendas and 910 *trapiches* (sugar mills). In the city of Nueva Guatemala alone there were eight houses of religious men: Santo Domingo (Dominican), a Franciscan school for young men showing talent in the sciences, Nuestra Señora de Merced (Mercedarian), the school of San Lucas established formerly by the Jesuits, an Augustinian school, the convent of Nuestra Señora de Belén, the colegio of Cristo Crucificado for apostolic missionaries propagating the faith among the Indians, and an oratory of the order of San Felipe de Neri. In addition, in Nueva Guatemala there were five convents, three *beaterios* (houses of *beatas,* or pious women who wore religious habits but were not actually members of religious orders), and two schools just for women. There were convents for the order of the Immaculate Conception, for Santa María Catalina Martir (founded in 1606), for Discalced Carmelites (begun in 1677), for Poor Clares, and for Capuchin nuns. The beaterio of Nuestra Señora de Rosario protected and instructed Indian girls in womanly arts, beginning at ages seven through twelve and continuing to twenty or twenty-two years of age. That of Santa Rosa de Lima taught sewing, cooking, reading, and embroidery. The beaterio of Bethlén had opened in 1781 to teach reading and cooking. There were two schools for girls and women—

the Colegio de la Visitación de Nuestra Señora (founded in 1796 for young girls) and the Colegio de la Presentación de Nuestra Señora (first established for poor girls, but after 1637 a refuge for the correction of evil women and for penitents). Finally, there were nine houses for third orders (such as the Third Order of Saint Francis, or the Franciscans) and five hospitals, all run by the religious orders. The Hospital of Santiago was founded by Bishop Marroquín for Spaniards and mixed-bloods in 1553 and administered by religious of the order of San Juan de Dios. The Dominican Hospital of San Alexis was founded to care for Indians, with an annual grant of six hundred pesos from the king. The Hospital of San Pedro cared for ecclesiastics. On the outskirts of the city, two others, La Misericordia and San Lázaro, cared for lepers.[77]

During the nearly three centuries of the colonial period the Roman Catholic Church was of considerable importance in the province and kingdom of Guatemala, both for its religious work and its political tie to the king of Spain. It was an institution transferred from the mother country and modified in Guatemala by circumstances, the people there, and problems that required adjustments. The church ministered to the needs of Spaniards, Indians, mixtures of races (ladinos), and toward the end of its long tenure, black Caribs. Its missionary work among the hundreds of thousands of Indians began in the early days of the conquest and colonization. Although some missions endured at the end of the colonial period, especially in such isolated regions as Verapaz, the congregation policy adopted in the period from 1537 to 1550 and the extensive control of the secular rather than the regular clergy were much more effective and long lasting in converting and administering the Indians of Guatemala than the missionary process. Both congregación and secularization served to evangelize the natives, to establish and maintain Catholicism, and to instruct Indians in religious dogma and ceremony, as well as European customs and practices. It should also be emphasized, as Jesús María García Añoveros has done, that the motives for congregating Indians into towns were not only religious but also economic and political. Certainly, as he notes, the foundation of such towns was a historical phenomenon that radically transformed Indian ways of life.[78]

Yet, the establishment of Indian towns was not the only achievement of the church in colonial Guatemala. From the capital, the church also administered to the needs of the growing numbers of Spaniards and mixed-bloods in successive locations in rural villages across the countryside. The church hierarchy and organization became increasingly complex over time, paralleling the growth in numbers, officers, and overlapping functions of the civil administration. In the first 170 years of the church's presence in Guatemala the secular clergy multiplied and became the dominant element within the organizational structure. Under the control of the bishop after the mid-1530s, the Cabildo Eclesiástico, the numerous religious orders, and parish priests by the hundreds came to represent the Catholic Church and the authority of the Spanish monarch in religious affairs. Thus the church became prestigious and wealthy in the colonial life of Guatemala. Then, with the advent of the Bourbon kings in Spain, ecclesiastical reforms and emphasis on centralization and secularization diminished the powers and prestige of the church. Secularization relieved the government of all financial responsibility for mission establishments, where the Indians were to become Spanish citizens with tax-paying obligations instead of wards of the state. Therefore secularization decreased the influence of the regular clergy while reinforcing the strength of the secular church under the control of the state. That movement and the ecclesiastical reforms also reduced respect for the church as an institution and for the regular clergy, thereby weakening their authority, their role as unifying factors, and the respect of both Spaniards and Indians for the church in the last years of Spanish rule. Even earlier, the quarrels between religious orders and regular clergy, and the conflicts over the control and jurisdictions of Indian communities, such struggles with civil officials as that surrounding the transfer of the capital, all had weakened respect for the church and its officials.

Still, it should be recognized that—in spite of its quarrels, the exploitation and mistreatment of Indians by civil and religious persons, the prejudice against Indians, and the corrupt practices of some religious—the church accomplished much and played an important ideological role in the colony.[79] In addition to establishing Indian towns and administering to the "gente de razón" ("civilized people," meaning Spaniards and the Christianized mixed-bloods and Indians), the clergy introduced European crops, animals, plants, and methods of animal husbandry, as well as agricultural practices, to the Indians. They also built and administered churches, chapels, convents, aqueducts, irrigation canals, hospitals, and schools in which care and instruction were provided for Spaniards, mixed-bloods, and Indians men, women, and children. It should be remembered that all of these innovations were not necessarily imposed on the Indians, for they chose those that appealed to them or for which they found a purpose.[80]

Finally, as many have observed, Christianity among the Indians of Guatemala, as elsewhere in the Spanish domains, became a syncretic, mixed form of the religion. The natives selected features of Catholic doctrine and ceremony that appealed to their spiritual, emotional, aesthetic, and practical interests. They complied with Christian obligations in the confession, communion, the Mass, baptism, observing holy days and Sundays, and the performance of last rites; and they also adopted many Christian observances after the arrival of the Spaniards, such as the worship of Our Lady of Guadalupe and that of the Black Christ at Esquipulas. However, they were not really ideologically converted. Instead they memorized the catechism and rituals while preserving and practicing some pagan rituals that were idolatrous within the Christian churches, such as adoring the sun and making sacrifices to other deities when illnesses or calamities overtook them.[81] Thus, as Robert Ricard has noted, in New Spain there was a survival of "paganism at the side of, and outside of, Catholicism."[82] Ricard observes that "what was founded, before and above all, was a Spanish Church, organized along Spanish lines, governed by Spaniards, in which the native Christians played the minor part of second-class Christians."[83]

The Catholic Church in colonial Guatemala, important as it was for religion, society, administration, and the economy, was only one facet of Spain's relations with the Indians. From the arrival of the first Spaniards, conflicts and confrontations developed with the hundreds of thousands of Indians in Guatemala. Thus Spanish-Indian relations, and especially the labor policies and practices adopted by the Spaniards for the Indians, were important, continuing, components of colonial Guatemala's historical experience over the course of nearly three centuries.

CHAPTER 5

Spanish-Indian Relations and Labor Practices

THE ARRIVAL of a few hundred Spaniards in Guatemala in 1524 brought about an immediate confrontation with the 500,000 to 800,000 Indians living in its highland region (perhaps 1–1.5 million if the Petén and coastal regions are counted).[1] Two cultures came into conflict— one representing the Old World in Europe, and the other the New World of the Americas. Although there were temporary alliances between the two, and some accommodations between Spaniards, on the one hand, and Indians, on the other, the conquest understandably was a period of Spanish imperialism and Indian resistance, usually in open, violent warfare and rebellions of the natives against the intruders. By the late 1530s this age of warfare had begun to subside. Although there were occasional Indian revolts thereafter, they were generally localized and fewer and farther between over the course of the nearly three centuries of Spanish rule. When contrasted to the Mixtón War, the Chichimeca wars, the Pueblo Indian revolts of 1680 and 1696, the Great Northern Revolt, and the wars with Tepehuanes, Tarahumares, Yaquis, Seris, Conchos, Tobosos, Navajos, Utes, Apaches, and Comanches in northern New Spain during the same time frame, Guatemalan Indian revolts were relatively few and did not seriously threaten the continued Spanish occupation. Overall, the threat of Indian raids and attacks was not so continuous as on the *frontera septentrional* of New Spain.

That does not mean that there were not problems between the two cultures or conflicts in relations between them. In place of warfare, the early missionary enterprises of the Catholic Church and the congregation policy of reducing Indians to towns had an enormous impact on the Indians during the sixteenth century in Guatemala. So too did the early enslavement of Indians during the first generation of the Spanish presence in the province and throughout the Kingdom of Guatemala. During most of the sixteenth and the first half of the seventeenth century, the dense Indian population found on initial contact dwindled rapidly and in considerable numbers. When after about 1650 it began to recover, much accommodation and acculturation took place as during the eighteenth century Indians learned to speak Spanish, developed their own understanding and practice of Catholicism, increasingly wore European clothing along with their traditional garb, raised European crops, animals, and fowl, learned European trades and artisanry, and sometimes practiced European customs and traditions, often by their own choice. Simultaneously, they resisted the importation of other European customs and institutions, retaining many features of their pre-Columbian way of life. In many ways they preserved and protected their autonomy and their cultural identities.

Perhaps the most important conflict in these nearly three centuries was between the Spanish Crown and the Spanish inhabitants or colonists of Guatemala. From the beginning, the kings of Spain adhered to their responsibilities and the policy of Christianizing, preserving, protecting, and Westernizing the Indians. This brought conflict with the settlers in Guatemala and throughout the kingdom since the Spanish and ladino residents wanted to exploit the Indians' labor, lands, and personal services. The result was an almost constant clash of policy and practice, sometimes bringing changes in Crown policies and inconsistent enforcement of them, which contributed in turn to corruption and mistreatment of the natives, and encouraged efforts by the colonists to encroach on Indian lands and gain control over Indian labor and services. The conflict centered around protection of the Indians by the Crown and royal authorities, on the one hand, and exploitation of the Indians by Guatemalans, on the other.

Spanish relations with the Indians of Guatemala were constantly changing, as were labor practices. They involved the Crown, royal administrators, and the colonists in addition to the clergy of the Catholic Church and the hundreds of thousands of Indians themselves. Having examined the ecclesiastical effort and the church's relationship with the Indians in chapter 4, here we will emphasize overall Spanish policies employed in dealing with the natives and with the practices of the settlers in Guatemala. This chapter also discusses the different labor policies and practices employed by Spaniards for Indians and the presence of black slavery in the colonial province.

CROWN POLICIES AND SETTLER PRACTICES

When Christopher Columbus returned to Spain from his first voyage he brought with him Indians in chains. Queen Isabella promptly freed the Indians and rebuked Columbus for enslaving them. The Castilian queen was a devout Catholic monarch and took seriously her responsibilities after the papal bull of 1493 assigned her the duty of evangelizing and extending Christianity to the Indians of the Americas. She established the policy of incorporating them "into the Spanish scheme of colonization by converting them, acculturating them, and putting them to work."[2] Thus the overall objective of Spanish policy was to convert and patronize the Indian population, although the conquerors and settlers desired to exploit them.[3] After Queen Isabella's death in 1504 her Habsburg successors continued this policy of Christianization and Westernization of the Indians, although sometimes they backed off in response to the colonists' opposition to specific regulatory practices.

Early in the conquest and settlement period, when only the islands of the West Indies (Española, Cuba, Puerto Rico, and Jamaica) had been occupied, the Crown issued its first set of regulations defining its position on Spanish-Indian relations for the Caribbean Antilles and regulating the pay and conditions of Indian work. These Laws of Burgos, issued in 1512–13 and consisting of thirty-two articles, were the first codification of laws attempting to define Crown policy toward Indians in the Americas.[4] Thirty years later Carlos I of Spain (Charles V of the Holy Roman Empire) issued what have come to be called the New Laws. At that time, in 1542, as a result of lobbying protests by Dominican friars and Bishop Bartolomé de las Casas concerning the mistreatment of Indians by Spaniards, the Crown outlawed Indian slavery, stated that no new encomiendas would be granted, provided that encomenderos who could not prove their titles to their Indians would lose them to the king, and ordered that on the death of an encomendero, his (or her) Indians would escheat to the Crown. The resulting outrage of colonists in America, including those in the Kingdom of Guatemala, led to formal protests such as that by Viceroy

Antonio de Mendoza in New Spain and a civil war in Peru, in which the first viceroy there was assassinated. Consequently, in 1545 the king amended the New Laws, suspending the termination of encomiendas but still outlawing slavery.[5] Later in the sixteenth century King Felipe II also issued laws regulating Indian relations and labor, and his successors did likewise throughout the seventeenth century. All of these regulatory measures were codified in 1681 with the publication of the *Recopilación de leyes de los reinos de las Indias,* of which one whole book contained laws relating to Indians and Spanish-Indian relations, especially the treatment of Indians by Spaniards.[6] Thus the Crown early established a distinct juridical status for Indians, created courts to hear their complaints, appointed the first "Protector de Indios" (Bishop Juan de Zumárraga, in New Spain, was the first Protector, followed later by others in various American kingdoms, including Bishop Marroquín in Guatemala), and exempted the Indians from the jurisdiction of the Holy Office of the Inquisition.[7]

In 1537 Crown policy endorsed the position of Pope Paul, who declared, "We . . . consider . . . that the Indians are truly men and that they are not only capable of understanding the Catholic Faith, but according to our information, they desire exceedingly to receive it."[8] Following that statement of policy, a great debate occurred in midsixteenth-century Spain between Bartolomé de las Casas and Juan Ginés de Sepúlveda concerning the status of the Indians and how they should be treated. Las Casas advanced the idea that "all mankind are one" and that Spaniards should not enslave and mistreat Indians. Ginés de Sepúlveda, a noted humanist, argued the Aristotelian philosophy that all men are slaves and Spaniards must supervise the Indians and lead them from their native state to civilization. Although the debate failed to reach a universally accepted conclusion, it was the first in Europe to address the status of the Indians and their rights in relationship to the Spaniards.[9]

All of those regulatory policies and differences of opinion concerning the status of Indians applied to colonial Guatemala, as did the Crown's objective of keeping Spaniards in America separate from Indians and applying the system of congregation of Indians into towns established specifically for them. By 1550 in Guatemala the Crown policy of separating Spaniards and Indians had become the cornerstone of Spanish-Indian relations. The king's idea was to isolate the Indians and protect them from the bad examples and encroachments of Spaniards by forbidding the latter from living in Indian towns and requiring the Indians to live in them. Thus two types of urban settlements were created: *pueblos de españoles* (towns of Spaniards) and *pueblos de indios* (Indian towns). The natives had a semiautonomous status under their own elected officials and cabildos, which were similar to those of the Spanish residents elsewhere. This system of Indian self-government was, however, under the strict control of Spaniards— ecclesiastical officials, such as parish priests, and civil authorities, ones such as alcaldes mayores and corregidores, to whom the Indian officials were subordinate. The Crown endeavored to establish two governmental entities known as the República de Españoles (Republic of Spaniards) and the República de Indios (Republic of Indians).[10] In fact, although clerical officials tried to keep Spaniards out of the Indian towns and Indian barrios of the city of Santiago de Guatemala, for example, the system of separation was impossible to enforce and maintain. As Christopher H. Lutz has shown clearly in his study of Guatemala's capital, Indians who lived in the barrios of the city worked as servants and apprentices in Spanish districts, and poor Spaniards and mixed-bloods (castas or ladinos) moved into the Indian barrios. The Crown's preoccupation with establishing urban communities all over Guatemala worked at cross-purposes with the theory of separation. Racial and cultural *mestizaje* (mixing of peoples) began in the sixteenth century, continued into the seventeenth, and accelerated in the eighteenth century. Although both the Crown and the Audiencia de Guatemala issued decrees to keep Spaniards out of the Indian barrios, such as that of 1626 prohibiting Indians in the San Francisco district of Santiago de Guatemala from selling their houses, lots, or fields to any Spaniard, mestizo, mulatto, or black, they failed to halt the ongoing process of racial mixing, the encroachments by Spaniards in Indian districts, and the movement of Indians into Spanish barrios. Indian movements from their villages into Spanish towns, intermarriage, liaisons between Spaniards and Indians, and work relationships contributed to the breakdown in the policy of separation, so that by the late eighteenth century it had lost its original meaning almost completely.[11]

Furthermore, the policy of congregation of Indians into towns contributed to the failure. Begun by royal instructions of 10 June 1540 to Bishop Marroquín, who had requested three years earlier that Indians be rounded up and established in towns specifically for them, the practice caused the majority of Indians to be incorporated into towns and Christianized.[12] By the early 1570s there were three hundred of these Indian towns with a total of 40,000 to 45,000 inhabitants.[13] From the viewpoint of Spanish authorities, the practice was an overwhelming success for the Christianization of the Indians, teaching them to live like "civilized" people, regularization in the collection of tribute, and administrative control by Spanish officials. Congregation of the Tzutujil Mayas, for example, began at Santiago de Atitlán in 1547, and most of the Indian towns surrounding Lake Atitlán had been founded by the end of the sixteenth century. Although the policy of congregation aided acculturation and also enabled Indians to preserve their cultural identity, it was harmful in that it accelerated the decline of the native population, increased contacts with Spaniards, and vacated rural lands so that they could be occupied by Spaniards and ladinos, who frequently employed Indians from nearby towns, triggering bitter disputes between ecclesiastics and civil officials over the use of Indian labor.[14]

Throughout the Spanish colonial era in Guatemala civil officials, encomenderos, and Spanish residents of urban and rural areas abused and mistreated the Indians. Some abuses by ecclesiastics have been discussed in the previous chapter, but it is appropriate here to stress that Spaniards, from the outset of the conquest period to the end of Spain's rule, encroached on Indian lands in rural areas and on Indian barrios in towns. Furthermore, they desired to exploit native labor in one form or another during the entire colonial era. In opposition to Crown policies, employers of Indians, especially in areas where cash crops and minerals were produced, overworked the Indians to the point of exhaustion and sometimes death.[15] Although they complied with many laws, it was in the interest of individual colonists to impede enforcement of them. Colonizers soon understood that the "great American wealth was the Indians, their services, their tributes, [and] their strength of work."[16] To the Spanish inhabitants economic realities were stronger than the good wishes of the king.[17] Although the

Indians of the *altiplano,* or highland Guatemala, were not exploited as much as those of the coastal regions,[18] according to Bishop Juan Ramírez (1601–1609), all Indians were worked as if they were slaves.[19] Furthermore, the principal caciques (Indian chieftains) in native towns collaborated in the exploitation of their own people. In return for such privileges as exemption from tribute, they selected Indians from their towns for labor services and engaged in the same corrupt practices as other civil officials.[20]

Civil officials—especially alcaldes mayores and corregidores, who had direct personal contacts with Indians and were poorly paid by the Crown—practiced widespread corruption and exploitation by using the natives for personal services of their own and retaining tributes for their own use.[21] Not only did Archbishop Pedro Cortés y Larraz denounce the practices of the Spaniards and ladinos living among the Indians and of the native caciques wielding great power over the Indians in their towns, but also he specifically charged five alcaldes mayores with exploitation of their charges. Among them was the alcalde mayor of Sonsonate, who had assigned Indians for three months of service at the indigo factory or mill, thereby making it impossible for them to sow corn or farm their own fields. The alcalde of Chiquimula de la Sierra was denounced for his use of Indians in spinning yarn, public works, and to conduct a load of freight to the gulf of the Río Dulce. This alcalde also reduced payments to Indians for their work and increased their annual tributes. In general, Archbishop Cortés y Larraz observed that alcaldes whipped excessively in punishing offenses—thirty stripes for drunkenness, twelve to fourteen for minor offenses, and thirty to forty for major ones—thus causing the natives to remain silent for fear of being whipped.[22]

Silence was only one form of the Indian resistance in Guatemala. Other practices included passive resistance, running away from communities to the mountains, and in some cases, rebellions and revolts. After their conquest of the Quiché Mayas and the establishment of Iximché as the capital, Spaniards enslaved and brutally treated their Indian allies, thereby causing a major revolt of the Cakchiqueles that lasted almost three years before it was suppressed.[23] In 1558 a Spanish expedition, commanded by Pedro Ramírez de Quiñones and accompanied by two thousand Indian allies, campaigned in northwestern

Guatemala against the revolt of the Lacandones and other Indians in Vera Paz, suppressing the uprising and taking 240 captives, of whom 80 were hanged.[24] Although Indian revolts occurred sporadically in the sixteenth and seventeenth centuries, they were not so frequent or serious as those in the 1700s.

The Indians were greatly affected by the centralization of Bourbon power, changes in the economic structure of the colony, expansion of trade and integration of Central America into the European commercial sphere, the decline in the wealth and power of the religious orders as well as the numbers of the clergy, dislocations of natives, and the kings' desires to create a free peasantry by abolishing the use of encomiendas and repartimientos. Demands for Indian labor increased, and Spaniards encroached repeatedly on native rural properties. Indians were forced into debt peonage or forced to work in cities or towns, or on haciendas. Although the Bourbons theoretically recognized the Indians as the equals of the Spanish and ladino colonists, and they applied ideas of the Enlightenment, such concepts were foreign to the indigenous religions and societies. As the importance of their authorities in Indian towns declined, Indians increasingly resorted to alcoholism as an escape from their persecutions, and revolts grew in number, intensity, and severity.[25]

Increased pressure on the Indians of Chiapas for labor and tribute, along with seizures of valuables from the cofradias in Indian towns by the bishop, were among the causes of the revolt of the Tzeltales and Tzendales Indians in 1712. This serious and widespread rebellion in Los Altos and Chiapas reportedly was led initially by an Indian woman, named María Angel, who claimed inspiration from the Virgin Mary. It raged for nearly two years before it was suppressed by Spanish authorities and military forces at considerable cost. As a result tribute payments were reduced, while the expense of maintaining a permanent defensive force in the region increased.[26] In the late eighteenth and early nineteenth centuries local revolts opposed abuses by specific authorities of established labor and tribute customs. For example, a widespread rebellion in highland Guatemala was sparked by the earthquake of July 1773. It was caused not by the huge labor draft to rebuild the capital of Nueva Guatemala, but by the Indians' belief that a king, named Martín, had come from Spain to free them from tributes and other obligations and to restore to them what Spaniards and ladinos had usurped. Manuel Antonio Montaña, a Spaniard married to an Indian woman at San Sebastián, reported that this king—whose name was a corruption of that of an Indian prophet named Martum—had prophesied that he would return to destroy all the Spaniards and that the Indians would then be left alone, free from labor drafts and tributes, to resume their earlier life before the arrival of the Spaniards. Believing that King Martín had destroyed the city of Santiago de Guatemala, they rose in rebellion in October 1773 and fled from their nearby pueblos to Nueva Guatemala to support President Martín de Mayorga, who they believed was their deliverer. It appears that there was little violence and warfare during this rebellion, but officials had great difficulty persuading the Indians to return to their towns.[27] Fifteen revolts occurred between 1801 and 1821, the last apparently among Quichés in the region of Totonicapán in 1820.[28]

Increased drunkenness among the Indians, as well as the Spanish residents, was evident in the reports of officials in the late eighteenth and early nineteenth centuries and in decrees by the Royal Audiencia to control alcoholism. Bishop Cortés y Larraz in the early 1770s reported that intoxication was one of the principal offenses in 70 of the 123 parishes in his diocese and that cofradias contributed to excessive drinking because the Indians consumed great amounts of chicha and aguardiente during the conduct of their ceremonies.[29] While Indians drank and got drunk before the arrival of the Spaniards, he observed that the practice had gotten worse because the colonists brought new types of alcohol and new ways of drinking. Alcaldes and ladinos had become the principal producers of liquor. Thus, the bishop observed, "everyone drank and got drunk frequently"—a comment reiterated by historian Jesús María García Añoveros when he stated that immoderate consumption of liquor has continued throughout "all the history of Guatemala."[30]

That the Audiencia de Guatemala endeavored to control public intoxication and drinking habits in the province and kingdom is evident in its bandos of 1793 and 26 November 1801. The latter, recognizing that the former had not been obeyed by the populace of Nueva Guatemala, established a set of regulations and punishments for drunkenness. Spanish residents, Indian caciques, justices, and principales who were drunk in the streets or in public places, truly intoxicated, were sentenced to one month of service on public works. For Indians who were not chieftains or principal officials but were drunk, the sentence was twenty-five lashes; but mulattos or mestizos served for two months on public works instead. To all the rest of the people not applying themselves to their work—loafers, vagabonds, beggars, and strangers— the punishment was twenty-five lashes and one month of service on public works. Spanish women who were drunk received fifteen days of confinement or seclusion, while Indian women got thirty days of the same punishment. Those who made or sold chicha, or any other strong drink, would have the same punishments for the first offense, double the sentence for a second one, and a lawsuit and punishment fitting the circumstances for third and subsequent offenses. Scandalous conduct in taverns was prohibited, and all drinking establishments were ordered to close at 9:00 P.M., with a fine of twenty-five pesos for each reported violation.[31] Thus it is evident that intoxication among Spaniards, Indians, and ladinos was a major social problem and that punishments were meted out differently according to the race and gender of the offender.

INDIAN LABOR

Three salient features stand out concerning the Spanish use of Indian labor in colonial Guatemala. First, there was the demand for it. The Crown desired that the Indians be put to work and imposed annual tribute on them, thus requiring them to work to pay their tributes in cash, although more commonly they paid in products and animals. There were few Spaniards in the sixteenth century, and numerous Indians who could produce food products to sustain the early colonists. As cash-cropping and commercial agriculture developed with cacao, indigo, sugar, and cochineal production tied to an export economy, the demand for Indian labor intensified, especially as the native population declined during the first century of the Spanish occupation, but also in the latter half of the seventeenth and throughout the eighteenth century, when labor was needed for the major indigo crop.

Second, the Spanish policy toward Indian labor was not static but ever changing from slavery, the encomienda, repartimiento, free wage labor, and debt peonage to the ultimate goal of the Bourbons, to integrate the Indians into a society where the natives would be paid for their work and their labor would be treated the same as that of Spanish residents. Thus the labor practices progressed from forced unpaid Indian labor to free wage work, although even at the end the Indians still did some forced work.

Third, Crown policy was continually in conflict with the needs and desires of Spanish and ladino inhabitants, who in turn were frequently at odds among themselves over the use of Indian laborers. Not only did the kings and their appointed officials struggle with the colonists over the employment of Indian workers, but royal authorities sometimes condoned, and participated in, the exploitation of the very Indians they were endeavoring to protect and regulate. While the civil officials contested with the religious, ecclesiastical orders argued interminably with one another over jurisdictions and control of the Indians, and settlers challenged both the Crown and the church over the right to use Indian laborers.

These features of the Spanish system must be borne in mind when one examines the highly complex, decentralized, and controversial uses of Indian labor. It will be helpful to examine in more detail five labor policies and practices: Indian slavery, the encomienda, repartimiento, free wage labor, and debt peonage *(peonaje)*.

INDIAN SLAVERY

The institution of slavery was not introduced into the Americas, or to Guatemala specifically, by the Spaniards. Indeed, as William L. Sherman has correctly observed, it "was well established among the indigenous peoples of Central America long before the coming of the Spaniards."[32] In fact, slaves in the pre-conquest period were usually prisoners taken in warfare between native tribes or nations, or they were criminals enslaved by their own society, although their children sometimes were born free. Slave raids by one Indian group on another were common, usually to obtain slaves for either labor or sacrifice. Others were enslaved by their own people. All slaves were considered as pieces of property that could be traded or sold to others.[33]

However, the employment of Indian slaves by the conquering Spaniards introduced new techniques of slavery, systematizing the original institution of Indian labor and producing serious social dislocations among the natives. Notwithstanding the subsequent fusion and accommodations between Indians and Spaniards, the latter became dependent on the Indians for many forms of labor. Bishop Marroquín noted this relationship when he remarked that "Spaniards in these parts [Guatemala] are worthless without native friends."[34]

In Guatemala and the rest of Central America the Spanish use of Indian slaves was established during the conquest and persisted for about thirty years, or until the early 1550s. Two types of slaves existed within the system: those taken in a "just war" and those who were slaves among their own people.[35] Indian slavery and the encomienda were the first forms of Indian labor employed by the Spaniards, but they were different systems even if they did exist simultaneously. The Crown permitted hostile Indians to be taken as slaves in a "just war" if, after they refused to accept peaceful overtures and the Catholic faith, they continued their resistance to Spanish conquistadores, making it necessary to campaign against and subdue them. Bartolomé de las Casas opposed Indian slavery whether the slaves were taken by warfare or tribute, barter, or trade. He specifically fought against the early Spanish practice of raiding native settlements in Honduras, Nicaragua, and Vera Paz to obtain slaves. His complaints and efforts affected Carlos I's policies greatly in the period from 1530 to 1542. A Crown cedula of 1530 outlawed slavery and was protested by the cabildo of Santiago de Guatemala, forcing the king to backtrack and permit slaves taken in a "just war"; however, in 1531 he ruled that slaves could not be taken outside of Guatemala, and eight years later he ordered that no Spaniard could ransom or buy slaves from Indian caciques or other leaders. The New Laws of 1542 prohibited all slavery throughout the Spanish kingdoms in the Americas, but they were not enforced in Guatemala and Central America until the arrival of Alonso López de Cerrato as president of the audiencia and governor–captain general of the kingdom in 1548.[36]

Branding of slaves and enslavement of women and children evidently took place in the first twenty years after the arrival of the Spaniards. The Crown did not question the practice of branding Indian slaves, even those taken in warfare, and it is evident that slaves were branded, for example, when the town of Santiago de Atitlán received 400 to 500 slaves from the caciques as tribute. Eventually the king ordered that no female could be branded as a slave and that boys under age fourteen could not be enslaved, but there were many violations of that law. Finally, in 1552, a royal cedula prohibited all branding of Indians.[37] It is apparent from these laws that branding of slaves was a common practice among Spaniards who possessed them from the 1520s to the early 1550s.

Common also was the Spanish practice of using female slaves for personal service. Many Indian rulers placed little value on females, and they often used them as commodities to trade for favors from their conquerors. These slaves became the objects of the invaders' lust; sometimes they were raped, but on "many occasions," according to Sherman, they consented to sexual acts with their masters. Female Indians were sometimes taken by force, given to Spaniards by caciques, or attracted by gifts from the conquistadores. One bishop wrote in 1547 that there were not ten Spaniards in the whole province of Honduras who did not have Indian slaves as mistresses. As personal servants these women were employed to prepare food, spin cloth, and perform heavy labor, for example, as burden bearers, or *tamemes.* Although the royal decree of 1534 forbade the enslavement of women or children under the age of fourteen, it permitted women taken in a "just war" to be used as *naborías* ("free" Indian servants) for personal services. While not technically slaves, in reality they were bound to their masters, some of whom eventually married their *indias.*[38]

While the capital city of Santiago de Guatemala was not a center for the Indian slave trade, the port cities of Central America and the entire province of Guatemala were a "fruitful ground for slave raiders."[39] In 1533 the value of a single slave was only two pesos, but it increased to fifty to sixty pesos during the following decade. Before 1549 the value of a female slave was considerably more than that of a male one— sixty to seventy pesos for each female, in contrast to twelve to fifteen pesos for each male. Although Indians were captured and impressed into slave cuadrillas, or gangs, they were sold individually to Spaniards at slave markets scattered around the province and kingdom after one-fifth of them were set aside for the royal *quinto.* In Guatemala in 1530, for example, proceeds from the sale of the *quinto* brought the Crown 345 pesos and 6 *tomines.*[40]

When Alonso López de Cerrato took possession as president of the

Audiencia de Guatemala and as governor and captain general of the kingdom on 26 May 1548, he found "none of the royal provisions being followed": tribute assessments for the Indians were excessive; the audiencia was inefficient, disorderly, and immoral; and the oidores lacked dignity and integrity.[41] As a reformer dedicated to enforcing the king's policies and laws, he had freed the Indian slaves of Honduras and El Salvador en route to Santiago de Guatemala, where he arrived early in 1549. There he immediately set free all the illegally held slaves of the province of Guatemala, some three thousand to five thousand Indians in the capital and surrounding areas alone.[42] Thereafter he cut Indian tributes significantly, took naborías from their masters, curtailed the use of Indians as tamemes, and issued an order forbidding personal services as a form of tribute. As chief executive of the kingdom and province, López de Cerrato, who was nearly sixty years old when he arrived, stirred up a major controversy with inhabitants, the cabildo of Santiago de Guatemala, and Bishop Marroquín over the course of his six years in office. Although he left the Dominican friars alone in Vera Paz and had the support of Bartolomé de las Casas in Spain and of one oidor of the audiencia, Alonso de Zorita, he incurred the wrath of the cabildo and of Bishop Marroquín, along with a newly arrived oidor, Tomás López, who supported the views of the local residents of Guatemala. They complained about López de Cerrato's mannerisms and haughty attitude, and accused him of favoritism and nepotism when he granted his brother two encomiendas near Granada, Nicaragua, thereby replacing two conquistador families. Also, he awarded his brother a corregimiento, an expense account, and the title "Protector of the Indians." Settlers complained that the reduction in tributes decreased their incomes and economic status. They pointed out that Indians had become vagabonds while farms and mines in the kingdom were neglected and there were no Indians to guard livestock. This controversy persisted until López de Cerrato's death on 5 May 1555,[43] but the reforms he initiated and carried out not only brought about the end of Indian slavery in Guatemala but changed Indian labor throughout the kingdom in the latter half of the sixteenth century.

Sherman notes objectively that the total number of Indian slaves in all of Central America during the period from 1524 to 1549 can be estimated as not more than 150,000. As in New Spain, the percentage of Indians who actually were slaves "was relatively small," but Indian slavery, along with the encomienda, resulted in post-conquest forced-labor systems that during the first two decades of Spanish contact were "clearly dreadful" for the Indians.[44]

THE ENCOMIENDA

The encomienda was the other early labor practice employed by the Spaniards in the first generation of their contact with the Indians of Guatemala along with slavery. While Indian slavery died out after the middle of the sixteenth century, the encomienda system continued, although it declined in importance until it was abolished by the Bourbon kings in the eighteenth century.

An encomienda was an official grant of Indians to an individual Spaniard or a corporation. The holder of the grant, the encomendero, was entrusted with the care, welfare, and education of his charges in European ways. The encomendero also had an obligation to bear arms and provide for the defense of the kingdom. In return, the king or his royal officials delegated to the encomendero the right to collect tribute from, and use the personal services or labor of, the Indians entrusted to him. Usually an encomienda was made to a deserving Spaniard or a corporation, such as the church (the *encomienda eclesiástica*), as a result of some service to the king, such as participation in an exploration, conquest, or colonization venture. The encomienda also was originally intended to promote settlement of a specific region while providing for the control and welfare of the Indians. In the beginning, an encomienda was only for the life of the original encomendero, but protests of American residents and their entreaties subsequently caused the king to extend encomiendas to a second, third, and even a fifth generation in some regions, thereby extending the grants into the eighteenth century in some kingdoms and making the encomienda hereditary. However, an encomienda was not a land grant as many writers have assumed. In the district of an encomendero's grant the natives retained possession of their lands, and other lands were apportioned to the settlers, including the encomendero, by royal land grants known as *mercedes de tierra*.[45]

The institution of the encomienda did not originate in the American kingdoms, but in medieval Spain. It was revived and transferred first to Santo Domingo, on the island of Española (Hispaniola), in the early 1500s, then to the other islands of the Antilles, and finally to the mainland kingdoms during and immediately after the conquests. It came to Guatemala and the rest of Central America with the expedition of Pedro de Alvarado. King Carlos I of Spain granted encomiendas to Alvarado and delegated to him the responsibility of awarding them to others of his followers and to early settlers. Bernal Díaz del Castillo, a participant and chronicler of the conquest of Mexico, became one of the encomenderos of Guatemala when he settled there in 1541. He received three encomiendas of Indians, including those of the towns of Zacatepec, Joazagazapa, and Mistán, although he and his family actually resided in Santiago de Guatemala. While living there, he wrote the first sixteen chapters of his *Historia verdadera de la conquista de Nueva España* ("True History of the Conquest of New Spain") between 1552 and 1557. He completed it after 1564, although it was not published until 1632.[46]

Technically, the encomienda was not the same as Indian slavery, but it was another system of forced labor. Instead of being acquired by warfare or being bought, sold, bartered, or traded as Indian slaves were, natives held in encomienda were acquired by an assignment or commendation. Although they became serfs in the European tradition and had the freedom to return to their villages when their work was done, as well as to feed themselves from their own fields, the encomienda was another kind of forced labor without pay since the Indian was required to work for the Spaniards to pay his annual tribute. The system exploited the Indians and became a virtual subterfuge for slavery, especially because of the many Spanish abuses of the institution. Treatment of the Indians depended on the goodwill (or badwill) of the encomendero. The mistreatment of natives—common during the first fifty years of Spanish occupation—appears to have declined by the late sixteenth century, as the institution itself declined in importance because Indians increasingly escheated to the Crown and because other forms of labor began to replace the encomiendas.[47]

From the outset of the colonization by Spaniards in Guatemala and the rest of the kingdom, the Crown endeavored to regulate the conditions of encomiendas. It is evident that the king intended grants to encomenderos to be only expedient, temporary measures for the control and labor of the Indians. This caused a heated and continuous conflict with those who wanted new encomiendas granted and the old ones protected and extended to their heirs. Encomenderos opposed the king's policy of having Indians held in encomienda escheat to the Crown on the death of the present holder. As early as 23 March 1528 the cabildo of Santiago de Guatemala ordered all encomenderos to have their Indians begin constructing houses on the lots of Spaniards and public buildings within the city.[48] This order favoring the residents of the capital was one of the first uses of Indian labor in a way not intended by the original grants of encomienda. It and subsequent misuses of encomienda Indians were resisted by the Crown. In 1538 a royal decree ordered encomenderos to marry within three years or forfeit their Indians.[49] Article 35 of the New Laws in 1542 forbade the issuance of new encomiendas and required that the existing ones escheat to the Crown on the death of the present encomendero.[50] This led to an uproar of opposition throughout the American kingdoms, including a civil war in Peru that resulted in the death of the first viceroy. In Guatemala encomenderos protested, and the cabildo of Santiago de Guatemala on 10 September 1543 addressed a letter to King Carlos I protesting the abolition of encomiendas.[51] Bernal Díaz del Castillo was sent to Spain as a delegate of the opposition forces in Guatemala to present their complaints to the king.[52] As a result, after careful consideration by the Council of the Indies, the king suspended that part of the New Laws pertaining to the abolition of encomiendas and permitted their continuance.[53] Meanwhile, the reforms of Alonso López de Cerrato and those of Governor Diego García de Valverde (1578–88) corrected such abuses of the encomienda in Guatemala as collecting tributes from Indians based on ancient head counts that were no longer valid because of the declining native population, collecting tributes from dead or absent Indians, selling encomienda Indians to other Spaniards, and beating Indians excessively.[54]

Indians in encomienda were required to contribute their labor without compensation and to pay tribute to their encomenderos. They were controlled by overseers known as *calpixques* or mayordomos. Historian William L. Sherman summarizes the Indians' work in four categories: service in agriculture, mining, stock raising, and industry; service in construction, and repair; transporting merchandise and personal effects; and domestic service in Spanish households.[55] On 3 February 1563, Licenciado Juan Núñez de Landecho, president of the Audiencia de Guatemala, observed that the Indians of Guatemala performed three types of work: cultivating the fields of the Spaniards, construction and public works, and "servicio ordinario" (routine tasks or services), such as house work, cooking, hauling water, supplying firewood, and grooming horses.[56]

That encomiendas were numerous and important by the middle of the sixteenth century in Guatemala is revealed in a list of the encomenderos in the jurisdiction of Santiago de Guatemala between 1548 and 1555 with the numbers of Indians assigned to them. In summary, it shows 79 encomenderos with the number of Indians for each and 15 others without figures of assigned Indians. For the 79 encomenderos who were listed with their Indians, there were 23,859 encomienda Indians in total. The Crown held 2,864 of them, while three encomenderos held over 1,000 Indians each, with Don Francisco de la Cueva possessing the greatest number, 2,100 Indians. The remaining 75 encomenderos possessed numbers of Indians ranging from a high of 880 to a low of 4.[57]

After 1549, when personal service was removed from encomienda grants and the Crown required that Indians be paid for their labor, the encomiendas declined in both numbers and importance.[58] Increasingly, Indians held by encomenderos reverted to the Crown's possession and control, and other labor systems replaced the institution. It is evident, however, that encomiendas continued to exist even in the late seventeenth century. In 1686 a report of Captain Joseph Aguilar Rebolledo on the encomiendas of the Condesa de Alba at Chimaltenango, about nine miles north of Santiago de Guatemala, revealed that at her death Alba held six towns of Indians in encomienda. Her tributes were collected twice a year, usually in kind (corn, beans, chile, and chickens, for example), but the income did not cover expenses. With some 4,500 tributaries, or a total of about 18,000 persons, Chimaltenango represented the decay of the encomienda to a system used largely to pay the pensions of descendants of the conquistadores.[59] Obviously, encomiendas were held by women as well as men. The last encomienda of the Lake Atitlán region, that of the Conde de Oropesa, ended in 1707. In 1720, King Felipe V abolished the encomienda completely, although certain families continued to receive pensions supported by the tribute of Indians, as in the case of the Condesa de Alba, until the 1760s.[60]

Although it existed for nearly two centuries in colonial Guatemala, the encomienda was really important as a system of forced labor only during the first generation of Spanish contact and colonization. It fell victim to Crown opposition and control, as well as to other labor systems and practices increasingly employed after the middle of the sixteenth century. It declined in importance and perished because of a variety of factors: Crown opposition and increasing royal control of the Indians; the abolition of personal services after 1549, which diminished the numbers of Indians at and migrating to congregaciones under royal control; new economic circumstances requiring other labor systems; the precipitous decline in the Indian population from the 1520s to about 1650; and finally the Bourbon pressure to do away with an obsolete and outdated system of labor and tribute. Thus the encomienda was "basically a transitional institution," as Sandra Orellana has described it,[61] but during the sixteenth century it did perform its economic function of sustaining the Spanish population, giving Spaniards the feeling that they were noblemen with vassals, and becoming the "economic base of the Spaniards and their institutions during the process of consolidation of the new society."[62]

THE REPARTIMIENTO

With the demise of Indian slavery and the decline of the encomienda, Spaniards in Guatemala turned to, and the Crown endorsed, labor by repartimientos. Although an early system of repartimiento had existed in the Antilles, where the Indians were divided among the conquerors and settlers, in Guatemala repartimiento came to mean a labor system in which Indians were conscripted to work according to quotas for a set number of days every month.[63] Although both terms, "encomienda" and "repartimiento," were used widely and often interchangeably in Guatemala during the sixteenth century,[64] and writers have frequently confused them since, the repartimiento was an entirely different labor system from the encomienda. In fact, as the latter declined in use and importance, the former increased and remained a principal source of labor into the eighteenth century and later.[65]

Technically known as the "repartimiento de indios," the system required Indian men between the ages of sixteen and sixty, excepting only their caciques and those who were ill, to contribute their labor to a rotating quota representing about one-quarter of those living in each native village. The conscripted Indians would report to the main plaza of a nearby Spanish town, where they were met and counted by a Spanish official such as the *juez del repartidor* (repartimiento supervisor or justice). This official received requests from Spanish landowners, agriculturalists, and others requiring labor. He assigned the required number of Indians for the prescribed days and longer periods of work, being careful that they were used legally, that is, only according to the laws pertaining to repartimiento labor. Overall, the Audiencia de Guatemala controlled the repartimiento system and assigned labor drafts to private individuals, religious institutions, municipalities, and government offices. Thus Indians could be used on public projects as well as to meet the needs of individual Spaniards. By law those who employed repartimiento Indians had to pay their laborers a fixed wage, usually one real (one-eighth of a peso) per day, and provide tools for their work, an adequate diet, and satisfactory housing for the period of their employment. Furthermore, at the conclusion of their work period, the Indians did not remain under the control of their employers, but returned to their villages. Thus repartimiento work was paid and temporary.[66]

While it may appear that this system provided the Indians with payment for their work and freedom to live in their own villages and to work on a rotating basis, the truth was that the repartimiento benefitted landowners and other Spaniards more than the Indians and the system was subject to all sorts of abuses. Employers of Indian labor under the repartimiento no longer had an obligation to protect their workers as they had under the encomienda system. Authorized by the New Laws of 1542, and supplemented by royal decrees in 1574, 1601, and 1609, the repartimiento system was under Crown control and use of the Indians was determined by royal authorities. However, once the natives were assigned to individuals or agencies beyond the control of those officials, employers rarely paid their charges in cash and often charged them for the goods they consumed. Furthermore, Indians lost additional time in transit walking to and from their villages to the appointed places of assembly. Poorer Indians were repeatedly conscripted while wealthier ones paid their local caciques not to be drafted, thereby ensuring that the poor missed harvesting and planting their own crops and served in repartimiento more frequently. In addition, the repartimiento disrupted village and family life and was subject to the corruption of the juez repartidor, who was a poorly paid lesser official and the willing target of employers who offered him a bribe and kept the assigned Indians longer than specified under their jurisdiction. Some employers even required their Indians to furnish their own tools and food.[67]

Although Indians, the Crown, and Spanish employers found the system irksome, repartimiento grew to be "a major supplier of labor after the epidemics of the 1570s, and during the half century of transition between then and the 1630s it was widely used."[68] While it suffered from the decline in the Indian population by the middle of the seventeenth century, repartimiento labor continued into the eighteenth century, and the colonists continued to exploit the Indian labor. Although the Crown endeavored to regulate the conditions of repartimiento and recognized some of its inequities, the royal ordinances of 1609 tolerated the system as a necessary evil until the Indians could become educated to working as free men for wages,[69] and officials permitted some of the abuses to continue.[70]

During the eighteenth century village Indians frequently complained to local officials, the juez repartidor, and to the Audiencia de Guatemala of abuses of the repartimiento. In 1734, during the administration of Pedro de Rivera (1733–42), Captain Nicolás Mencos, the juez repartidor of the valley of Comalapa, reported that Indians of the village protested that their own justices extorted from them one real per person each week as a legal fee, leaving them with only five reales for six days of work. Mencos rebuked these Indian leaders severely and ordered that the practice of collecting such a fee cease. He also sought the support of the audiencia and its president, Rivera, who ordered on 9 March 1735 that this surcharge be prohibited and that the governor and justices of the pueblo protect the Indians according to law and help them.[71] Five years later, the officials and people of the village of Jumay complained that because of their diminished numbers they could no longer supply their quotas of twelve Indians for the sugar mill at Cerro Redondo and ten for that at La Vega. Also, they pointed out that the sugar mills were seven leagues (approximately twenty miles) from their fields, that they had to cross the dangerous Esclavos River to ge to them, and that the pay was not enough to enable them to support their tribute payments and their families. The attorney of the audiencia supported their complaints, and that body ordered the alcalde mayor of Escuintla to halt repartimientos for the two sugar mills.[72]

Those two examples illustrate both the decline of the repartimiento system and the complaints of the Indians about the injustices and burdens they faced. From the 1730s to 1798 there were numerous requests for repartimiento Indians by employers who promised to pay them for their labor, and numerous protests by Indians and officials in various villages and districts (for example, Chiquimula, Amatitlán, Chimaltenango, Sololá, Jilotepeque, Iztapa, and San Pedro Sacatepéques) and in the capital, Santiago de Guatemala.[73] One such petitioner was Don Juan Carrascosa, who on 20 October 1773 requested repartimiento Indians to work on his hacienda at Arqueta near Sololá, which produced wheat and maize for the city of Santiago de Guatemala. His petition contained the following schedule of the numbers of Indians required for 4 to 6 days of work per month and the tasks they were expected to perform:

February	400 Indians to clear land with hoes
March	500 Indians to clear maize fields
April	100 Indians to fence maize fields
May	400 Indians for planting wheat
June	600 Indians for weeding maize and wheat fields.
July	600 Indians for "hilling the maize."
August and September	600 Indians for clearing the land for the next season.
October	No Indians needed—only voluntary workers for plowing with oxen, a task the village Indians do not know how to do.
November	600 Indians for harvesting wheat.
December	600 Indians for harvesting maize.
January	200 Indians for storing maize.[74]

By the early 1770s there were three types of repartimientos in Guatemala, according to a recent historical study. They were the apportionment of labor for the haciendas in the southeastern region near the

Pacific coast the apportionment of porters in eastern Guatemala near the Atlantic coast, and the apportionment of spinners of yarn and makers of "utensils," for the most part in the highland region.[75] While those uses of the repartimiento were evident, another employment of the system was equally important. After the destruction of Santiago de Guatemala by the earthquake of 29 July 1773, and the king's order in July 1775 to transfer the capital to the Valley of La Hermita, repartimiento Indians were employed to build the new capital of Nueva Guatemala de la Asunción. So many Indians were taken from the nearby villages for this work that protests were registered by *hacendados* (owners of haciendas) and by authorities concerned about the scarcity of laborers for their normal repartimientos. One such complaint came from Doña Ana Taracena, a *hacendada* of Sierra de Canales, who noted that officials were taking her Indians for the construction of the new city. She had requested twenty repartimiento Indians from the town of Amatitlán at a wage of 1½ reales per day, a request that was granted by the Audiencia de Guatemala; however, when this repartimiento was assigned to the towns of Santiago and San Lucas, officials there complained to the commissioner of the town of Mixco, that it was difficult to supply the laborers because so many men had been taken from both villages to build the new capital. Also, claims for exemptions from repartimiento because of the scarcity of Indians around Mixco were registered often in the years 1774 and 1775.[76]

Thus the system of repartimiento was established early in the Spanish colonial period and endured into the late eighteenth century and beyond. It was another form of forced labor by the Indians, and furthermore, it was not satisfactory for either the Indians or the Spaniards. It was subject to abuses, to uncertainties and problems in supplying the growing needs of the Spaniards, and to complaints by the Indians, by officials, and by employers of the repartimiento Indians.

FREE LABOR AND DEBT PEONAGE

While under the early policies of the Spanish Crown, beginning with Queen Isabella in the first years of the sixteenth century, the Indians were viewed as free vassals, the monarchs of Spain contradicted themselves by requiring the Indians to work and by tolerating Indian slavery until the middle of the sixteenth century. They allowed the natives to be placed under forced-labor labor systems such as the encomienda and repartimiento, neither of which proved satisfactory. As William Sherman has observed, the conviction of the Crown that conquered peoples should be kept busy was a fundamental aspect of the Crown's Indian policy. This royal policy, without success, tried to ensure that Indians were paid for their work.[77] While the use of "free labor" increased gradually, and some Indians learned trades so that a sizeable number of native artisans were skilled in European trades by the end of the sixteenth century,[78] the majority of Guatemalan Indians were bound to their employers by the beginning of the seventeenth century.

As the numbers of Indians declined, the Spaniards moved into rural areas, where they acquired lands vacated by the natives, who in turn moved into congregaciones, where they began producing commercial crops for export. As the demand for labor consequently increased, the Crown's objective of "free labor" was circumvented by the rising system of debt peonage. Beginning in the seventeenth century, this form of Indian labor became significant in the eighteenth century when the Bourbons sought to create a free peasantry with an agricultural, wage-earning class that included Indians. Along with the abolition of the encomienda and opposition to the repartimiento at the end of the eighteenth century, the Bourbons attacked the Catholic Church's control and protection of their Indian wards. Legislation was passed requiring the Indians to pay tribute in cash, thereby forcing them to leave their pueblos and move to cities and haciendas, and favoring the use of Indians in indigo workshops and fields. Debt peonage had begun in the early 1600s when Indians began to find life in their villages intolerable because of continued repartimientos, taxes, and other obligations that caused them to move onto Spanish haciendas. The new type of labor at first complemented the repartimiento, but by the eighteenth century it had replaced it:[79] The Indians were not free laborers at all, but now were bound to their employers by debt.[80]

The institution of debt peonage satisfied the increasing demands of Spanish hacendados for labor and the Indians' desire to escape from oppression in village life. At first the relationship was an informal contract for a specific period of time, often as long as six months, and was mutually beneficial to the hacendado and the Indian. Hacendados advanced Indians pay against future work to induce them to hire themselves out to Spaniards. At the end of the contracted period Indians were still in debt, and so they accepted another advance, thus perpetuating their debt relationship. While government officials at first opposed this system, they had ceased trying to prevent it by 1610. Consequently, Indian agricultural laborers came to reside permanently on haciendas and farms where they became virtual serfs. A variation of the arrangement developed when Indians became sharecroppers. They were given a plot on the hacienda for their own use, and on which they could build a hut for their families. In return for that they were obligated to work a specified number of days each week for the landowner. Hacendados and other owners of landed properties would provide these Indians with food, clothing, and sometimes housing, as well as a small wage. The landowners would agree to pay the Indians' tribute to the authorities and protect them against such intrusive forces as the repartimiento assignments that the Indians faced in their villages. Thus the Indians labored now for the hacendados and could be bought and sold along with the estate where they lived.[81]

Although some improvements were gained by Indians under this system, and the hacienda may have seemed preferable to them over their village,[82] they were subject entirely to the control and the exploitation of their labor by the hacendados, who kept their charges in debt and subject to the landowner's prices for food, clothing, tools, and other necessities. In addition, this system broke down the unity of the Indian villages and decreased the tributes collected there, as well as the amounts of food that village-dwelling Indians could produce for Spanish cities and communities.[83]

While government control over labor declined and "free labor" became more prevalent in the eighteenth century,[84] debt peonage increased. The Bourbon monarchs attempted to integrate the Indian pueblos into society by compelling their residents to enter the money economy and by bringing village institutions increasingly under the control of secular authorities.[85] They wished to establish a free peasantry, including Indians, with wage earning as its base. In their attempt, however, they also contributed to the breakdown of Indian communities, tolerated and sometimes even encouraged debt peonage, and intensified the demand of other Guatemalans for Indian labor. Employers of Indians favored debt peonage because it ensured a steady labor supply, something that was unattainable under the repartimiento system. Therefore, at the end of the eighteenth century Indians continued to be exploited for their labor, and free Indians had become displaced in Spanish communities, where they displayed characteristics of vagabondage, instability, criminal behavior, and drunkenness. During this century also, there occurred the rising use and importance of blacks as slaves in Guatemala and elsewhere throughout the kingdom.

BLACK SLAVE LABOR

African slaves first arrived in the Caribbean islands during the second decade of the sixteenth century, and in Guatemala and Central America soon after the conquest by Pedro de Alvarado. Obtained at first by private contractors, and later by Spanish *asientos* (slave contracts) with Portugal and Great Britain, the slaves, known by Spaniards as *bozales,* came initially from the Sudan and the coast of Guinea, and later were captured Bantu people from Angola. Spain did not participate in the capture of blacks within Africa or at the "factories" established on the African coast by the Portuguese and the English. Instead, the Spanish Crown negotiated contracts with both those nations (with Portugal after 1580 until the midseventeenth century, and with Great Britain in the eighteenth century, especially after the War of the Spanish Succession and the Treaty of Utrecht). In each contract the supplying nation was authorized to deliver a set number of slaves yearly to Spanish ports, such as Santo Domingo, in the Indies. Slave markets at port cities in Spanish domains then disseminated black slaves to individual buyers. By 1570, no more than 31,200 such slaves had entered Spanish-American ports over a period of fifty years, and they were only a "tiny fraction of the total labor force."[86]

In Guatemala blacks were introduced in 1524 with the conquering expedition of Pedro de Alvarado from New Spain, and around the middle of the sixteenth century they were being regularly supplied to eastern Central American ports, largely in Honduras.[87] By 1570 there were an estimated 10,000 blacks and *mulatos* (mixtures of black and other races) compared to 550,000 Indians, in a total population of 575,000 in all of Central America.[88] The slave population increased somewhat until about 1635, but the economic depression and the decline of Central America's export industry (largely cacao) caused the

financially strapped Crown to reject the cabildo of Santiago de Guatemala's petition to the king to subsidize the importation of five hundred
black slaves per year. Thereafter the importation of African slaves
dropped to almost nothing, and it did not revive until the beginning of
the eighteenth century.[89] By 1650 there were an estimated 20,000
blacks and 10,000 mulattos among Central America's total population
of 650,000, which included about 540,000 Indians.[90]

Guatemalans, like other residents of the Spanish kingdoms of the
Americas, and like the Spanish Crown, viewed blacks, and especially
slaves, as "piezas de Indias" (literally "pieces of the Indies") who were
not subject to the royal patronage over Indians that the popes had
granted to the monarchs of Castile.[91] As such, blacks were thought of
as property to be bought and sold, and it is obvious that neither the
Crown nor the church felt an obligation to Christianize them, although
some clergymen did. Black slaves were considered not as a part of the
"Republic of Spaniards" or the "Republic of Indians," but as a separate group, along with free blacks and mulattos, in the ordering of
society.[92] While some blacks served in urban areas, such as Santiago
de Guatemala, as domestic servants, traders, mule drivers (arrieros),
and craftsmen, and by 1620 others lived in the sugar-growing village
of Amatitlán (about one hundred men, women, and children, living in
thatched houses),[93] the great majority was employed in regions of
Central America outside the province of Guatemala, largely in the
silver-mining area of today's Honduras and the indigo-growing regions of the Pacific coastal zone. Black slaves were allowed to marry
free men and women, although their offspring were nonetheless born
into servitude. They also could purchase their own freedom, and often
they were manumitted by their owner, usually at the latter's death.[94]

After 1700, and particularly after the Treaty of Utrecht ended the
War of Spanish Succession in Europe in 1713, Spain agreed to an
asiento permitting Great Britain to import black slaves into the Americas. This contract lasted until 1739, when the War of Jenkins's Ear
between Spain and Great Britain began over British violations of the
treaty and reported instances of smuggling into the Spanish kingdoms.
Although an asiento in 1765 provided four hundred slaves yearly for
Campeche and Honduras, it appears that only about two hundred (or
fewer) arrived annually. Throughout the eighteenth century the asientos

failed to meet the demand for slave laborers, even though they lowered the prices for individual slaves to 150 to 300 pesos. As a result, Guatemalans continued to bring black slaves into the province from New Spain, Panama, and Nicaragua, and they continually resorted to a contraband trade with the English on the Mosquito Coast of Honduras and Nicaragua. Christopher H. Lutz concluded that no more than 21,000 black slaves were imported to Central America between 1520 and 1820,[95] a figure that may be quite low in view of the number already imported between 1524 and 1635 and during the continued importation of them during the eighteenth century.

Various documents between 1713 and 1809 in the Archivo General de Centro América in Guatemala City contain information on the slave trade, the cost of blacks, freedom for escaped slaves, regulation of slave sales, marking and branding of slaves, and their education, occupations, treatment, and places of residence. A patent of 23 March 1713, issued in accordance with the concession granted to the English in the Treaty of Utrecht, authorized Captain Thomas Dillon to bring into Central America[96] 72 black slaves (51 men and 21 women) branded with the mark of the English trading company. The prices of 100 slaves brought from Jamaica to Omoa in 1756 by an *asentista* (holder of a slave contract), Gaspar Hall, indicate that the individual price was 184 pesos, to be paid by the royal officials of Guatemala. The same individual figure was quoted when 100 blacks were imported in 1769, and for 217 such slaves imported by Don José Piñol, "apoderado del asiento de negros esclavos" ("holder of a power of attorney for the black slave contract"), to work on the construction of the fortress at Omoa.[97] Gaspar Hall submitted a bill in 1760 for 200 blacks ("piezas de negros," or individual blacks—100 men and 100 women) who were imported at Hall's expense on the brigantine *Honduras,* Captain John Moncrief commanding, for the president and governor of Guatemala. Hall requested payment for the 200 blacks at 184 pesos each, or a total of 36,800 pesos. New clothes were furnished for the slaves at 12 reales each (300 pesos total), plus one hundred caps for the men at 2 reales each (25 pesos total) and one hundred shawls for the women at 2 reales each (25 pesos total). Thus Hall claimed a total payment of 37,150 pesos.[98]

Granting freedom to slaves who escaped from the British colony of Belize and the manumission of black slaves were both evident in colonial Guatemala during the eighteenth century. One resident of Petén, in a 1778 letter to the president and captain general, Martín de Mayorga, reported that on 28 April a black, about twenty-six years old, had fled from "Balis" (Belize) with three companions recently arrived from Jamaica, seeking refuge and baptism. This Spanish inhabitant of the presidio of Petén explained that he had taken all of the refugees into his household with his family to teach them the Christian religion and baptize them. The president's attorney advised him that the governor could grant freedom to slaves seeking baptism because of the royal cedula of 19 December 1739. Evidently Mayorga granted liberty to these blacks, but there is no official statement of that in the document.[99] That Guatemala's chief royal official did grant freedom to blacks is apparent in a concession of Governor Matías de Gálvez in 1783. Recognizing the services of a black named Manuel Antonio Udenta, who had served at Gálvez's side since 1779 on the northern coast of Central America during the governor's campaigns against the English, Gálvez gave Udenta his freedom and provided him with a house, "in the name of His Majesty," located in the barrio of La Hermita of Nueva Guatemala. Udenta could live and dispose of the house as he wished, "as his own." Accompanying this grant was a map, indicating in black where Udenta could live.[100] On 12 July 1789 a royal order prohibited the return of black slaves escaped from British colonies, and it was enforced in Guatemala by a writ issued at Nueva Guatemala.[101]

According to entries in the royal books between 1808 and 1810, nineteen women and five men, all slaves at Omoa on the northern coast of today's Honduras, were freed at a total cost of 3,065 pesos, evidently paid by the individuals to the royal treasury. The value of each slave ranged from 60 to 300 pesos. For example, in 1808, Gertrudis Mavacala and Perrona Duran obtained their freedom on 1 September at values of 175 and 225 pesos, respectively. On 10 November, María Víctor Musinga was freed at a value of 70 pesos, while the next day Margarita Arroyo, Gregoria Guala, and Juana María Guisebe obtained their freedom at values of 225, 60, and 75 pesos, respectively. Juana Francisca de Arroyo was freed on 22 November at a value of 235 pesos, thus bringing the total value of all seven of these women to 1,065 pesos.[102]

The Spanish Crown and royal officials also established regulations for the education and treatment of black slaves between 1784 and 1790. In 1784, King Carlos III, "moved by sentiments of great humanity" for the betterment of the black slaves who had been taken to his dominions in the Indies, decreed the abolition of the customary practice of branding slaves on the face and back when they entered port cities of the Americas. In the same decree he ordered that all the branding irons used for the purpose be sent to the office of the Minister of the Indies in Spain so that they could never be used again.[103] The order was decreed in Nueva Guatemala by the governor and captain general on 16 March 1785, and all of the branding irons were shipped to the Council of the Indies on 25 May 1785.[104]

Furthermore, King Carlos IV issued detailed instructions on 31 May 1789 for the education, good treatment, and employment of slaves to make them "useful citizens." He required that all owners instruct their slaves in the principles and "truths" of the Catholic faith so that they could be baptized not later than one year after their arrival in his dominions. Furthermore, slaves were to be clothed according to standards of dress set by the justices of the various regions and with consideration of the climate in which the slave lived. Blacks should be employed principally, according to the king, in agriculture and other occupations in the fields, usually from sunrise to sunset but with two hours set aside each day for work on their own fields. They should not be idle, but justices should give slaves consideration for their age, strength, and robustness when employing them. Owners were not permitted to have slaves work on fiesta days, and they were to be instructed to attend mass to hear the Christian doctrine. The king permitted slaves to have their own simple diversions, but sexes were to be separated, excess drinking was prohibited, and all celebrations were to end before the bells tolled calling them to prayer and vespers. Owners were instructed to provide housing, separately for unmarried slaves, plus beds, blankets, and clothing for all of their charges. Slaves who were ill were to be sent to hospitals in nearby towns, and those who were too old or too sick to work were to be treated in the same way as children. All black slaves were to receive food from their owners. Also, the king encouraged slaves to marry and to avoid "illicit agreements." They were obligated to show obedience and respect for their masters, who could castigate them for their offenses by imprisonment, shackling, chaining, and whipping, but not on the head and not to exceed twenty-five lashes. Only owners or their mayordomos could execute punishments, and none could use instruments that drew blood. For major crimes against owners, wives, children, or mayordomos, the punishments did not apply. In such cases the justices of the audiencia or the appointed "protector of the slaves" would determine punishment according to the law and the gravity of the crime. Owners were charged not to mistreat their slaves, and punishments were set for those who did so or who injured their slaves. Finally, the king directed that owners prepare and present annual lists of their slaves, distinguishing their ages and sexes, to the ayuntamientos of towns near their haciendas; and he ordered town councils to establish a special "caja de multas" (financial branch for fines) into which deposits derived from punishment fines would be made.[105]

While those royal regulations may have been considered humane, it should be emphasized that reported mistreatment of black slaves continued into the early nineteenth century[106] and that slaves died, for example, in the construction of the fortress of Omoa.[107] The institution of black slavery continued until 1821 with the exception of a brief period when the Constitution of 1812 in Spain outlawed it. Although the number of slaves declined toward the end of the eighteenth century and during the first two decades of the following one, the government used black slaves to populate frontier regions along the Mosquito Coast.[108] Four black slaves were brought from Omoa to Nueva Guatemala in 1796 so that they could learn the trades of blacksmith, gunsmith, and carpenter. Two of them were assigned to the king's armorer, Don Francisco Planas, and the other two were assigned to a carpenter's master, Tomás Benítez. Each of the apprentices was paid a daily wage of one real, and they received four and one-half reales for each piece of their handiwork. All four were furnished four varas (about 132 inches, or 11 feet) of cloth for their clothing, a poncho, and a blanket.[109]

Lists of black slaves at various places early in the nineteenth century indicate that such labor continued. Near the end of 1803, for example, the commandant at the fortress of Omoa, Antonio González, reported that there were 372 slaves there, representing a decline of one-fifth from over the previous year. The figure did not include the 60 blacks in the artillery company of the garrison. One-fourth of the 372 slaves were women, children, disabled men, or old people, called *ancianos*. Discounting them, along with other blacks who were engaged in fixed occupations, worked for the garrison (five of whom were in Nicaragua, two in Trujillo, and six in Guatemala), and discounting those who had died during the year, the commandant reported that he had only 74 blacks available for labor.[110] A list of black slaves in the villa of Santísima Trinidad de Sonsonate (in today's El Salvador) on 2 March 1809 showed 16 (12 females and 4 males) ranging in age from three to forty years and living in the houses of six Spaniards. Only 7 of the 16 were adults over twenty years old, and 2 actually were owned by persons in Guatemala.[111]

A census of 1821, at a location in Guatemala or possibly Honduras simply named Pueblo de los Esclavos (town of the slaves), lists a total of 771 persons (395 women and 376 men) along with their ages, marital status, and occupations. Francisco López, a widower, was reported as one hundred years old, and 6 others (3 women and 3 men) were in their eighties and nineties, while the youngest was a boy of five months. There were 69 married men, 69 married women, 69 single men, 47 single women, 10 widowers, and 24 widows in the total population of this town. While 2 were reported as blind, 118 were engaged in various occupations—89 as farmers, 16 as servants, 3 as vaqueros (cowhands), 3 as day laborers, 2 as hacendados, 2 as mayordomos, and 1 each as sacristan, carpenter, and weaver.[112]

Thus it is evident that black slavery continued on the eve of independence, that many were of advanced age, that they generally were married and had families with children of all ages, and that most had occupations and skills (including two who were landowners in their own right) to pursue their own lives without any mention whatever of their being owned by others. Apparently Pueblo de los Esclavos was established as a community of black slaves in Guatemala or Honduras under the jurisdiction of the Audiencia de Guatemala, not by individual owners in some part of the kingdom.

In summary, Spanish relations with the Indians of Guatemala began with violence in the conquest period, but soon thereafter developed during a long era of accommodation and acculturation. Throughout the nearly three centuries of Spain's occupation and control of the province and kingdom of Guatemala, the hundreds of thousands of Indians presented major problems for Spanish administrators and settlers, on the one hand, while the natives suffered, on the other. Royal policies conflicted with the needs and practices of the Spanish inhabitants, causing disunity, strife, and struggles that often resulted in vacillation of policies and neglect. Indian labor was of paramount importance to both religious and civil officials. It progressed from outright slavery and the encomienda to repartimiento and supposedly free labor for wages; but ultimately debt peonage became widespread. The Bourbon efforts to reform the system brought Indians under Crown control and endeavored to integrate the Indians into a general society of free farmers at the cost of increasing debt peonage, vagabondage, and intoxication among the natives. In areas such as the Atlantic and Pacific coastal regions, Indian communities and their residents nearly vanished, while in the highlands, where there were no indigo fields and few sugar factories, and where products usually were for local consumption, Indians preserved their languages, traditions, and community orientation, thereby surviving after the Spanish colonial period to the present day.[113] While the numbers of the Indians declined precipitously until the middle of the seventeenth century, they gradually increased thereafter, and they still constituted about 65 percent of the total population at the end of the Spanish colonial era.[114]

Blacks were present as slaves from the outset of Spanish colonization. Although their numbers were relatively small when compared with the Indian population and with the overall totals of the inhabitants of the province and kingdom, they constituted an important labor source. Black slaves were concentrated principally on the Atlantic coast of Central America with pockets of them near the Guatemala-Salvador border as well as a few within Guatemala itself. Black slavery persisted until the end of the colonial period, although the Bourbons made improvements in the treatment and conditions of work of the slaves. Relatively few black slaves existed within what is today the republic of Guatemala, although there were some in rural communities and others worked for their owners in Santiago de Guatemala and other Spanish towns.

The labor of Indians and blacks, along with Spanish policies and practices toward both races, were only parts of Spain's total presence in the province and kingdom of Guatemala. The Spaniards also had interests in landholding, establishing communities, and developing the economy of both the province and kingdom—subjects that will be addressed in the next chapter.

CHAPTER 6

Land, Towns, and the Economy

ALTHOUGH THE PRESENCE of Indians in considerable numbers for conversion to Christianity and education in Western ways, and the exploitation of their labor, attracted Spaniards to Guatemala, land was an increasingly important motive for Spanish settlement and expansion throughout the colonial period. Lyle N. McAlister emphasized that for most of colonial Latin America land was "the basic natural resource of the Indies."[1] Guatemala's diverse landforms, climates, and regions attracted settlement both in urban communities and the rural countryside during the long period of Spanish colonization. The highland region with its temperate climate, large numbers of Indians, and agricultural and stock-raising possibilities, was the focal point of attraction. Yet, largely for economic and military reasons, Spaniards also came to settle the Pacific coast, the boca costa (piedmont), and the Atlantic coast, thereby ensuring that all the geographic regions were developed between the sixteenth and the early nineteenth century.

From the early days of the conquest to the end of Spanish rule, Spaniards established and lived in urban communities, as they had for thousands of years in Spain itself. Thus the institution of the Spanish municipio became the heart and soul of permanent settlement over the entire area of colonial Guatemala, as well as in the rest of Central America during this era. Various types of towns became the centers of administration, religion, trade and commerce, other economic activities, and social and cultural life. Inhabited by Spaniards, Indians, and ladinos, these communities demonstrated the true characteristics of settlements by Spanish men, women, and children, contrary to the view of many North American and European writers that Spaniards sought only wealth and consequently wiped out the Indians, while only the English were true colonizers in the Americas. Having discussed

118

Indian towns in the previous chapter, we shall examine here the Spanish communities founded and sustained in colonial Guatemala.

Economic motives had much to do with why and how Spain established communities in the province and kingdom of Guatemala. Indeed, as Ralph Lee Woodward has noted, "the principal motive for colonization in Central America was economic."[2] While the lure of wealth from gold and silver originally attracted Spaniards, it proved illusory except for a silver-mining boom of short duration in what is today Honduras. Although some mining occurred in isolated locales or pockets within the province of Guatemala, the industry never played a major role in the economy during the colonial era. The development of agriculture and the export of such commodities as cacao, indigo, and cochineal, along with the availability of Indian labor to construct and maintain agricultural properties, served to keep Spaniards in Guatemala and elsewhere in Central America when mining became less lucrative than they had hoped.[3] In colonial Guatemala agriculture and stock raising dominated the province, as it did the rest of the kingdom, displaying boom-and-bust cycles that depended on external demand as well as internal market conditions. In addition to the big three agricultural crops exported to Spain, Guatemalans raised sugar, wheat, maize, fruits, and garden vegetables largely for local trade and consumption. Other inhabitants became involved in manufactures such as textiles, and many became skilled artisans in various trades. During the last century of Spanish jurisdiction over Guatemala, largely as a result of Bourbon economic reforms, wealthy persons who resisted Crown efforts to control the economy became an important counterforce to the king, opposing royal policies. Their cadre demanded loosening economic restrictions in favor of free trade and expanded economic opportunities for themselves and for the province.

LAND SYSTEMS

Although in the first generation of the Spanish presence in Guatemala there had been relatively little interest in acquiring and possessing land,[4] Spaniards after about 1550 showed increasing desire to possess it, largely for economic reasons but also for prestige, respect, and advancement in society. Their needs differed from those of the Indians. Whereas the natives had been content with small plots of land on which they raised their crops for subsistence and local trade, Spaniards wanted land in large increments where it could be productive and economically rewarding.[5] Corporations and private individuals occupied and purchased land increasingly in the late sixteenth century. As Indians abandoned rural areas for congregaciones established by Spanish authorities, Spaniards acquired these vacant lands and increased the size of their holdings, both by purchase and intermarriage. At the end of the sixteenth century and during the first half of the seventeenth, Spanish landowners moved from cities like Santiago de Guatemala into the countryside and established themselves on properties outside the control of the king and his royal officials. Land also acquired a social value to its owner and served as a status symbol. It was held in pieces of various sizes: haciendas were large, privately owned estates, while ranchos, were small, privately owned plots for subsistence. Although the Spanish landholdings increased in number and size, some Indian lands, especially those near native communities that were already in existence when the Spaniards arrived, were preserved and protected by Crown grants and regulations. Nonetheless, through the course of Guatemala's colonial history, there was steady encroachment by Spaniards and ladinos on Indian lands.[6]

All land originally was owned by the king as his royal domain, but to encourage its settlement the monarch authorized royal officials, such as the governor, to grant land in towns and the rural countryside to individuals and corporate bodies such as the church. This was done through the mercedes de tierra, beginning after the arrival of the conquistadores and the first colonizers *(primeros pobladores)*. A surveyor laid out a town plan by "line and rule," first defining the location of the plaza mayor. The governor then distributed town lots *(solares)* and agricultural plots *(suertes)* to the founders and first settlers of the community who often were the vecinos, or principal residents of the town. Other lands were reserved for the common use of the community's residents *(ejidos)* and for the Crown *(tierras realengas)*. In later years the cabildo might make and confirm these grants. Those who received such lands were required to build a house on their town lots, make improvements to their properties, put rural lands to use, and live on their properties for a period of four to five years, during which the Crown retained title to the lands. Having met the conditions of the grant, recipients were then granted title to the land as their personal property, although ownership of the subsoil always remained in the hands of the monarch. If the conditions of the grant were not met, land reverted to the monarch and royal officials for redistribution. Initial distribution of the land was made by caballerías, (for the more important inhabitants) and peonías (for lesser people).[7]

As an example of early land distribution in Guatemala, Christopher H. Lutz discussed the apportionment of land in 1528 for Santiago de Guatemala, pointing out that lands were distributed by the caballería-peonía system. In addition to the town lots, each vecino, as a settler of the capital, received some fertile land along the nearby river and some choice woodland in the sierra outside the town. At first captured Indians were brought to work the surrounding *milpas* (maize fields) and as artisans in the town itself, but by 1541 to 1543 most such workers were freed Indians. They settled in barrios within the town, becoming wage earners, but they also continued to maintain small maize plots in semirural areas outside the community.[8] Thus from the outset both Spaniards and Indians had certain assigned town and agricultural properties in Santiago de Guatemala.

In the later colonial period community lands were held in "every imaginable combination of use tenure and private property," although custom prevailed and each community or municipality was recognized to embrace an area of one square league (a *sitio,* or about seven square miles).[9] In most areas of what is today the republic of Guatemala, especially in the western highlands, *latifundia* (large-scale landownership) hardly existed except for a few haciendas in the Indian-dominated region and the ladino cattle ranches that began to move onto lands abandoned by defunct towns on the southern coast. Small farms dominated the eastern regions. Village common lands included those that were available to all town residents for wood, water, temporary pasture of animals, and in some instances, rent for cultivation in small plots; land purchased by and for the community from either private individuals or public lands, often by a *composición,* a payment made to regularize long-term but technically illegal possession; land owned or possessed by individual families or clan groups; and tracts claimed by residents of the town because of customary use without any legal basis.

All legal residents of the town had access to community lands for subsistence agriculture and stock raising.[10]

Thus landholding was not simple but complex in colonial Guatemala, involving private and corporate ownership, common lands, and Crown holdings. Like labor, land was a valuable social as well as economic asset to the king, administrative officials, and inhabitants, both those who resided in towns and others in the rural countryside.

SPANISH TOWNS

"The Spaniard, then, was by tradition a town dweller. His strongest loyalty was to his *comunidad* [community]. . . . His town, or at most his province, was *patria* [homeland], which he loved (and loves) with an astonishing strength"[11]—so wrote Lesley Byrd Simpson about residents of Spain, the "mother" country. This belief of Spaniards in Europe came with them to all the American kingdoms, including Guatemala, and remained with their descendants for the next three centuries. Everywhere they went conquerors, settlers, and their successors founded a town or a *población* as a base of operations and the symbol of their presence. Among the first acts of Spaniards who came to America was to organize themselves into *comunidades,* and such municipal corporations were recognized as the proper source of civil authority along with the Crown itself. The Castilian municipio, including not only the village but also all land used around it for its support, became the main instrument of European colonization in Central and South America. In fact, to Spaniards the "republic was a city."[12]

Moreover, the Spanish Crown throughout the colonial period recognized the municipality legally as a symbol of royal control and authority. Both Carlos I (Charles V of the Holy Roman Empire and king of Spain from 1516 to 1556) and his son Felipe II (Philip II, king of Spain from 1556 to 1598) established regulations for the founding, laying out, and governance of towns, in laws promulgated in 1523, 1563, and 1573. The monarchs allowed founders of such communities to appoint the first officials and establish a cabildo for the settlement, and towns became the primary units of territorial jurisdiction. Site selections required attention to geographical features, conditions, climate, the presence of wood and water, and the availability of Indians for conversion to Catholicism and labor, although Spanish town founders were strictly enjoined to build their communities away from Indian ones that were still inhabited. Surveyors laid out town plans *(trazas)* by "line and rule," and using the gridiron pattern of the community of Santa Fe de Granada, which had been established before 1492 as a general model by the Catholic monarchs during the siege of Granada in Spain. They first designated a plaza mayor, from which they laid out the streets at right angles so that they intersected the plaza at its corners, and then they delineated the town plots. Common lands, plots for agriculture and stock raising, and royal lands were all parts of the town plan. Founders distributed urban and agricultural lots to individual vecinos, reserving certain plots for the construction of a church, a residence for the governor or founder, and offices for royal administrators, which usually were on the plaza mayor. The Spaniards then employed nearby Indians to construct their towns.[13]

While Spanish towns in the Americas followed those general guidelines, important alterations were made, depending on such factors as geography, climate, and demography. Towns also were designated as a ciudad, a villa, a pueblo, a poblacion, or a puesto, according to their size and importance. A *ciudad,* or city, was a major community of civil and religious significance having rights, privileges, and a coat of arms as did cities in Spain. For example, a bishopric, necessitating the construction of a cathedral, could be established only in a ciudad. A villa generally was a first or frontier town with a charter granting its residents the right to have a cabildo, along with other privileges. Only the monarch could authorize the establishment of a ciudad or villa, but that authority for villas often was delegated to town founders or governors in accordance with the terms of their *capitulación,* or contract, arranged between the Crown and the founders. *Pueblo, población,* and *puesto* were terms often used interchangeably to designate smaller, unchartered towns, villages, hamlets, and other inhabited places.[14]

Armed with these royal regulations and the terms of their contracts with the Monarch, conquistadores and town founders established communities all over the Americas. Between 1502 and 1515 Spaniards founded twenty-seven towns on the four major Caribbean islands,[15] including such places as Santo Domingo, Santiago de Cuba, San Juan (originally called Puerto Rico), and Havana. By 1531 they had founded fifteen municipalities in New Spain, including today's Mexico City,

Veracruz, and Guadalajara, and there were six European towns in what is today's Guatemala and El Salvador.[16]

Panamá became the first Spanish community in Central America. Today's Panama City was founded originally in 1519, although earlier settlements had been established temporarily at Santa María la Antigua del Darién and Nombre de Dios. Other Spanish communities followed at Santiago de los Caballeros in Guatemala (1524), Granada and León in Nicaragua (founded in 1524 and 1525, respectively), Trujillo and Gracias a Dios in Honduras (1525 and 1533, respectively), and the *real de minas* (mining town or district) of San Miguel de Tegucigalpa (1578) near the earlier site of Comayagua, originally founded in the 1530s.[17] By 1570 there were about 2,200 to 2,300 Spanish vecinos living in nineteen towns in Central America, although Santiago de Guatemala alone contained about 500 of them.[18] Vecinos were permanent residents of a community, property owners, usually the heads of families, and active participants in local affairs, according to William L. Sherman. Therefore, the total population of Spaniards in Central America living in Spanish towns in 1570 can be estimated between 8,800 and 10,000 people, and the population of Santiago de Guatemala was between 2,000 and 2,500. By 1620 there were fifteen towns in Central America with some 2,400 vecinos, of whom about 1,000 were at Santiago de Guatemala (about 5,000 people), according to the chronicler Antonio Vásquez de Espinosa.[19]

The founding of the Indian congregación towns in Guatemala, beginning in the late 1530s and early 1540s, has been discussed in the preceding chapter, and it is appropriate here to examine the establishment of Spanish towns, commencing with the Spanish conquest and colonization of Pedro de Alvarado and continuing with later communities established by Spaniards. Soon after entering what is today's Guatemala, Alvarado left a garrison at Quezaltenango under the command of Captain Juan de León y Cárdona to serve as a rearguard while the conqueror advanced into the interior.[20] Although this may have been the first Spanish community within present-day Guatemala, it cannot be considered the initial civil settlement inhabited by Spanish vecinos, which was the town of Iximché, founded by Alvarado's official act on 25 July 1524. The conquistador named it Santiago de los Caballeros de Guatemala, established its first cabildo, appointed its

Quezaltenango: "Plaza principal y parroquia" (main plaza and parish church) (Samuel Katz Collection, Special Collections, Nettie Lee Benson Latin American Library, University of Texas at Austin).

initial officials, and issued the first orders for the vecinos in the villa there.[21] Subsequently the Cakchiquel Indians who had resided at Iximché abandoned the town, and the Spanish community became just a paper settlement.[22] In the absence of his brother, the acting governor, Jorge de Alvarado, and the cabildo moved the site of the capital to the depopulated valley of Almolonga, establishing the town at the new location officially on 23 November 1527. Almolonga was chosen as the new site because of the absence of Indians, the temperate climate, the defensible nature of the terrain, a better water supply, accessibility of building materials, and availability of lands for cultivation. Thus Santiago de Almolonga (today called Ciudad Vieja, or the "old city") became the new residence of the Spaniards, as well as their Mexican, Tlaxcaltecan, and Cholutecan Indian allies who had accompanied Pedro de Alvarado's army.[23]

Panoramic view of Antigua (INGUAT, Guatemalan Tourist Commission)

This new community was laid out according to its traza in a grid pattern, with four solares in the center reserved for the plaza major and with streets running north to south and east to west. One *manzana* (block), consisting of two town lots, was designated on the plaza for the construction of a church dedicated to Santiago (Saint James); four lots fronting on the plaza were allotted for the building known as the cabildo *(casa del cabildo);* one lot was reserved in the town for a chapel dedicated to Nuestra Señora de los Remedios (Our Lady of the Remedies, or Miracles); one lot was assigned for a jail; two lots were reserved for the benefit of the townspeople of the community; and the remaining lots were distributed to the 100 to 150 vecinos of the town.[24] There the community remained until the disastrous flood and earthquake of three days culminated in the inundation of 11 September 1541

Iglesia de Ciudad Vieja (church of Ciudad Vieja) (Samuel Katz Collection, Special Collections, Nettie Lee Benson Latin American Library, University of Texas at Austin).

and the town was transferred after 1542 to a third site in the valley of Panchoy. This last change of location and the development of Santiago de Guatemala (today's Antigua), along with the transfer of the capital to Nueva Guatemala de la Asunción after the earthquake of 29 July 1773, will be discussed later in this chapter.

Santiago de Guatemala was not the only town founded by the Spaniards during the sixteenth century in what is today's Guatemala. Pedro de Alvarado also founded the original villa of San Salvador in 1524. It was moved in 1528 and again refounded in 1534, and though it is now the capital of El Salvador, in the colonial period San Salvador was part of the jurisdiction of Guatemala.[25] Amatitlán and Chiquimula were founded a few years after San Salvador. Amatitlán united five Indian towns that were scattered about the district.[26] Alvarado likewise founded the town of Huehuetenango after a battle with the Mames there in

1525.[27] To Captain Pedro de Portocarrero is attributed the founding of
the town of Chimaltenango in 1526, and Chichicastenango was named
by Tlaxcaltecans who accompanied Alvarado, on a site where Dominicans constructed its colonial church about 1540.[28] Totonicapán evidently was officially founded as a town by Captain Juan de León y
Cárdona on 13 January 1544 with Tlaxcaltecan, Cholutecan, and
Quiché Indians as inhabitants, and Licenciado Juan Rogel, an oidor of
the Audiencia de los Confines, founded the town of Sololá near Lake
Atitlán on 30 October 1547.[29] Thus by the middle of the sixteenth
century Spaniards had established many of the communities of present
day Guatemala, both Indian settlements and those inhabited by Spaniards and ladinos. Although Sidney D. Markman has observed that
Spaniards did not settle on pre-Columbian sites in Guatemala as they
did in Mexico,[30] that is not strictly true, because some Spanish towns
in the countryside and the original capital at Iximché were founded
where Indians already lived. It also is notable that Spanish towns from
their origins were inhabited by Europeans, Indian allies, and nearby
Guatemalan Indians, as illustrated by the capital of Santiago de
Guatemala.

In general, Spanish communities were laid out and occupied following royal regulations, but with some variations. The site selectors and
town founders considered prescribed conditions in making their decisions, and there always seems to have been a *traza* drawn up before-
hand. Yet, plazas mayores differed in their measurements from one
community to the next and did not always follow the guidelines set
forth in the royal regulations. Vecinos received town lots, usually one-
fourth of a block, which measured 100 varas on each side or 10,000
square varas.[31] The construction of public and religious buildings and
homes evolved sometimes over the course of many years. The first
towns looked much alike because the structures, even those of the
churches and public buildings, displayed a rudimentary architecture
and building materials were of little durability. Usually the initial
buildings were of wood with reeds covered with mud for walls and
straw for roofs. Others were made of adobe bricks. By the early seventeenth century colonial construction had begun to embrace more aesthetic and durable architectural forms, making use of more permanent
building materials. During the next two centuries structures became

Antigua: "plaza principal—Palacio y Catedral (main plaza, palace, and cathedral) (Samuel Katz Collection, Special Collections, Nettie Lee Benson Latin American Library, University of Texas at Austin).

more durable, larger, and more ornate, often employing the baroque and churrigueresque architectural forms, including magnificent arches, domes, and intricately carved facades, especially on public and religious buildings.[32]

Of all the Spanish municipalities in colonial Central America, Santiago de Guatemala was the largest, most beautiful, and most important administrative, economic, religious, and social center. After the transfer of the capital to the valley of Panchoy from Ciudad Vieja a few miles away, this community became the hub of the Spanish presence and activity for the entire region between New Spain and Panamá (which belonged to the Viceroyalty of Peru after 1570 and to the Viceroyalty of New Granada after its establishment in 1739). Santiago de Guatemala, as we have seen, was the capital of the Kingdom of Guatemala and also the seat of civil authority for the province of Guatemala. It was the headquarters of the bishopric and later the archbishopric of Guatemala. Furthermore, it was the focal point and center of economic, social, and cultural life of colonial Central America. After 1676 it had an established, widely recognized university, that of San Carlos de Guatemala, the only such institution of higher learning between Mexico City and Bogotá in New Granada. Indeed, Santiago de Guatemala was viewed by many as the third city of importance after Mexico City and Lima in Spain's kingdoms in the Americas.[33]

The villa of Santiago de Guatemala was granted ciudad status by King Carlos I in a royal cedula of 28 July 1532, while the capital was still located at Almolonga (Ciudad Vieja). After the destruction of that site on 11 September 1541, the capital was moved to the new location in the valley of Panchoy. There it remained, being granted the title of the "Muy Noble y Muy Leal Ciudad de Santiago de los Caballeros de Guatemala" ("Very Noble and Very Loyal City of Santiago de los Caballeros de Guatemala") by King Felipe II on 10 March 1566, until its transfer to Nueva Guatemala de la Asunción following the earthquake of 29 July 1773.[34]

Today known as Antigua Guatemala or simply Antigua, the new city was laid out according to a traza after the cabildo voted on 27 September 1541 to move the capital. The cabildo met again before the end of October to decide on the valley of Panchoy as the new location. The new city contained a plaza mayor, streets running east to west and north to south, town lots to be distributed to individual vecinos according to their status, twenty-four plots for public and private buildings, and one block for a public market. Although some writers have attributed this plan to the engineer Juan Bautista de Antonelli, Christopher Lutz doubted that he could have played a part in the city planning because Antonelli did not come to Guatemala until the late sixteenth century.[35]

Beginning the following year, 1542, civil offices, individual homes, and churches were constructed at the new site and gradually occupied. Franciscans, Dominicans, and Mercedarians built churches in separate areas of the city (La Merced north of the plaza mayor, San Francisco southeast of it, and Santo Domingo northeast of it). The cathedral site covered most of the block on the east side of the plaza mayor, while the Palace of the Captains was on the south side, and the cabildo was on the north side. Indian barrios also were designated, where Mexican, Tlaxcaltecan, and Guatemalan Indians settled and were provided with their own cabildos, officials, chapels, buildings, jails, police forces, and militias. However, the Spaniards strictly subordinated the native officials of those districts to Spanish authority.[36]

The city expanded greatly in the following decades from its original 41 blocks to 50 to 60 blocks in 1560, 90 in 1604, and 215 in 1773; but it never had any walls around it, and its boundaries were only vaguely defined.[37] In the early 1770s Santiago de Guatemala was described as a city of about 25,000 people, over a mile wide, with streets at right angles and well paved, and having an abundance of water. Facing the plaza mayor were the governor's and archbishop's palaces, the city hall (the meeting place of the cabildo or ayuntamiento), the royal mint, and a magnificent cathedral over 300 feet long, 120 feet wide, and 66 feet high with a huge nave and eight chapels on each side. Throughout the city there were nineteen churches, eighteen convents, and eleven chapels.[38]

Although the city was subjected to numerous earthquakes and periodic volcanic eruptions, those of 1717 and 1751 caused the most damage. After the earthquake of San Miguel in August and September 1717 authorities and vecinos considered moving the capital to the valley of La Hermita, but they chose instead to rebuild the capital and repair the damage at the city's present site.[39] But the earthquake of 29 July 1773 caused such extensive and heavy damage that city authorities petitioned the king to authorize the transfer of the capital and build a new one in the valley of La Hermita, a request that King Carlos III subsequently approved.

About a year after the disaster, which took 123 to 130 lives and damaged, if not totally destroyed, hundreds of buildings (including the cathedral, (which was a total ruin with its ruined domes, and cracked walls), Governor and President Martín de Mayorga and the Audiencia de Guatemala wrote to the king. Their correspondence had been delayed so that they could report on the later earthquake of 13 December 1773, which destroyed many of the buildings left standing after the one of 29 July. They advised the king of their carefully considered opinion

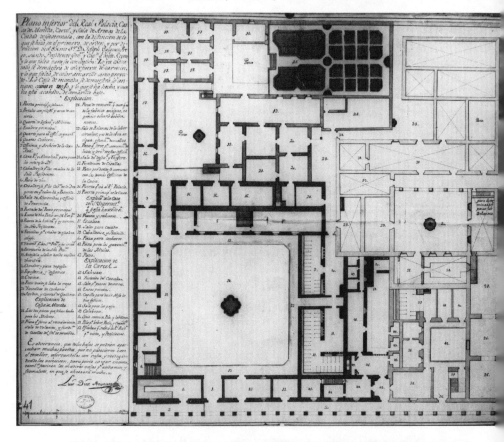

"Plano inferior del Real Palacio, Casa de Moneda, Carcel, y Sala de Armas de la Ciudad de Goatemala" (interior plan of the royal palace; treasury, or mint; jail; and armory at Guatemala City), by Luis Díez Navarro, 1755 (AGI, Sevilla, Mapas y Planos, 157).

favoring the transfer of the capital to the valley of La Hermita (or as it was sometimes called, the valley of the Virgin). Mayorga, speaking for and supported by the oidores, reviewed the destruction of the capital since its location at nearby Almolonga in 1541. He pointed out that Santiago de Guatemala had suffered greatly in the earthquakes of 1717 and 1751, but that before July 1773 it was still a city of many large public buildings and "five or six thousand private [ones]," whose total property value was in millions of pesos. Indeed, according to the

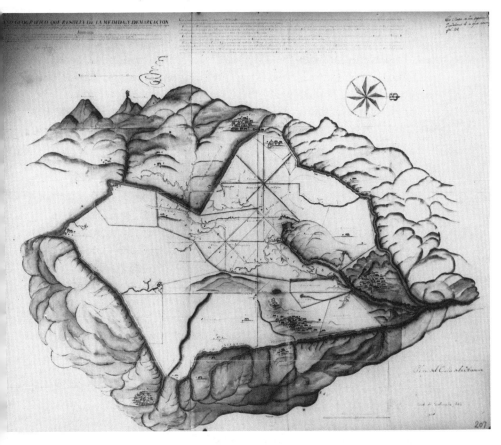

"Plano Geográfico que resulta de la medida y demarcación del Valle y Llano de la Hermita" (geographical plan resulting from the measurement and demarcation of the valley and plain of La Hermita), by Josef Gregorio Rivera, 12 March 1774 (AGI, Sevilla, Mapas y Planos, Guatemala, 207).

governor, the city would have "competed perhaps with Mexico and Lima if the fury of the weather had not pursued it." Now, after much study and deliberation, he and the audiencia had decided that the best course for the future was to transfer the capital to the plain or valley of the Virgin, rather than remain under the shadow of the Agua and Fuego volcanoes. Mayorga emphasized that the proposed new location had "always been . . . the preferred and desired place for effecting a formal transfer"; it was already inhabited by Spaniards, including some from the principal families, at a *ranchería* (small settlement). He also observed that after the 1717 earthquake, the bishop had asked to transfer the capital to La Hermita, but circumstances and the superior government then had decided otherwise. Now Archbishop Pedro Cortés y Larraz opposed the proposed move from the valley of Panchoy. His continued residence in the old city resulted in a shortage of clergy in the new capital (to which the governor had already moved) and a *"lack of respect for God and the Church" ("la falta de respeto a Dios y a la Yglesia")*.[40]

The plan developed by the president and the oidores of the Audiencia de Guatemala contained eighty-six numbered paragraphs. They proposed to buy two to four square leagues (about thirteen to twenty-five square miles) of land at La Hermita at a cost of one hundred pesos per caballería. The cost to the royal treasury would be reduced by a "voluntary" contribution from all the haciendas of the kingdom corresponding to the number of caballerías of which each was composed, at the rate of one peso per caballería. The new city would have a plaza mayor and lesser plazas larger than those of the old city, and streets wider than those in the damaged capital. The blocks in the new city would be proportionate and equal in size, well arranged and of such disposition that they would facilitate communication and easy transit for the people. Concessions were to be made for public buildings, churches, and other structures as they had been in "devastated Guatemala." All vecinos of the new capital would receive their own plots of land in the same locations as they had held in the old capital. Buildings in the new city were to be kept low in height, not to exceed 4½ varas (about 12½ feet) except for the "compact and secure jail" that would be designed to house the "multitude of delinquents of past years" and to provide for the increased crime rate in the new capital. The audiencia also provided for the building of a new Palacio Real to house the governor, other royal officials, and the treasury and customs officers. In addition, the proposal included religious buildings such as churches, hospitals, convents, and schools. It suggested also that the Royal University be located near the new cathedral for the "political and moral benefit of the people, especially the secular and regular clergy."[41]

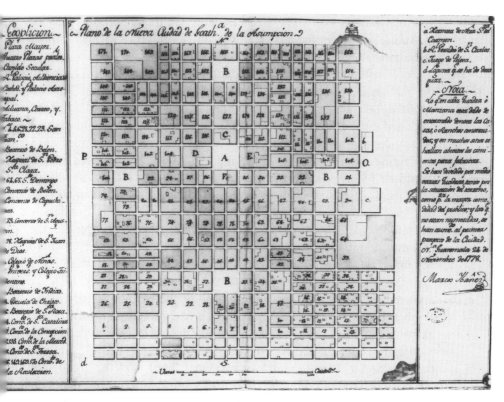

"Plano de la Nueva Ciudad de Goatha. de la Asumpción" (map of the New City of Guatemala de la Asunción), by architect D. Marcos Ybañez, 24 November 1778 (AGI, Sevilla, Mapas y Planos, Guatemala, 234).

To support their decision and proposal, one oidor of the audiencia submitted an *expediente* (dossier) in tabular format comparing the two inspected sites, which were on the *llano,* or plain, of La Hermita and the plain of Jalapa, to the royal laws for establishing new towns. Both sites had good terrain and climates, could permit the raising of live-stock, had mountains and forests nearby, possessed materials for build-ing houses and public buildings, and had entrances and exits permit-ting easy access to the new capital. However, La Hermita had more haciendas for raising livestock; had extensive lands nearby for raising crops and fruits; was blessed with benign skies, gentle and pure air, and many sources of water; had vast lands for many purposes and for the future growth of the city; and was surrounded by a greater number of Indian villages.[42]

Notwithstanding the recommendation of the president-governor and the audiencia, Archbishop Pedro Cortés y Larraz and the cabildo opposed the transfer of the capital and advocated the rebuilding of the damaged city of Santiago de Guatemala. The archbishop addressed a twenty-eight-page report and letter to the king on 1 December 1773, explaining his reasons for opposing the move. He believed that it would be inconvenient to transfer the capital either provisionally or permanently, that there was no other site for visiting the Indian pueblos that had not suffered during the earthquake, that it was financially wasteful to spend hundreds of pesos to lay out plazas and streets in the new city, and that churches, convents, schools, and the university could not make the move without great loss and suspension of studies for many years.[43] In another letter to the king on 1 January 1774, he reported on the destruction and damage of the earthquake of 13 December 1773 and its aftershocks, which had ruined one-third of the existing buildings, and he reiterated his determination to remain at Santiago de Guatemala until the president and audiencia re-examined the sites at La Hermita and Jalapa.[44] On 1 April 1774 the archbishop again reported to the king, giving further information about the damages caused by the earthquakes and tremors (although they had ceased by then), as well as the numbers of clergy in the convents of Santo Domingo, San Francisco, and La Merced, along with the prelates dispersed throughout the province.[45] The cabildo also continued to oppose moving the capital, even though the king had so ordered; except for Don Nicolás Obregón, its members excused themselves from such a relocation with various pretexts. According to President Mayorga, in his letter of 5 January 1776, this left the public abandoned by the municipal administration, and he had to perform some of the cabildo's functions for the new city.[46]

In Spain the *contador general* (auditor general or controller), considered with thanks the representations of the president-governor, the audiencia, the archbishop, the secular clergy, the Cabildo Eclesiástico, and the royal ministers of Guatemala, and on 13 January 1774 approved "the indispensable transfer of the city as certain and opportune." Then the Royal Council of the Indies added its endorsement.[47] Two days later the *fiscal* (auditor of public finances) reported that he had seen the dossier on the "absolute desolation of the city of Guatemala," and he recommended that the king permit the construction of the new city on another site that would not be so exposed to the "horrible ravages" that the old city had experienced, surrounded as it was by four volcanoes that "probably had been the cause of the earthquake."[48] With these recommendations, King Carlos III recognized the ruined state of the old capital, the temporary transfer of the capital to La Hermita in January 1774, and the archbishop's desire to rebuild on "the same site where the ruined one was." He issued a decree or order on 21 July 1775, from San Ildefonso north of Madrid, approving and authorizing the permanent establishment of Nueva Guatemala de la Asunción.[49]

Yet, this royal authorization was not the end of the problem of relocating the capital. While construction began at the new site and people commenced moving there, opposition continued from the vecinos of the old city and the cabildo there, and especially from the archbishop, who still refused to move.[50] Officially transferred on 2 January 1774,[51] the new capital of Nueva Guatemala contained buildings, both public and religious, constructed in the neoclassical style of architecture.[52]

The engineer Don Luis Díez Navarro was named "delineador oficial de la ciudad" (official planner of the city). The plan he drew assigned the sites for barrios and towns surrounding the capital, oriented the streets to run from east to west and north to south, designated the site for the plaza mayor, and provided lots for the principal buildings of religious and civil officials. However, while the building of the city proceeded, and over 700,000 pesos had been spent at Nueva Guatemala by early 1775,[53] the members of the cabildo and the archbishop still resisted moving to the new capital. Two regidores refused to move in January 1776, and one renounced his position on the cabildo.[54] On 22 March 1777 the king issued another order, directing that the complete and final transfer from "Antigua Guatemala" be concluded within one year. On 28 July 1777, President Mayorga ordered all the inhabitants to move within the prescribed period, and he directed the Cabildo Eclesiástico, prelates, university members, and religious orders, as well as civil authorities, move within two months, without delay or excuse, to Nueva Gua-

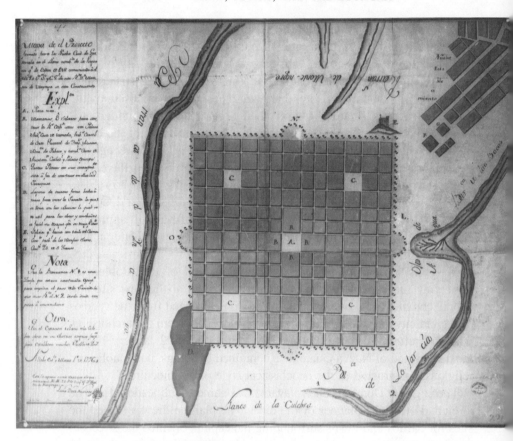

"Mapa de el Proyecto formado para la Nueba Ciudad de Guatemala," by Luis Díez Navarro, 1 March 1776 (Sevilla, AGI)

temala.[55] Yet, the archbishop stated that he would not move without a license from the Pope. Thus the Cabildo Eclesiástico, canons, and parish priests remained in the old city, forcing President Mayorga to explain that one-half of the people in Nueva Guatemala had not yet been organized into parishes. He suggested replacement of the four *capitulares* (capitularies) who supported Archbishop Cortés y Larraz and recommended that the archbishop be given another see in Spain.[56]

Not until the appointment and arrival of a new archbishop, Doctor Cayetano Francos y Monroy, and the arrival of Matías de Gálvez as the

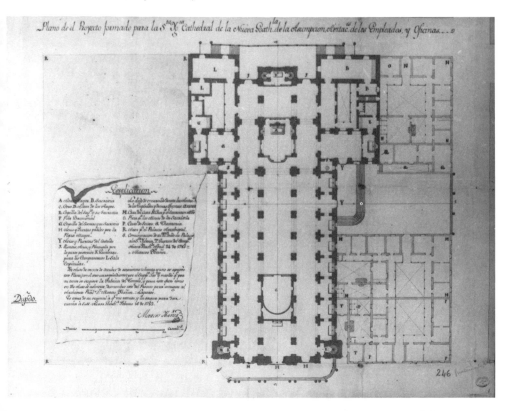

"Plano de el Proyecto formado para la Sta. Ygla. Cathedral de la Nueva Goathla. de la Asumpción . . . (plan of the project constituted for the Holy Church of the Cathedral of Nueva Guatemala de la Asunción), by architect D. Marcos Ybañez, 24 April 1781 (AGI, Sevilla, Mapas y Planos, Guatemala, 246).

new president, captain general, and governor of the Kingdom of Guatemala in 1779, was the transfer to the new capital completed. With the consent of the new archbishop, Gálvez moved the Audiencia de Guatemala into its new offices in the royal palace on 3 May 1779, and he relocated the royal treasury and customs officials there soon afterward. On 6 June he issued a bando directing all other governmental authorities to move to the new capital within fifteen days. With the king's approval, he also transferred the archbishop's residence and those of the religious orders to Nueva Guatemala. To enforce his

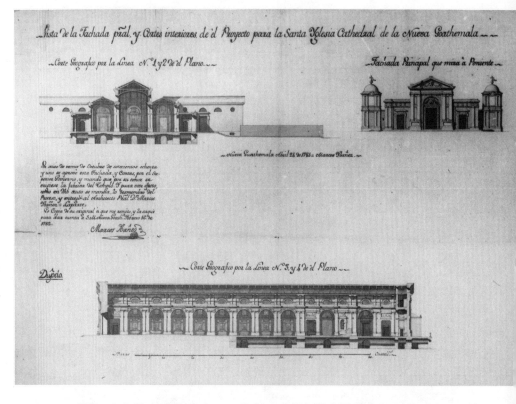

"Vista de la Fachada pral. . . . para la Santa Iglesia Cathedral de la Nueva Guatemala" (view of the front facade of the Holy Church the Cathedral of Nueva Guatemala), 1781–82? (AGI, Sevilla, Mapas y Planos, Guatemala, 247).

orders, he dispatched a detachment of infantry and another of cavalry to Antigua.[57]

Thus ended the five-year period of the transfer of the capital of the Kingdom of Guatemala from Santiago de Guatemala to Nueva Guatemala de la Asunción. In 1782 the new city contained slightly more than 13,000 inhabitants;[58] the municipal, provincial, and royal authorities; and the religious headquarters of the realm. Yet, Santiago de Guatemala, although it was no longer the seat of authority, was not totally abandoned, and some parish churches continued to function there for those residents who remained in Antigua.

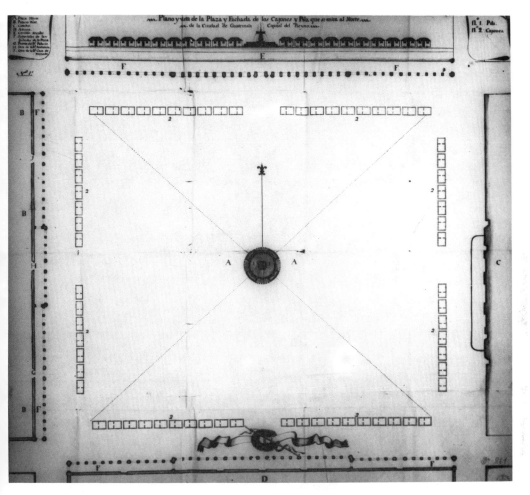

"Plano y vista de la Plaza, y Fachada de los Cajones y Pila . . ." (plan and view of the plaza and facade of the boxes and basin or trough) in Guatemala City, by architect Antonio Bernasconi, 1785 (AGI, Sevilla, Mapas y Planos, Guatemala, 261).

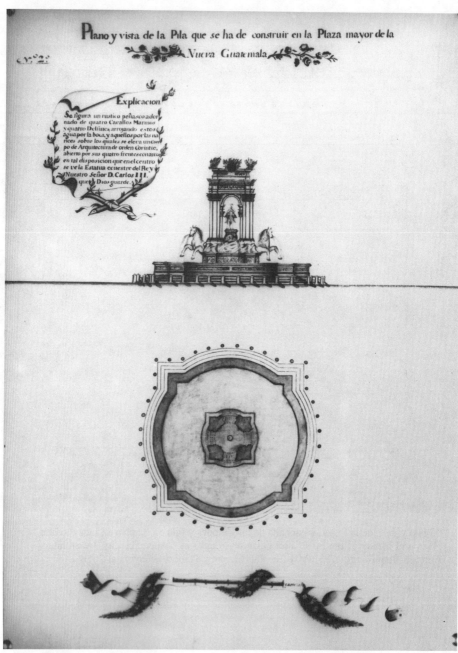

"Plano y vista de la Pila . . ." (plan and view of the basin or trough) in the main plaza of Guatemala City, by architect Antonio Bernasconi, 1785 (AGI, Sevilla, Mapas y Planos, Guatemala, 262).

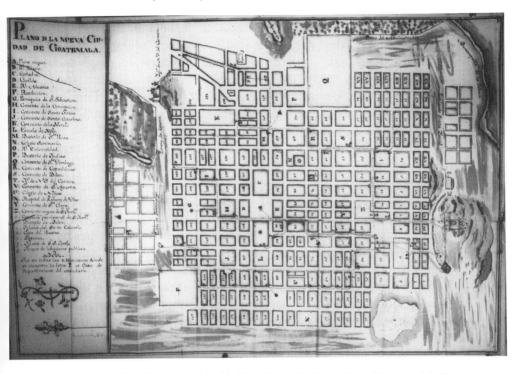

"Plano de la Nueva Ciudad de Goatemala" (plan of the New City of Guatemala), 17 March 1787 (AGI, Sevilla, Mapas y Planos, Guatemala, 264).

The development of and the changes in Central America's and Guatemala's principal community have been examined here to illustrate the degree to which the Spaniards planned their towns and the importance of the colonial capital. Yet, the land and the towns would have been useless if they had not played the roles that they did in the overall economic life of Guatemala during the colonial period.

THE ECONOMY

Initially, during the conquest and occupation of Guatemala, Spaniards came to the province for many reasons, but primarily seeking wealth. When the region failed to supply vast riches of silver and gold as settlers had hoped, agriculture and stock raising became the principal economic pursuits of the first settlers and their descendants. Both remained important means of livelihood throughout the Spanish colonial period in Guatemala. As the first subsistence farming, practiced by both Indians and Spaniards, developed into cash-cropping and an export-oriented economy, the province (like the rest of Central America) went through periods of boom and bust, depending on European demands for cacao, indigo *(añil),* cochineal, and sugar, as well as the availability of capital, labor, and technology.[59]

While mining may have been an initial goal, it proved illusory except for small enterprises in Guatemala and the silver mining in the Tegucigalpa region of today's Honduras, which had begun by 1580 and reached its peak in the first half of the eighteenth century. Honduran mines expanded from one silver site in 1712 to seven silver and two gold regions, with thirty-three mines in the Tegucigalpa area and twenty-five mines near Comayagua by 1737. All the silver produced was sent to Santiago de Guatemala, where the mint was established in 1733. While it is true that Honduran silver attracted Crown interest, immigrants there, and English ships in the Bay of Honduras, Guatemalan historian Francis Polo Sifontes observed accurately that the Kingdom of Guatemala was very poor in exploitable mines and that the province of Guatemala produced only small amounts of gold and silver at isolated locations in Huehuetenango, Chiquimula de la Sierra, Quiché, and Verapaz.[60] Certainly, mining in the province and kingdom of Guatemala (except perhaps in Honduras) did not rival the extensive silver production of Peru and New Spain and the gold mines of Nueva Granada (today's Colombia).

Without such spectacular mining activity, the basic economic activity of Spaniards and Indians became the husbandry of plants and animals, or on a larger scale, agricultural and rural development. Since supplies of capital were limited and unstable, inhabitants of Guatemala favored land and labor enterprises that concentrated on raising maize, wheat, cacao, indigo, cochineal, sugarcane, beans, squash, grapes, melons, and other fruits such animals as cattle, horses, swine, sheep, goats, oxen, mules and fowl.[61] Murdo J. MacLeod classifies Central American economic life during the sixteenth and seventeenth centuries in two systems. The first he calls a "cattle and cereals" system of Indian and Spanish staples (such as cattle, sheep, wheat, maize, and beans) raised for local consumption or for trade through urban markets. The second system consisted of cash crops raised largely for an export-oriented economy. This more-dynamic economy comprised foreign trade, shipping, and the presence of merchants. It was a source for wealth for many Guatemalans and other Central Americans, but it also impoverished some because its boom-and-bust cycles resulted in periods of great prosperity followed by stagnation and decline.[62] Thus this economy was less stable over time than the cattle-and-cereals market. Because cash-cropping and the export of cacao, indigo, and cochineal, trade and commerce became important parts of the economy of both the province and kingdom of Guatemala. For example, they led to the rising importance of wealthy Creoles (Spaniards born in America) during the eighteenth century, men who became liberals and challenged the controls of the Spanish Crown especially during the economic depression of the late eighteenth and early nineteenth century.

The subsistence economy dominated the early years of the Spanish presence in Guatemala. It included the Indians' raising of traditional crops such as maize, beans, melons, and chiles, for example, among the Tzutujil Mayans near Lake Atitlán. To those the Spaniards added figs, pomegranates, and apples, as well as the production of cotton, sugar, and salt in the lowland regions of the province. The machete and the *asadón* (a two-sided metal hoe) replaced the stone axe and digging stick formerly employed by the Indians.[63]

Cacao became Guatemala's first important cash crop exported to New Spain, South America, and Spain by the middle of the sixteenth century.[64] It was used for food and as coinage before then, but the European and American demand for it as a source of chocolate in drinks increased its importance. Grown in trees in hot, humid climates along the Pacific coast, especially in Soconusco (mostly in today's southern Mexico, in the state of Chiapas), and in the Sonsonate region of Guatemala and El Salvador, cacao, had become a booming trade item by 1560, when 20,000 *cargas* (loads), worth a total of 60,000 pesos, were being shipped annually, primarily to New Spain with some to Peru. Soconusco was about 300 miles long and 25 miles wide and largely flat, with a hot, humid climate and intense thunderstorms and lightning as well as rain for eight months of the year from March to October. It contained small Indian settlements and the principal town of Huehuetlan, which had twenty Spanish vecinos and some Indians by 1573, according to its governor. All of Soconusco's villages belonged to the Spanish Crown; there were no encomenderos there. The region produced 4,000 cargas of cacao annually in 1573, but labor shortages contributed to its decline, as did competition later from Caracas and Maracaibo, in Venezuela, and especially from Guayaquil, Ecuador. Soconusco cacao was generally considered the best available during the seventeenth century. In 1598 the province of Guatemala was still producing 20,000 cargas of cacao worth more than 200,000 pesos yearly, according to one source.[65]

Although cacao declined in importance thereafter, it did not disappear entirely as an export crop. Spaniards began to drink large quantities of it in the 1590s, and it was exported as far as Spain, Holland, and England by the 1630s. While Indians, Creoles, and Europeans all drank it in Guatemala, the upper classes preferred it mixed with vanilla, cinnamon, and sugar for flavoring. When hurricanes in 1641 and 1659 damaged the cacao plantations on the Pacific coast, cultivation spread inland to Chiquimula de la Sierra and Zacapa. Yet, Soconusco was not abandoned, and cacao production continued there. By 1684 the district still had a population of 100 or more Spanish vecinos and 259 mestizos, mulattos, and Negroes as heads of families. As competition from Guayaquil cacao intensified after 1628, the Audiencia de Guatemala banned its importation in Central American ports. Spaniards and others preferred the smooth and mild *criollo* (Creole) cacao from Guatemala over the bitter *forastero* (foreign) type from Guayaquil. However, the Nicaraguans resented the protectionist policies emanating from Santiago de Guatemala, and this became an early factor in the growth of separatism there. While cacao cultivation continued in Soconusco and Guatemala to the end of the Spanish colonial period, their plantations "never approached their sixteenth-century levels of production."[66]

Indigo, called *xiquilite* by the Indians and *añil* by the Spaniards,[67] became a prosperous, rapidly expanding commodity in the period from 1580 to 1620. By 1600 it was "the major export industry of Central America."[68] Grown as a plant three to six feet high on tropical savannahs and along riverbanks, its leaves contained most of the blue dye needed in Europe for the textile industry. It grew extensively along the Pacific coast of Central America, especially in El Salvador and Nicaragua, but also in Gracias a Dios and Comayagua, in today's Honduras, and in the present state of Chiapas in Mexico. Harvested yearly in July, it had an offensive odor, tended to burn the skin, and attracted bothersome insects; however, it did not demand as much labor in the fields as cacao cultivation did, except for one or two months during the year. The processing of indigo in *obrajes* (dye works) led to the widespread employment of Indians (under Crown protection), slaves, free Negroes, mulattos, and mestizos in a considerable industry during the seventeenth century. By 1620 there were forty such obrajes within a thirty-mile radius of Santiago de los Caballeros de Guatemala, and over two hundred of them in the jurisdiction of San Salvador. Royal interest in indigo production was high, leading to laws to protect Indians in the obrajes and causing periodic inspections to evaluate and regulate working conditions in them. Although the industry stagnated in the seventeenth century, it enjoyed its greatest prosperity in the eighteenth century when the demand was high in Spain and the rest of Europe, especially in Great Britain.[69] During this indigo boom Creoles amassed fortunes in Guatemala. The subsequent decline and economic uncertainty early in the nineteenth century greatly affected political and imperial relationships during the independence era.

Cochineal, known to the Spaniards as *grana cochinilla,* became the third crop of importance to Guatemala during the colonial period. The brilliant red dye was derived not from a plant or a tree but from the cultivation of insects that infested the leaves of the nopal cactus. It was used first by Indians and later by Europeans in the production of textiles. Known and used by the natives of Mexico and Central America before the arrival of the Spaniards, it was cultivated principally in Mexico and somewhat in Guatemala, mostly by Indians. One authority estimated that about 25,000 live insects and 70,000 dried ones were necessary to make one pound of dye. The Spaniards were slow to learn the process of raising the insects on cactus leaves, brushing them off the leaves, and drying them, either in the sun or by artificial heat. The industry was largely left in the hands of the Indians, who employed traditional methods to produce the dye. In the latter half of the sixteenth century the Spanish Crown permitted intensified production of cochineal, and in 1617 Governor Conde de Gómara encouraged large plantations in the boca costa of Guatemala and the warmer foothills of the Pacific coastal area.

The cochineal industry expanded largely in New Spain, however, and Guatemala's production did not meet its high hopes. After 1621 there was little mention of the crop. Locusts destroyed the cactus, rainfall was too high for cochineal raising and processing, and the reduced Indian populations and their employment in cultivating other crops, all precluded the growth of a strong, stable industry that might have offset the decline in cacao production. New Spain remained the major producer of cochineal, although average amounts were grown in the vicinity of Sololá, according to Governor Josef Estachería's report of October 1785.[70] To counteract the economic depression during the independence period, Governor José de Bustamente introduced the nopal cactus and production of cochineal around Antigua in 1815 to replace the depressed cotton and indigo trades. The renewed industry had produced about 4,350 pounds of cochineal by 1820, and approximately 135,000 pounds had been exported, at a value of three pesos per pound, five years later. Thus cochineal developed into a major profitable industry that had become important to Guatemala and Central America by the 1830s, after their independence from Spain.[71]

Among the other crops and animals raised during the Spanish colonial years in Guatemala was the sugarcane grown in Chiapas, Verapaz, and around Amatitlán, near Santiago de Guatemala. Refined at sugar mills, it was a source of wealth for some Guatemalans, especially the Jesuits, but the industry "never developed on a large scale."[72]

According to Governor Josef de Estachería's report of 1785, wheat was abundant in the Quezaltenango district and average ("mediana") in Sololá and Totonicapán, while scarce in Chimaltenango, Escuintla, and Sacatepéques; maize was abundant in Sacatepéques, Chimaltenango, Escuintla, and Sololá, but average in Quezaltenango, Verapaz, and San Antonio; bean production was average in Sololá, but scarce or nonexistent elsewhere; rice and cotton were abundant in Escuintla; sugarcane was abundant in Verapaz; indigo was abundant in San Salvador, Comayagua, and Nicaragua, but just average in Chiquimula, and scarce in Sonsonate; cacao was abundant in Nicaragua, but scarce in Guatemala, or nonexistent; cochineal was average in Tuxtla in Chiapas, but did not exist or was scarce elsewhere; chickpeas were average in Sololá; and chile was abundant in Sacatepéques, average in Verapaz. Other products reported were salt, tobacco, and *achiote* (a red dye from a plant with heart-shaped leaves), but none were abundant or even average compared to those listed above.[73]

Although Spaniards seem to have left the stock raising and the care of herds largely to Indians, and the increase in the numbers of draft animals was "agonizing slow" after the arrival of the Spaniards,[74] the husbandry of animals later developed into a major economic pursuit. As the Indian populations in rural areas fell, sheep and cattle raising took on increased importance with the establishment of privately owned haciendas.[75] Valuable for their meat, hides, skins, fleece, lard, and tallow, livestock became important to the urban populations, where slaughterhouses and meat markets were established, such as the one slaughterhouse at Santiago de Guatemala, and butcher shops provided for the sale of meat products.[76] Although there were periodic shortages of beef, the cattle and sheep industry was still a significant part of the economy in the late eighteenth century. Largely in the hands of the Indians and free *castas,* the stock raising, especially in Nicaragua and the highlands of Guatemala, was described in 1785 by Governor Estachería in his report complying with the royal order of 10 May 1784 for information about the crops and animals raised throughout the kingdom. According to Estachería, cattle were abundant in Sacatepéques and Escuintla, and their numbers were average in Chimaltenango, San Antonio, Quezaltenango, Verapaz, Sololá, and Totonicapán; sheep were abundant in Sacatepéques, average elsewhere; horses, "common" in Sacatepéques, scarce in Escuintla, and average in the other provinces; and mules were "common" in Sacatepéques and Chimaltenango, average in Quezaltenango, Verapaz, and Sololá, but scarce in Escuintla and Totonicapán.[77]

The economic policy of mercantilism, employed by the Spanish Crown and other European nations in the colonial era, emphasized that colonies existed for the benefit of the mother country and that they should produce only raw goods to be refined and manufactured in the mother country. The theory did not work completely in Guatemala and the other Spanish kingdoms in America. Instead, manufacturing and industry developed there to process raw materials and meet local needs. Ralph Lee Woodward has observed that "manufacturing played a minor though essential role in the kingdom's economy."[78] Although Spanish authorities did not look favorably on the development of competitive industries in Guatemala and the rest of the kingdom, the isolation of the region, the high cost of transporting European goods to Central America, and the fact that the principal trade routes between Spain and the Americas neglected or ignored the Kingdom of Guatemala, all ensured that many items had to be manufactured locally. Home manufacture of clothing, leather goods, housewares, and other everyday necessities took place in the urban communities and sometimes in the rural areas. Artisans abounded in towns: blacksmiths, shoemakers, silversmiths, hat makers, tailors, masons, carpenters, and many others. Usually they were organized into craft guilds to maintain standards and limit competition in their respective crafts. Their products were purchased and consumed largely by townspeople. Added to the general category of manufacturing were such Indian crafts as textiles, pottery, clothing, and crude furniture, which were sold or bartered at local markets to Indians and ladinos as well as Spaniards.[79] Finally, manufacturing also included textile mills, sugar mills, and factories for producing leather goods, soap, pottery, glass, gunpowder, and furniture, and also even shipbuilding, which took place primarily in ports outside the province of Guatemala. All of the products, including wine and other alcoholic beverages, were intended for local or regional purchase and consumption.[80]

Other aspects of the colonial economy in Guatemala were commerce and trade, transportation, and finances. According to the Spanish Crown's mercantilistic and monopolistic practices, trade with the mother country was closely regulated by the Consulado of Seville, which was a merchant monopoly, and the Casa de Contratación (board of trade), also in Seville, both of which, with the port of Cádiz, exclusively controlled the economic affairs, including commerce, of Spain's American kingdoms. In the western hemisphere only certain ports were allowed to export to and import from Spain: Nombre de Dios and later Portobelo, in Panama; Cartagena, in Nueva Granada; Veracruz, in New Spain; and Havana, Cuba. Connecting the Americas and Spain were two fleets, the *flota* to New Spain and the *galeones* to Cartagena and Panama, which were supposed to sail annually under a naval escort to protect the merchant vessels from foreign attacks. These fleets brought European goods and passengers to the far-flung American kingdoms in exchange for gold, silver, and other American products, in a trade regulated by Crown officials and *consulados* (merchant guilds) that were responsible to authorities and similar guilds in Seville and later in Cádiz. Thus the trade was designed to benefit the mother country, was in the hands of merchant monopolists, and was supposed to be regulated closely by Spanish officials who inspected cargoes and passengers, regulated the prices of goods, and imposed the numerous royal taxes. Among the taxes were the *almojarifazgo,* or customs duty, of 5 percent on imports and exports; the *avería,* for the expenses of the fleets; and the *alcabala,* or sales tax, on all exchanges of goods, which sometimes was high as 10 percent and at others as low as 2 percent. All of the regulations served to collect revenue, increase the prices of goods, and restrict trade. Tributes and tithes also furnished considerable sums to the royal coffers and to the church.[81]

This commercial system caused American merchants and colonists to participate in contraband trade with Frenchmen, Canary Islanders, African slave traders, and especially Englishmen, during the eighteenth century.[82] In colonial Guatemala and throughout Central America there was widespread evasion of Spanish laws and regulatory practices. Isolated from the routes of the fleets and the approved ports of Veracruz and Portobelo, the region depended on overland transportation from and to New Spain, some seagoing contacts with Peru and New Spain along the Pacific coast, and occasional trade, legal and illegal, through Atlantic ports. Since the Golfo Dulce, with its shifting sandbanks, poor soundings, and difficult surrounding terrain made access to Guatemala difficult, Puerto Caballos, in today's Honduras, became the principal port on the Caribbean Sea for the Audiencia de Guatemala between the 1570s and 1604. After pirates sacked it in 1591 and 1596, Governor Alfonso Criado de Castilla sent Francisco Navarro to examine the Golfo Dulce as a possible port facility. He surveyed the region and recommended that a port be established along the shores of the Bay of Amatique, which borders northeast Guatemala and southeast Belize. By 1604, Santo Tomás de Castilla had a small fort and several warehouses, but it was never a major port and declined in importance after 1617.[83] Instead, Guatemalan indigo, cacao, and other products were exported from Puerto Caballos or Trujillo (also in Honduras), transported overland to New Spain, or shipped from Pacific ports to Peru and New Spain when limited trade was allowed by the Spanish Crown.[84] Because of these overseas trading problems, the province and kingdom of Guatemala had experienced early and extensive contraband trading and smuggling by the 1630s.[85] Such practices continued and had become a major threat to legal commerce with Spain by the eighteenth century.

Colonial Guatemala continued to sustain two kinds of commerce throughout its existence, export-oriented and local. While a barter economy existed at first, a monetary one, based on the Spanish peso, had replaced it by the last half of the sixteenth century. Yet, because of Guatemala's unfavorable balance of trade and the economic depression by the 1630s, a severe shortage of currency developed in the middle of the seventeenth century and continued until the establishment of the first royal mint at Santiago de Guatemala in 1733–34.[86]

The local trade within Spanish Guatemala occurred mostly in urban centers and in Indian villages at public markets. Goods were transported over roads that at first were merely trails. Pack trains of mules conducted by arrieros and tamemes were commonly employed at first to carry products. The Spaniards did not originate the use of Indian burden bearers, for they had long served native society in pre-Columbian times, but the arrival of the "more materialistic Spaniards only increased the demand for tamemes."[87] Throughout the sixteenth century the Spaniards evidently abused Indians in this work by requiring them to carry excessive loads and undertake conduct long journeys, recruiting them by force and intimidation, working them without pay, providing them an inadequate diet resulting in malnutrition, and generally mistreating them. Encomenderos also sought income by renting out their Indians as burdenbearers.[88] Although the Crown disapproved of the practice and wanted to abolish the use of tamemes in favor of using animals and constructing better roads, it made only half-hearted efforts to regulate the conditions of Indians so employed because "it was cheaper to use humans, who cost little or nothing," and the nature of the terrain seemed to dictate their use.[89] The Audiencia de Guatemala began to enforce the Crown's restrictions on the use of tamemes in 1548, but the human-carrier system was not replaced by animals until after the development of better roads and larger herds of livestock, and the increased use of *carretas* (two-wheeled carts) and *carros* (large wagons) drawn by mules.[90] Human carriers are still employed in present-day Guatemala, particularly in regions of mountainous terrain.

The province and kingdom of Guatemala during the Spanish colonial era experienced periods of prosperity and depression depending on many factors, including the supplies of capital, demands for exports, demography, settlement development, climate, natural disasters, and imperial relationships. Murdo J. MacLeod identifies four distinct periods between the 1520s and 1720. After the conquest came the first, extractive period of encomiendas, slavery and the slave trade, and especially, the booming production of cacao. Beginning in the late 1570s and extending until about 1630 was the second period, marked by a rapid decline in cacao production, movement of Spaniards from urban to rural areas vacated by the declining Indian population, and the rise of indigo as a prominent export. The third period, from the 1630s to about 1680, was characterized by depression or economic stagnation and the beginning of the haciendas. Finally, in the last decades of the seventeenth century until about 1720, there occurred a revival of trade (largely based on contraband) and a gradual increase in the Indian population.[91]

The period from 1720 to the 1780s, was represented by population growth and especially indigo prosperity. Then, from the end of the eighteenth century until Guatemala achieved independence from Spain in 1821, a period of economic distress resulted from the decline of the indigo market, warfare in Europe and throughout Latin America, new economic and political ideas, and Guatemala's new relationships with the rest of Central America, on the one hand, and Spain and Europe, on the other.

The advent of the Bourbon dynasty in Spain at the beginning of the eighteenth century and its continuance thereafter brought great economic changes to colonial Guatemala and Central America. As Ralph Lee Woodward has noted, the Bourbon kings (Felipe V, Fernando VI, Carlos III, and Carlos IV) emphasized commercial reforms to increase production and trade between Spain and the Indies, while attempting to eliminate contraband trading and competitive trade with Spain's rivals, particularly Great Britain.[92] With those goals in mind, the

Bourbon monarchs sought to gain complete royal control over their subjects and kingdoms in America by centralizing both the political and the economic administration of their empire, and to improve the efficiency and economy of both the mother country and the far-flung kingdoms, which increased in size and population during the course of the eighteenth century. While some of the reforms achieved their purpose, others did not and instead introduced new problems that led to increased unrest, demands for change, and finally even to the idea of independence from Spain on the part of Guatemalans, other Central Americans, and inhabitants of Mexico and South America.

Among the many reforms or changes implemented by the Bourbons and their officials in Spain, some had considerable impact on the economy of Guatemala and the rest of Central America. One of the earliest was the establishment of a royal mint at Santiago de Guatemala to promote the growth of mining, provide control over the production of Honduran silver, and resolve the shortage of currency. With dies for coining money sent from New Spain, the Casa de Moneda (royal mint) cost about 19,000 pesos to build, which proved a worthwhile investment since it was damaged very little by the earthquake of July 1773. From 1733 to 1757 the mint produced a total of 3,618,387 pesos, or an average of 150,766 pesos yearly over the twenty-four period, with the peak years from 1737 to 1739 and again from 1741 to 1743. After the royal officials moved to Nueva Guatemala after the 1773 earthquake at Antigua, a new mint was built adjoining the governor's palace on the main plaza. Its superintendent always served on the audiencia, and the mint employed an accountant, a treasurer, a weigher, an engraver, and two assayers, among other employees.[93] In 1765 and 1766 the king established royal monopolies and offices to administer them for the production of tobacco and aguardiente. Designed to increase royal control and improve revenues, these monopolies also provoked local opposition to the administrators and resulted in intensified antagonism between Creoles and peninsular Spaniards.[94] In the same period of the 1760s, the Spanish Crown responded to the reports of its two visitadores describing frauds practiced by alcaldes mayores, abuses of the tributary system, and farming out of sales tax collections. The king ordered the establishment of a new tax administration separate from the audiencia and appointed Francisco de Valdés to administer it.[95]

From the 1760s to 1778, King Carlos III and royal officials issued a series of reforms to expand Spanish-American trade, loosen the dependence of Central America on New Spain, and counter the substantial contraband trade with the British. These changes resulted from an inspection originally made in 1743 by the engineer Luis Díez Navarro, who reported the extensive incursions by English commercial houses on the Atlantic coast of Central America, their development of Roatán Island as a supply base, and their contraband trade arrangements. Díez Navarro also recommended that Spain fortify the Caribbean ports of Puerto Caballos and Omoa.[96] Bourbon reforms also abolished the old fleet system and monopoly trading ports, replacing them with free trade within the Spanish empire. Finally, in 1794 the king authorized the establishment of the Consulado de Guatemala (merchant guild of Guatemala) to promote economic development of the province and kingdom and to regulate trade. With its own tribunal and *fuero* (code of privileges), and a 5 percent avería to finance its operations, the consulado became a major force in both politics and the economy thereafter.[97]

While the eighteenth century was characterized by continued contraband trade and smuggling, as well as the Bourbon economic reforms, it was also dominated by the rise of the indigo and livestock industries and the emergence of a new, powerful merchant class in Guatemala. By the late 1740s European demand for indigo had increased dramatically, particularly in Spain and Great Britain, causing the price to increase notably and attract the capital of Spanish investors. Meanwhile, stock raising increased to feed the expanding populations of Central America (especially Guatemala) and to provide hides for leather goods, as well as wool for clothing. These developments led to the establishment of a new landowning aristocracy who bitterly resisted Spanish officials and opposed the monarchs who tried to break the merchants' ties with Cádiz, eliminate contraband trade, and establish direct royal control over Guatemalan commerce.

Juan Fermín de Aycinena was an example of the new landowning and merchant aristocracy. A Spaniard from Navarra who came to Guatemala from New Spain in 1754, he accumulated a fortune through a series of propitious marriages, acquisitions of land in Guatemala and San Salvador, and domination of the indigo trade, as well as by raising livestock. His wealth enabled him to purchase in 1780 the title of Marqués de Aycinena, so that he became the only resident holder of a title in Guatemala, and to build a home of fifteen rooms and seven patios fronting on the plaza mayor of Nueva Guatemala, across from the cathedral and government offices and next to the customshouse. Controlling trade and serving as a banker for both the government and private citizens, he had amassed a fortune estimated at more than one million pesos by the end of the century, and he possessed indigo plantations and commercial houses with connections in Lima, Mexico City, Cádiz, Jamaica, and Great Britain. He and his sons were only one family among the new merchant elite. Others were José de Vidaurre (a native of Vizcaya, Spain), Simón Larrazábal, Gaspar Juaros, Martín Barrundia, and Gregorio Urruela. All were closely linked to merchant houses in Cádiz and opposed the Spanish Crown's efforts to break that tie. Ultimately they became important leaders in the independence movement.[98]

Throughout the latter half of the eighteenth century the Bourbon kings attempted to gain control of the commerce of Guatemala and sever the merchants' ties with Cádiz and Great Britain. Miles Wortman described two distinct phases in the Bourbon offensive against the wealthy entrepreneurs. At first, the state allied itself with these merchant families to eliminate Habsburg institutions, the encomenderos, and the church. Then the government turned against the new merchants who had developed power during the first six decades of the eighteenth century. Reforms, such as the revision of the tax structure and the establishment of tobacco-liquor monopolies beginning in the 1760s, were intended to limit merchant finances and provide royal fiscal controls.[99] Also, in this second phase the Crown endeavored to aid the cattlemen and the *provincianos* (provincials, or those living in regions outside the capital) against the Guatemalan merchants. Although edicts were issued to open additional Central American ports to trade, to restructure the tax system, and to provide more direct royal control of the economy, the end result was intensified resistance by the merchants, increased hostility between Creoles and Spaniards, and rivalry between provincials and the merchants in the capital.[100] Meanwhile, government revenues increased because the revised tax structure and the monopolies, and because the freeing of commerce allowed import duties on goods from outside the empire. Reaching over 100,000 pesos annually by 1780, the military costs of the almost constant warfare involving Spain in Europe during the last twenty years or so of the eighteenth century, and the economic burdens of the expanded empire at that time, both ensured that Central America could not support itself.[101] An example of the burdens of empire was the cost of the foundation of the new capital of Nueva Guatemala. While it had become "a major center of commercial activity" by the end of the century,[102] so much so that income from the sales tax surpassed tribute for the first time in 1777,[103] the costs of establishing the new capital were borne by the king, who ceded the collection of alcabalas for ten years between 1775 and 1784 for the construction of Nueva Guatemala and for distributions to the poor necessitated by the earthquake at Antigua.[104] This concession yielded a total of 1,685,515 pesos and 2¼ reales against a debt of 1,998,524 pesos and 3 reales incurred for the transfer of the capital and the building of convents, monasteries, parish churches, the cathedral, hospitals, the university, the archbishop's palace, schools, and the secular cabildo.[105] Thus the merchant monopoly remained intact,[106] and its political power, its control of the Guatemalan economy, and its ties with the Cádiz and British merchants continued as a counterforce to royal authorities.

The Guatemalan merchant elite was at its height between 1783 and the early 1800s. Most of the profits from the prosperous indigo trade fell into the hands of these entrepreneurs and their allies in Cádiz, while farmers and small stock raisers remained in debt, and Guatemala frequently faced shortages of meat, wheat, maize, flour, and other provisions, especially after the mid-1770s during the construction of the new capital.[107] During the last decade of the eighteenth century two notable economic developments occurred. The first was the foundation of the Sociedad Económica de Amigos del País de Guatemala in 1794–95, an extension of an Enlightenment institution, originally founded in Switzerland, that had spread to France and Spain. King Carlos IV granted the Guatemalan economics society a charter in 1794, and it commenced to have regular meetings the following year. It had many functions, including promoting the economy, the arts, education, and industry, as well encouraging agricultural improvements and other advances to the general welfare of the kingdom. The society supported the first regular newspaper of Central America, the *Gazeta de Guatemala,* published between 1794 and 1812, and sponsored classes in political economy, bookkeeping, mathematics, foreign languages, and drafting. Reflecting the ideas of the Enlightenment, the society's members, drawn largely from the elite, questioned the idea of monopolies, special privileges, the role of the church, and Spanish restrictions on trade, while advocating freer economic institutions, representative government, and a more open political process.

Among those who participated in the Sociedád Económica were the indigo merchants and such persons as Ignacio Beteta (publisher of the *Gazeta*), José Antonio Liendo y Goicoechea (who promoted curriculum reform for the University of San Carlos), Juan Bautista Irissari (a Salvadoran planter and merchant who advocated freer trade and port construction on the Pacific coast), and José Cecilio de Valle (a Honduran lawyer who had moved to Nueva Guatemala, received his bachelor of arts' degree from the university there in 1794, and promoted the study of political economy in the colony by writing essays for the *Gazeta* on geography, history, the sciences, education, and politics, all reflecting the ideas of the Enlightenment). Because of its liberal views and its challenges to the authority of the Spanish Crown, the Sociedad Económica was suppressed by the king, who prohibited its further meetings by a royal order of 14 July 1800. Restored in 1811, after the rise of the liberals in Spain and the captivity of King Fernando VII in France, the society became the nucleus of opposition to the absolute powers of the monarchy. It promoted change and progress according to the rational and scientific concepts of the Enlightenment, advocating free trade and popular sovereignty, and advancing ultimately the idea of independence from Spain.[108]

Another economic development of the late 1790s was a result of Spain's wars in Europe, first as an ally of France, but later as an enemy of that nation and an ally of Great Britain. In a royal order of November 1797 the king permitted his American colonies to trade with neutral nations. This was interpreted as applicable to Central America by Jacobo Villa Urrutia, the chief judge of the Audiencia de Guatemala, in the absence of the president. The edict permitted English and North American ships to call openly at the port of Omoa, and merchants immediately established contacts with Boston, Philadelphia, and Jamaican commercial houses. Trade opportunities developed between Guatemala, on the one hand, and Great Britain and the United States, on the other. When the privilege was rescinded a few years later, contraband trade continued and increased. Guatemalan indigo and Honduran silver went to islands in the Bay of Honduras (principally Roatán) and Belize; Nicaragua sent indigo and cacao via the San Juan River to Curacao and Jamaica; along the Atlantic coast, Mosquito and Sambo Indians traded with Jamaican shippers; in the Pacific, foreign ships picked up goods at Realejo in Nicaragua; and the British traded Manchester textiles to Central Americans.[109] Thus the easing of Spanish commercial restrictions and the inability to enforce them when they were reinstituted promoted the growth of illegal commerce once again and exposed Guatemalan merchants to the benefits of trade outside the Spanish empire.

The economic hard times of the late eighteenth century[110] degenerated into depression during the first two decades of the nineteenth when the demand for indigo declined precipitously and European nations were engaged in warfare almost continuously because of Napoleon Bonaparte. Since Guatemalan trade had been dependent on European demands for indigo,[111] the collapse in Europe led to a severe depression from the early 1800s until the establishment of independence in Guatemala and the rest of Central America. Actually the decline began in 1798, when international commerce was suspended as a result of the war between Spain and Great Britain. A surplus of indigo had accumulated in the warehouses by 1799, and attacks of locusts in 1802–1803 devastated both the indigo and the food harvest, not only affecting commerce but also leading to severe food shortages. High prices for the production of lesser-quality indigo also contributed to the collapse of the market, particularly since Venezuelan competition expanded greatly in the last twenty years of the eighteenth century and the quality of its dye was much better than that of Guatemala. In 1780 the British also had begun to cultivate indigo in Bengal, India, and exports of the dye from there to Great Britain reached 5.5 million pounds annually between 1805 and 1814. In contrast, Guatemalan and Central American exports of indigo, at their height of about one million pounds yearly between 1787 and 1801, declined to 637,227 pounds annually in the years from 1802 to 1804, and 230,000 pounds yearly in

1812–13, with annual production averaging 405,781 pounds in the years 1801 to 1804 and 1806 to 1808, which was only 40 percent of the average for the previous fifteen years. By the 1820s production of indigo had dropped about 60 percent since the first years of the century.

Thus, the loss of capital, declines in the production and later the demand for Guatemalan indigo, increased competition from Venezuela and India, the forfeiting of farms by small producers indebted to Guatemalan merchants, the destruction of the Honduran cattle industry, the foreign wars of Spain and increased military costs, and also ravages of locusts, all contributed to food shortages and famines, and an economy that "came crashing down."[112] This economic disaster became a major factor in the intensified interest of Guatemalans, the formerly wealthy merchants as well as small farmers and livestock raisers, in promoting free trade and changes in their relationship with Spain, and ultimately in the general desire to establish Guatemala's independence from the mother country.

The exploitation of the land, the towns, and the economic life of Guatemala during the Spanish colonial period depended greatly on the people who resided within the province. While land was owned and developed in various ways, it was important principally for its economic uses. The towns, both Spanish and Indian, that were established during and after the conquest remained centers of political, economic, and social activities throughout the nearly three centuries of the Spanish presence and administration. Santiago de los Caballeros de Guatemala and its successor, Nueva Guatemala de la Asunción, were the most important urban communities not only for the province of Guatemala but also for all of Central America during the entire Spanish colonial period. Economic life, both internal and external, revolved around the production of agricultural and pastoral products and their trade in local and regional markets, and especially in foreign ones. The emphasis on a monocultural economy including at various times the slave trade, the production of cacao and indigo, and orientation toward exports, contributed to the sustenance of Guatemalans and, more important, to the periods of prosperity or depression experienced during this era. We now turn to these Guatemalans who resided on and worked the land, lived in the towns, and determined the economic life of the province and kingdom, to discuss their population, society, and cultural activities.

CHAPTER 7

Population, Society, and Culture

CONTRARY TO the prevailing opinion of many otherwise respectable historians and the beliefs of the general public that only the English came to America to settle and till the soil while Spaniards came solely to plunder,[1] Spain established true settlement colonies in its kingdoms in the Americas, which were populated by Spaniards, Indians, blacks, and a wide variety of mixtures. Furthermore, the family was the heart and soul of Spanish colonial society. All of this was evident in colonial Guatemala as it was throughout Central and South America and New Spain (today's Mexico, approximately). The colonial populations worked the land, established and lived in the towns and rural areas, and carried on the economic life and development of the province as discussed in the previous chapter. Indeed, without the settlers, Spanish Guatemala would not have existed at all.

The population of Guatemala in the colonial era was considerable, both the Amerindians descended from the Indians of the pre-Columbian period, and those of Spanish descent living in the province. Of course, the original inhabitants were the 1,000,000 to 1,500,000 Indians who dwelled in the highland region and along both coasts when the Spaniards first arrived.[2] While their numbers declined in the first 150 years of Spanish-Indian contact because of warfare, forced labor, disease, acculturation, and mestizaje, their population stabilized about the middle of the seventeenth century and increased during the next 150 years. The Spaniards came next, in limited numbers during the sixteenth century, but reaching tens of thousands as early as 1650, and increasing greatly thereafter. The term "españoles" (Spaniards) came to include many born in America who lived and practiced a Spanish lifestyle, largely in towns of various sizes and descriptions, but also in the rural countryside. Negroes from Africa and other Spanish colonies constituted the third major ethnic group of colonial Guatemala, arriving in small numbers during the sixteenth century and much larger numbers in the centuries that followed.

To mention only those three groups in Guatemala's colonial population is a gross oversimplification and injustice. Beginning in the early years, the process of mestizaje created a growing number of mestizos and ladinos (mixtures of Spaniards and Indians), mulattos (mixtures of blacks and Europeans), and *zambos,* or *sambos* (mixtures of Indians and blacks). Within those racial mixtures there existed all sorts of subordinate castes identified by such terms as *pardos, coyotes, lobos, colores quebrados,* and *bozales,* just to name a few.

Mestizaje not only produced the new class of mestizos, but also established an American multiracial society that differed greatly from the society of Spain, where only three groups—nobility, clergy, and commoners—existed. In Guatemala, as in other parts of Spanish colonial America, society, while hierarchical by nature, developed the concept of coexisting states, or *repúblicas,* that were cohesive because of associations of race and mutual interests, but which experienced together the exigencies of everyday life on this earth. Thus there was a "republic of Spaniards," or "gente de razón," to which one might belong based on one's place of birth, *limpieza de sangre* (purity of blood), education, economic position, and life-style. Separate from it was a "republic of Indians" with a distinct juridical and societal status and its own institutions of government patterned on Spanish models. It preserved Indian customs and traditions despite the European desire to Christianize and Westernize Indians. Blacks did not belong to either order or republic. Overall, within colonial society the social order was unstable, displaying a high degree of flexibility, and social mobility within the structure was dynamic, ever changing, and common.[3] Society was not simple and static as it has often been portrayed by historians, and it was not a reproduction of the social system that existed in Spain. Instead it was complex, changing, and new.

Nor was colonial Guatemala a cultural desert. Schools were established for Indians as well as Spaniards early in the colonization period, and they continued thereafter. They were run almost entirely by religious orders, but there were some secular schools near the end of the colonial period. The most notable cultural advances were the early presence of a printing press at Santiago de Guatemala and the foundation of the University of San Carlos there in the last quarter of the seventeenth century. Writers, architects, sculptors, musicians, painters, and other artists and intellectuals abounded in colonial Guatemala beginning in the sixteenth century. Indeed, colonial Guatemala, especially its capital, became the cultural center for all of Spanish Central America.

POPULATION

Santiago de los Caballeros de Guatemala, when it was established at Almolonga in November 1527, contained a population of twenty-four vecinos. Three years later there were 150 vecinos, including Juan Rodríguez Cabrillo, who was later the discoverer of California and the harbor of San Diego.[4] By 1549 the capital of the newly founded Audiencia de los Confines had about 100 vecinos, but by 1585 the municipality had grown to include approximately 700 vecinos.[5] These early figures must not be misinterpreted as the total population in the city. They do not include Indians, especially those allies brought from New Spain by Pedro de Alvarado. Nor do they reflect the total population of either Guatemala or Central America at those times. The overall population of the town may be estimated by using the multiplier of five persons per family commonly accepted by anthropologists and historians, but recognizing that this factor may have been only an average more or less of persons per family. Thus we can arrive at populations of about 120 for 1524, 750 for 1530, 500 for 1549, and 3,500 for 1585. While the numbers may be inexact and open to question, they reflect the earliest records for Santiago de Guatemala alone, and they indicate trends in the development and growth of that community.

According to the late Adriaan Cornelis van Oss, "the demographic history of Latin America is a ground of relatively new investigation."[6] He pointed out some of the difficulties one finds in the study of populations for both colonial Guatemala and Central America. Among the problems are the scarcity of sources, incomplete reports by secular and clerical officials, inconsistencies in the reports, omissions of sectors of the population, and of course, reports specifying numbers of vecinos instead of total inhabitants. Not until the latter part of the eighteenth century and early nineteenth century did systematic reports by officials (such as Pedro Cortés y Larraz and Domingo Juarros) and census returns (for example that of 1778) become more detailed and reliable, although even those sources are incomplete and inconsistent. Furthermore, Van Oss noted that, lamentably, the greater part of the general census of 1778 has been lost, although its summary appeared in the *Gazeta de Guatemala* in 1802[7] (a fact that the present author of this book corroborated after painstakingly searches in the Archivo General de Indias in Spain and the Archivo General Centro América in Guatemala City for the original document).

Therefore, any analysis of the populations of Central America, the province of Guatemala, and individual communities is the result of bringing together bits and pieces of information from various manuscript and published sources. Recognizing that the data are incomplete, sometimes erroneous, and inconsistent, and based on scattered, limited sources, an attempt was made to compile and present table 3, giving figures for the populations of Central America, Guatemala, and Santiago de Guatemala–Nueva Guatemala.

From those figures it can be seen that the population of colonial Guatemala constituted the majority of the inhabitants of the Kingdom of Guatemala, and the inhabitants of the capital, Santiago de Guatemala–Nueva Guatemala, were the majority in the province of Guatemala. For example, in the 1778 census (in which the capital was not included) the 421,147 residents of Guatemala comprised 52.8 percent of the total number of people (797,214) in the entire kingdom. By 1796 that percentage had increased to 62.9 percent, and in 1825, four years after independence, the population of the new nation of Guatemala still constituted 39.8 percent of the total in Central America. The decline in the percentage can be attributed to the detachment of Chiapas (then a Mexican state) and the loss of Soconusco to El Salvador. Furthermore, the population of Santiago de Guatemala (Antigua) increased from 100 vecinos and their families in 1549 to about 1,000 vecinos, or an estimated 5,000 people, in 1620; and between 1768 and 1770, only a few years before the earthquake of 29 July 1773, the capital had 26,411 residents. Nueva Guatemala grew from nothing to 5,917 inhabitants in 1776 (during the transfer of the capital), and to 23,434 persons in the census of 1793.

Within the province of Guatemala the number of Indians, both living in the capital and in the countryside, was considerable, and it dwarfed other sectors of the population. In 1570 and 1650 the estimated Indian populations of 550,000 and 540,000, respectively, constituted 95.6 percent and 83.1 percent of the total inhabitants of Central America, thereby illustrating the decline in their share of the total population by the middle of the seventeenth century. The majority of these Indians lived within the province of Guatemala, with only scattered groups elsewhere in the kingdom. Archbishop Pedro Cortés y Larraz indicated that of the 471,556 inhabitants counted in his "Descripción" between 1768 and 1770, 50,000 were "Spaniards," blacks, and mulattos, while 295,805 were Indians and 75,342 were ladinos.[8] Thus in 1770 about 62.7 percent of the total population were Indian. In 1802, of the 496,504 residents of colonial Guatemala, 143,632 were Spaniards and ladinos (28.9%), while 352,872 were Indians (71.1%). During the last decades of Spanish administration, the numbers of blacks and mulattos were still relatively small, as they had been in earlier centuries, for all of Central America (they were estimated at 10,000 in 1570 and 30,000 in 1650 for all of Central America). By the early 1800s black slavery had declined, and the small numbers of slaves were confined to the Caribbean coast; only a few lived in colonial Guatemala itself. Thus Ralph Lee Woodward's appraisal indeed is reasonable that in the kingdom as a whole at the end of the Spanish colonial period 65 percent of the total population were Indian, 31 percent were ladino, and 4 percent were Spaniards and Creoles,[9] although in the province of Guatemala, Indians were still about 70 percent of the population.

Two other conclusions can be advanced concerning the population of colonial Guatemala. First, while the number of Spaniards had increased notably by the beginning of the nineteenth century, the presence of over 350,000 Indians ensured that those of European heritage remained a distinct minority. Second, the ladino sector of the population had reached sizable proportions by the late eighteenth century. Largely dwelling in the eastern part of Guatemala and in the capital of Nueva Guatemala, the ladinos numbered 75,342 persons, or 17.9 percent of the total of 421,147 residents, according to the figures compiled by Archbishop Cortés y Larraz between 1768 and 1770.[10] Of that total,

TABLE 3. **The Populations of Central America, Colonial Guatemala, and Santiago de Guatemala–Nueva Guatemala during the Colonial Period**

Year	Vecinos	Inhabitants	Remarks
			Central America
1570	2,200–2,300	575,000 (est.)	Estimated 15,000 Europeans, 550,000 Indians, 10,000 blacks or mulatos
1594	1,760	8,800 (est.)	Only Europeans
1620	2,840	14,200 (est.)	Only Europeans
1650	—	650,000 (est.)	Estimated 50,000 Europeans, 540,000 Indians, 20,000 blacks, 10,000 mulattos, and 30,000 mestizos.
1768–70	—	471,556	Estimated by Cortés y Larraz.
1778	—	797,214	Census published in *Gazeta de Guatemala*, 26 April 1802.
		805,339	Juarros's correction of the census because it did not use all parish registers.
		793,615	Adriaan van Oss's correction.
1796	—	822,579	Adriaan van Oss's computation.
1800	—	923,538	Adriaan van Oss's computation.
1802	—	972,579	
1803	—	1,037,421	
1804	—	421,955 (?)	Incomplete report in AGCA, A144.1, exp. 22150, leg. 2646, f. 19
1825	—	1,287,491	
			Colonial Guatemala
1571–74	—	41,300–45,300 (?)	Estimated 1,300 Spaniards and 40,000–45,000 Indians.
1768–70	—	471,556	Cortés y Larraz's estimate, including Salvador.
		264,685	Cortés y Larraz's estimate, excluding Salvador but adding Verapaz.
1778	—	421,147	Estimated 50,000 Spaniards, blacks, and mulattos; 295,805 Indians; and 75,342 ladinos.
1796	—	517,518	
1800	—	336,103 (?)	
1802	—	496,504	143,632 Spaniards and ladinos; 352,872 Indians.
1804	84,391	421,955 (est.)	Incomplete report in AGCA, A144.1, exp. 22150, leg. 2646, f.19.
1825	—	512,120	

TABLE 3. continued

Year	Vecinos	Inhabitants	Remarks
			Santiago de Guatemala–Nueva Guatemala
1527	24	120 (est.)	
1530	150	750 (est.)	
1549	100	500 (est.)	
1565–75	500	2,500 (est.)	
1585	700	3,500 (est.)	
1594	500	2,500 (est.)	
1604	890	4,450 (est.)	
1620	1,000	5,000 (est.)	
1657–59	1,000	5,000 (est.)	
1675–85	1,000	5,000 (est.)	
1768–70	—	26,411	Cortés y Larraz's figures, including 7,512 Indians and 3,416 ladinos.
1773	—	25,000 (est.)	
1776	893	5,917	Early census of Nueva Guatemala.
1778	—	—	Not included in general census.
1782	—	13,338	Villacorta Calderón, *Historia*, 439.
1793	—	23,434	Census.
1804	4,686	23,434 (?)	Based on census of 1793.

SOURCES: Archbishop Pedro Cortés y Larraz, "Descripción," AGI, Guatemala, 984; Mapas y planos, tomo II, 74–186. Jesús María García Añoveros, *Población y estado*, 16, 135, 193. Adríaan C. van Oss, "La población de América Central hacia 1800," 293. Christopher H. Lutz, "Santiago de Guatemala," 2:516–17. Domingo Juarros, *Compendio de la historia de la ciudad de Guatemala* 1:66–67. Domingo Juarros, *Statistical and Commercial History of Guatemala*, 497. *Gazeta de Guatemala*, num. 256, del lunes 26 de abril de 1802, AGI, Gacetas; "Resumen General de las Familias de españoles y ladinos domiciliadas en el reyno de Guatemala . . . ," 7 May 1804, AGCA A144.1, exp. 22150, leg. 2646, f. 19. "Testimonio del Pedimiento del Sor Fiscal," AGI, Guatemala 658. Bancroft, *History of Central America* 2:97, 718. Wortman, *Government and Society in Central America*, 49, 67, 289–90. McAlister, *Spain and Portugal*, 131, 344. Sherman, *Forced Native Labor*, 8. MacLeod, *Spanish Central America*, 218–19. Villacorta Calderón, *Historia*, 109. Angel Rosenblat, *La población indígena y el mestizaje en América* 1:59–88. Sidney D. Markman, "Pueblos de indios y pueblos de españoles en el Reino de Guatemala," 81. Francisco de Solano Pérez-Lila, "La población indígena de Guatemala, 1492–1800," 68–69, 308. Francisco de Paula García Peláez, *Memorias para la historia del Antiguo Reyno de Guatemala* 3:138–39, 202. *Enciclopedia Universal Ilustrada* 26:1616.

52,211 ladinos lived in towns, and 23,131 were dispersed outside of formal settlements for various reasons, including some who fled tribute obligations, or desired to live free of town restrictions, or were avoiding punishments, or were trying to improve their economic status. Archbishop Cortés y Larraz believed that these rural ladinos often were undesirables, "a congregation of persons without subjection to God, the Church, or the King," and that they should be "reduced" to living in towns.[11] According to Woodward, almost one-third of the population of the kingdom of Guatemala at the end of the colonial period was ladino.[12]

It is unfortunate that the demographic history of the Spanish colonial province of Guatemala, and the kingdom as a whole, is so much a matter of estimation and conjecture because of the lack of definitive sources and the incompleteness, inaccuracy, and inconsistency of statistics. Even though King Carlos III on 10 November 1776 ordered that censuses be taken annually throughout his American dominions, and the president of the Audiencia de Guatemala on 7 November 1777 ordered the governors, alcaldes mayores, and curas to carry out the king's orders, it is evident that in Guatemala and throughout the kingdom regular censuses were not accomplished thereafter. A few general censuses, were completed, beginning with that of 1778, but they were undertaken only sporadically. One reason was the opposition of Archbishop Cortés y Larraz to the transfer of the capital to Nueva Guatemala. According to the report of the Consejo Real de las Indias (Royal Council of the Indies) to the king on 11 May 1778, the archbishop had advised the priests in his jurisdiction not to assist the civil officials in conducting the census and not to open the parish registers to them unless those royal officials had a specific authorization from him.[13]

This foot dragging may have contributed to the incompleteness and delays in accomplishing the general census of 1778. Thereafter, the sheer magnitude of the task of conducting yearly censuses among nearly half a million people, the shortage of officials to carry out the king's wishes, and the preoccupation with other imperial and provincial governmental duties and responsibilities during the period of almost continual Spanish warfare with foreign nations from 1789 to 1815, interfered with the accomplishment of regular censuses. Indeed, one report from the Audiencia de Guatemala to the king on 6 December 1778 emphasized the magnitude of the task of conducting an annual census and pointed out that it was "impossible" for an oidor of the audiencia to make such a count of all the Indians because of their large numbers, the many towns in which they resided, and the distances involved. Indeed, the audiencia observed that if an oidor were so employed, he would lose his health and possibly his life in canvassing twenty-two provinces, 685 towns, 103,005 tributaries, and 2,660 naborios in a domain where there were over 8,044 leagues (21,000 miles) to be traveled between the towns, requiring an estimated 125 months and 17 days to reach all of them. The oidors cited the lack of adequate shelter in the towns; the scarcity of food; the unpopulated regions to be crossed; the rough, severe, and mountainous roads (some could not be traveled in summer on horseback, and in winter were not passable even on foot); the risk to life of being transported on the shoulders of Indians; and the many rivers that in times of heavy rain could not be crossed. The audiencia explained these obstacles and the inconveniences that one faced in trying to carry out the king's orders. While the audiencia supplied a statistical account for the "provinces that comprise the kingdom of Guatemala," it also asked that the counts be made every three years, or every five as was the current practice.[14]

With some idea of the size and composition of Guatemala's colonial population, along with the problems of sources and the conduct of the regular censuses, we can now devote our attention to the social structure and society of the Spanish province.

SOCIETY

Spaniards, Indians, blacks, and ladinos essentially made up the social structure and society of colonial Guatemala. Miles Wortman has observed that a new American social order in Central America emerged following the violent years of the conquest: "a settled and relatively peaceful colony comprised of Amerindians, castes, and Creoles under a Habsburg monarchy and a Spanish, Christian god."[15] In the sixteenth century the term "Spaniard" seems to have been applied only to those whose native country was Spain, but by the latter part of the eighteenth century it is evident in reports of officials and censuses that "Spaniards" had come to mean not only those from Spain but also persons of European descent born in America and those who practiced a life-style that displayed the customs, traditions, religion, and overall civilization of Spaniards.

The Indians (Amerindians), who were the overwhelming majority of people in Guatemala, dwelled in either their pre-Columbian towns or in the congregaciones established for them by Spaniards, or they fled to Spanish communities, where they lived in barrios but sometimes mixed with the rest of the population. The first group were said to be part of the "Republic of Indians," having a distinct juridical status with regulatory laws of the Spanish Crown to protect them, and preserving their own municipal governments (under the overall supervision of Spaniards), their customs, and their traditions.

The numbers of the blacks, who originally came to Guatemala and Central America as a result of the slave trade in the sixteenth century, declined in the 1600s. They increased in the first half of the eighteenth century, but as the slave trade and slavery declined notably in the last half century of Spanish administration, they tended to be concentrated along the Atlantic and Pacific coasts, with few in the heartland of Guatemala. They were not treated as part of either the Republic of Spaniards or the Republic of Indians, but toward the end of the eighteenth century they and the zambos were viewed as threats because they were not Catholic and because of their trade and other relationships with British interlopers.

Of special note in the structure of society was the rise of the ladino sector. Christopher Lutz has observed that in the city of Santiago de Guatemala mestizaje accelerated and the arrival of African slaves, free Negroes, mulattos, and mestizos during the latter half of the sixteenth century caused the separation of Indians and Spaniards to crumble as non-Indians took up residence in the Indian barrios of the city.[16] Thus the cornerstone of the Spanish policy dividing the two groups of people—Spaniards and Indians—began to wither away in an urban environment, and eventually it failed. Since Indians worked as servants and apprentices in the Spanish sectors of the city, and Santiago de Guatemala came to have a "numerous slave and free population of African descent" by the middle of the eighteenth century, the growth of castas in the urban setting brought a "demographic revolution" there.[17]

Archbishop Cortés y Larraz in his "Descripción" of the diocese of Guatemala not only examined Indian towns and parishes, but also made extensive observations concerning the ladino population of Guatemala between 1768 and 1770, by which time the ladinos numbered 75,342 persons.[18] Noting that half of the ladinos lived in San Salvador, and another quarter were in the coastal and eastern zones of Central America (including eastern Guatemala),[19] the archbishop observed that many of them lived outside of settled communities.[20] Since they often were undesirables and not closely regulated by the church or the king, he recommended that they be settled in towns.[21] According to the archbishop, many of the ladinos lived in violation of Spanish laws in Indian towns, where they were a destabilizing element of society and often clashed with the Indians over possession of the ejidos of the villages.[22] He claimed that ladinos always were less under the control of the authorities than was the Indian population, and that, like the Spaniards and Indians, they were prone to intoxication, sexual excesses, theft, gambling, extramarital relations, homicide, incest, and other sins and vices.[23] In summary, he thought that ladinos were "loafers, given to vice, thieves, and disorderly persons."[24]

By 1776 the new capital of Nueva Guatemala de la Asunción had 893 families totaling 5,917 persons. Of those, 230 families, or 1,876 persons, were classified as *españoles,* or Spaniards. There also were 234 families of 1,668 persons described as "vecinos antiguos" (old or ancient householders, in other words, Indians), while 429 heads of families with 2,373 persons were classified as mestizos, pardos, or another casta.[25] While those figures reveal the hierarchical nature of the city's society, they also show the flexibility and mobility of that society, as well as the growth of the mixed portion as a result of mestizaje.

Although Spaniards resided principally in the urban centers during the period from 1524 to 1580, they also began to move to the countryside between 1580 and 1630 for the production of indigo and the raising of food crops. Throughout the seventeenth century they established haciendas, which were not large-scale agricultural enterprises because of the lack of manpower and capital; however, on the Pacific coast of Guatemala, as well as in Nicaragua and San Salvador, they "overwhelmed" the Indian populations and created a Westernized, Spanish-speaking ladino rural peasantry that was predominately mestizo in its racial origins.[26] Yet, when the cabildo of Santiago de Guatemala took a count of the city's vecinos in 1604, for example, it revealed that the city's population still was considerable. Among the 890 heads of families were 76 encomenderos, 108 merchants, 76 officials at various levels, 13 traders, 13 storekeepers, 22 owners of factories or workshops (obrajes), 10 owners of sugar mills, 11 candlemakers or confectioners, 7 blacksmiths, 10 widows of traders, 7 millers, 8 kiln operators or weavers, 82 farmers, and 33 raisers of livestock.[27] With the indigo boom in the eighteenth century and the rise of Spanish entrepreneurs in the indigo trade, once again both Spaniards and Creoles contributed to the growth of urban populations. Merchants, officials, artisans, and even landowners constituted the majority of the inhabitants of such major communities as Santiago de Guatemala, along with the religious, day laborers, servants, and storekeepers.[28]

While the Spaniards principally lived in urban settlements (with some in the countryside), the rural population consisted largely of Indians (although there were some Indians in Spanish towns), blacks (both slave and free), and ladinos. The rural population worked as farmers, livestock raisers, and laborers on properties owned by others. Increasingly after 1550 they, along with some artisans and a growing class of mestizo merchants, tended to live in small towns. Caciques were permitted to govern their people under Spanish supervision and were rewarded for their loyalty with coats of arms, permission to bear arms and ride horses, and encouragement to have their sons educated.[29] Although the Indian cultures in the eastern and Pacific coastal regions of Guatemala were almost totally obliterated and replaced by ladinos, in the highland area there were no indigo plantations and factories, few sugar mills, and products were primarily for local and regional consumption. Protected by Spanish law, the Indians were not so exploited in this region, according to José María García Añoveros, and they preserved their own languages, many of their customs, and became impervious to Castilian influences.[30] However, it must be emphasized that Añoveros did not take into account the sixteenth-century Spanish practices of forced labor—slavery, encomienda, and repartimiento—among the highland Indians, which resulted in their population decline, resettlement, diseases, and often loss of lives.

Toward the end of the 1780s and until Guatemala achieved independence from Spain in 1821, authorities attempted to do something about the threat from blacks, pardos, and Mosquito Indians on the Atlantic coast of Central America, particularly because of British activities there and contraband trade with these residents. This military and economic threat had grown for nearly a half century since the 1740s, when the governor of Jamaica had sent Robert Hodgson to the Mosquito shore to attract trade, destroy Spanish hegemony, produce dyewoods, and possibly conquer Guatemala with two or three thousand Mosquito Indians as allies. Hodgson, over the course of nearly forty years, expanded British trade stations along the Atlantic coast of Central America, established contraband trade with Spanish merchants and officials, and directed Mosquito raids against Spanish settlements.

After the British conflict with the Spaniards during the American Revolution, in which Governor and Captain General Matías de Gálvez recaptured the fortress of Omoa, seized the British trading headquarters on Roatán Island, and defeated British forces along the Honduran and Nicaraguan coasts, Spain embarked on a policy in 1787 of populating the coast with settlers from Asturias and Galicia in northwest Spain and winning the support of the Mosquito Indians and the zambos and pardos. Don Bernardo Herbella (or Erbella) recruited 130 families (109 from Asturias, 21 from Galicia) of an authorized 150 for this venture in 1787. Conducted by Juan de Ponte, there were originally 123 male heads of households, all married except for two servants and one widower, and 7 widows, together with 344 children and 52 others, amounting in all to a total of 646 persons. Many became ill with fever and smallpox by the time they reached La Coruña in Spain, and some died, including many children. On 1 June 1787, Juan de Ponte reported that only 91 families comprising 426 people had reached La Coruña. The survivors were issued white bread, wine, sardines, wax candles to light their abodes, fuel to heat the sardines, seeds, food, and tools, as well as passports. These poor "farmers and artisans" were supposed to occupy four settlements in the kingdom of Guatemala, and the English colonists already there were required to evacuate the communities. Evidently the colonists did not leave from La Coruña until late in 1787, arriving thereafter at Trujillo in today's Honduras. Many more became sick of "smallpox and other types of illnesses," and some died, according to Ponte's report of 14 September 1788.[31]

Four years later the Spanish government hired Robert Hodgson, its very enemy during the past forty-five years or so, as its representative on the Atlantic coast of Central America, thereby ensuring English contact and creating the potential for expanded illicit commercial relations. On 28 June 1791 the king issued an order to the viceroy of Nueva Granada stating that Hodgson should be permitted to enter Guatemala with the grade and the salary of a colonel paid to him by the treasury of Cartagena, in today's Colombia. Hodgson could choose where he wished to reside in Central America, taking from the "Laguna de Bluefields," north of the Río San Juan in Nicaragua, all that belonged to him. Also, the Crown gave permission to the English colonel Francisco Meany for a term of three years to introduce to the Atlantic coast of Central America one "ship loaded with English textiles for the supply of and trade with those natives [the Mosquito Indians] without prejudicing our Spanish traders sending also what they want." The president of the Audiencia de Guatemala was instructed to deal with Colonel Meany to establish fixed prices on the buying and selling of goods to the Mosquitos, and their commerce was declared to be a monopoly. Presents also were to be distributed to the Indians as determined by the president of the audiencia, but their total value was not to exceed 4,310 pesos every three years.[32] Thus the king—in an effort to control the flow of contraband, impede English influence in the region, and win the support of the Mosquito Indians—by legalizing the trade, actually contributed to the growing threat represented by the clandestine trade between the English and Spanish and Creole merchants in Guatemala.

In summary, society in Spanish Guatemala may be characterized as hierarchical but ever changing. In the fifteenth century the different sectors were decentralized, segmented, and separate, but by the middle of the seventeenth century society was multiracial, and finally it became homogeneous in the early or mid eighteenth century, as Lutz has concluded the city of Santiago de Guatemala was.[33] Ranks and classes of people depending on race, color, and class were pronounced during the era of the "primeros pobladores" (first settlers) in the sixteenth century, and still were present in the last century of Spanish control, but they had diminished in importance by the late eighteenth and early nineteenth centuries because miscegenation and social mobility had made it impossible to maintain clear-cut boundaries between the various classes and castes of the people. Indeed, Spain created a new American society in Guatemala, as elsewhere in her kingdoms, not a reproduction of the society in the mother country.[34]

CULTURE

Although the large majority of Guatemalans in the Spanish colonial period worked long, hard hours in both the urban settlements and the rural countryside, important cultural achievements were made in education, literature, the arts, and publishing. Most of these developments understandably occurred in the capital, where the living conditions and concentrations of people permitted access to supplies and provided a small market for writers and artists, as well as a corps of teachers and students for schools. Perhaps the most notable cultural phenomena were the founding of the Real y Pontificia Universidad de San Carlos de Guatemala (hereafter referred to as the University of San Carlos) in the last quarter of the seventeenth century and the arrival of the ideas of the Enlightenment stressing reason, science, and natural laws toward the end of the eighteenth century. High culture was limited to a small sector of colonial Guatemalans. The people and the province were not the equals of the same sector in Mexico City, Lima, and Bogotá, but the cultural achievements were notable. In fact, Santiago de Guatemala and its successor, Nueva Guatemala, were significant as the cultural hubs of Central America and as important centers of such developments for all of Spanish colonial America.

Catholic friars brought many institutions of Western civilization and culture to Guatemala, among which were the earliest schools established by the Franciscans, the Dominicans, the Augustinians, the Mercedarians, and principally, the Jesuits. These colegios educated Spaniards and Indians separately. Privately run by the orders, they were often in buildings constructed near churches and within convents.[35] Their curricula emphasized reading, writing, mathematics, and religious dogma. With limited enrollments and facilities, the subjects were taught by the friars themselves. Church funds from tithes, tributes, and the sinódos of the friars supported the schools, in addition to contributions from the citizenry, especially wealthy individuals. These educational institutions were religious by nature, and they often had a relatively short existence because of the many problems they faced, although some schools in the colony lasted throughout long periods. Among their problems were the scarcity and unreliability of long-term funding, the limited numbers of students, restrictive facilities, the lack of qualified teachers, and difficulties with the Indian languages since the religious had to deal with about twenty-five different tongues spoken in the Kingdom of Guatemala.[36] Not until the late eighteenth and the early nineteenth century were secular schools established as a result of the ideas of the Enlightenment and the Spanish Crown's anticlerical emphasis.

Bishop Francisco de Marroquín was among the earliest, if not the first, to promote education for Guatemala's Indians. He founded a Franciscan school to teach grammar to youths in 1548 and a college of arts and theology, the Colegio de Santo Tomás Aquinas, in Santiago de Guatemala before his death in 1563. He began working toward the establishment of a university in 1559, hoping that his college of arts and theology would evolve into such an institution. Although he bequeathed much of his property to such a venture in his last will,[37] nothing was done to implement his idea for more than a century, and his school evidently ceased to exist some time after his death.

Yet, religious orders did found other schools thereafter. Dominicans founded the Colegio de Santo Domingo in 1548 (it did not grant degrees until 1625), while Jesuits established the Colegio Universitario de San Lucas in 1621. Regidor Nicolás Justiniano Chaverría of the cabildo of Santiago de Guatemala donated a sum of 30,000 pesos in 1646 to the Jesuits to support their schools.[38] These schools educated the children of families associated with their orders, and others were founded for specific congregations, such as the highly successful school founded in the 1690s for the congregation of San Felipe Neri in Santiago de Guatemala, which was taught by the clerical presbyter Don Carlos de Coronado y Ulloa and was founded without cost to the royal treasury.[39] Many schools were established, both in the capital and in rural settlements, solely for Indians.

During his extensive inspection of his diocese between 1768 and 1770, Archbishop Cortés y Larraz compiled statistics concerning Indian schools and made observations about their students, teachers, and problems. In the 431 poblaciones in the diocese of Guatemala, 56 percent of the parishes responding to his survey had schools for Indians. This represented a total of 103 such schools. There were 2,388 students enrolled in these schools, but 41 of the 103 parishes did not report the number of students in their school. José María García Añoveros estimated that the total of Indian students may have been as high as 3,996. Cortés y Larraz observed that each school instructed the Indians in the Castilian language and Christian doctrine. He believed that seventy-six of the schools had good teachers and that only two received poor instruction. The salaries of the teachers were paid from community funds, yet, the archbishop noted, attendance was poor and Indian parents often strongly resisted sending their children to the schools. Both boys and girls were students, but he noted that learning was reduced to "reciting by memory the prayers and doctrine," and he urged that all Indian children be required to attend school, beginning at age five.[40] It is obvious that the education of Indians in Guatemala and throughout the kingdom, even at this late date in the colonial period, was not comprehensive and was fraught with difficulties.

After the expulsion of the Jesuits in 1767, the Spanish Crown issued a series of cedulas between 1775 and 1778 ordering the establishment of schools to teach "primeras letras" (basic subjects) in all of the Indian towns and barrios. The children were to learn Castilian Spanish and Christian doctrine as well as the fundamentals of reading, writing, and arithmetic. Teachers were to be paid from the "bienes de la comunidad" (community funds). Most of the schools were taught by a choirmaster who instructed his pupils only in the Christian doctrine, and they were largely failures. The Indian parents opposed them ideologically and economically and took their children out, believing, for example, that learning Castilian would create an "open door" for an invading culture. Community leaders and treasurers also opposed the costs of maintaining the schools.[41]

Although the general topic of secular schools in colonial Guatemala needs further investigation, it is evident that they existed for both boys and girls toward the end of the eighteenth century and in the early years of the nineteenth. Most of them were supported by subscriptions, either from community funds, where available, or by donations of the parents. By a decree of the Regency in Spain during the absence of the king, on 14 October 1812, prelates of religious communities were ordered to establish primary schools at all convents to teach reading and writing. In the cities the curriculum was to include Latin and Spanish grammar.[42] It is doubtful that this education order was carried out extensively in the last nine years of Spanish administration, because of the fall of the Regency and the return of King Fernando VII, and the unstable political and economic situation in the brief period from 1812 to 1821. One prominent individual, Don Antonio de Larrazábal, a canon of the cathedral of Guatemala, reflected in 1812 on his educational experience in a "colegio internado" (boarding school). He observed that the school he had attended was for both boys and girls between the ages of four and twelve, and the pupils were totally separated from their parents. Boys were taught to speak Castilian correctly and were instructed in elementary writing. Girls were taught "the appropriate labors of their sex, like sewing and making stockings."[43] The scarcity of public schools in the early nineteenth century was observed by historian Ramón A. Salazar, who noted that there were only three such schools in the whole Kingdom of Guatemala, all of them in the capital. He concluded that the general ignorance of the people at that time was "not strange."[44]

While the educational opportunities and levels of public literacy were limited at best, such was not the case for higher education, especially after the establishment of the University of San Carlos in the years following 1676. This institution was the outgrowth of Bishop Marroquín's original idea and his bequest in the years 1559 to 1563, together with the establishment of the Colegio de Santo Tomás Aquinas, which was originally founded in 1562, but reestablished in 1620 as an institution for advanced learning.[45] Founded initially on 9 March 1562 to teach philosophy, theology, and Latin grammar, the Colegio de Santo Tomás was intended by Bishop Marroquín as the first step toward a full-fledged university.[46] However, it had little activity, no lectures, and few, if any, students before 20 October 1620, when the first classes were held in the convent of Santo Domingo by Dominican fathers. Established in the city of Santiago de Guatemala officially to counteract the Jesuit school of San Lucas, it conducted classes in theology, philosophy, and canon law. Yet, this predecessor to the University of San Carlos had no rector, few students, and no formal discipline or set of regulations, although it did occasionally grant degrees. Still in existence in 1659, it had accumulated funds that could be used in founding a real university, not just one in name.[47]

On 5 March 1667 the president of the Audiencia de Guatemala addressed a letter to the king emphasizing the need for a university in Santiago de Guatemala. He noted that it would provide a good education for the youth of the kingdom, teach them the "sciences," defend the Catholic faith, improve health and save lives by teaching medicine, better prepare the religious to administer their pueblos, and provide for a "well-governed republic." He cited the contributions of universities in Europe, as well as the distance of more than three hundred leagues, over nearly inaccessible roads and perilous rivers, from Guatemala to Mexico City, where the nearest university was. To support his request, he emphasized that there was only one learned person in the city who was a lawyer, that there was a shortage of doctors, and that language professors were needed to deal with the innumerable Indian pueblos. Finally, the president added that the colegio founded by Bishop Marroquín, with its lecture halls, could be converted into a university, and that fourteen professorships and a secretary could be established at a total cost of just 4,690 pesos, of which Santo Tomás already had 1,525 pesos, leaving a deficit of 3,165 pesos, which he suggested could be made up from vacant encomiendas. He proposed professorships of canon law, vespers, civil law, statutes, theology, the arts, scriptures, medicine, and two of the "principal and universal languages of these provinces," with remunerations ranging from 150 to 500 pesos each.[48]

King Carlos II issued a royal cedula on 31 January 1676 authorizing the founding of La Real y Pontificia Universidad de San Carlos de Guatemala.[49] Over the course of the next eleven years before its official dedication on 10 January 1687,[50] the "Royal and Pontifical University of San Carlos de Guatemala" obtained its first secretary and rector, began holding classes, acquired students, hired faculty, and developed its curriculum. It also granted its first degrees and obtained financial support. The king, in his founding order of 1676, had authorized the creation of seven chairs, or professorships, one each in theology, scholasticism, ethics, medicine, civil law, canon law, and Indian languages (the last professorship was divided between the Cakchiquel and the Mexican, or Nahuatl, language). In 1680 another royal order added a professor of philosophy and *instituta* (constitutional or statutory law). Thus there were nine professors (the languages were taught by two) before the first courses began. No one taught grammar or rhetoric, although knowledge of Latin, grammar, and rhetoric were required of students admitted to the university. Salaries were established for the faculty, and the king also ruled that Indians could be enrolled and graduated.[51]

A Junta Universitaria (university board) was formed in Santiago de Guatemala to carry out the king's orders and oversee the planning, financing, and establishment of the University of San Carlos (which was not titled "San Carlos de Borromeo," as some writers have said). The board's members were President Fernando Francisco de Escobedo y Cabrera (governor and captain general of the Kingdom of Guatemala, and president of the audiencia), two oidores of the Audiencia de Guatemala, the fiscal (attorney) of the audiencia, and the bishop.[52] Two interim rectors, oidores Jacinto Roldán de la Cueba and Juan Bautista de Urquiola y Elorriaga, headed the administration of the university before the official appointment of José de Baños y Sotomayor (archdeacon of the cathedral and a graduate of the University of Osuna in Spain) as rector. Don Pedro de Barceno became university secretary in 1677. The university's initial bills and the faculty salaries were paid with 2,200 pesos that were remitted in memory of Bishop Marroquín by Alferez Juan de Cárdenas and by private contributions such as those of the two board members from the audiencia (Jacinto Roldán de la Cueba and Juan Bautista de Urquiola) and 3,000 pesos donated by the executors of the estate of postmaster Pedro Crespo y Suárez.[53] Another individual provided considerable guidance and direction for the university: Don Francisco de Sarasa y Arce, an oidor of the audiencia and by 1681 the university's rector, was its "ideological founder," according to José Mata Gavidía. Sarasa promoted life at the university, authored its constitutions and regulations, defended its fueros, and eliminated all teaching monopolies.[54] The first stipends for the nine professors totaled 2,750 pesos: 500 for each law position, 200 for *instituta,* 400 for medicine, 300 for theology, 250 for "moral theology," or ethics, and 200 each for arts and crafts *(artes),* the Cakchiquel language, and the "Mexican" (Nahuatl) tongue.[55]

Classes began on 7 and 8 January 1681 in four disciplines, and Father Agustín Cano had more than seventy students in his philosophy course.[56] Franciscans, Mercedarians, and two educated lawyers with bachelors degrees comprised the initial faculty, but in May 1681, instruction had yet to be given in medicine because Licenciado Joseph Salmerón had not yet arrived to teach class in that discipline. Nor had any course in Nahuatl been presented, because of the "lack of a competitor" in the faculty selection process.[57] Rector Francisco de Sarasa reported that in the first classes Fray Raphael Castillo (a Dominican) had three or four students in his theology class by May 1681; Fray Agustín Cano, who had begun his philosophy course with sixty students, now had forty; Licenciado Don Antonio de Avila (who had replaced Licenciado Jacinto Jaime Moreno because Moreno had gone to Spain) had six or seven students in his law course; and Fray Joseph Angel (a Dominican) had seven or eight students in his course in the Quiché and Cakchiquel languages.[58]

The first graduations occurred in mid-October 1683 when sixteen of the twenty petitioners had passed their examinations and were granted bachelor's degrees. Soon afterward a second graduation took place when nine philosophy students obtained bachelor's degrees after having passed their examinations, two with marks of "suficiente" (passing), one with "más que suficiente" (better than passing), and six with "suficientísmo" (excellent).[59] Authorized by the king to grant degrees at the bachelor's (bachillerato), master's (licenciado), and doctoral (doctor) levels, the University of San Carlos continued to do so throughout the Spanish colonial period. For example, in the decade before the great earthquake of July 1773, it conferred 122 bachelor's and 30 higher degrees. In the next decade, after the university's transfer to the city of Nueva Guatemala, it conferred 119 bachelor's and 42 higher degrees. Between 1812 and 1821 it awarded 375 bachelor's and 40 superior degrees, for an annual average of forty-one and a half degrees per year.[60]

Francisco de Sarasa wrote the *constituciones* (constitutions or codes of laws) for the University of San Carlos in compliance with the king's order of 6 June 1680, and submitted them on 17 May 1681 to King Carlos II for approval.[61] Modeled on the University of Salamanca in Spain, and named San Carlos because, according to the king, the saint was "of my royal patronage,"[62] the Guatemalan university received the king's approval of its code of laws in 1686 in a document printed in

Madrid. This code or set of regulations gave formal direction to the University of San Carlos. Its 168 printed pages contained titles and specific constituciones (codes) governing such subjects as the patron saints of the university (San Carlos and Santa Teresa de Avila, the Spanish founder of the Carmelite nuns in the sixteenth century), the election of the rector in November, and the election of the eight council members who elected the rector. The rector had to be thirty years of age or older, be a graduate of a university, and possess a doctoral degree. He could be a civil but not a religious official, and could not be a medical doctor or a *maestro* (master) in the arts.

At eleven o'clock every 11 November the elected rector was to swear his loyalty to the Crown and profess his faith to his predecessor, and the students were to "swear and give obedience to the said rector." On the following day in the chapel of the university all the students would again swear their obedience to the rector and the council members. In addition, the code specified the rector's duties and responsibilities (which included a visit to each professor every two months), the enrollment of students within forty days after the rector's election, regulations for the schoolmaster ("maestre de escuela"), who evidently was in charge of instruction and assembled the council members to elect a new rector within a period of three days in the event of a rector's death, and the laws governing the professors ("doctores y maestros"), who had to be at least twenty years of age. Concerning students, the code required that they enroll every year and pay a fee of two reales (one-fourth of a peso), one for the secretary and one for the coffers of the university. All students were required to be proficient in Latin, rhetoric, and grammar before they could be admitted to the university.

Students were required to live in decent houses ("casas honestas") without scandal and to wear suitable clothing (it was not to be trimmed in gold or with embroidery, and no colorful stockings were permitted). Nor could the students have long locks or tufts of hair. The wearing of a priest's cloak and the bearing of arms by students were prohibited. The code also specified the requirements for the three degrees, which (included oaths of loyalty to the king and civil officials, profession of "our Holy Catholic Faith,") and enrollment in one course per six-month term. The code also stated that no one associated with the Holy Office of the Inquisition nor "negros, nor mulattos, nor those commonly called Chinos, Morenos, nor whatever type of slave," would be permitted to enroll, although Indians, as vassals of His Majesty, could be enrolled and awarded degrees. Finally, there were regulations for fiestas, funerals for professors, masses for the deceased, the treasury of the university, the salaries of professors, the fees charged students, enrollment, courses, and the awarding of each degree, along with the penalties or punishments for violations any of the laws in the code.[63]

The University of San Carlos was the only university in Central America during the colonial period. Located in Santiago de Guatemala until the earthquake of July 1773, it was moved to its new site in Nueva Guatemala in 1777. Its curriculum was radically altered following Spain's participation in the war against Great Britain as an indirect ally of the American Revolution. Influenced by the Enlightenment in Europe, two of its faculty members, Fray José Antonio Goicoechea (a Franciscan) and Fray Fermín Alcas (a Dominican) led the movement to change the curriculum after 1782 and became symbols of academic progress in Guatemala. They and José Felipe Flores, a medical doctor, introduced such new courses as experimental physics, geometry, optics, astronomy, geography, and anatomical studies. With emphasis on social sciences, natural laws, and the application of useful sciences, the revitalized curriculum brought the university to the forefront of modern ideas and influenced a whole generation of students who became the liberal leaders of Guatemala in the period from 1790 to 1821. These advocates of change in the government and economy of the province and kingdom were the leaders in the movement for independence from Spain.[64]

The University of San Carlos was not, however, the only cultural or intellectual agent of reform in Guatemala at the end of the eighteenth century and during the first two decades of the nineteenth. The Sociedad Económica de Amigos del País, chartered in 1794 and founded the following year in Nueva Guatemala, not only promoted ways to improve the economy, as its name implied, but also concentrated on improving the arts, education, and industry. Its members included such persons as Fray Goicoechea and Dr. Flores of the university, who with others sponsored classes in political economy, bookkeeping, mathematics, foreign languages, and drafting in the community of Nueva Guatemala when such classes were not being taught at the university.[65]

Many of the society's members were graduates of the University of San Carlos, were liberals in their ideas and philosophy, and looked forward to change and progress. Their support of and writings in the *Gazeta de Guatemala* from the 1790s onward promoted the ideas of the Enlightenment and advocated change. The Sociedad Económica's efforts were reinforced by the visit of two members of the Royal Scientific Expedition from Spain after 1797. Arriving in the Americas via New Spain, José Mariano Moziño, a botanist, and José Longinos Martínez, a naturalist, reached Nueva Guatemala by separate routes across Guatemala, seeking to extend the work of the Royal Scientific Expedition by gathering information and rendering reports of their observations. Although their work was primarily scientific, they also investigated and reported on such subjects as Guatemalan society. In 1798, Moziño climbed volcanoes in southern New Spain and Guatemala to study eruptions, made geological and physical studies of the terrain, analyzed the cultivation of indigo, and met with members of the Consulado de Guatemala concerning the possibilities of trade between Central America and Spain. He also studied and classified flora and fauna, investigated agricultural production and manufactures, and observed the population of Guatemala.[66] These activities not only advanced knowledge about Guatemala but also stimulated the intellectual climate of educated Guatemalans, especially members of the Sociedad Económica, with whom the visiting scientists came into frequent contact.

Throughout the colonial period Spanish Guatemala was also a center of literary activity and of the arts of music, architecture, sculpture, and drama. In the western hemisphere only Mexico City, Puebla, and Lima had printing presses before that established at Santiago de Guatemala in 1660. Although most of the Guatemala press's publications were religious,[67] many secular writers also made use of it, especially in the eighteenth century. Guatemala also was the scene of the first periodical published in Central America. The *Gazeta de Guatemala* began publication in 1794 after its editor, Ignacio Beteta, solicited and secured a license for what he intended as a monthly periodical.[68] After two more numbers appeared in 1795, the *Gazeta* suspended publication until 1797, when Beteta resumed the periodical, asking that historical documents, especially acts of the cabildo be given him so that he might publish extracts in the newspaper.[69] From 1797 to 1812 the *Gazeta de Guatemala* appeared weekly. Its issues contained information and indexes pertaining to agriculture, the arts, population (such as the extract from the 1778 census in 1802, discussed earlier in this chapter), the economy, commerce, literature, education, medicine, and the Indians. The *Gazeta* also included government documents and laws, domestic news, and articles on miscellaneous subjects. In 1812 its name changed to the *Gazeta del Gobierno de Guatemala,* and publication continued even after Guatemala declared its independence.[70]

Guatemalans excelled in literature during the colonial period. Important, voluminous chronicles of a historical nature were written by religious and secular residents. For example, Bernal Díaz del Castillo, an infantryman during the conquest of Mexico by Cortés, lived in Santiago de los Caballeros de Guatemala (today's Antigua) after 1541 and married and raised nine children there. He finished his manuscript at age seventy-two in 1568, although it was not sent to Spain until 1575, nine years before Díaz del Castillo's death.[71] His *Verdadera y Notable Relación del Descubrimiento y Conquista de la Nueva España y Guatemala,* under various titles, has appeared in print in both Spanish and English for centuries and is considered one of the classic accounts of the conquest of Mexico and Guatemala. Other important historical works by residents of Guatemala were Dominican Fray Antonio de Remesal's *Historia General de las Indias Occidentales y Particular de la Gobernación de Chiapa y Guatemala;* Francisco Antonio Fuentes y Guzmán's *Recordación Florida: Discurso Historial y Demostración Natural, Material, Militar, y Política del Reyno de Guatemala;* Franciscan Fray Francisco Vásquez's *Crónica de la Provincia del Santísimo Nombre de Jesús de Guatemala;* Fray Francisco Ximénez's *Historia de la Provincia de San Vicente de Chiapa y Guatemala de la Orden de Predicadores;* and Domingo Juarros's *Compendio de la Historia de la Ciudad de Guatemala.* [72] Other residents of Guatemala, especially of the capital, wrote poetry, such as Friar Pedro de Lievana, who arrived in Guatemala in 1530 and died in 1602 and the Jesuit Rafael Landívar y Caballero (1731–92), who was expelled from Guatemala in 1767 along with the other Jesuits, but wrote his *Rusticatio Mexicana,* dedicated to his homeland of Guatemala, while in exile before his death in Bologna, Italy.[73]

Nor was there a lack of artists in colonial Guatemala. Painting was dominated by religious themes. Examples are Pedro de Liendo's retablos in the church of San Luis Obispo, accomplished in 1611; Tomás de Merlos's painting of the Virgin of Pilar, now in the church of the Capuchins in Guatemala City, and his paintings in the interior of El Calvario in Antigua; and the works of Antonio de Montúfar (1627–68), who did six miniature paintings of the Passion of Christ now at El Calvario in Antigua.[74] The notable sculptors, many of whom had become maestros by training in Spain, New Spain, or Nueva Granada (today's Colombia), included Quirio Cataño, who created the sculpture at Esquipulas, and Alonso de Paz, the seventeenth-century sculptor of the statue of Jesús Nazareno now in the church of La Merced in Antigua.[75] Baroque influence was evident in the eighteenth-century architecture of Pedro Garci-Aguirre, at the Casa de Moneda or mint; Agustín Núñez, who in 1687 was given the title of "Maestro Mayor de Arquitectura y Retablos" (superior master of architecture and retablos); Bernardo Ramírez, who participated in drawing the plan for the city of Nueva Guatemala and the construction of the ayuntamiento and Capuchin buildings there; José Manuel Ramírez, who built the University of San Carlos; and especially Diego de Porres and his sons, who in the eighteenth century worked on various churches, the Casa de Moneda, the cathedral, the ayuntamiento, and other buildings in Antigua. One of Diego's sons, Felipe de Porres (1710–59), also built the church of Esquipulas, where he later died.[76] Music was cultivated continuously, and in the middle of the eighteenth century Francisco Mariano López constructed a beautiful organ for the cathedral at Antigua at a cost of 16,000 pesos.[77]

Thus it may be observed that by the late eighteenth century Spanish colonial Guatemala was heavily populated by a multiracial society of Spaniards, Indians, blacks, and many mixed-bloods. The social structure was dynamic and ever changing, and cultural life was constant throughout the period, producing remarkable achievements.

CHAPTER 8

Disasters and Defense

THE PEOPLE of colonial Guatemala faced many types of calamities and disasters during their lifetimes. Men, women, and children experienced all sorts of biological and environmental threats to their lives— high infant mortality, diseases, epidemics, and other human miseries in addition to periodic food shortages, damaging fires, occasional hurricanes along the Caribbean coast, and above all, frequent earthquakes and volcanic eruptions. Indeed, Guatemalans well illustrated the generalization made by Domingo Juarros in the late eighteenth century that "from the time the first transgressors were expelled from Paradise, miseries, misfortunes, and calamities have formed a very prominent part in every history."[1]

Loss of life was evident for both Spaniards and Indians during the tumultuous conquest period, especially in the warfare that characterized the period from Pedro de Alvarado's entry in 1524 to the early 1530s. After the Cakchiquel rebellion, which occurred less than two years after the arrival of the Spaniards, and the severe punishments that Alvarado's inflicted upon the Indians, an almost constant state of tension existed among the living because of the numbers of dead from the conflict and warfare. During this period the Cakchiquel attack on Santiago de Guatemala forced Spaniards to abandon the capital and move to Almolonga, but the threat did not subside until Alvarado returned from Spain and subjugated the Cakchiqueles and other resisting Indian nations.[2]

Thereafter, in the next twenty years or so, the native populations began their precipitous declines because of diseases, enslavement, and the dislocations due to the establishment of the encomienda, the repartimiento, and the congregaciones. Periodic epidemics of smallpox, measles, and other diseases took heavy tolls of Indians over the course of the nearly three centuries of Spanish occupation. Spaniards and castas also suffered greatly during these calamities because of unsanitary conditions, the lack of doctors and medicines, and the limited number of hospitals and other facilities. Not until the late eighteenth century did the situation improve with the establishment of professional medical education at the University of San Carlos, the presence of comparatively well trained doctors in Nueva Guatemala, and the introduction of vaccination to combat smallpox. Even then the availability of doctors, medicines, and facilities in the countryside remained woefully inadequate.

Earthquakes, floods, and volcanic eruptions constituted major disasters and continuing threats for the people of Guatemala. These spectacular disasters began as early as the mid-1520s and continued for the remainder of the colonial period. They resulted in loss of life and property, extensive damage to agriculture and other economic pursuits, and increased expenses to repair damages and restore production of crops, animals, and products. Furthermore, the people lived with constant psychological tension and fear of impending disaster as "sons of the shaking earth," according to Eric Wolf.[3]

In addition to those problems, colonial Guatemalans faced the prospect of new Indian uprisings, of local revolts, and especially, the constant menace after the midsixteenth century of foreign interlopers, privateers, pirates, buccaneers, filibusters, and outright invasions of Guatemala and Central America by the subjects of foreign powers. These conditions and events necessitated constant Spanish preoccupation with the defense of the Kingdom of Guatemala, especially in the eighteenth century when Great Britain was a serious threat in Belize and along the Mosquito Coast from Nicaragua through Honduras and along the Río Dulce in Guatemala. That threat led to many Bourbon reforms for the defense of Guatemala and Central America, as well as increased expenses for the intensified military and naval preparations. The Crown had some successes in warfare against the British during the administration of Matías de Gálvez (1779–83). Finally, in the tumultuous years of the European wars during the Napoleonic era (1793–1815) the threats of insurgency, foreign invasion and expansion, and internal conspiracies necessitated defensive measures by Spanish authorities in Guatemala.

TABLE 4. **Earthquakes and Their Severity**

Category	Name	Severity Remarks
1.	Instrumental	Detected only by seismographs.
2.	Feeble	Noticed only by sensitive people.
3.	Slight	Resembling vibrations caused by heavy traffic.
4.	Moderate	Felt by people walking; rocking of free-standing objects.
5.	Rather Strong	Sleepers awakened; bells ringing; widely felt.
6.	Strong	Trees sway; some damage from overturning and falling objects.
7.	Very Strong	General alarm; cracking of walls.
8.	Destructive	Chimneys fall; some damage to buildings.
9.	Ruinous	Ground begins to crack; houses collapse; pipes break.
10.	Disastrous	Ground badly cracked; many buildings destroyed; some landslides.
11.	Very Disastrous	Few buildings stand; bridges and railways destroyed; water, gas, electricity, telephones out of action.
12.	Catastrophic	Total destruction; objects thrown into the air; much heaving, shaking, and distortion of surface.

SOURCE. D. G. A. Whitten and J. R. V. Brooks, *The Penguin Dictionary of Geology* (Harmondsworth, Eng.: Penguin Books, 1972), 142.

Yet, with all those calamities, disasters, and threats, the people of Guatemala persevered and endured. They showed their resolve and ability to rise anew and reconstruct their lives and their material surroundings from the despair and damages wrought by each calamity, disaster, and threat.

DISASTERS

The most spectacular and damaging disasters of the Spanish colonial period were the frequent earthquakes and volcanic eruptions that brought panic, loss of life and property, and extensive damages, necessitating reconstruction and rebuilding. With thirty-three volcanoes and Guatemala's location along a major fault line, the province experienced numerous natural catastrophes in addition to minor eruptions and earth tremors.

Earthquakes in Guatemala were both major and minor on the Modified Mercalli Scale shown in table 4, which classifies the severity of earthquakes from 1 to 12. This twentieth-century classification, provides some guidelines for evaluating the severity of the quakes in light of contemporary descriptions at the time of their occurrence in colonial Guatemala. Different types of wave motion are generated by earthquakes,[4] one being the undulation of the earth's surface described by Felipe Cádena for the 29 July 1773 earthquake at Santiago de Guatemala, related in chapter 1.[5]

The first recorded earthquake occurred in 1526, accompanying the eruption of the volcano called El Fuego near Almolonga, or today's Antigua. Bernal Díaz del Castillo described the event as being so violent that he and the Almolonga troops (then located at Iximché) could hardly remain on foot.[6] Fifteen years later the eruption of the volcano El Agua (also near Antigua) was accompanied by an earthquake on the night of 10–11 September 1541 after three days of steady rain, causing a mud slide that inundated the capital, Santiago de Guatemala (Ciudad Vieja). This disaster resulted in the deaths of many Spaniards and Indians, including Governor Beatriz de la Cueva, the destruction of the capital, and the decision to move to the valley of Panchoy in 1543, where the new community of Santiago de Guatemala was established.[7] Pacaya Volcano, south of today's Guatemala City, erupted in 1565, and earthquakes in August and September of that year caused extensive damage to the city of Santiago de Guatemala. Other ruinous earthquakes occurred in 1575, 1576, and 1577, while on 26–27 December 1581 a volcanic eruption rained ashes on the capital so densely that the sun was obscured and people could not see each other in the dim light.[8]

Thirty volcanic eruptions and earthquakes occurred in the seventeenth century, according to the compilation of José Antonio Villacorta Calderón, beginning with the damage to Santiago de Guatemala in 1607. Pacaya Volcano again erupted in 1651, and a severe earthquake on 12 February 1689 caused extensive damage once again to the capital.[9]

Although such events continued throughout the eighteenth century, the most disastrous episodes occurred between 27–29 August and 29 September 1717 (the earthquake called San Miguel), on 4 March 1751 (the earthquake called San Casimiro), and on 29 July 1773 (the strongest earthquake of all, called Santa Marta). At eleven o'clock on the night of 27 August 1717, for example, the people of Santiago de Guatemala observed a plume of fire emanating from the summit of Fuego Volcano, growing in size and accompanied by noise and the slow shaking of the earth. When these conditions increased and intensified the following day, the flaming, roaring, and smoking volcano and the rumbling of the ground caused great fright and consternation among the residents of the city. They sought divine help and implored the aid of the saints by praying, conducting processions, and uttering *novenas* (special worship over the course of nine days), asking for God's mercy. Although the shaking of the earth calmed down over the next month, the fire and smoke from the volcano did not cease.

Just when the people assumed that the worst was over, a terrible earthquake occurred at nightfall (seven o'clock) on 29 September, causing widespread destruction not only to the capital but also to surrounding towns, and even to some at considerable distance from the city. "So horrible an earthquake had never been felt," the royal officials reported to the king on 29 October. In less than an hour it destroyed over two thousand buildings, leaving the churches and most of the public buildings still standing useless. Most of the surviving people fled in confusion to outlying villages, some of which were totally destroyed, and their religious accompanied them. Indians abandoned their villages and fled to the nearby mountains and hills. Although the governor and captain general estimated that only about twenty persons had lost their lives, the confusion among the populace was widespread, and damage to buildings was extensive.[10]

Governor Francisco Rodríguez de Rivas met the emergency by placing one hundred armed guards in the principal plaza and near the royal buildings (including the treasury and armory) to prevent looting, and by stationing others near the principal religious structures to prevent desecration and robberies. He also distributed food rations and beef supplies to the people remaining in and returning to the city.[11] He appointed Captain Joseph Bernardo Mencos de Coronado, alcalde ordinario of the town council, and Captain Alexandro Pacheco, alderman of the cabildo, to make an intensive inspection of the ruined buildings of the city and to estimate the cost of rebuilding and repairing them. These two officials reported on the damages to churches, convents, schools, and public buildings, estimating the costs of repair and rebuilding at a total of 345,050 pesos.[12] That figure did not include restoration of damaged homes of Spaniards, Indians, and ladinos in the city and surrounding villages, which the governor estimated amounted to three thousand houses.[13]

Serious consideration was given to moving the capital to a more favorable site as a result of the disaster. On 8 October 1717 the president of the audiencia proposed the move, and evidently the bishop supported the proposal. So too did the Marqués de Valero, the viceroy of New Spain. However, the members of the cabildo believed that it would be better to repair and rebuild the city at its present location, and it appeared as if a royal commercial concession permitting trade with Peru would help meet the costs of repairing buildings. By June 1718, Governor Rodríguez de Rivas had changed his mind, even though the bishop, his secular cabildo, and the oidores of the audiencia still preferred to transfer the capital to another site. Having continued "the maintenance of this city for the usefulness of the public benefit," and believing that it was one of "the most beautiful and plentiful cities that Your Majesty has in these dominions," the governor now favored continuing Santiago de Guatemala at its present location.[14] The king's cedula of 7 July 1720 reflected his concurrence and his decision to rebuild the city instead of moving it to another location.[15]

Although other earthquakes and volcanic eruptions took place thereafter, especially in 1749, 1762, and 1765 (the last caused the bells of the cathedral to ring), the most serious one before the catastrophic event of 29 July 1773 occurred on 4 March 1751. This earthquake of San Casimiro, at eight o'clock in the morning, was of such force that within the short space of one minute it ruined the vaulted ceilings of various churches and badly damaged the cathedral and the royal palace. It also left the majority of the houses of city residents in a lamentable condition. The destruction led to a new burst of construction in the Baroque style that had begun after 1717.[16]

Still the worst was yet to come in the midsummer 1773, when the earthquake of 29 July, called Santa Marta, might have been classified in category 11 or 12, "Very Disastrous" or "Catastrophic" on the modern scale presented in table 4. Actually, this event had been preceded by a series of shocks of considerable duration that were felt by the residents of Santiago de Guatemala beginning between three and four o'clock in the afternoon on 11 June and that continued periodically until 25 July. They damaged houses and roofs in the city, as well as the churches of the Carmelites and the Dominicans and the Royal Hospital of San Juan de Dios; and they caused the residents of the city to remain apprehensive and uneasy.[17] The new governor, captain general, and president of the audiencia, Martín de Mayorga, arrived on 12 June in the midst of the tremors and found the royal palace badly damaged. During the following days the archbishop of Guatemala and the new bishop of Comayagua, Don Antonio Macarulla (en route to his diocese from the bishopric of Durango in northern New Spain), were forced to live for some days at the Potrero de Retana outside of the city because of the damage caused by the 11 June shock.[18]

During the afternoon of 29 July, "the saddest, most pitiful, and terrible day,"[19] between 3:25 and 3:40 P.M., according to different sources, a strong earthquake struck the capital following some brief shocks two and one-half hours earlier and another at 3:15 P.M.[20] These earlier tremors had alerted the people of Santiago de Guatemala, some of whom fled from the capital while others made preparations to seek safety.[21] The strongest quake, of only a few seconds' duration, was so violent that everyone experienced "that sad and fatal hour." People were reported by one eyewitness "kneeling, others lying prone on the ground, others looking toward the sky, many confessing themselves [and] the rest receiving absolutions, and all asking God for mercy."[22] According to Felipe Cádena, the thrusting and undulating of the earth's surface, accompanied by widespread cracking and collapsing of buildings, brought terror and panic to the people, who had difficulty remaining on foot. Some fell into the huge cracks while attempting to flee when the ground gave way beneath them. Some inhabitants lay flat on the surface, where they were joined by animals, which also could not remain upright. Many persons suffocated in the huge dust cloud that blanketed the city, and others were killed or injured by the falling buildings. Although only 123 bodies were found in the ruins after the earthquake, Father Cádena reported that he could not estimate the total numbers of dead and injured other than to say that they were "many"; some persons were probably still buried in the rubble.[23]

Yet the catastrophe of the afternoon earthquake did not end the misery of the Guatemalans or the destruction of the buildings. During

Antigua: ruins of San Francisco and the Volcán de Agua (Agua Volcano) (Samuel Katz Collection, Special Collections, Nettie Lee Benson Latin American Library, University of Texas at Austin).

the night of 29–30 July a storm struck the city, bringing heavy rainfall while the tremors continued. Rain mixed with dust destroyed valuable merchandise, costly furniture, beautiful paintings, archives, papers, and books.[24] Throughout the night the president, archbishop, and city officials worked to help and meet the emergency. Oidor Juan González Bustillo described one instance where he and other officials heard five women crying from inside a building where they were trapped. Although the officials could only provide spiritual help, the women were freed the next morning.[25]

When dawn came on 30 July, one could see everywhere "the most pitiful spectacle," according to González Bustillo. Wherever you looked, he reported, there was a multitude of ruins, especially "in all four corners of, and the houses immediate to, the Plaza Mayor."[26] Militia and regular troops of the Cuerpo de Dragones (dragoon corps)—of whom there were not seventy— were dispatched to various locales to help people, maintain order, and prevent robberies and other evils. All the churches, the cathedral, and the convents, with the exception of the church of the Mercedarians, were destroyed or so weakened that they could not be used. "Completely ruined" also were the royal palace, the Cabildo Secular, other public buildings, and the homes of families.[27] Inhabitants who had suffered through the cold and rainy night without light, coats, and food, now faced a severe shortage of both food and clothing. Displaced too were the religious, many of whom took up temporary residence in *jacales* (huts) within the barrios of the city and in nearby towns.[28] To resolve the food shortage, efforts were made to find and recover wheat, maize, and vegetables from the ruins. In addition, meat, maize, and two hundred cases of biscuits were sent from the royal port of Omoa, where they had been destined for the garrison of the fortress.[29]

Another earthquake occurred on 7 September, and the severe shocks at one o'clock on that afternoon and during the night of 13 December, which González Bustillo reported as stronger than those of 29 July, were accompanied by rockslides in the hills around the city and by openings of the earth in various places within the capital. Most of the damaged buildings left standing by the earthquake of Santa Marta fell, and nearby villages were extensively damaged by the 13 December quake.[30]

In the following year, after extensive inspection of the damage and destruction of Santiago de Guatemala, González Bustillo rendered a report to the king on the status of religious and public buildings. He stated, for example, that the cathedral, was "threatening to be a total ruin." Completed in 1679 after ten years of construction, at a cost of more than 200,000 pesos, and dedicated in October 1680, it had been inspected after the 29 July disaster by engineer Don Antonio Marín, who had found its vaulted arches completely ruined and its walls cracked or split. It imperiled the nearby university since only a small street separated the two structures. The remainder of the cathedral

Antigua: ruins of El Carmen (Samuel Katz Collection, Special Collections, Nettie Lee Benson Latin American Library, University of Texas at Austin).

collapsed during the earthquake of 13 December. The church and convent of Santo Domingo, among others, were described as completely ruined.

Concerning the royal buildings, González Bustillo observed that engineer Marín's evaluation of the royal palace was that it was mostly ruined, including the arch of the main door, the barracks of the royal dragoons, the principal patio, and the four facades of the porticos. The jail was unserviceable, and the royal treasury (Casa de Moneda) was also severely damaged. Although the University of San Carlos did not sustain damage in the 29 July earthquake, it did in that of 13 December when the cathedral collapsed. Engineer Marín's inspection of the archbishop's palace revealed that its upper part had been ruined, and the lower part was out of plumb, cracked, and split. The ayuntamiento or cabildo building was cracked, and the vaulted ceiling of the capitular meeting room had fallen.

After master architect Bernardo Ramírez and escribano Josef Sánchez inspected and surveyed the damages to individual houses, Sánchez estimated that only five or six were intact while an estimated five or six thousand had been destroyed. González Bustillo also noted that the streets were in terrible shape, with great cracks in them, and the public fountains had been badly damaged when the pyramidal or columnar bowls from which the water flowed had fallen.[31] Father Cádena explained that the earthquake of 29 July had also destroyed the conduits or water pipes that brought water to the public and to the city's fountains, while the ruin of ovens and mills contributed to the intensified hunger of the people.

Governor and Captain General Mayorga and the members of the cabildo, in addition to their immediate actions to help the people on 29–30 July, took vigorous and sustained measures to alleviate the suffering of the city's residents. These officials issued orders to have Indians come down from the mountains where they had fled and bring food from their villages to the city; and they appointed Regidor Don Nicolás de Obregón and others to leave the capital to bring grains from the Sierra de Canales and other places; had some of the ovens and mills repaired; ordered the corregidores of Sololá and Quezaltenango to bring wheat and flour; and directed Don Juan de Carrascosa to bring in supplies of maize. To prevent "some individuals of the populace" from robbery and pillage, Governor Mayorga not only placed troops around the city but also issued a bando providing grave punishments for transgressors—two hundred lashes for stealing property valued over ten pesos and ten days in jail for those who robbed less-valuable items. Since the jail had been destroyed, it is hard to imagine how the latter provision could have been implemented, but the gallows he had erected in the main plaza probably served as a deterrent.[32]

Archbishop Pedro Cortés y Larraz provided spiritual and material aid to the suffering people, while the Royal Hospital of San Juan de Dios and the Niñas del Real Colegio de la Presentación rendered aid to the poor. The alcalde mayor of San Salvador, Don Francisco Antonio de Aldama y Guevara, sent cattle to the archbishop for distribution among the people.[33] Furthermore, the archbishop reported to the king in April 1774 that very few religious were remaining in the city, the overwhelming majority having fled to the countryside and the surrounding villages because of the destruction of their churches and habitations, leaving the residents of Santiago de Guatemala without the protection of the prelates. For example, he noted that in the convent of the Dominicans, where there had been sixty to seventy religious before the earthquake, only twelve remained. In the convent of San Francisco, where there had been one hundred religious, only about twelve remained, and the Franciscans in their convent did not know where half of their members were. In the convent of La Merced only twelve of approximately fifty were still present, and the rest, the archbishop complained, lived "of their own free will without my notice."[34]

In the midst of all the suffering, damage, and relief efforts, plans began to transfer the capital to another site. On 4–5 August 1773 the governor held a meeting with officials of the audiencia to discuss the possibility, and they evidently decided to undertake an intensive study of two proposed sites—the llanos of Culebra and Hermita and the llano of Jalapa—and of the Laws of the Indies in relation to each location. These studies had been accomplished by 21 October 1774, when the oidores of the audiencia voted to transfer the capital to the valley of La Hermita. In an earlier letter to the king on 30 June 1774, Governor Mayorga and the members of the audiencia had cited their "enemies," the nearby volcanoes Fuego and Agua, as the real cause of the earthquakes during the previous year, to explain the necessity to move the capital. They also had indicated their preference for the valley of the Virgin or La Hermita, emphasizing that it had been the preferred site for such a transfer since 1717 and that some people, including principal families of Guatemala, already lived there. Furthermore, they noted for the king's information that Archbishop Pedro, who still resided in the old capital, opposed the move. Evidently some officials and other people had already moved to the new site by June 1774, because the governor and oidores reported a lack of clergy in the new community.[35] King Carlos III, after receiving the opinion of his fiscal favoring the transfer, ordered the official move of the capital by a cedula issued on 21 July 1775.[36] Over the course of the years 1775 through 1782, the move took place, although not without opposition from Archbishop Pedro, until he was replaced in 1779, and from the cabildo of the old capital. By 1782, Nueva Guatemala had 13,250 inhabitants—3,338 españoles, 4,268 mestizos, 4,021 mulattos, and 1,623 Indians. Included in the total were 128 clergy, 230 friars, 233 nuns, 297 married couples, 468 single male Spaniards, 608 single female Spaniards, 866 children, and 194 widowed persons (35 widowers and 159 widows).[37]

While the earthquakes of July and December 1773 were the most catastrophic in the history of Spanish colonial Guatemala, they were not the last such natural disasters. In July 1775 a volcanic eruption spread considerable destruction. Pacaya Volcano was south of today's Guatemala City and only six leagues (about eighteen miles) from the old ruined capital of Antigua, or Santiago de Guatemala. Beginning on the night of 2 July, it once again burst forth in a "prodigious eruption of fire," and the eruptions continued through that month, scattering ash and rocks as far north as far as Antigua, where a dense cloud obscured the sun for three days. Pacaya also opened new vents over an area that was one and one-half leagues (about five miles) in length and fifty varas (about 140 feet) in width; scattered ash, rocks, and sand over a considerable distance southward toward the Mar del Sur (Pacific Ocean); and issued a "watery river of fire" that ran south for a distance of two leagues (about six miles), accompanied by a strong odor of sulphur, until it ended in a ravine or gorge. Although that eruption caused nearby Indian villages to be abandoned, it did not produce any tremor at Nueva Guatemala. President Mayorga observed, however, that explosions like shots from a cannon were heard there, and seven or eight tremors were felt in the old capital of Antigua, where Fuego Volcano emitted some fire and smoke.[38]

Earthquakes and volcanic eruptions continued in colonial Guatemala. On the night of 21 July 1816, for example, according to Governor and Captain General José de Bustamante y Guerra, a series of earthquakes began in the Totonicapán district, inflicting much damage on the capital of that province and throughout the district. Some churches fell, according to information sent by parish priests to the governor;[39] however, no details or further information on this event exist in the Archivo General Centro América to provide one with some idea of the severity of and the destruction caused by this earthquake.

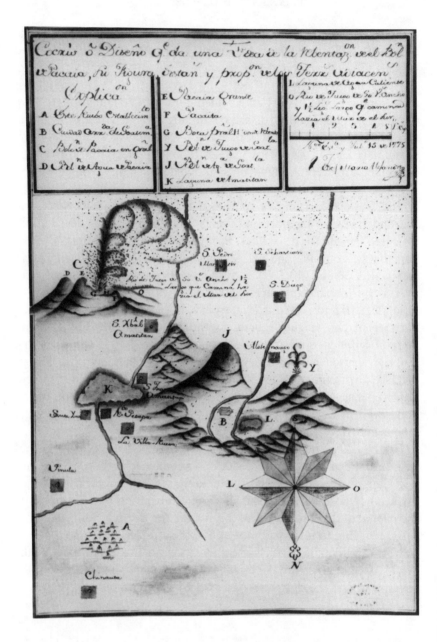

"Croquis . . . que da una idea de la Rebantazón del Bolcán de Pacaia" (rough sketch that gives an idea of the blow up of Pacaya Volcano), by Josef María Alexandre, 15 July 1775 (AGI, Sevilla, Mapas y Planos, Guatemala, 219BIS).

"Croquis de Volcán de Pacaya y terrenos adyacentes" (rough sketch of Pacaya Volcano and adjacent terrains), by Josef María Alexandre? (AGI, Sevilla, Mapas y Planos, Guatemala, 315).

FIRES

Natural disasters were not the only calamities experienced by Guatemalans during the colonial period. Other human miseries were both local and widespread throughout the province. Local threats included such events as a mountain lion descending from the volcano of El Agua to attack herds of cattle near Santiago de Guatemala (Ciudad Vieja) in 1532, ravaging the neighborhood for six months before the animal was killed.[40] Fires, food shortages, crimes, and epidemics also took lives.

Damaging fires were a constant menace, especially in the early years of settlement, when construction of buildings was usually primitive and temporary. Domingo Juarros noted that an extensive conflagration in February 1536 destroyed many thatched houses at Santiago de Guatemala (Almolonga, or Ciudad Vieja).[41] Although such disasters became less frequent in the capital in the late eighteenth century because of improved construction, the flimsy buildings in the barrios of the city and those in many of the provincial towns were susceptible to extensive damage from fires.

One such conflagration occurred during a fiesta in the town of Chiquimulilla in the province of Guazacapán on 7 December 1775. At noon on that day fireworks, caused by launching of rockets during the public celebration of "La Concepción de Nuestra Señora," sparked a fire in the roof of a small house. This spread to other houses and the royal buildings, ultimately destroying, according to the *justicia mayor* (principal justice) of Escuintla, the royal buildings, the cabildo, and fifty-three houses, from which residents could save little. Governor Martín de Mayorga reported that only the archives and the personal belongings of the inhabitants had been saved. The fiscal who reviewed this episode for the king felt such fires could be prevented by absolutely prohibiting the making and launching of fireworks throughout the kingdom. However, Governor Mayorga reported that, in spite of this unfortunate event at Chiquimulilla, the king did not want to prevent the use of fireworks, but emphasized that necessary precautions should be taken to prevent fires in the future resulting from their use.[42]

FOOD SHORTAGES

The periodic food shortages that caused hunger and suffering among the people of Guatemala were more pronounced in the late eighteenth and early nineteenth centuries because of the increased population and unsettled economy. This was especially true in 1776 at Nueva Guatemala after its founding and in the old capital (Antigua) after its destruction. The fiscal of the Audiencia de Guatemala reported that about 24,000 people still resided in the former capital and about 6,000 in the new one. The population in Nueva Guatemala was being rapidly augmented by the arrival of the aldermen of the cabildo with their families and servants, and all sorts of tradesmen (carpenters, bricklayers, masons, and others) who came looking for work. As a result there was a serious shortage of such provisions as meat, flour, and maize.

The shortages often led to violence, as in the case of Monica de la Cruz Salazar, an Indian about forty years old from the pueblo of Santa Ana. She was a patient in the hospital of San Juan de Dios because her hunger, due to the maize and beef shortages, led her into a riot or violent scene in the granary of Nueva Guatemala. Don Manuel Mariano Rodríguez del Valle, professor of medicine and surgery, became her doctor. She explained that she had only one real (one-eighth of a peso) for her entire family and could not pay the established price of two reales for one and one-half pounds of meat. The doctor examined her and found that, crippled from blows received in the scuffle at the granary, she was having difficulty breathing, displayed a high fever, and was experiencing tremors and a great pain in the right forward lateral part of her chest. Although the doctor said he took immediate remedies, after seven days of treatment she developed a large tumor on her right chest. Rodríguez del Valle consulted with Don Manuel Sanz, chief surgeon of the capital, and Don Manuel de Molina, professor of medicine, about her condition. Doctor Don Francisco Saavedra y Carbajal also examined her and reported that the cause of her illness was indeed the tumor on her chest, which had resulted from elbow blows at the granary when the crowd of Indians there became violent.

Monica de la Cruz Salazar died at four o'clock in the morning of 10 September 1776, still in bed number three of the hospital of San Juan de Dios. The escribano reported that a priest testified to the time of her death, and the scribe certified that she had come to the granary seeking to buy maize there, had developed a tumor during her hospitalization, and had died as a result of blows received at the granary. In connection with this case, the alcalde mayor and Manuel Maldonado de Matos, parish priest of San Lucas, testified regarding the scarcity of meat and its inflated price. The alcalde mayor noted the inadequate supplies of meat, wheat, and maize, and pointed out that many hungry people had come to him and complained of the meager distributions that had been made in the capital. Father Maldonado stated that in his parish of San Lucas "there is no meat, neither for him nor for the Indians, who go down to La Hermita so that they can buy meat there, or go with their alcalde who goes around with them."[43]

Another food shortage was recorded in the town of Chiquimulilla in 1811. Governor José de Bustamante y Guerra reported in July that he had been advised of the needs and sufferings of the people in that village, that neither the town nor its environs had enough food and there was a shortage of funds to purchase food. Many had abandoned the town, and those who remained had sought help from the parish priest every day and night, who had used up all his parish funds to purchase food. He had asked for help from the alcalde mayor of Escuintla, but had not received any; and now he requested aid from the governor. After soliciting information on the funds needed, Governor Bustamante noted that the royal treasury had placed 189 pesos at the disposition of the parish priest to help the "naturales" (natives) of Chiquimulilla.[44]

CRIME

As in all societies, past and present, crime caused great misery among the people of colonial Guatemala as well as losses of property. Frequent homicides caused President, Captain General, and Governor Don Joseph de Araujo y Río to issue a decree on 2 December 1748 prohibiting all persons of "any rank from having in his possession or carrying with him pistols, a knife, a dagger, a machete, or any other kind of small arm." The punishments for violation of this order were three consecutive days in chains, for twelve hours each day; two hundred lashes, given the offender in the public streets of Santiago de Guatemala; or a two-year sentence to galley service without salary.

In 1749, Governor Araujo reported on the state of crime in the capital that he had found on succeeding his predecessor, Don Tomás de Rivera y Santa Cruz, in 1748. He reported to the king, in a seven-and-one-half-page letter, that he found the city of Santiago de Guatemala in a "pitiful state" with public drunkenness, gambling, and "other excesses, abuses, and vices." Among the disorders he cited was the manufacture of "aguardiente de caña" (raw rum) and other "noxious drinks," causing scandalous drunkenness, many deaths, wounds, and other public wrongs. Araujo also denounced the widespread gambling in the barracks of the royal palace, where slaves, children, officials, and vagabonds gathered to play games of chance. As well as the many people who carried daggers and small arms, the governor criticized those who went out on the roads to buy provisions in order to resell them in the city at higher prices, forcing the Indians to sow crops and yet causing widespread shortages because of the increased cost of foodstuffs. To combat vice and crimes, he issued decrees and established punishments, as he did in prohibiting the possession and carrying of small arms. As a result of his efforts, Governor Araujo explained that forty-one criminals had been sent to the galleys and fortresses, and some other persons were in chains, thereby making the city "free of its vices."[45]

As one might expect, crime did not cease even with the severity of the punishments imposed by that governor. In 1787, Don Juan Hurtado de Mendoza, scribe of the Royal Audiencia, listed twenty-nine criminal cases heard during the year. They covered transgressions in Guatemala, Honduras, San Salvador, and Costa Rica, ranging from homicides and wounds inflicted by small arms to thievery, robbery, drunkenness, attempted escapes from jail, and simple resistance to law enforcement. In one case, Roman Lorenzo Polanco had simply thrown a rock at the head of Josef María Ortega. Possession and use of small arms against another person were the most common offenses, for which punishments were six to twelve months in the jail ("presidio") of the capital or days spent working on public or religious buildings. Clemente Mendoza y Meléndez, convicted of thievery, was sentenced to three years in jail, but was relieved of the fifty-lash punishment imposed on him by the alcalde ordinario of the cabildo. Mariano Ortiz, found guilty of wounding some soldiers in the capital, was given four years in jail, but the audiencia and chief attorney reduced the sentence to two years. The same punishment was ordered for Josef Sebastián, Miguel, and Antonio Julajuh, who were brought to justice by the alcalde mayor of Sololá for robbing two bulls from Doña Josefa Morales. Dionicio (alias "El Panadero") received two years in jail for wounds inflicted on Cesilia Obregón in Sololá, and Gaspar Xep of the same village was sentenced to the same confinement for blows given an Indian woman there that caused her death nine days later. Drunkenness and fraudulent purchases of cattle in the province of San Salvador resulted in one year in jail, fifty lashes, and a fine ranging from 25 to 500 pesos. One Indian there received a sentence of ten years in the jail of Nueva Guatemala for killing his servant. None of the punishments specified execution of the offender,[46] but one death sentence appears among the 198 civil and 129 criminal cases tried by the Audiencia de Guatemala in 1788.[47]

DISEASE

Diseases and epidemics took many Guatemalan lives during the colonial years. Disastrous epidemics in 1558 and 1586 were noted by Domingo Juarros, the earlier one accompanied by violent nosebleeds and the later one killing one-tenth of the residents at Santiago de Guatemala.[48] A measles epidemic between 1768 and 1770 was a major disaster. Bodies lay in the streets of the capital and roads leading to it. An estimated 10,000 children died in Amatitlán and Sacatépeques, and in the curacy of Alotenango, 74 percent of the infants and 8 percent of the adults died. From 1771 to 1772 a disastrous epidemic in Chiapas brought the deaths of 20,000 Indians, according to the bishop's estimate. The village of San Juan Naqualapán, near San Antonio Suchitepéques, was annihilated in 1764, and in 1796 some 441 tributaries out of a total of 775 died in San Francisco el Alto, while 1,000 women and children died of a rampant disease, as did two-thirds of the village of Jacaltenango. Two years later the residents of Quezaltenango were decimated by a localized, unnamed disease.[49] In 1814 a whooping cough epidemic caused great suffering among the children of Guatemala. Doctor Narciso Esparragosa and Licenciado Pedro Molina issued instructions for combatting the illness, and President José de Bustamante sent copies to the ayuntamientos of all towns in the province, advising them to keep him informed of the increase or decrease of the epidemic.[50]

Of all the diseases, the specific natures of which are often obscure, the most serious, continuous, far-reaching, and deadliest was smallpox. While it decimated the Indian population beginning in the sixteenth century, it also took its toll of Spaniards, Indians, and castas in periodic epidemics. Some of the epidemics listed in the preceding paragraph may have been caused by smallpox. Domingo Juarros specifically cites the smallpox epidemic of 1733 in which more than one thousand inhabitants of Santiago de Guatemala alone died in the space of one month.[51] Other such disasters attributed to smallpox occurred in 1752, 1761, 1780, and 1789.[52] The disastrous epidemic of 1780 struck not only the province of Guatemala but the entire kingdom.[53] Although drought, famine, and the Indians' lack of resistance were factors in the spread of smallpox, poor sanitation, climatological changes, and inadequate medical personnel and facilities also contributed to these disastrous events.

For centuries only a limited number of physicians and hospitals existed in Guatemala to combat the periodic outbreaks of smallpox and other diseases. Usually medical care was more readily available in Santiago de Guatemala, but even there, the hospitals, which were operated by religious orders, were severely limited. In addition to the Royal Hospital of San Juan de Dios, by the eighteenth century the capital had one other, named for San Pedro. With a financial concession of one-ninth and one-half from the annual tithes authorized by the king, the annual revenues of San Pedro totaled 16,279 pesos and 4 reales between 1719 and 1727, ranging from a low figure of 1,601 pesos and 5 reales in 1727 to a high of 2,011 pesos and 5 reales in 1721.

The expenses of the San Pedro hospital in that nine-year period totaled 15,789 pesos and 1 real, leaving a favorable balance of 490 pesos and 3 reales for the nine-year period. They included 300 pesos yearly for the doctor; 30 pesos for the surgeon; and 12 pesos for the *sangrador* (bloodletter); 100 pesos for medicines; 100 pesos for the "rector" (head of the hospital); 100 pesos for the person administering the funds; 24 pesos for the lamp that burned in the church; 24 pesos for the hosts, wax, and wine used in the Mass; 36 pesos for the gardener who took care of the vegetable garden; and a total of 252 pesos for the sacristan, cook, doorman, and other servants. Those expenses totaled 978 pesos.

For the maintenance of the patients, who were all religious and numbered between three and nine in 1727, for example, expenses were itemized monthly for chickens (24, at a total cost of 6 pesos), bread (2 pesos, 7 reales), mutton, chocolate, sugar, candles, little boxes, and beef tortillas. In addition to the cost of firewood, monthly salaries, mattresses, lamps, wine, wax, and hosts, the monthly expenses totaled 77 pesos and 2 reales in January and 86 pesos and 2 reales in February 1727.[54]

During and after the smallpox epidemic of 1780 vast improvements were recorded in the doctors, medical practices, and the availability of hospitals. Accompanying this overall improvement, and partially responsible for it, were the reforms at the University of San Carlos and the establishment of a medical school there. Although a board of doctors (Real Tribunal del Protomedicato) was not created to examine doctors (protomédicos), physicians, bleeders, surgeons, and druggists in Guatemala until 1793, the ayuntamiento or cabildo of Santiago de Guatemala and later Nueva Guatemala, along with the Audiencia de Guatemala, did perform the same function. In June 1780, following the smallpox epidemic of that year, Dr. José Felipe Flores asked permission of Governor and Captain General Matías de Gálvez to introduce inoculation to prevent smallpox. The process consists of opening the skin and introducing the virus from a diseased person into a well one in the hope of causing a light case of smallpox and therefore future immunity to the disease. After some opposition from other physicians, in 1785 the government of Guatemala issued an order requiring inoculation throughout the kingdom and provided a set of instructions describing how to inoculate correctly.[55]

Later a more-effective preventative of smallpox was discovered by Edward Jenner in Europe after twenty years of research and observation. In his 1796 work, *An Inquiry into the Causes and Effects of the Variolac Vaccine,* he described the inoculation of well persons with cowpox vaccine. Although Jenner had predicted that Spaniards would be the last people to embrace vaccination, astonishingly, they were among the first.[56] The first vaccine arrived in Guatemala from Oaxaca in New Spain after articles in the *Gazeta de Guatemala* during the year 1802 repeatedly emphasized the validity of the process and the life-and-death need for the vaccine in the kingdom.[57] Of greatest importance in the widespread introduction of vaccination was the Real Expedición Marítima de la Vacuna (royal maritime smallpox expedition) headed by Francisco Javier de Balmis between 1803 and 1813.

The expedition, authorized and financed by King Carlos IV, traveled to New Spain, the northern frontiers of that kingdom, Central America, South America, and even the Philippines and the Far East after its departure from La Coruña, Spain, on 30 November 1803. It consisted of Dr. Balmis, two assistants, two male nurses, and twenty-two boys, aged between three and nine, who carried the cowpox serum in their arms for transmission to persons in the Americas.[58]

Some years earlier Dr. Flores had gone to Spain, where he had described his use of inoculation and how smallpox was the "first and principal cause of the depopulation of America." The expedition was solicited also by the captain general of the Kingdom of Guatemala on 3 July 1803 when an epidemic developed around Ciudad Real in Chiapas.[59] The vaccine, sent by José Pavón y Muñoz from New Spain on 22 April 1804, took twenty days to arrive in Nueva Guatemala. There the doctors Narciso Esparragosa y Gallardo and José Antonio de Córdoba, using a vaccinating needle, performed the process by pricking the arms of each of six children four times. Seven days later a vesicle was observed on the arm of one of the boys (Alfonso Wading), indicating a successful vaccination. Dr. Esparragosa, who kept a detailed diary, then vaccinated twenty more children. With the arrival of more vaccine from New Spain, transmitted on threads between two glass slides, both doctors continued the process and trained physicians as well as professors and students from the university to administer the cowpox serum. Doctor Córdoba published a vaccination guide, and by 23 June 1804 an estimated four thousand persons had been given the vaccine in Nueva Guatemala and its surrounding towns. Dr. Esparragosa alone vaccinated some 1,132 of them in the first month. A special Mass and ceremony were held in the cathedral on 17 June to give thanks for the vaccine.[60]

Private individuals carried the vaccine to the provinces, including San Salvador, where Dr. Nicolás Monteros vaccinated 9,220 persons shortly after its arrival, and to Nicaragua and Costa Rica. At Antigua, Dr. Esparragosa distributed the serum to the residents of the former capital at houses designated as vaccination centers. He administered the vaccine personally, trained two other doctors to do so, and then at his own expense visited neighboring Indian villages to vaccinate their residents. By the time he had returned to Nueva Guatemala on 8 August he had vaccinated over 9,000 persons in Antigua and its surrounding villages. The Franciscan padre Santiago Pérez of Panajachel brought two boys with him to Antigua, where he watched Dr. Esparragosa vaccinate them. Thereafter he returned to Panajachel and went to four other Indian villages, where he himself vaccinated 784 persons after overcoming some initial resistance to the process.[61]

Francisco Javier de Balmis, the head of the royal expedition, dispatched one of its members, Francisco Pastor, to conduct vaccine to Guatemala. In early July 1804, Pastor and four boys from Mérida in Yucatán proceeded by schooner to Campeche and Laguna de los Términos, then overland to Villahermosa, where 170 persons were vaccinated, including the daughter of the governor. Thereafter Pastor proceeded to Ciudad Real in Chiapas, and finally reached Nueva Guatemala.

In the capital Pastor found little to do since Dr. Esparragosa and Dr. Córdoba had already vaccinated persons in great numbers and had instructed others on the administration of the serum. However, Pastor delivered instructions from Doctor Balmis to create a special vaccination board in Guatemala. This governing body, headed by Dr. Córdoba, consisted of three permanent members, three elected ones, and a secretary, all serving without financial compensation. It also supervised provincial and local *juntas* (boards) charged with the administration of the vaccine in their jurisdictions. A "Reglamento para la Propagación y Estabilidad de la Vacuna en el Reyno de Guatemala" (regulation for the dissemination and stability of the [smallpox] vaccine in the Kingdom of Guatemala) was published in Nueva Guatemala in 1805, and President Antonio González Mollinedo y Saravia sent a full report to the king on vaccination in Guatemala and the establishment of the board. King Carlos IV approved the regulation and authorized the use of public funds to finance the board on 4 September 1805.[62]

Although vaccination and the board administering its use continued until 1817, the administration of the cowpox vaccine was haphazard, and the serum was often in short supply or lost.[63] An 1806 report of the Junta Central de Vacuna (central board of [smallpox] vaccination), which had been established in Nueva Guatemala on 22 March 1805, indicated that in 1805 some 1,462 persons were vaccinated in the capital and 43,982 people in all received the vaccine there by the end of the year, and in the provinces of Jocotenango, Totonicapán, Verapaz, San Salvador, and Sonsonate.[64] Only one document in the Archivo General Centro América relates to continued vaccination in Guatemala after 1805: On 16 February 1815 the *protomédico* (examining doctor) indicated his support of Dr. Don José Ygnacio Palomo's qualifications to vaccinate the pueblo of Chinauta, which was only one of the towns in "absolute need of vaccination."[65]

The introduction of inoculation and vaccination was only one of the major improvements in medical practices that led to an overall population increase in the province and kingdom of Guatemala during the last generation of Spain's presence. There was a notable increase in the

Indian population: the number of tributaries grew from 99,156 in 1788 to 115,935 in 1802, and to 138,505 in 1811.[66] Furthermore, between the 1780s and the end of the Spanish the administration in 1821, medical education and practice in Guatemala were greatly improved by professional medical personnel such as doctors Flores, Esparragosa, and Córdoba, by the establishment of a school of medicine at the University of San Carlos, and by the adoption of the experimental method, along with the creation of the Real Tribunal del Protomedicato in 1793.[67] Those improvements affected the quality of life and helped to overcome or diminish human miseries and the incidence of the disease, especially the periodic, widespread disasters caused by smallpox, although they did not entirely remedy the scarcity of medical personnel and the limited facilities.

DEFENSE

Spain also never entirely succeeded in defending the province and kingdom of Guatemala, which embraced most of today's Central America, from Indian uprisings in the early days and the threat of foreign intrusions and interventions beginning in the late sixteenth century. A succession of internal and external problems only increased the need for Spain to defend colonial Guatemala, where throughout the period of the conquest and initial colonization (1524–40) Spaniards had warred with resisting Quichés, Cakchiqueles, and other nations of Indians. After the early subjugation of the native groups, rebellions and uprisings extended into the 1530s, causing losses of life and property among both Spaniards and Indians. Then attacks by English, French, and Dutch corsairs, buccaneers, privateers, and pirates during the latter half of the sixteenth century and the seventeenth century wreaked havoc and destruction on both the province and kingdom of Guatemala. Actual assaults and fear of foreign attacks led Spain to establish its first defenses to protect its commerce and people in the 1580s and to meet new, intensified threats during the first half of the eighteenth century.[68]

As a result, the principal port and the fortifications of the Kingdom of Guatemala on the Caribbean Sea were changed many times. Until 1573 the major commercial port of the kingdom was Puerto Caballos in what is today Honduras. Because of the port's bad climate, Governor Pedro de Villalobos ordered its commercial activities transferred to the Golfo Dulce. After attacks of English and French pirates in 1578 and 1586, Governor Francisco de Sandé in 1596 ordered a circular tower with firing platforms constructed at the outlet of Lake Izabal. Named Fuerte de Bustamante (Fort Bustamante), it was the beginning of a fortification later known as Castillo de San Felipe.[69] Soon afterward, in 1603, pirates destroyed the fort, and the port of Santo Tomás de Castilla was discovered. Since it was considered more suitable for merchant vessels, Santo Tomás became the Crown's principal port, and a fortress named San Francisco was authorized to protect its harbor. Yet the exposed site near today's Puerto Barrios proved vulnerable to the continuing attacks by pirates in the early 1640s, and in 1644, Governor and President Diego de Avendaño ordered the reoccupation of the Golfo Dulce site with the addition of a trench in front of the abandoned tower of Fort Bustamante, a moat, a parapet, and some redoubts manned by Indians from Verapaz and by ladinos from Amatique. Constructed between 1645 and 1655, the fortress was named San Felipe de Lara in honor of the king and Antonio de Lara, the governor who authorized its building. It served not only to prevent pirate attacks but also as a prison. It burned in 1662 and was reconstructed, only to be attacked by pirates in 1679 and by the Dutch pirate Juan Zanques, with three vessels, in December 1683. Zanques attacked the fort again on 27 April 1684. Its twenty soldiers were no match for the two hundred attackers. The fort surrendered and the Dutchman burned it to the ground.[70]

A *junta de guerra* (war council) was held at Santiago de Guatemala, and the governor decided to reconstruct and fortify Fort San Felipe. On 30 May 1684 he sent a master mason, accompanied by a second mason, officers, and eight soldiers, to recover the cannon and munitions left by the pirates, to study the site and condition of the fort, and to make a report to the president. Having accomplished those tasks, the inspection party estimated that the reconstruction would cost 50,000 pesos if stone nearby were used for the foundation. On 24 July a second junta de guerra endorsed that proposal, and the fiscal of the Consejo de Indias (Royal Council of the Indies) in Spain supported the fort's reconstruction as "the only defense of the province of Guatemala." In 1688, Captain General, Governor and President Jacinto de

Barrios Leal ordered engineer and sergeant major Andrés de Ortiz y Urbina to reconstruct Fort San Felipe, a process that continued into the early 1690s. At the beginning of that decade 110 shotguns were sent to the fortress, and by 1691 some 40,000 pesos had already been spent in rebuilding it. The commander of the garrison served at an annual salary of 500 pesos, and he also performed as alcalde mayor of the village of Amatique. Evidently desertion was a problem, because in 1694 the commander reported the flight of four soldiers from the garrison; but life continued at San Felipe until the 1720s. Then in 1723 merchants proposed to the King, with the support of an oidor of the Audiencia de Guatemala, José Rodezno y Rebolledo, that a new fort be erected at Omoa, near Santo Tomás de Castilla, and that San Felipe be abandoned. The new fort was not built, but in 1726 Fort San Felipe burned once again, and evidently it was not rebuilt until the mid-1740s.[71]

In 1743 reconstruction of Fort San Felipe became a project of Luis Díez de Navarro as part of the engineer's overall plans for the defense of the realm against English expansion and threats along the Caribbean coast. Great Britain's increased commercial activity and expansion from Belize along the Mosquito Coast of Nicaragua and Honduras alarmed Governor and Captain General Pedro de Rivera. Two years after his arrival at Santiago de Guatemala in 1732, he advised the king of the British threat and the influence of Great Britain among the Mosquito Indians and zambos, urging increased defensive measures and military augmentation of the Kingdom of Guatemala. On 1 October 1736, Governor Rivera sent the king a map of Castillo de San Felipe together with a list of its existing properties.[72]

Three years later, when the so-called War of Jenkins's Ear had begun between Great Britain and Spain (allied with France), the king, the Guatemalan authorities, and the people of the province faced serious problems of defense. King Fernando VI ordered Rivera to take measures to prevent a British attack and to construct a fortress on the Río Matina in Costa Rica. Three hundred guns were also shipped from Spain to the president of the audiencia. Engineer Díez de Navarro was sent by the king to inspect the defenses of the Kingdom of Guatemala and make improvements there, including repairs for the fortress of San Felipe. Evidently it had been reoccupied by 1740, when its commander,

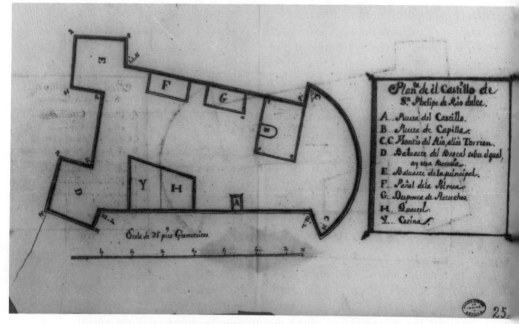

"Plano de el Castillo de San Felipe de Río Dulce," 1740 (AGI, Sevilla, Mapas y Planos, Guatemala, 25).

Don Antonio de Castillo, sent Governor Rivera a report on 5 June concerning its condition and garrison. The walls, according to Castillo, were five varas high (about fourteen feet) and three cuartas wide (about twenty-four inches). There were four bastions at the corners of the fortress, three covered by palm fronds and one by boards. Forty soldiers comprised the garrison, and they were armed with shotguns, flasks, muskets, and powder flasks.[73]

In 1743, Díez de Navarro personally visited and inspected Fort San Felipe. He reported that it was a "small fortification, mistreated, of quadrangular form on one side and circular on the other." Its garrison then consisted of sixty-three men—one commander, one lieutenant, one sergeant, two corporals, one constable or gunner, four artillerymen, thirty-two soldiers, and a Negro corsair captain with twenty soldiers attached to the fortress who went "out privateering in small *piraguas* [pirogues, or small vessels]." Of the thirty-seven bronze

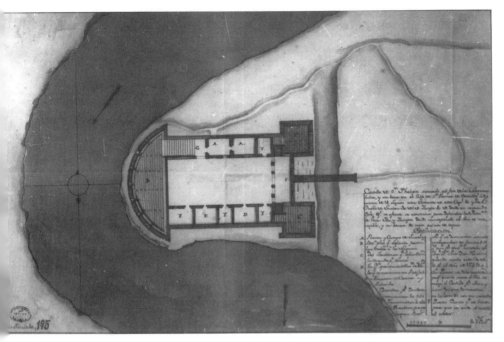

Plan of the Castillo de San Felipe, by Luis Díez Navarro, 1773 (AGI, Guatemala, 195, Mapas y Planos).

cannons, Díez de Navarro noted that twenty-seven were useless and the other ten were of small calibre. For the cannon there were two hundred "and some" balls, but no powder and no serviceable *fusil* (flint fuse). The engineer concluded that the fortress was not capable of resisting attacks from other maritime powers, but urged that it be maintained because of its strategic location and as the port of the "Mar del Norte" (North Sea, meaning the Caribbean) closest to the capital of the kingdom. After he became "ingeniero director" (directing engineer) in 1765, Díez de Navarro advanced ideas for the improvement of San Felipe, sent drawings of the fortress, and at age seventy-three in 1772, initiated projects to repair and improve the fortification. Although it suffered from fires, and from hurricanes such as that in 1772, after which the fortress was in a deplorable state, and from an earthquake in 1785 that split or cracked the walls,

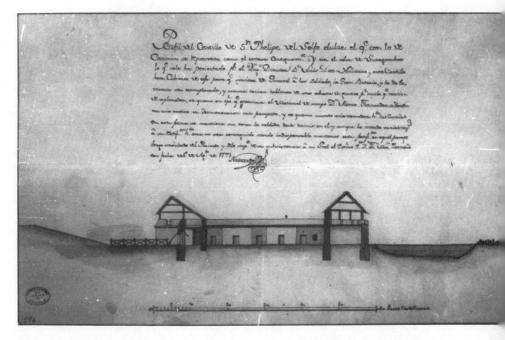

"Perfil del Castillo de San Phelipe del Golfo Dulce" (profile or cross section of the Castle of San Felipe of the Golfo Dulce), by Luis Díez Navarro, 1773 (AGI, Sevilla, Mapas y Planos, Guatemala, 196).

San Felipe continued to be garrisoned until the independence of Guatemala from Spain.[74]

The maintenance and periodic reconstruction projects at San Felipe were only part of the military and defensive measures undertaken by the Bourbon monarchs during the eighteenth century for the Kingdom on Guatemala. Among the military reforms were the repair of fortifications and the construction of new ones from Yucatán to Panamá, campaigns against woodcutters from Belize, the establishment of militia units as the basis for defense, and increases in the numbers of royal troops beginning at the time of the American Revolution in the late 1770s. In spite of such measures, the British expansion and influence among the Mosquito Indians, and the contraband trade, continued to increase. By 1748 the British had established settlements not only at

Castillo de San Felipe de Lara (INGUAT, Guatemalan Tourist Commission)

Belize, but on Roatán Island in the Bay of Honduras and along the Mosquito Coast at Black River, Cape Gracias a Dios, and Bluefields. From those bases they raided Spanish ports, developed an extensive contraband trade, invaded Spanish territory to cut dyewood, and allied themselves with Mosquito Indians and zambos to oppose Spanish authorities. For nearly half of the eighteenth century the confrontation between Spain and Great Britain continued unabated for control over the Kingdom of Guatemala.[75]

Among the countermeasures taken by Díez de Navarro during his long years of service to the kingdom, in addition to rehabilitating the fortress of San Felipe, were his surveys of the military needs of the colony, his efforts to halt infiltration of English settlers and stop the contraband trade, and his promotion of stronger defenses. Realizing the strategic importance of the port of Omoa, he recommended that a fortress be constructed there, a suggestion that had originated with oidor José Rodezno y Rebolledo's proposal to the king on 4 May 1723.[76] Díez Navarro had arrived in Comayagua, Honduras, by 23 February 1743 as instructed by the king's cedula of 24 March 1741 to construct a fort at the mouth of the Río Matina in Costa Rica and another at the port of Trujillo in Honduras. He held a junta de guerra to discuss the possibility of constructing the fort at Omoa instead of at Trujillo.

After a reconnaissance and inspection of the port of Omoa by his lieutenant and assistant engineer, Jerónimo del Rosal, Díez de Navarro informed the king of his preference for the Omoa site because it would serve as a place of embarkation for His Majesty's corsairs, was an "open port" for the registered vessels arriving from Spain, would provide a shipyard for the careening of naval ships, would serve as an impulse for the natives to cultivate nearby lands, was by the way better for Spain's commerce than the Trujillo site, would contribute to the population at Omoa by foreigners from nearby districts, would provide a secure defense for the kingdom, and could be reached by a road extending 140 leagues (about 350 to 400 miles) from the capital of Santiago de Guatemala, and it would be better for Spain's commerce than the Trujillo site. Construction of the fort would stimulate the natives to cultivate nearby lands and would attract settlers to Omoa from nearby districts.[77]

Received in Madrid on 25 January 1746, this report, accompanied by letters of support from Governor Tomás de Rivera y Santa Cruz, was referred to the Council of the Indies and to the fiscal, or attorney general, who approved the establishment of the fortress of San Fernando de Omoa. After considerable delay, King Fernando on 27 March 1752 ordered the construction of the fortress on a reduced scale and for less than the 1,000-man garrison proposed by Díez de Navarro. Evidently President, Captain General, and Governor José Vásquez Prego Montaos y Sotomayor had received earlier instructions to begin the construction of the fortification, because he had ordered the formal beginning of the work on 28 January 1752, financed initially with 50,000 pesos, and later a total of 61,642 pesos, from the royal treasury.

San Fernando de Omoa took twenty years to complete, during which periods of active construction alternated with relative inactivity. Most of the construction was by workers from Honduras and by Negro slaves, such as the 245 who were assigned to it by the president of the audiencia on the death of their owner, José de Palma, in 1769.[78] The costs of building the fortress were paid with royal-treasury funds from Guatemala, Havana, and Comayagua. Between 28 January 1752 and 20 July 1773 they totaled 1,652,793 pesos and 7½ reales.[79] Two years later Governor Martín de Mayorga wrote to Julián de Arriaga in Spain that the fort would be finished the following June. In 1775 construction of the walls was officially completed, but other works, such as the embankments, terraces, and ramparts, were not yet finished. On 28 December 1777 the governor and captain general declared construction completed and garrisoned the fort with militiamen who had been working on it. He also advised the governor of the province of Comayagua to supply one hundred men every two months to man the new fortification of San Fernando de Omoa.[80]

Militia forces constituted the bulk of military personnel organized for the defense of the Kingdom of Guatemala during the last half of the eighteenth century. President and Governor Don Alonso de Arcos y Moreno advised the King, in a letter of 17 February 1755 to his principal minister for the American Kingdoms Julián de Arriaga, that he (Arcos y Moreno) had established companies of fifty-three men each, including sergeants, corporals, and drummers. Commanded by captains, lieutenants, and sublieutenants *(alféreces),* these companies were grouped into regiments and governed by written regulations.[81] The governor's detailed regulations praised the militia and the great "heroes" it had produced as part of the military profession. They also emphasized that militia service was a valorous occupation, a "school of good policy, and a stimulus to good work, generosity, prudence, and honor." Citing the example of Pelayo's heroic resistance with citizen soldiers to the Moslems at Covadonga in northern Spain during the early eighth century, Governor Arcos y Moreno urged all inhabitants of the Kingdom of Guatemala to serve promptly for their sovereign, the republic, and their own interests.[82]

The regulations provided for the organization, privileges, armament, clothing, recruitment, marching order on campaigns, and inspections of militia forces throughout the kingdom. Each regiment, commanded by a colonel or lieutenant colonel, was composed of twelve companies, each of fifty-three men, including sergeants, four corporals, and a drummer in addition to their captains, lieutenants, and sublieutenants. Officers serving as battalion commanders (colonels and lieutenant colonels) were supplemented by a sergeant major and an assistant, but these personnel were to be independent from the companies themselves. Militiamen, whether officers or soldiers, were to have the distinctions and privileges of the *fuero militar* (privileges of the military) at all times, and the chain of command was to be respected and obeyed from the colonel down to the soldiers. Reviews of militia units were to be conducted every six months by the governor of the province or his lieutenant, and the king was to name the colonel of the militia regiment for the city and valley of Guatemala. This officer was to be salaried.

All militia, except for the officers, were to be equipped with firearms maintained in the armory of the town where their unit had been formed and stationed. Soldiers were to be furnished blue uniforms with trousers of the same color and jackets or waistcoats trimmed with a red ruffle. Officers wore the same uniform, but with a hat trimmed with "gold and half white."

Recruits had to be older than eighteen and not more than fifty-six years of age. No defective person or anyone incapable of bearing arms or going out on campaigns was to be enlisted. The sergeant major and his assistant were to maintain a service record for everyone and conduct inspections of the companies, instructing their sergeants and corporals in the handling and use of arms and the proper manner of assembling and marching. The battalions of Spaniards were to be separate from those of the mestizos and mulattos, who were always to march behind the whites ("los blancos"), although they would have the same privileges as the Spaniards. Captains and sublieutenants were to march at the front of their company with the banner, while the lieutenant would station himself at the rear of the company while mustering the troops, and would move to the front thereafter in advance of the sergeants. The sergeant major and his assistant were to keep a list of boys between the ages of fourteen and eighteen in their communities, but were instructed not to enlist anyone before his eighteenth birthday. Eight to twelve cavalry companies were also to be formed, each with a captain, lieutenant, sublieutenant, sergeant, three corporals, and forty soldiers for a total of forty-seven men. A squadron of cavalry consisted of three companies. The officers and men of these companies were to wear a blue uniform with a red ruffle, and buskins, or half boots, and they carried both a sword and firearms—musket, carbine, and pistols.[83]

A report of 20 August 1756 gave detailed information about the infantry and cavalry regiments of militia for the entire Kingdom of Guatemala. One regiment, commanded by a colonel with the assistance of a sergeant major, was garrisoned in the governancy of Guatemala, meaning the city of Santiago de Guatemala and two districts in the valleys of Chimaltenango and Sacatepéques. There were twenty-one infantry companies within the capital, three in Chimaltenango, and eleven in Sacatépeques. Each company had one captain, one lieutenant, and one sublieutenant. The total number of militiamen was 1,475 for Santiago de Guatemala, 197 for Chimaltenango, and 1,287 for Sacatepéques. In addition, there were six cavalry companies in the capital, two at Chimaltenango, and one at Sacatepéques, each officered by a captain, lieutenant, and sublieutenant. There were 349 mounted cavalrymen in the capital, 123 in Chimaltenango, and 71 in Sacatepéques. Thus the militia forces for Santiago de Guatemala and its two districts totaled 3,636 men: one colonel, one sergeant major, 132 officers, and 3,502 soldiers and cavalrymen.

There were two regiments of twelve infantry companies each, and a total of four cavalry companies, organized at Ciudad Real in Chiapas. Each regiment there was commanded by a colonel, a lieutenant colonel, a sergeant major, and an assistant, while each company, infantry and cavalry, was led by a captain, lieutenant, and sublieutenant. There were 1,564 infantrymen and 130 cavalry in these companies. In addition, there were four infantry companies in the jurisdiction of Soconusco, four at Huehuetenango, two at Quezaltenango, one at Sololá, five at Guaiscapán, and five cavalry companies at San Antonio, all within the province of Guatemala. When added to the units of militia stationed in Costa Rica, Nicaragua, Honduras, and San Salvador, the total was impressive: nineteen regiments, 343 infantry companies, and 184 cavalry companies, including 1,103 infantry officers and 21,952 soldiers, along with 585 cavalry officers and 9,493 mounted men—for a grand total of 33,133 militiamen for the defense of the Kingdom of Guatemala.[84]

The total numbers and the organization of the militia may have made it appear capable of defending the kingdom, and they reflected the increased military emphasis of President and Governor Arcos y Moreno (who was also a field marshal in the Spanish army). But the truth of the matter was that the militia were poorly and inadequately armed, lacked provisions, and were undisciplined and shoddily trained. One year after the organization of the militia units, President Arcos y Moreno reported on the shortages of firearms. Although some had been received and distributed to the garrisons of Omoa and in Tegucigalpa, Costa Rica, Sonsonate, and in the province of Guatemala itself, especially in the *alcaldías mayores* (districts) of Chiquimula and Zacapa. The president noted that although the city of Santiago de Guatemala had 660 weapons on hand, it could use an additional 3,000 for its own defense and that of the provinces under its jurisdiction. While Arcos y Moreno observed that 3,000 firearms had arrived and been distributed, he requested that 8,340 more be sent for the defense of the capital and the entire kingdom.[85]

The condition of the militia forces, perhaps never very good, was in a deplorable state by 1764, and had not improved by the end of the 1770s. On 11 December 1764, Don Julián de Arriaga wrote to Pedro de Salazar Nátera y Mendoza, who had been appointed to relieve Alonso Fernández de Heredia as governor, captain general, and president of the Kingdom of Guatemala. Arriaga advised the new official that the kingdom's "sole defense" until then had been its militias and that they were "so badly armed and with such poor discipline that they scarcely merit the name." Except for procuring some arms and providing some early instruction for militiamen, almost nothing had been done, according to Arriaga, by the present governor, Fernández de Heredia, who felt that it was not possible to organize them since pardos, other mestizos, and Negros had gone "unclothed and barefooted" all their lives and it was impractical to dress them with uniforms and shoe them "so that they could not move." Furthermore, according to information Arriaga had from the present governor, these militiamen would defend only their own houses, haciendas, and families. The few Spaniards who were there (in the capital) were so well off as tradesmen that they disdained service in the militia and were fed up with wearing the blue uniforms. However, Arriaga emphasized that the king, Carlos III, supported the idea of militias, not garrisons of royal troops. Therefore, the minister instructed the new president to dedicate himself to disciplining and training the militias, uniforming them, taking necessary defensive measures, and keeping the roads open, especially the one to the port of Omoa from the capital and those to the "small forts in their places."[86]

Three years later, President Salazar sent a status report to Arriaga on the state of the kingdom's militias. At the end of 1767 there were 109 infantry companies of Spaniards (españoles), 236 of mulattos, and 28 of mestizos. In addition, there were 75 cavalry companies of Spaniards, 88 of mulattos, and 21 of mestizos. With 21,814 infantry militiamen and 8,927 cavalry, there were in all 30,741 militiamen for the defense of the entire kingdom. However, in April 1768, Inspector Alexandro O'Reilly reported to Arriaga that he considered the numbers of mulattos excessive and the total militia forces "much more than needed." The inspector believed that in time of war there would be no funds to maintain the militia, and he observed that no other force existed in the Kingdom of Guatemala beside the sixty dragoons of the regular Spanish army stationed in the capital. He feared that these royal troops would be unable to put down a popular rebellion and that the militia forces, so well armed, could establish their independence from the king. Therefore, he urged that the size of the militias be greatly reduced, that more emphasis be placed on recruiting Spaniards, and that the kingdom continue to count on the loyalty of certain militia units to maintain its defenses.[87] Indicative of the poor state of the militia forces by 1778 was their status at the fortress of San Fernando de Omoa when the new commandant and inspector of troops, Lieutenant Colonel Matías de Gálvez, arrived on 29 June 1778. His inspection of 4 July revealed that the garrison's second company was in a "deplorable state" with its captain and many others ill, the position of lieutenant vacant, the sublieutenant absent in Nueva Guatemala, and only fifteen of an authorized complement of twenty-seven men present for duty.[88]

In 1778–79, in addition to the militia forces, there were some two hundred Spanish regular troops stationed in Nueva Guatemala. They included the original sixty in two companies of dragoons, augmented by the arrival of one hundred Spanish *tropa veterana* (veteran troops) in 1777.[89] At that time the company of *granaderos* (grenadiers, or artillery) and that of *fusileros* (riflemen, or musketeers) each had a captain, a lieutenant, a sublieutenant, two sergeants, two corporals, a drummer, and an unspecified number of grenadiers or soldiers as was appropriate to the company. Pay scales reveal that rifle-company personnel were paid less than grenadiers. For example, the captain of grenadiers received 70 pesos monthly; the lieutenant, 44; the sublieutenant, 34; sergeants, 18 or 16; corporals, 12 or 11; the drummer, 11; and each grenadier, 10. The captain of a rifle company, on the other hand, was paid 62 pesos monthly; the lieutenant, 40; the sublieutenant, 32; sergeants, 16 or 14; corporals, 11 or 10; the drummer, 10; and each soldier, 9. In addition, at headquarters there were a colonel (paid 218 pesos monthly), a lieutenant colonel, a sergeant major, an assistant, a standard-bearer, a chaplain, a surgeon, an armorer, a lead drummer, and two fifers (the latter paid 12 and 10 pesos). Furthermore, a subsidy of 2 reales and 14 maravidies for each position provided for the expenses of the soldiers or grenadiers, for their training with arms, and the costs of hiring a barber and a washerwoman. The soldiers also received 1½ reales per day for their mess. "No slave, nor Negro, nor pardo, even if they be free," was admitted into the tropa veterana.[90] Although the militia forces supplemented these regulars, they were mostly mulattos with poor discipline who had arms for only half of their numbers and no armorer to repair and maintain the weapons, and they lacked skill in the use of their firearms.[91]

During the presidency and governorship of Matías de Gálvez (1779–83) the British threat to the Kingdom of Guatemala, and Spain's declaration of war against Great Britain in 1779 during the American Revolution, necessitated vast improvements in military defenses, as well as offensive operations against the enemy. After ten months as inspector of the troops and second-in-command to Captain General Martín de Mayorga, Gálvez became president of the Audiencia de Guatemala and captain general and governor of the Kingdom of Guatemala officially on 15 May 1779. He had performed in an exemplary fashion as inspector of the troops and had initiated military reforms with the support of President Mayorga. On taking office he immediately took measures to improve the garrison at San Fernando de Omoa, which he felt was the "key and outer wall of the kingdom."[92]

Although Gálvez faced and resolved many problems during his four years as head of the Spanish administration—for example, pursuing an aggressive policy of completing the removal of civil and religious authorities from Santiago de Guatemala (Antigua) to Nueva Guatemala—Gálvez concentrated on his role as captain general in the defense of the kingdom. Soon after he took office, Spain declared war as an ally of France against Great Britain, thereby indirectly aiding the cause of the patriots in the American Revolution. Within months Gálvez had filled vacancies in the officer ranks, had arranged for the purchase of supplies and munitions, had improved and mobilized both regular and militia forces, had requisitioned ships and men from Havana, Campeche, and Cartagena, and had planned an offensive against the fortress of Omoa, which the British seized on 20 October 1779.[93]

Gálvez's plans and preparations were not carried out from afar, nor were they hastily conceived. He personally took charge of an army of approximately one thousand men to recover the fortress for Spain. Marching from the capital to San Pedro Sula in Honduras, after months of detailed planning and meticulous preparations, he prepared for the siege and assault on Omoa, which he conducted successfully during the last week of November 1779. On 28 November the British defenders, commanded by William Dalrymple, fled on ships to Jamaica, and Gálvez peacefully reoccupied the fort the next day. For this successful campaign, Gálvez was promoted to brigadier.[94]

Yet, that was only the beginning of Gálvez's offensive against the British, who had expanded their operations along the coasts of Honduras and Nicaragua and had invaded as far west as the port of Trujillo in today's Honduras. Concentrating first on the British invasion of Nicaragua and the threat to Granada there, Gálvez planned, prepared, and conducted a defense of the region and an offensive against the enemy. He reached the Nicaraguan capital on 22 February 1780 and personally saw to its defenses, organizing a patrol of vessels on Lake Nicaragua, mobilizing the local militia, and transporting them across the lake to its eastern shore. At that site he supervised the construction of a new fort, named San Carlos in honor of the king, one hundred yards in diameter and with a moat protecting it from the land side.

Protected by sixteen cannon facing landward and by small schooners, each with a single cannon, from the lakeside, Fort San Carlos thwarted

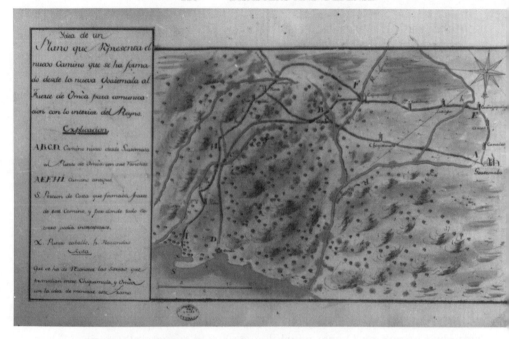

"Idea de un plano que representa el nuevo camino que se ha formado desde la Nueva Goatemala al fuerte de Omoa" (idea of a plan for a new road from Nueva Guatemala to Fort Omoa), sent with letter of Matías de Gálvez, 6 August 1779 (AGI, Sevilla, Mapas y Planos, Guatemala, 238).

the British advance along the Río San Juan to seize control of Lake Nicaragua and advance on Granada. From it Gálvez subsequently provided for an advance down the Río San Juan, seizing British posts at Fort Inmaculada by the end of December 1780, and at San Juan del Río, which his forces seized from the enemy on 4 January 1781. Although Gálvez did not personally lead this Spanish force, his plans were carried out by Captain Tomás de Juliá with some two hundred troops, all of whom Gálvez praised for their success in a letter to the king. In his correspondence to Minister of the Indies José de Gálvez, the president and captain general proclaimed, "I promised the king to frustrate the British designs and projects in this part of his dominions, and now enjoy the honor of giving proof . . . that in it I promised to continue it to the natural result, taking from the enemy the armament with which he occupied the mouth of the Río San Juan to sustain the [Spanish] garrison at the fort."[95]

Before the end of this Nicaraguan campaign, Gálvez was back in Nueva Guatemala planning and preparing for an offensive against the British along the Honduran coast and the British headquarters on Roatán Island in the Bay of Honduras. Throughout the year 1781 he planned and organized a military and naval campaign by land and by sea against the British garrisons and their Mosquito Indian allies. His strategy was to capture Britain's headquarters and supply center for the mainland by using naval vessels requisitioned from Campeche, Havana, Cartagena, and Portobelo, together with troops from those locations, in addition to his own Central American forces.

Once assembled, Gálvez's land forces were to advance along the Honduran and Nicaraguan coasts from Trujillo to the Río San Juan, seizing the enemy's posts at Black River and Bluefields along the way. Now promoted to field marshal, Gálvez reorganized and increased the size and the training of his militias; extended the fuero militar to all militiamen, including drummers and fifers; brought battalions up to authorized strengths; reshuffled his officers on the basis of meritorious service in Nicaragua; obtained arms, supplies, and funds for an army that totaled 15,000 troops, with an equal number of reserves, by the end of 1781; and requisitioned ships from other Spanish jurisdictions around the Caribbean.[96]

On 17 December 1781, Gálvez marched out of Nueva Guatemala to Omoa, where three Spanish ships transported him and six hundred troops to the assembly point at San Jorge Olanchita, about eighty miles from Trujillo, Honduras. Arriving there on 12 February 1782, the captain general organized his forces for the land campaign against Trujillo and beyond, while simultaneously assaulting Roatán Island. Between 10 and 14 March he embarked his troops—one hundred regulars and five hundred militiamen—with supplies for a twenty-day campaign against Roatán. A flotilla of twenty-eight vessels, including three frigates, one corvette, and twenty-four smaller craft of varying sizes and capacities, convoyed the soldiers under Gálvez's personal command to Roatán, where they arrived the morning of 15 March. After bombarding the fortress protecting Port Royal, Gálvez sent an officer, Don Enrique Reinaldo MacDonnell (the only person who spoke

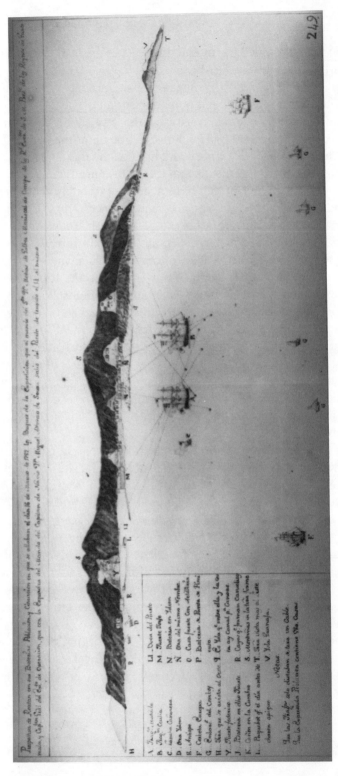

"Perspectiva de Roatán . . . (Roatán in perspective), sent with letter of Matías de Gálvez, 20 March 1782 (AGI, Sevilla, Mapas y Planos, Guatemala, 249).

English), to negotiate the surrender of the port. When the British refused to capitulate, the bombardment resumed until the enemy surrendered on 17 March. Having captured 135 English of both sexes as prisoners, including 60 troops, plus 203 Negro slaves, along with 26 cannon, 232 rifles, 35 quintals of powder (about 3,500 pounds), and 6 enemy flags, Gálvez said that he treated the prisoners with "humanity and liberality" before he sent them to Havana. Thereafter, he burned the town, destroyed the fort, and took the cannon, rifles, and powder with him when he sailed back to the mainland, where he reported to José de Galvez on 20 April that the "English establishment at Roatán has been destroyed."[97]

Meanwhile, Gálvez's land forces had taken Trujillo from the British, but were bogged down beyond it. Gálvez took personal charge at Trujillo and dispatched an army to take the British post at Black River, while he returned to Nueva Guatemala. Between 30 March and 2 April the Spanish force of 1,500 troops succeeded in capturing five enemy forts along the Río Tinto, but it bogged down and was attacked by British forces and their Mosquito allies. The seagoing portion of this campaign did land at Black River, but the Spanish garrison established there was subsequently attacked by the enemy and massacred on 21 April 1782, while the land force, which had not yet reached that point, retreated westward. Thus the final campaign of Gálvez along the Caribbean coast was only partially successful, and it had suffered severe setbacks by the time the preliminary treaty of peace between Great Britain and Spain was signed on 30 November 1782.[98] Gálvez in the following year was promoted to lieutenant general and appointed as viceroy of New Spain, a position that he held until his death on 3 November 1784.[99]

The defenses and campaigns of Matías de Gálvez in this critical period reveal much about colonial Guatemala in the last quarter of the eighteenth century. The increased size of the militia and regular forces is evident throughout the expeditions to Omoa, Roatán, Nicaragua, and Honduras. With relatively small numbers of royal troops, augmented by well-trained, disciplined, and provisioned militia, both the province and kingdom of Guatemala were defended successfully from the serious British threat. Although Spain did not succeed completely in eliminating this threat or in ending the contraband trade, the Spanish forces did thwart British expansion. Finally, the intense emphasis on defense and on establishing effective military forces accentuated the role of the captain general in the administration of the Kingdom of Guatemala. After Gálvez a succession of senior military officers served as president of the audiencia, governor of the province and kingdom, and captain general of its military forces until Guatemala declared its independence from Spain in 1821.

Brigadier José de Estachería, successor of Gálvez, reported in 1785 on the state of the kingdom's military forces, especially their rifles, bayonets, cartridge belts, and broadswords. While his report covered the entire kingdom, he specified that the capital of Nueva Guatemala, for example, had 493 rifles in good condition, 422 in a mediocre state, and 2 that were useless. At Omoa there were 1,743 rifles in good condition, 411 classified as mediocre, and 277 that were useless. At the Castillo del Golfo (the fortress on the Gulf at the mouth of the Río Dulce, or San Felipe) there were no rifles in good condition, 25 that were mediocre, and 35 that were useless, while the fortress of Petén Itzá (in Yucatán) had 59 in good condition, 41 that were mediocre, and 14 that were useless. Similarly, Estachería detailed the numbers and quality of rifles, bayonets, cartridge belts, and broadswords for the districts of Chiquimula, Quezaltenango, Realejo, Chimaltenango, Sacatapéques, Sololá, Totonicapán, San Antonio, Ciudad Real, and Verapaz. All the weapons at these locations within colonial Guatemala evidently were possessed by local militias.[100]

During the independence era from 1808 to 1821 the threat to the province and kingdom of Guatemala was not foreign but internal. Defensive measures were against a possible invasion of insurgents from New Spain and against conspiracies and possible revolts within the kingdom, especially during the administrations of Lieutenant General José de Bustamante y Guerra (1811–18) and his successors, who were all senior military officers. The military preparations and policies belong appropriately to the tumultuous period discussed in the following chapter.

CHAPTER 9

Instability and Independence

COLONIAL GUATEMALA during the last twenty years or so of the Spanish presence was wracked by economic decline, the collapse of the indigo trade, factionalism, an intense struggle between liberals and conservatives, conspiracy, and finally an increasing desire among discontented intellectuals for independence from Spain. In this period of instability and turmoil the Spanish authorities, headed by the governor, captain general, and president, were usually allied with the audiencia in the struggle to maintain the authority of and loyalty to the absolutist principles of the king and administrative bodies in Spain. Arrayed against them were the members of the ayuntamiento or cabildo of Nueva Guatemala, a powerful group of liberal merchants advocating free trade and popular sovereignty in government, and such institutions and organizations as the Sociedad Económica de Amigos del País, the faculty and graduates of the University of San Carlos, who advocated the science and reason of the Enlightenment, and the editors of the *Gazeta de Guatemala*.

Added to the problems within Guatemala, and crucial in the course of events leading to independence, were the instability of the government in Spain between 1808 and 1821 and nearby developments in New Spain during its long struggle for Mexican independence. The rise of Emperor Napoleon Bonaparte in Europe, Spain's involvement in European conflicts and diplomatic changes of face, and the decline in the quality and prestige of the Bourbon monarchy during the later years of the reign of Carlos IV, led to his replacement by Fernando VII in 1808, all contributed to developments in Guatemala, the kingdom, and the rest of Spanish America. Napoleon's invasion of Spain in 1807–1808, while attempting to force his Continental System on Portugal, resulted in the captivity of both Carlos IV and Fernando VII at

Bayonne, as well as the imposition of Joseph Bonaparte as king of Spain. Spaniards opposed this usurper of the Crown, expressed their loyalty to the Bourbons, and rose in armed resistance against the French army on their soil. They formed temporary governing bodies, or juntas, in the absence of Crown authority, which were ultimately consolidated into the Junta Central de Cádiz, a liberal body that wrote the Constitution of 1812 based on popular sovereignty, a constitutional monarchy, the legislative supremacy of the Cortes (the Spanish parliament), free trade, and above all integration of the American colonies into the Spanish government via a representative system. When Fernando VII was restored in 1814, he abolished the liberal Constitution of 1812 and endeavored to restore conservatism and the absolute rule of his forefathers. Six years later, on 1 January 1820, Colonel Rafael Riego, with troops assembled at Cádiz for use in suppressing uprisings in America, revolted at the instigation and with the support of Spanish liberals. They succeeded in restoring the Constitution of 1812 and requiring Fernando VII to profess his support of that document, thereby reluctantly agreeing to rule as a constitutional monarch for the next three years.

These events destabilized Spain and also caused reactions in New Spain and the Kingdom of Guatemala. Liberal and conservative elements waged war in New Spain from the time of the calling of the *cabildo abierto* (open town meeting) in Mexico City, through the insurgencies of Fathers Miguel de Hidalgo y Costilla and José María Morelos, to the Plan de Iguala and the establishment of independence for Mexico in late September 1821. While the struggle between conservatives and liberals waxed and waned in New Spain between 1808 and 1821, eventhough conservatives controlled the government in Mexico City, that struggle and the resulting clashes of arms had an effect on the Kingdom of Guatemala. Especially in the capital of Nueva Guatemala, Spanish officials feared the possible spread of ideas and insurgencies from nearby regions of New Spain and they took measures to prevent rebellions and conspiracies that might lead to independence.

During the first two decades of the nineteenth century colonial Guatemala was ruled only by senior military officers as the president, captain general, and governor (the *jefe político superior,* or supreme political chief, after 1812). Two of them were authoritarian and conservative in their views and practices: Antonio González Mollinedo y Saravia and José de Bustamante y Guerra. Their opposition to new influences—both internal and external—and their attempts to adjust to the rapid changes in Spain were evident in the last decades before independence in an early period from 1800 to 1811 and in the middle period from 1811 to 1818. Between 1818 and 1821 Guatemala, was increasingly unstable before the declaration of independence on 15 September 1821, influenced by the Riego Revolt in Spain and the establishment of Mexico's independence in the same month and year as Guatemala's.

CONSERVATIVE REACTIONS, 1800–1811

Bourbon reforms continued to tighten and centralize the Spanish administration of the Kingdom of Guatemala at the end of the eighteenth century. The reforms, along with the decline and collapse of the indigo market and the continued contraband trade, intensified differences between the government bureaucracy, on the one hand, and the local aristocracy, on the other. In addition, the provinces, especially San Salvador, increasingly opposed being administered and controlled from Guatemala.[1] Such foreign ideas as those of the Enlightenment, disseminated through University of San Carlos, heightened the conflict. Having enjoyed trade temporarily with the United States and Great Britain at the end of the 1790s, as a result of Spain's changing alliances in Europe, the Guatemalan elite thereafter campaigned for its permanent establishment as a solution to the economic woes caused in part by the decline of the indigo trade. This caused intense rivalry between the indigo growers and the *consulado*, or merchant guild, which endeavored to maintain Spain's economic controls over commerce.[2]

Among those who promoted free trade, popular sovereignty, and relaxed Spanish restrictions on commerce were such persons as the wealthy Juan Fermín Aycinena (who had purchased the title of a marqués), Mariano Aycinena, José de Aycinena, Pedro Molina, José Cecilio del Valle, Ignacio Beteta, Alejandro Ramírez, and Juan Bautista Irisśari of San Salvador. In the 1790s many of them and others had formed the core of the Sociedad Económica de los Amigos del País, through which they embraced science, democratic ideas, and concepts of reform in the Spanish political and economic administration of the kingdom. The Sociedad's liberalism led to its suppression between 1800 and 1811, but the ideas of change and progress lived on in the pages of the *Gazeta de Guatemala* thereafter.[3] Since most of the opponents of Spanish policies and restrictions were criollos, this intensified the struggle between them and the peninsulares, creating a power struggle between the two upper classes of colonial society. This conflict reached its peak between 1812 and 1821, but its origins were forged in the earlier period.

José Cecilio del Valle merits special attention because of his influence from 1800 through independence, as well as during the years of the United Provinces of Central America (from 1824 until his death at age fifty-seven on 2 March 1834). Born in Choluteca in Honduras in the fall of 1776 (22 November), he moved with his family to Nueva Guatemala in 1787, where he enrolled in the Belén school. By 1790–91 he had become a fourteen-year-old student at the University of San Carlos, where he was exposed to the enlightened ideas of Fray José Liendo y Goicoechea, Dr. José Felipe Flores, and Dr. Narciso Esparragosa. Valle received his bachelor's degree in 1794, passing his examination and defending his thesis on general and specific physics. He then began to study law. Although he found it irritating and tedious, by 28 August 1803 he had passed his examination, paid the required tax, and submitted documents to receive his law degree. Admitted to the bar, he also became the censor for the *Gazeta de Guatemala,* for which he also wrote essays ranging over geography, history, the sciences, education, and politics, promoting the ideas of freedom and the Enlightenment. He remained, however, a loyal servant of the king between 1808 and 1818, and served Governor José de Bustamante as secretary and later as interim attorney. His friendship with Bustamante caused Valle to be out of favor with Bustamante's successor, but he participated in the meeting of the cabildo abierto on 15 September 1821 and accepted the idea of independence, which he had advocated since he began publishing *El Amigo de la Patria* on 6 October 1820, and he drafted the Central American declaration of independence.[4]

Jefe de Escuadra (chief of a cavalry squadron) José Domas y Valle governed the Kingdom of Guatemala from 1794 to 1801, a period in which Spain experienced warfare and changing alliances in Europe and permitted trade with such neutral nations as the United States and, temporarily, with Great Britain. In 1799 a government order required all communities of one hundred taxpayers or more to provide elementary schools, but there is no evidence that this educational advance was ever implemented.[5] During the administration of Domas y Valle, the Sociedad Económica de los Amigos del País was founded and suppressed, but in 1801, when the decrepit and senile Domas y Valle retired from office, he was succeeded by Lieutenant General Antonio González Mollinedo y Saravia.[6]

General González served as governor, captain general, and president of the Audiencia de Guatemala from 1801 to 1811, a period marked by the declining economy, the growth of contraband trade, the increasing authority and power of the cabildo of Nueva Guatemala, and uncertainty, as well as tension, after the Napoleonic invasion of Spain. When he arrived in Guatemala on 28 July 1801, González found the kingdom in a "state of misery," according to historian Ramón A. Salazar.[7] Of middle age and distinguished as a valiant soldier who had campaigned at Ceuta, Oran, and on the Iberian Peninsula, González was modest and well intentioned. Since Nueva Guatemala was still in a state of construction, the new governor and captain general addressed himself to completing the churches, including the cathedral, which was finished during his administration. He also issued orders prohibiting drunkenness, processions of penitents, and the granting of repartimientos, as well as establishing a nightly curfew in the capital. Furthermore, he complied with a royal order permitting freedom of trade at the Pacific port of Acajutla in Sonsonate; allowed Guatemalan merchants to establish commercial relations with companies in Boston, Philadelphia, and Jamaica; and granted the trading house of Juan Bautista Irissari permission to trade in "foreign merchandise." While trying to maintain public order and inhibit crime in the capital, González's permissive policies contributed greatly to the growth of illegal commerce. Inflation, crop failures, interdiction of legal trade because of Spain's involvement in European wars after 1804, and the declining indigo market, all added to the economic woes of the province and the kingdom.[8]

Contributing to those economic problems were the continual and increasing military expenditures of the mother country, for which Guatemalans had to contribute voluntary *donativos* (donations) from time to time. For example, the kingdom contributed 100,231 pesos and 3½ reales in 1808 to support King Fernando VII "or whoever governed Spain in his sovereign name." This sum, not really voluntary, had been collected from the corregimientos of Chimaltenango, Chiquimula, and Quezaltenango, as well as the alcaldías mayores of Escuintla, Sacate-péques, Verapaz, Sololá, Totonicapán, Suchitepéques, and Sonsonate. In addition, donations came from the intendencies of León (Nicara-gua), San Salvador, Comayagua (Honduras), Ciudad Real (Chiapas), and the governancy of Costa Rica.[9]

However, the crisis in Spain after Napoleon invaded the country—the abdication of King Carlos IV and the imprisonment of his suc-cessor, Fernando VII, in Bayonne, France, when Joseph Bonaparte was placed on the Spanish throne—initiated a series of momentous events in Guatemala. News of these European developments reached Nueva Guatemala on 13 August 1808, whereupon Governor and Cap-tain General González convoked a junta of principal authorities in the assembly room of the royal palace the next morning. Attending were the governor, oidores of the audiencia, members of the cabildo, the rector of the University of San Carlos, representatives of several con-vents, the archbishop, members of the ecclesiastical council, principal officers of the army, and officials of the consulado. They listened to a reading of the dispatch from Mexico City informing them of the abdi-cation of the royal family and cession of the Spanish throne to the emperor of the French, who had installed his brother Joseph as king of Spain. The junta unanimously declared these abdications null and void, and rejected the acts of Napoleon Bonaparte. They refused to recognize any foreign authority and reaffirmed their loyalty to the "legitimate sovereign" of Spain.[10]

On 5 September, González ordered the publication throughout the kingdom of the Spanish declaration of war against the French. He closed all Central American ports to the French and ordered that properties belonging to the enemy be confiscated. Fourteen days later the governor issued an edict establishing a public subscription for a "donativo patriótico y voluntario" (patriotic and voluntary donation) for Spain to use in the war against the French, which was to be at the disposition of whoever governed there. As indicated earlier, this dona-tion of more than 100,000 pesos became the first in a long series of such contributions to support governing authorities in Spain during the absence of the king. On the night of 17 October a public celebration took place in Nueva Guatemala, presumably in the principal plaza, with two orchestras, forty musicians, and a military band, illuminated by eighty-seven double flares. After denunciations of Napoleon and *vivas* (shouts for long life) for Fernando VII, the crowd proceeded in a parade to the royal palace nearby, carrying a portrait of the king.[11]

While this expression of unanimity and patriotism in Guatemala appeared to give authorities and the people direction, it did not resolve the new problem of what officials or which government in Spain the Guatemalans should support. They differed in their views about supporting the Junta Central in the mother country or establishing their own juntas. On 22 January 1809 the Junta Central in Seville issued an order declaring that the American kingdoms were no longer colonies but an integral part of the Spanish monarchy. As such, Americans were given the right to take part in the government of Spain in the absence of the king. They were instructed to elect representatives and send them to Spain for a meeting of the Cortes called by the Junta Central. On 30 April 1809, Governor and Captain General González published this order and established a system for elections. Each town council was instructed to name three persons of "honesty, talent, and education," choose one of them by lot, and send his name to the "Real Acuerdo" (governor and audiencia), which would then pick a name from the three considered persons in the capital. From those nominated, the Real Acuerdo would select the one representative authorized to be a member of the Junta Central and subsequently of the Cortes.[12]

It took Guatemalans eleven months to determine who their representative should be. During this interim period the Junta Central fled in advance of French troops from Seville to Cádiz, where it appointed a regency of five men to govern and prepared for the calling of the Cortes with elected representatives from Spain and the Americas on 4 February 1810. Only nine delegates from the Americas and the Philippines were to be selected in all for the Cortes, which would be dominated by thirty-nine Europeans. In this same period Guatemalans, unaccustomed to elections as they were, proceeded slowly with their elections to select their delegate, and González issued orders prohibiting foreigners in the kingdom from carrying out Napoleon's reported plan to foment insurrections. On 15 May 1810 he also established a reward of five hundred pesos for anyone denouncing or discovering a spy, or informing him of some information relating to spying in the kingdom.[13]

From the thirteen candidates for Guatemala's representative to the Cortes, the Real Acuerdo on 24 July 1810 selected Doctor Don Antonio Larrazábal from the faculty of the University of San Carlos, who was canon of the cathedral. Senior regidor José María Peinado of the cabildo of Nueva Guatemala wrote instructions on 13 October 1810 for Dr. Larrazábal. In four parts, these instructions contained, among other requirements and statements, exhortations that the representative recognize the ideas of liberty and equality, Rousseau's concept of popular sovereignty, the idea of a constitutional monarchy with Fernando VII as king, and government by a national cortes in which Americans had proportional representation. Larrazábal was also instructed to work for changes in the Spanish economic system and for reform of specified laws. On 23 November 1810, having been paid five thousand pesos from the tobacco revenue, Larrazábal left Nueva Guatemala for Jalapa in New Spain. Still there awaiting transportation from Veracruz in February 1811, he did not reach Cádiz until 17 August, almost a year after the Cortes had been convened, and therefore he contributed little to the formation of the Constitution of 1812, promulgated in March.[14]

Meanwhile, Governor and Captain General González was taking measures to establish a *tribunal de fidelidad* (loyalty court) to hear cases of reported spies, and on 12 July 1810 he reestablished the Sociedad Económica de los Amigos del País. He also permitted the freedom to write and publish ideas without first obtaining a license to do so, and abolished the practice of whipping the common people and Indians as punishment for their crimes. Early in 1811 González received the news of the Hidalgo revolt in New Spain, but before he could take any action to prevent a similar insurrection in Guatemala, he was replaced by Jefe de Escuadra and later Lieutenant General José de Bustamante y Guerra.[15]

THE BUSTAMANTE PERIOD, 1811–1818

Bustamante took possession as the governor, captain general, and president of the audiencia on 14 March 1811, thereby beginning a period of seven years of turmoil, conspiracy, and struggle for power between the chief executive and the cabildo of Nueva Guatemala, which represented the interests of liberal merchants and entrepreneurs. Born in Santander, Spain, in 1759, Bustamante had a long and distinguished naval and military career, including service on the scientific expedition to the northwest coast of North America and California under the command of Alejandro Malaspina in the early 1790s. By 1796 he had become governor of the Banda Oriental (today's Uruguay), and at the time of his appointment to Guatemala by the regency in Spain for Fernando VII, he was serving as commandant general and president of the Royal Audiencia of Cuzco, Peru.

Intensely loyal to the Bourbon monarchy, Bustamante was a highly principled absolutist who was opposed to Creoles' beliefs in liberty and freedom from Spanish restrictions. Likewise, he opposed the groups or conventions that they formed to discuss the destiny of the colonies and their relationships to the monarchy. According to Ramón Salazar, he believed in a policy of "hierro y el fuego" (literally, iron and fire, that is, strong measures and force) to cure the ill of revolutions against legitimate monarchs.[16] After receiving his appointment over the objections of the cabildo of Nueva Guatemala,[17] Bustamante wrote in his acceptance a pledge of his loyalty to the regency in Spain. Expressing his willingness not to spare any effort or sacrifice that came his way in the performance of his duties, he professed that his objective was to promote the "happiness and general prosperity of that beautiful country [Guatemala] and the growth and decoration of its dignified capital."[18]

Bustamante's expression of good intentions toward the ayuntamiento of Nueva Guatemala belied his real objectives. He was well aware that its members had opposed to his appointment, and on his arrival from New Spain, accompanied by his wife, a sister, a nephew, and a friar named Manuel de la Madre de Dios, he denounced the ayuntamientos of the kingdom for their decadence in his inaugural speech. Furthermore, he would not approve the ayuntamiento's ordinance to form and organize trade guilds, thereby opposing liberal merchants and those interested in fewer royal restrictions on commerce. Reinforced by the arrival of Archbishop Ramón Casaus Torres y Plazas on 30 July 1811, Bustamante and the new prelate shared many of the same ideas and objectives over the next few years. Archbishop Casaus, who had lived in New Spain for the past twenty-three years, was a great orator. An enemy of the insurrectionists in New Spain, he denounced Father Hidalgo for his revolt there, and he wrote against heretics and the ideas of the philosophes. He was also a Spaniard, loyal to the Bourbons and denounced Napoleon for his captivity of the royal family and for his traitorous invasion of Spain. On 2 May 1812, in a stirring, passionate address from the pulpit of Santo Domingo church in Nueva Guatemala, Casaus denounced Napoleon in front of the congregation.[19]

On 11 November 1811 a rebellion occurred in the town of San Salvador, led by Doctor Matías Delgado and Don Nicolás de Aguilar, against the governor of that intendancy, Antonio Gutiérrez Ulloa. The rebels seized 3,000 new rifles from the armory there and took more than 200,000 pesos from the royal treasury. Governor and Captain General Bustamante appointed Colonel José de Aycinena as the new intendant and sent him with José María Peinado (both men were Creoles) to subdue the rebellion and restore order by force of arms. They led an army of regular troops and newly formed militia that had been established by Bustamante as proposed by the ayuntamiento of the capital. This Nueva Guatemala militia consisted of four companies of Spaniards "without distinction of classes" and another one of "empleados" (employees or servants). In the "honorable name of distinguished Guatemalan volunteers of Fernando VII," these enlisted militiamen, together with their appointed officers, were created to "preserve and defend our sacred religion, the rights of our beloved and captive monarch, and [for] the maintenance of order and public tranquillity in this capital,"[20] but they were also dispatched to suppress rebellions in San Salvador and later, in 1812, in León and Granada, Nicaragua.

On 16 January 1812, Bustamante established a "preventive tribunal of police" for the entire Kingdom of Guatemala to establish a system of "precautions" against the spread of revolutionary ideas from New Spain and to discover internal conspiracies within the kingdom. In twenty-two articles, regulations organized and specified the duties and practices of the police force. Doctor Don Joaquín Ibáñez, the chief advisor to the presidency and military auditor or legal advocate of the captaincy general, was appointed as the superintendent of police, to serve without additional salary but with functions throughout the kingdom. He was specifically instructed that his authority did not include normal police functions, since they were the responsibility of the ayuntamientos and their specific justices. Instead the Tribunal of the Superior Police, as it was titled, was to prevent crimes and transgressions, especially those that could result from meetings, for example, in private homes, contrary to the laws and the public order.

The tribunal was also to discover and report foreigners who entered the kingdom without permission; libelous "politicians" who wrote seditious and defaming information or corresponded with rebels and enemies; propaganda falsifying disasters and national misfortunes, or pretending victories of the enemy; satires; and plans of both external and internal enemies. In general, the Tribunal of the Superior Police was to concern itself with any act or event that might disturb the peace of the kingdom, induce sedition, or cause or sow discord in the towns. For the welfare and security of the towns, the regulation specified that the tribunal was to prevent crimes instead of punishing them after they happened. Once transgressors were discovered, they were to be sent to the tribunal in Nueva Guatemala, which would act as a court in accordance with the laws of the kingdom.

Ayuntamientos and alcaldes were instructed to keep and correct yearly lists of their inhabitants, as were Catholic fathers, heads of families, teachers, and homeowners in towns or on haciendas. They were to list the numbers of persons, their origins, ages, and occupations, or lack of work. These lists were to be sent to the superintendent of the tribunal, together with a sworn statement by the official charged with the town or district administration. Furthermore, professors of the University of San Carlos, teachers in the schools, lawyers, doctors, scribes, and notaries were directed to have each of their students, assistants, or clerks place in their hands a note or report telling their name, origin, age, rank, time in their present position, and places of residence for the past four years. The professors and these professional people were to add notes about their students' or employees' aptitudes, their conduct, and especially their patriotism, sending these reports to the superintendent. The rector of the royal university was instructed to send Governor Bustamante current lists of all residences occupied by *cursantes* (students or scholars), and district and barrio officials were to inform him of all idlers, vagrants, and others living freely and licentiously. Furthermore, innkeepers were required daily to identify to the governor any strangers who arrived in their establishment, and no householder was allowed to admit any guest or visitor without informing his immediate justice.[21]

The regulations also restricted people's movements from one place to another and specified punishments for all transgressors. The royal justice for the neighborhood had to issue a stamped pass for a person who wished to move his place of residence within the same jurisdiction. To depart for another jurisdiction within the kingdom, one needed a passport from the chief or principal justice, or the provincial alcalde. To leave the kingdom, one needed the permission of the superior government, as had always been required in Guatemala and all the Spanish dominions in America. Indians were excepted from this policy since they could be identified readily from their dress and physical features. If a stranger should be among them, he could be easily identified, detained, and arrested. Punishments varied according to the seriousness of the offense and the class of the transgressor. The fines for simple offenses done without malice for the first time were not to exceed one peso for Spaniards and the loss of one day's income for castas. Fines were doubled for the second offense, and third offenses resulted in arrest and summary punishment determined by the justice. Each ayuntamiento of the provinces was to name a commissioner of the Superior Police to enforce the regulations, and special commissioners were to be appointed by justices to visit, on orders from the governor, barrios, houses, and places of a suspicious nature where possibly dangerous persons had been introduced by the French to foment insurrection. Rewards of 500 to 1,000 pesos were offered to those who informed or denounced offenders to the governor or the superintendent of the Superior Police. The tribunal was funded from the fines of the offenders and voluntary contributions by organizations and individual "good patriots" of the city of Nueva Guatemala and other towns of the kingdom.[22]

After the Constitution of 1812 had been proclaimed in Cádiz, and the news of its liberal contents had reached Guatemala, a crisis arose. The document, which applied to Spain and the American dominions, provided for the establishment of a constitutional monarchy with a Bourbon king (Fernando VII); for the supremacy of the Cortes; for popular sovereignty and representation in the Cortes, including representatives with a voice and a vote from the American possessions; freedom of the press; free trade; and the abolition of the Inquisition and tributes. For the Audiencia de Guatemala and other such bodies in the Americas, the title of "presidente" was to be replaced by that of "jefe político," and the political chief was to have an advisory body, called the Junta Provisional, composed of five representatives from the kingdom to assist him.[23] Thus the absolutism and many of restrictions of former Spanish political and economic systems were to be replaced by a constitutional government that was still under the Bourbon monarchy but incorporated many of the liberal principles and ideas of the Enlightenment.

Jefe Político Bustamante swore his allegiance to the Constitution of 1812 on 24 September 1812 in Nueva Guatemala's Plaza de Armas, now renamed the Plaza de la Constitución. Two days later, Archbishop Casaus and the clergy did the same.[24] Both Bustamante and the archbishop must have performed these acts with reluctance. Certainly the jefe politico had already begun a serious scrap with the new ayuntamiento of Nueva Guatemala, which had been elected after a decree of the Cortes in Spain, on 24 May 1812, required that the old regidores and other officials of the ayuntamientos be replaced under the constitution after an election in which all community residents participated. Over the opposition of the upper class and the clergy, two new alcaldes and twelve regidores finally were elected. The new members, mostly liberals of the Creole aristocracy who had promoted the ideas contained in the constitution, encountered opposition from Bustamante, who they claimed did not comply with its provisions and did not want either the ayuntamiento or the elected Diputación Provincial (Provincial Deputation) installed in office. Furthermore, Bustamante required that he approve the manuscripts of all articles published in the *Gazeta de Guatemala*.[25]

This was the beginning of a long, heated confrontation between the liberal ayuntamiento of Nueva Guatemala and the conservative, autocratic views and policies of Jefe Político Bustamante, extending over the next six years. In addition to his censorship of the press and use of the Tribunal of the Superior Police as a widespread spy system to prevent insurrections, Bustamante took many other measures in conflict with the Constitution of 1812 and the policies desired by the members of the ayuntamiento. In April 1812 he had already decreed a "voluntary contribution" from all citizens of the kingdom, especially those of the "primeras clases" (the Creole aristocracy as well as civil officials and clergy), to support the war in Spain against the "most barbarous and powerful" French army and Joseph Bonaparte.[26] Later, after he swore to support the Constitution of 1812, and when he needed funds to replace the abolished tributes, he compelled the Creoles to make "voluntary contributions" to the war effort and depleted Indian community funds by taking moneys from them to meet expenses, promising to repay them in the future.

After suppressing news concerning the rebellion of José María Morelos in New Spain, the jefe político in 1813 finally informed the ayuntamiento of Nueva Guatemala about Morelos's success at Oaxaca, which constituted an immediate threat to Guatemala. He pointed out that, to defend the province, he would have to move troops from Omoa through the capital, before they were sent to the northern frontier. The members of the ayuntamiento vigorously protested this proposal, fearing that the troops, mostly mulattos, would initiate a racial attack on the local residents. The ayuntamiento ordered that the troops not enter the city. When Bustamante rejected that this mandate, the ayuntamiento proposed that a "Provincial Governing Board" take control from the jefe político and that the Marqués de Aycinena be appointed "jefe superior." Bustamante moved the troops anyway to the northern frontier, where they subsequently invaded Oaxaca against his orders. As a result the force was repulsed by the Mexican insurgents and pursued in retreat as far as Chiapas.[27]

Numerous similar confrontations occurred in 1813, a year of great tension in Guatemala, and in the following year before Fernando VII was restored to power in Spain in May 1814. On 3 January 1813 the ayuntamiento complained that Bustamante had interfered in the annual election scheduled for the tenth of the month to determine new deputies and the installation of the Provincial Deputation. The regidores protested his suspension of the acts governing these elections, and pointed out that Bustamante had a "hard and dominant" character.[28] The jefe político also suspended all of the Cortes's liberal legislation, especially that pertaining to freedom of the press and authorizing local autonomy. Attacking contraband trade and the liberal merchants who participated in it, he took control of the consulado, removing the Aycinena faction and replacing it with businessmen who did not traffic with foreigners. The house of Aycinena was deprived of government business, and after 1814 charges were brought against the Marqués de Aycinena for failing to pay taxes on English goods brought in during the liberal years before Bustamante's arrival. The jefe político also continued the policy of forced contributions to meet expenses, although by suspending construction of the Omoa fortress and public buildings in Nueva Guatemala and reducing the number of civil and military posts, Bustamante did succeed in reducing expenses by about a million and a half pesos in his seven years, compared to those of his predecessor, González.[29]

Late in December 1813 the confrontation between Bustamante and the liberal Creole merchants reached a climax with the "conspiracy of Belén." On 21 December, Bustamante, who had received information from one of the conspirators, issued a writ denouncing the conspirators, who had met at the convent of Belén in Nueva Guatemala. Among them were José Francisco Barrundia, José María Montúfar, Doctor Tomás Ruiz and his brother José, Cayetano and Manuel Bedoya, Lieutenant Joaquín Yudice, Sergeant León Díaz, Don Andrés Dardon, and lay brother Fray Manuel de San José. Most of them were young men, and some were members of the merchant community. Their plan was to rebel on Christmas Eve, aided by the one battalion of regular troops and militia forces. They intended to free the prisoners held from the 1812 rebellion in Granada, take arms, seize money from the royal treasury, capture the jefe político and high civil and military officials, proclaim independence, establish control over the interior, deport to Spain Bustamante and all who would not accept their actions, and finally unite Guatemala and southern New Spain into one country liberated from Spain. Bustamante took quick action as soon as he received the news, sending Captain Antonio Villar to take prisoners both at Belén and at the conspirators' houses. He imposed martial law for two months and imprisoned, as accomplices of the conspirators, some members of the ayuntamiento and principal Creoles. An abortive revolt also occurred a few months later in San Salvador.[30]

As one might expect, this abortive *golpe de estado* (coup d'etat), and Bustamante's repressive policies toward possible accomplices, heightened the tension between the ayuntamiento and the jefe político. Before the conspirators could be sentenced in September 1814, the news of King Fernando's restoration in Spain reached Nueva Guatemala on 24 June. Bells rang, cannons fired, and bands played in a joyous ceremony. Archbishop Casaus publicly attacked the ideas of the philosophes and proclaimed the "destruction of democracy." Bustamante, now relieved of any commitment to the Constitution of 1812 and to orders of the Cortes that the king declared null and void, sentenced twenty-eight criminals from the Granada revolt of 1812 to ten years' imprisonment at Trujillo in Honduras. In September the conspirators of Belén were sentenced: four were to die on the garrote (two were *hidalgos,* or lesser nobility, and two had status as priests); eleven were to be hanged, because they were commoners; one Catholic father was sentenced to ten years in jail in Africa and permanent exile from America; and two others had eight-year terms in jail.[31]

Evidently one of the imprisoned was Tomás Ruiz, the former prior of the monastery at Belén. José Francisco Barrundia, who allegedly had been a conspirator but now was sublieutenant of the squadron of dragoons in Nueva Guatemala, wrote in November 1817, describing what he knew about the conspiracy of Belén and his friendship with Ruiz. According to Barrundia, some young men had met in the cell of the prior of Belén in 1813. Their youth and feelings of liberty had caused them to oppose the illegal procedures of Bustamante before and after the Constitution of 1812 was promulgated. Barrundia stated that the jefe político had spoken of these *tertulias* (social gatherings) heatedly and with resentment. The young men were said to be influenced by other men of the "vilest and lowest order." Bustamante knew of the gatherings from the beginning because his spies kept him informed daily. At the end of the year 1813, Barrundia said, he went to Belén to visit Tomás Ruiz, with whom he had "friendly relations." Not finding him in his cell, Barrundia went to the prior's room, where he encountered eight persons, mostly unknown to him. According to Barrundia, they spoke with "imprudence and frivolously" about Bustamante, but he did not hear a plot or a plan, although the assembled young men did take an oath of secrecy. Barrundia stated that he did not utter a word, did not attend any meetings before or after this visit, and did not hear anything that even remotely indicated a conspiracy. As a regidor of the ayuntamiento loyal to the regency in Spain in 1813, Barrundia concluded that Bustamante had resolved to arrest those who participated in these gatherings as a pretext so that his "excessive and useless expenses would not be disapproved." Also, Barrundia believed that Bustamante had acted to counter the claims that the ayuntamiento of Nueva Guatemala had made against his government.[32]

A few months later, in January 1818, Tomás Ruiz, on behalf of four other prisoners and himself, wrote to the king appealing for clemency. In his letter Ruiz pointed out that the two meetings at Belén had been full of discussion about the critical state of affairs on the Iberian Peninsula, Bustamante's censuring of the Cortes, and the jefe político's opposition to the gatherings. Arrested and jailed on the night of 21 December 1813, Ruiz and the others had been held without being permitted to communicate with anyone. Although ecclesiastics, military persons, and *paisanos* (countrymen, or everyday people) had participated in the gatherings, Ruiz did not believe that the prisoners were criminals since they did not plan or execute any crime. Such was "the famous lawsuit of Belén in Guatemala," Ruiz concluded, adding that Bustamante had brought companies of Negro troops from Trujillo and mulattos from Chiquimula to maintain the tranquillity of loyal Nueva Guatemala, which really had not been disturbed, according to his view.[33]

Once restored, King Fernando VII decided to declare the Constitution of 1812 and acts of the Cortes null and void and to reestablish ayuntamientos as they had been in 1808. Bustamante complied completely during the remainder of 1814 and thereafter.[34] As a precaution against anyone who intended to disturb the public order and tranquillity, he imprisoned Don Antonio Larrazábal, former deputy to the Cortes, in mid-May 1814 in accordance with the king's instructions. Representations on Larrazábal's behalf had been made to the ayuntamiento, the Cabildo Eclesiástico, convents of male and female religious, and the rector of the university, but Bustamante believed these were all promoted by the Marqués de Aycinena, "the intimate friend of Larrazábal," and by his brother, José de Aycinena, both of whom he considered to be without merit for employment in responsible government positions.[35]

The struggle between Bustamante and the ayuntamiento of Nueva

Guatemala continued heatedly during the last four years of the governor's administration. Furthermore, Bustamante wrote to the king in September 1814 to review the sad situation of government in Spain and America since 1810, the instructions given by José María Peinado to Larrazábal in 1811, and the recent revolt of San Salvador that had deposed the legitimate governor-intendant. Reporting that all the provinces had been pacified, he asked the king to revoke Peinado's instructions as seditious and asked that Peinado, whom Bustamante had sent in 1813 to govern San Salvador, be deprived of that office and replaced with an honorable and meritorious military officer who was of "sane opinions." Also, he requested that all who had signed the instructions from the former liberal ayuntamiento be excluded from obtaining any public offices anywhere in America, with the exception of Don José Irissari, Don Sebastián Melón, Don Miguel González, and Don Juan Antonio Agueche, because they were all four Europeans of true loyalty and sane sentiments who had voted against the instructions.[36]

Supported by the pro-peninsular mercantile interests in the capital, the textile manufacturers, and the small landholders of the kingdom, Bustamante represented the government party in a struggle against the Creole aristocracy, who found allies with those who hated Bustamante and favored independence or the restoration of the Constitution of 1812. These opponents concentrated their efforts on removing Bustamante removed from office through their influence and membership in the ayuntamiento of Nueva Guatemala.[37] Basically the conflict revolved around Bustamante's efforts to counter the influence and power of the Aycinena family, who resisted vigorously and endeavored to have the king remove Bustamante from his position at the head of Spanish authority in the kingdom. Carrying out the king's determination in his royal order of 31 March 1815 that the instructions written by Peinado and given to Larrazábal in 1810 were "seditious and disturbing," Bustamante decided to have all copies burned in the principal plaza as a public display. This act, performed by the town crier and witnessed by the scribe of the "Superior Government," was accomplished on 22 December 1815, including copies recovered from different parts of the kingdom. Bustamante reserved two copies of the instructions from destruction, and he sent them to the governor of Chiapas at Ciudad Real for him to forward to the tribunal of the

reestablished Inquisition in Mexico City. During the year 1815, Bustamante also had deprived Peinado of his post as governor-intendant of
San Salvador, replacing him with Royal Artillery Colonel José Men-
dez, and he had ordered that all members of the ayuntamiento who had
signed the instructions, except those mentioned earlier, be deprived of
"exercising any profession or position in America."[38]

Furthermore, the governor and captain general explained his opposition to the Provincial Deputation's complaint to the Cortes in September 1813, and took immediate action to impede the appointment of
a new oidor from New Spain to the Audiencia de Guatemala. In his
manifesto on 18 March 1815 and a letter written on the same day to the
secretary of state and communications in Spain, he proclaimed his
vigorous support of King Fernando VII and denounced the members
of the ayuntamiento whose complaints about him he had read in *El
Universal,* a Madrid newspaper. Their statements that Bustamante had
not ordered the singing of the Te Deum for the election of deputies,
about his delay in installing them and his failure to comply with the
Cortes's order to establish freedom of the press, were, according to
Bustamante, not only untrue but damaging to his honor. Insulted,
although he said the members of the ayuntamiento complained only
because he did not share "the dangerous opinions of that damned age
[the Enlightenment]," Bustamante pointed out that he had worked day
and night to preserve the tranquillity of the kingdom, which the "hordes"
from New Spain had tried to disturb. In his opinion, those who had
complained about him were "more criminal than Morelos and his
hordes." Specifically he cited the opposition to him of Peinado, Larrazábal, Miguel Larraynega, Antonio Juarros, and Don Manuel Pavón, a
merchant of Nueva Guatemala and member of the Provincial Deputation who had for many years wanted to dominate Bustamante's administration and sought glory for himself. Bustamante denounced these
revolutionary leaders along with José Miguel Ramos Arizpe (delegate
from New Spain to the Cortes) and the journalists, who "served at the
mercy of those called liberals," for wanting to make the king only the
"primer ciudadano" (first citizen) and the legislature the property of
the nation, and for destroying the aristocratic elements as "monstrous"
and supporting the establishment of democratic states. The object of
his opponents, according to Bustamante, had been to put "total govern-

ment of the provinces in juntas composed of natives and leaders plagued with the tumultuous opinions of those damned times." He also denounced the ayuntamiento for having approved the instructions to Larrazábal on 16 October 1810, and he stated that in the first meeting of the Provincial Deputation Pavón and four other deputies on 7 September 1813 had signed the complaint to the Cortes and had asked for the removal and replacement of Bustamante as jefe político.[39]

Demonstrating his opposition to the spread of revolutionary ideas from New Spain, Bustamante opposed the appointment of Don José Ygnacio Ortiz de Salinas as one of the oidores of the Audiencia de Guatemala in 1816. Since Ortiz de Salinas had been the parish priest that Miguel de Hidalgo had appointed to the Audiencia de Guadalajara in western New Spain when the rebels captured that city, Bustamante consulted the other four oidores of his audiencia, all of whom agreed with the president that the new appointment should be prohibited. These judges thereafter advised the viceroy of New Spain and the minister of Gracia y Justicia in Spain of their decision. The king approved Bustamante's and the audiencia's recommendation and ordered that Ortiz de Salinas be denied the appointment.[40]

King Fernando VII, in another of his chameleonlike changes of policy, ordered Bustamante's removal from office in March 1817 and named a successor. Evidently this action occurred because of the ayuntamiento's petition for the captain general and governor's removal, because of letters from the Marqués de Aycinena and his friends to influential persons in Spain, and because of the presence of José de Aycinena in Madrid charging Bustamante with poor administration.[41] The Plenary Council of the Indies and the fiscal, in view of the petitions they had received, reviewed the complaints and requests of the ayuntamiento and others and issued an opinion on 28 February 1817. The members of the Council of the Indies noted their uncertainty that the instructions given by the ayuntamiento to Larrazábal had been responsible for the uprisings in San Salvador, León, and Granada, as Bustamante had reported in his letter of 18 September 1814. They also observed that those who had authored these instructions were not the only guilty parties. Guilty too were those who signed them and Bustamante also shared the blame for having permitted their circulation. Furthermore, the family of the deceased Marqués de Aycinena, José

María Peinado, and the regidores of the ayuntamiento who had participated in the formation of these instructions, all had by now voluntarily
abjured their earlier straying because of the generally contagious times
in which the instructions had been written. As a result, according to
the Council of the Indies and the fiscal, the king had granted these
individuals indulgences already in his declaration of 1 June 1814. Instead of meriting Bustamante's indignation against them now in 1817,
the council ruled that all these persons should be reinstated in their
employments and cleared in their honor and reputation. The Council
of the Indies therefore recommended that the conduct of the president
and governor be disapproved by the king, that Bustamante "be removed immediately from the government," but that he remain in Guatemala until the king decided who would replace him. Finally, it suggested that Bustamante's residencia be accomplished as recommended
by the Office of Justice.[42] On 3 March 1817, King Fernando, who
desired to restore good relations with the liberal merchants of Guatemala and end the controversy, removed Bustamante from office,
ordered him to remain in Nueva Guatemala until his replacement
arrived, and appointed Lieutenant General Carlos Urrutia y Montoya
to the position of governor, captain general, and president of the Audiencia de Guatemala.[43]

General Urrutia, who was serving at the time as captain general of
the island of Santo Domingo, did not take possession of his new office
for nearly one year. The Plenary Council of the Indies approved his
delay at Santo Domingo because of the "multitude of corsairs that
disgracefully infest these seas," but asked that the king appoint an
interim governor of Guatemala to sustain the diminishing authority of
royal officials there.[44] No such interim governor was appointed by the
king, and Bustamante continued in office until Urrutia finally arrived
and took possession on 28 March 1818. Meanwhile, the ayuntamiento
of Nueva Guatemala, in letters of November and December 1817, continued to express its opposition to Bustamante and his policies in the
interim, asking for his immediate suspension.[45]

Also, during August 1817, Bustamante had ordered the arrest of José
García Zelaya, whom the governor accused of aiding José Antonio
Rodríguez, a prisoner in Nueva Guatemala, to escape from his jail cell.
Expressing his innocence, García Zelaya was surprised on the night of

16 August by Don Francisco Cáscara and Don Ygnacio Cediles, who were armed and backed by troops. They took him with books from his bookstore to a jail cell in Chiquimula where there was no bed or furniture other than a shelf on the wall. García Zelaya's brother also was imprisoned, and his papers were seized the same night. On 12 September, Cáscara gave García Zelaya, in a package in a small box, a draft of the prisoner's confession, which he completed four days later, hoping that he would then be freed. Through the efforts of his mother, García Zelaya was finally transferred to the prison in Nueva Guatemala from which he wrote on 25 April 1818. Held without explanation of any formal charges against him, García Zelaya pointed out that the people of Guatemala had suffered the oppression of Bustamante for seven years and that they awaited "your [probably Urrutia's] coming like the Jewish people awaited the arrival of Otomil, king of Mesopotamia."[46]

Although Bustamante was replaced by Urrutia on 28 March 1818, his difficulties persisted for the next three years, during his residencia, which the king ordered to be conducted at first by Urrutia and after 1 October 1818 by Francisco de Paula y Vilches, regent of the audiencia. Urrutia met with the aldermen of the ayuntamiento and other distinguished persons at the cabildo on 24 April,[47] but his advanced age and his other responsibilities as governor led to his replacement by Paula y Vilches. Bustamante also may have influenced Urrutia's decision to give up the responsibility for his end-of-term inspection. In his letter of 31 March 1818 to Urrutia, Bustamante explained that his goals had always been to serve the king as honorably as he could and to preserve the tranquillity of the kingdom. Convinced that the royal order for his suspension and replacement had been based on the falsities of those who attacked him, his character, and his honor, he defended his actions over forty-seven years of loyal service.[48] Selected from a list of three persons nominated by the Council of the Indies in accordance with the provisions of the royal order of 24 August 1799 prescribing the method of conducting residencias in America,[49] Paula y Vilches did not receive his commission until 27 April 1819, almost seven months after his appointment initially on 1 October 1818.[50]

Bustamante's residencia proceeded very slowly because, as Paula y Vilches noted, it was a "laborious task" and it was difficult to determine the truth in the short space of four months that he had been allotted to complete his investigation. In fact, he did not even receive official replies of testimony from León, Nicaragua, until 9 May 1820, and from Cartago, Costa Rica, until 18 May of the same year, both responding to President Urrutia's writ of 15 April.[51] In his letter to the king on 16 October 1820, together with the testimony he had accumulated, Paula y Vilches exonerated Bustamante, pointing out that never had an official governed with more love and justice, conforming to with the laws, and that Bustamante had tried to govern softly and pleasantly in a period of "unfortunate ages." Paula y Vilches was convinced that Bustamante had been the primary reason for the retention of Spanish authority and the "failure of independence."[52] Defended also by the opinion of the Office of Justice in Spain and by Spanish official José Tejada, Bustamante was exonerated, and the king ordered the suspension of his residencia on 8 January 1821.[53]

THE LAST YEARS OF SPANISH ADMINISTRATION, 1818–1821

As noted earlier, General Carlos de Urrutia took charge of the administration of the Kingdom of Guatemala and its provinces in March 1818. He presided over a region in which centralist authority had ended while the power of the liberal ayuntamiento had emerged triumphant. Within two years open trade with foreign nations became a reality, and within three years the Provincial Deputation took power away from the president of the audiencia, which was unable to resist either development. With the Riego Revolt of 1 January 1820 in Cádiz, the triumph of the liberals in Spain, and the reestablishment of the Constitution of 1812, Guatemala drifted toward independence in September 1821.[54]

Members of the Creole aristocracy quickly established good relations with the mild-mannered, aged, and permissive Urrutia. Although he opposed contraband trade, he authorized trade with Belize in 1819, relaxed Bustamante's coastal defense measures, closed the port of Izabal, and removed the garrison from Fort San Felipe. Thus he not only opened up illicit trade but also encouraged merchants to expand their legal activities.[55] Urrutia began this last period of Spanish administration by issuing on 23 July 1818 a "bando de buen gobierno" (decree for good government) consisting of thirty-one articles that proved unenforceable. It prohibited taking the name of God in vain;

sanctified Sundays and other religious days; prohibited anyone from uttering obscenities, dishonesties, and curses; outlawed dancing at night behind closed doors in the company of both sexes; and set a curfew at ten o'clock at night, after which no one was to be on the streets unless engaged in urgent business.[56]

In fact, Urrutia was well liked, especially by the liberal aristocracy. His biggest problem arose from the factionalism of Guatemalans, who divided into two early-day parties: the *cacos,* favoring free trade and Creole rule through the cabildos, ayuntamientos, and provincial deputations, were opposed by the *gazistas* who were mainly the merchants and the Spanish bureaucracy, who were hurt by free trade and desired protectionism. Doctor Pedro Molina, a former student of Goicoechea at the University of San Carlos, became the spokesman of the liberal Cacos, while José Cecilio del Valle became the advocate for the conservative Gazistas who promoted protectionist ideas. After 1820 these two factions became Guatemala's first political parties. The Cacos favored Molina's advocacy of immediate independence, absolute individual freedom, and application of natural laws, including free trade and separation of powers in government. The more-moderate Gazistas favored protected commerce and gradual independence from Spain.[57]

This struggle intensified after the liberals seized power in Spain and reestablished the Constitution of 1812 following the Riego Revolt. President Urrutia, ill and unable to continue in office because of his advanced age, sent a circular on 10 March 1821 to all the ayuntamientos of the kingdom announcing that the subinspector of militias, Don Gabino Gaínza, was now "jefe político superior" of the Kingdom of Guatemala.[58] Urrutia was opposed to independence, while Gaínza, a younger officer fifty-three years old, was more receptive to the ideas of the ayuntamiento of Nueva Guatemala.[59] By then the restoration of liberal rule in Spain had led to the reestablishment of Provincial Deputations (as had been tried in 1814), which were largely controlled by Cacos who were members of the Aycinena faction. The latter announced their intention to appoint civil judges throughout Guatemala, Honduras, and San Salvador, thereby ensuring that liberals would interpret the laws, not Spanish sympathizers. Although Urrutia attempted to resist the Creole aristocracy and had the support of the audiencia and Archbishop Casaus, he could not overcome the opposing deputation, especially after the news was received of Colonel Agustín de Iturbide's revolt in New Spain and proclamation of the Plan de Iguala in February 1821. With Mexican independence proclaimed and Simón Bolívar's successes in northern South America, the Guatemalan Provincial Deputation forced Urrutia's resignation in favor of Gaínza.[60]

The secession of the provinces from Guatemalan authority and the rebellion of Agustín de Iturbide, which promoted Mexico's independence from Spain, brought a crisis in the administration of the Kingdom of Guatemala that spread from the capital, Nueva Guatemala. Political disintegration of the region's colonies began before independence was declared. With tribute abolished as a source of income, the treasury emptied, and Spain was in no position to help financially or politically after the Riego Revolt. Nor could Spain send troops to maintain order or suppress insurrections. The Salvadorans' demand for self-government had intensified with the establishment of the separate intendant system. When in 1820, Guatemalan Creoles created judgeships to be filled by them, Comayagua's intendant, José Tinoco, established a Provincial Deputation and appointed deputies to the Spanish Cortes from all of the Honduran regions. Tegucigalpa refused to accept those measures and pledged its support to the central authority in Guatemala, but Nicaragua (León) also declared its autonomy, while Costa Rica appealed to the Cortes for its independence from both Guatemalan and Nicaraguan jurisdiction. Thus all except Tegucigalpa resisted centralized control from Guatemala.[61]

INDEPENDENCE

By mid-1821 the principal issues facing Guatemalans were the disintegration of the Kingdom of Guatemala, financial problems, and especially, the concept of independence from Spain. Doctor Pedro Molina, as editor of his newspaper, *El Editor Constitucional,* and his allies of the Aycinena faction championed independence from the liberal-controlled Spanish government. José Cecilio del Valle headed the moderate faction, which, with its own newspaper, *El Amigo de la Patria,* opposed radical change and tended to support a loyalist position. Gabino Gaínza, the new "jefe político superior," followed a middle course, sometimes issuing public statements against independence, yet at the same time courting the favor of the radical Cacos and tolerating their goal of independence. Iturbide's successes in New Spain with the Army of the Three Guarantees, and the danger that he might send an army to "liberate" Central America, forced Guatemalans to do something on their own.[62]

Although the ayuntamiento of Nueva Guatemala met and discussed the possibility of declaring independence on 31 August 1821, and Gainza warned on 4 September that the public tranquillity was not to be disturbed,[63] it was not until 13 September that the issues of independence and possible military conquest from New Spain were forced. On that day news arrived that Ciudad Real in Chiapas had accepted Iturbide's Plan de Iguala for independence from Spain, the maintenance of the Catholic religion, and the union of Spaniards and Americans. The ayuntamiento met during the afternoon of the fourteenth, and Gainza issued an order for a meeting of authorities the next morning.[64]

At eight o'clock on Saturday morning, 15 September 1821, some fifty authorities and leading citizens of the capital assembled in the parlor of the palace of the captain general. They included both civil and religious officials. Although it was not called so at the time, this meeting can be described as a cabildo abierto of the town council. In attendance were, among others, Gabino Gaínza, José Cecilio del Valle (as judge advocate), José Matías Delgado, Manuel Antonio Molina, Doctor Antonio García Redondo, Miguel Larreynaga, the Marqués de Aycinena (Juan José de Aycinena, son of the first marqués, Juan Fermín de Aycinena), Mariano de Aycinena, and Canon José María Castilla. They represented the Provincial Deputation, the ayuntamiento of Nueva Guatemala, the audiencia, and the ecclesiastical cabildo, along with the Creole aristocracy. After a free but stormy discussion, the majority voted 23 to 7 in favor of declaring independence, and Valle was appointed to write the official declaration.[65]

The "Act of Independence of the United Provinces of Central America," consisting of nineteen articles, was adopted on 15 September. It was proclaimed publicly by the "Jefe Político Superior and Presidente de la Junta Consultativa" (superior political chief and president of the consultative body), Gabino Gaínza, on the same day and published on 16 September.[66] Its preamble expresses the desire of the Guatemalan people to be independent from the Spanish government and notes that proclamations of independence from Ciudad Real and Tuxtla (both in

Chiapas) furnished examples that Guatemalans wished to follow. The first article declares that "independence from the Spanish government is the general voluntary will of the people of Guatemala," and it calls for elections of representatives from the provinces to a congress. Article 8 specifies that the "Señor Jefe Político Brigadier Don Gavino Gaínza" is to continue in office as the "Gobierno Superior Político y Militar" (superior political and military government), and a provisional consultative "Junta," composed of the Provincial Deputation and regional alcaldes, was to govern Guatemala and the United Provinces of Central America. Article 11 preserves the Catholic religion as the only faith of the new government, just as the Plan de Iguala did for Mexico. The final article states that a special Mass was to be held to give thanks for the establishment of independence, accompanied by an artillery barrage and three days of *iluminación* (illumination, or lighting; but also possibly fireworks).[67]

Thus independence was declared and accomplished peacefully. Although there had been fighting to suppress insurrections in the provinces during the preceding ten years, there was no conflict with Spanish military forces as there had been in New Spain, Venezuela, Nueva Granada (today's Colombia), Ecuador, Peru, Chile, and Argentina. Gabino Gaínza continued as the chief executive, and Archbishop Casaus, who had opposed independence, reluctantly accepted it and continued as the head of the Catholic Church. Yet, the provinces were far from united as the declaration had stated, and subsequently they, especially El Salvador, would resist Guatemala's leadership and control. Gone were the allegiances to King Fernando VII and the Cortes of Spain. So too was the Kingdom of Guatemala destroyed, centralization of authority terminated, and the long administration of Spain over Guatemala and Central America ended.

CHAPTER 10

The Spanish Legacy

SPAIN ADMINISTERED Guatemala and Central America for 297 years. The Kingdom of Guatemala, gradually established as a political entity between 1524 and 1570, was only a part of the Spanish empire in the Americas, yet it was the most important jurisdiction between New Spain, on the one hand, and Nueva Granada and Peru, on the other. Ostensibly subject to the Viceroyalty of New Spain, the Kingdom of Guatemala with its governor, captain general, and president of the audiencia, and finally its supreme political chief, more often than not operated as an autonomous entity and maintained direct contact with the king and royal officials in the mother country. The region was governed by its executive, by the Audiencia de Guatemala, by cabildos or ayuntamientos, and by the district as well as local officials who maintained Spanish jurisdiction over the vast domain from Chiapas, in today's Mexico, to the present Costa Rica–Panama border.

In this extensive region the province of Guatemala and its capital—whether at Iximché, Almolonga, or Ciudad Vieja, Santiago de los Caballeros de Guatemala (today's Antigua), or Nueva Guatemala de la Asunción (present-day Guatemala City)—were the most important centers of administration, economic life, society, and culture in colonial Central America. Although silver mining was never so significant in the region and the province as it was in New Spain and Peru, other developments in the economy were. Agricultural and pastoral pursuits dominated economic life, both internally and externally. As a result, trade and commerce were vital and fostered the growth of a vigorous merchant sector and a contraband trade that defied the regulations and restrictions of the Spanish commercial system of mercantilism. Guatemala's population was large and diverse throughout the entire colonial period, and with its bishopric and later archbishopric, it served continuously as the focal point of the far-flung Catholic Church in Central America. Furthermore, its principal city was extraordinary because of its plazas, public buildings, cathedral, churches and convents, writers and artists, the University of San Carlos (the only such institution in colonial Central America), and its sizable population. The capital of Guatemala served as the center of Spanish administration and cultural life not only for the province but for the entire Central American region as well.

While it may appear that this was a stable and static period in the overall history of Guatemala, in reality these nearly three centuries were characterized by dynamic changes, controversies, conflicts, growth, and development. Changes were constant in administration, labor practices, economic life, and the organization and composition of society, some for the better and others for the worse. Yet, throughout these adjustments and in the face of national, environmental, and health disasters, Guatemala and its residents remained as a permanent settlement or colony.

In the conquest and colonization period from 1524 to about 1550 colonial Guatemala experienced important cultural encounters between the races, personalism in government, evangelization, and forced Indian labor. Spanish institutions were planted in the province and kingdom, some to last, others to be altered by the people, environment, and circumstances; and still others to be abandoned. While Catholicism, the Spanish language, and the system of town-founding, for example, survived, the early system of Indian slavery was found wanting and was replaced by encomiendas and repartimientos, as well as the beginning of congregaciones by the midsixteenth century.

These new labor and societal practices were part of Guatemala's second colonial period, an era of consolidation and maturing that extended from approximately 1550 to 1700. During those one hundred and fifty years the congregación and repartimiento systems were supplemented by the establishment of royal authority through the Audiencia de Guatemala and the governor, captain general, and president as the head of the province and Kingdom of Guatemala. These supreme Spanish authorities and a host of provincial, district, and local officials governed along with the cabildos at the municipal level. Likewise, in this period Christianity spread, and the economy became export-oriented with the development of cacao and indigo plantations. As colonial Guatemala became a monoculture, its economic prosperity, or disasters, depended on the European demand for crops. Although land ownership was still in private hands, and land was held in relatively small plots, especially in the towns, rural areas were increasingly dominated by large haciendas dedicated to the production and export of one crop. Society began to change through the introduction of black slaves, the acculturation and relocation of Indians, the eventual decline of encomiendas, and the emergence of a ladino sector of the population. Finally, it should be noted that the University of San Carlos was founded toward the end of this period, and foreign interlopers necessitated the development of Guatemala's defenses along the Atlantic coast with the founding and construction of the fortress of San Felipe where the Río Dulce leaves Lake Izabal.

During the eighteenth century, Guatemala's third colonial period, the dynamic changes initiated by the reforms of the Bourbon dynasty in Spain brought controversy, challenge, and new problems to the province. Devoted to the ideas of the Enlightenment—natural laws, reason, and science—and intent on government centralization and efficiency throughout the Spanish possessions, the Bourbons established new governmental institutions, such as the intendant, and increased royal control over the province and kingdom of Guatemala. They appointed, especially in the latter half of the century, military officers to the position of governor, captain general, and president of the audiencia to administer and enforce royal policies, and increasingly they concentrated on improvements in Guatemala's and Central America's defenses against British expansion, threats to Spanish sovereignty, and contraband trade. Matías de Gálvez's defensive and offensive operations during the period from 1779 to 1782 were the high points of the resistance to British penetration, although the Spanish authorities did not succeed in eliminating the contraband trade. Bourbon economic policies and political centralization led to the expulsion of the Jesuits in 1767, to limitations on the authority and power of the church and the cabildos, and to loosened restrictions that allowed trade even with neutral nations in time of war. In the 1790s, Spain authorized the founding of the consulado in Nueva Guatemala, the first in all of Central America. After the disastrous earthquake of July 1773 had seriously damaged Santiago de Guatemala, the king authorized the relocation of the capital to Nueva Guatemala, a process that took several years to complete.

All of those measures increased expenses and brought controversies to the Guatemalan scene. The changes in the curriculum of the University of San Carlos to the ideas of the Enlightenment, and the emergence of an educated group of professionals in Nueva Guatemala dedicated to the new concepts, led directly to demands for free trade, popular participation in government, and less control by the absolutist monarchy in Spain. Thus the origins of liberalism were sown in this period of dynamic change during the eighteenth century. Furthermore, the ladino and Creole sectors of the population became increasingly numerous and important. The Creole aristocracy subsequently began to challenge peninsular political and economic interests in the colony.

Guatemala's final colonial era extended from about 1800 to 1821. It was another period of turmoil, conflict, changing administrations, and new policies, including a decline in indigo production, insurrections in some of the provinces, challenges to royal authority, and finally, independence. Developments in Spain during the Napoleonic wars and afterward raised new problems and policies to which Guatemalans had to respond and adjust, thereby intensifying their own difficulties with factionalism, economic decline and uncertainty, the rising contraband trade, and the breakdown of centralized authority. While Governors González Mollinedo and Bustamante y Guerra tried to maintain loyalty to the Crown and enforce the policies of conservatism, absolutism, and authoritarianism, they were forced to accept the rapid and radical changes of government brought about by the French invasion of Spain, capture of King Fernando VII, establishment of juntas and a cortes on the Iberian Peninsula, and the promulgation of the liberal Spanish Constitution of 1812.

Those two governors also were examples of the continuous appointment of senior military officers as administrators of the province and kingdom of Guatemala. Throughout the period they faced increasing opposition to their policies from the growing liberal elements of society—the enlightened intellectuals, professors from the university, journalists, and especially the liberal merchants and indigo growers who formed a Creole aristocracy clamoring for free trade, partici-

Guatemala City: "Plaza de Armas y Catedral" (main plaza and cathedral) (Samuel Katz Collection, Special Collections, Nettie Lee Benson Latin American Library, University of Texas at Austin).

pation in government, prestige, power, separation of governmental powers, free speech, a free press, and ultimately independence from Spain.

Centralized authority broke down after 1818. Liberals challenged conservatives, federalists differed from centralists, and Creoles fought with peninsulares. This intense struggle culminated in the calling of the Junta Consultativa (Consultative Body), which met on 15 September 1821 in Nueva Guatemala and declared the independence from Spain of the United Provinces of Central America (of which Guatemala was one, and the principal leader). This proclamation, while ending Spanish rule peacefully without warfare against peninsular

Interior of the cathedral, Guatemala City (Samuel Katz Collection, Special Collections, Nettie Lee Benson Latin American Library, University of Texas at Austin).

troops, also marked the triumph of the liberal Creole element of society. Guatemala's independence was established by a small portion of its people serving its own interests, not by the majority of the population, who were never consulted. Nor did the general population participate in the decision to separate from Spain until the public celebrations of the Act of Independence, after it had been decided and proclaimed.

Spain's long presence in Guatemala left the new nation with an important and far-reaching legacy. Francis Polo Sifontes in his *Historia de Guatemala* has observed that Spain brought to the province and kingdom of Guatemala its language, culture, university, books, missionaries, Christianity, juridical system, artisans, new crops, livestock, and an "injection of new blood" (page 170) that definitely forged the character of the present republic of Guatemala. Yet that this is not all

Guatemala City: "Vista del 'Cerro de Carmen'" (view from the Hill of Carmen) (Samuel Katz Collection, Special Collections, Nettie Lee Benson Latin American Library, University of Texas at Austin).

Guatemala City: Cathedral and Colegio de Infantes (school of infants) (Samuel Katz Collection, Special Collections, Nettie Lee Benson Latin American Library, University of Texas at Austin).

that constitutes the legacy of Spain to Guatemala. Spanish inhabitants and authorities founded the towns from which today's cities and villages grew. The architectural achievements of the Spanish colonial period are still evident in the civil, religious, and military buildings of Antigua, Guatemala City, and the fortress on the Río Dulce. The Royal Palace of the Captains General on the plaza and the University of San Carlos (now a museum) in Antigua, the cathedrals and churches in both Antigua and Guatemala City, the plazas principales in the capitals of the colonial era and in many cities and towns throughout the republic, the fortress of San Felipe, and the many churches, including that at Esquipulas, are only some of the physical reminders of Spain's presence. The Spanish writers of the colonial period are the foundations of Guatemala's literature. Spanish artists—painters, sculptors, architects, musicians, and others—represent the beginnings of Guatemala's cultural heritage along with the Indians' arts and crafts, especially in the fine weaving of textiles. Likewise, Spaniards established a unified jurisdiction that endured for almost three centuries, a condition not equalled since independence. Spain's centralized administration from Santiago de Guatemala and Nueva Guatemala also caused opposition to Guatemalan leadership in other provinces such as El Salvador, Honduras, Costa Rica, and Nicaragua, resulting in their separation and the splintering of Central America into five nations and the state of Chiapas, now a part of the republic of Mexico. Furthermore, Guatemala's production of crops for export lives on as a reminder of the mercantilistic economy of the colonial period.

Most significantly, Spaniards effected a major change in Guatemala's society and its people. Colonial Guatemala was not only the center of political, economic, social, cultural, and religious life between Mexico City and South America, it also was the most heavily populated region of Central America. From its different races and separate peoples—the native Indians, blacks from Africa, and Spaniards from Europe—Spain forged a new society composed of Spaniards, Creoles, blacks, ladinos, mulattos or pardos, and other racial mixtures. Begun as an encounter of two worlds—Europe and America—and a conflict of civilizations and their cultures, this multiracial Guatemalan society, while it resulted in a radical decline of the Indian population for the first 150 years, did not annihilate the province's native inhabitants. Their descendants are everywhere apparent in Guatemala City, Antigua, Sololá, Quezaltenango, Chichicastenango, Totonicapán, Huehuetenango, and a multitude of other communities and rural villages, especially in highland Guatemala.

Spanish society with its many racial origins and mixtures in Guatemala focused on the family; on the *dignidad,* or respect, of the individual person; on the preservation of customs and traditions; and on the incorporation of such new elements as the emergence of the ladinos and the veneration of the Virgin of Guadalupe and Our Lord of

Esquipulas, just to name a few. With the flexibility and the complexity of the social structure by the eighteenth century came the development of new groups of people with new ideas and interests, especially those who, opposing Spanish control and restrictions in the last years of the colonial period, advocated their self-interests and independence from the mother country. The peoples of colonial Guatemala—Spaniards, Creoles, Indians, blacks, and castas—all faced, one generation after another, domestic problems, natural disasters, and foreign threats. In spite of their frustrations and setbacks, they rebuilt, adjusted, and endured, thereby providing a basis for the Republic of Guatemala.

Spain's nearly three centuries of jurisdiction over what today is the Republic of Guatemala left indelible marks upon the history of the nation, its land, and its people. A legacy is something that is bequeathed or handed down from the past to the present by an ancestor or predecessor. Spain's greatest legacy for today's Guatemaltecos is the establishment of their territory, language, religion, society, and customs. Having created a new society, Spain left this as a reminder of the Spanish presence and human contribution to the rich heritage of Guatemala. Indeed, Spanish colonial Guatemala was both an encounter and an accommodation of two worlds, Europe and America.

Appendix. Spanish Governors, Captains General and Presidents of the Audiencia of Guatemala, 1524–1821

Official	Took Office	Left Office
CONQUEST AND EARLY PERIOD (GOVERNORS AND CAPTAINS GENERAL)		
Pedro de Alvarado	27 July 1524	4 October 1525
Pedro de Valdivieso	4 October 1525	12 October 1525
Pedro de Alvarado	12 October 1525	3 February 1526
Gonzalo de Alvarado	3 February 1526	20 August 1526
Pedro de Alvarado	20 August 1526	26 August 1526
Pedro de Portocarrero and Hernán Carrillo	26 August 1526	20 March 1527
Jorge de Alvarado	20 March 1527	14 August 1529
Francisco de Orduna	14 August 1529	11 April 1530
Pedro de Alvarado	11 April 1530	20 January 1533
Jorge de Alvarado	20 January 1533	20 April 1535
Pedro de Alvarado	20 April 1535	2 March 1536
Gonzalo de Alvarado	2 March 1536	10 May 1536
Alonso de Maldonado	10 May 1536	16 September 1539
Pedro de Alvarado	16 September 1539	19 May 1540
Francisco de la Cueva	19 May 1540	29 August 1541
Beatriz de la Cueva	9 September 1541	11 September 1541
Bishop Francisco Marroquín and Francisco de la Cueva	17 September 1541	17 May 1542
Alonso de Maldonado	17 May 1542	20 November 1542
REAL AUDIENCIA DE LOS CONFINES/GUATEMALA (GOVERNORS, CAPTAINS GENERAL, AND PRESIDENTS)		
Alonso de Maldonado	20 November 1542	26 May 1548
Alonso López de Cerrato	26 May 1548	14 January 1555
Antonio Rodríguez de Quesada	14 January 1555	October 1555

Official	Took Office	Left Office
Pedro Ramírez de Quiñónes	October 1555	2 September 1559
Juan de Landecho Núñez	2 September 1559	30 May 1563
Francisco Briseño de Coca	30 May 1563	5 January 1570
Antonio González	5 January 1570	26 January 1573
Pedro de Villalobos	26 January 1573	4 February 1578
García de Valverde	4 February 1578	21 July 1588
Pedro Mayén de Rueda	21 July 1588	3 August 1594
Francisco de Sandé	3 August 1594	20 June 1596
Alvaro Gómez de Abaúnza	20 June 1596	19 September 1598
Alonso Criado de Castilla	19 September 1598	19 September 1611
Antonio Peraza de Ayala Castilla (conde de la Gomera)	19 September 1611	1 April 1621
Juan Ibarra	1 April 1621	April 1623
Antonio Peraza de Ayala Castilla (conde de la Gomera)	April 1623	21 April 1627
Diego de Acuña	21 April 1627	16 March 1634
Alvaro de Quiñónes y Osorio (marqués de Lorenzana)	16 March 1634	16 March 1642
Diego de Avendaño	16 March 1642	2 August 1649
Antonio de Lara	2 August 1649	11 March 1652
Gerónimo Garzés Carrillo de Mendoza (conde de Priego)	11 March 1652	21 November 1653
Real Audiencia (oidores)	21 November 1653	February 1654
Gerónimo Garzés Carrillo de Mendoza (conde de Priego)	February 1654	14 May 1654
Fernando de Altamirano y Velasco (conde de Santiago de Calimaya)	14 May 1654	January 1657
Real Audiencia (oidores)	January 1657	6 January 1659
Gen. Martín Carlos de Mencos y Arbizú	6 January 1659	8 January 1667
Sebastián Alfonso Rosica de Caldas	8 January 1667	28 October 1670
Bishop Juan de Sancto Mathía Sáenz de Mañozca y Murillo	29 October 1670	9 June 1672
Gen. Fernando Francisco de Escobedo	9 June 1672	22 December 1678
Lope de Sierra Osorio	22 December 1678	23 December 1681

Official	Took Office	Left Office
Juan Miguel de Augusto	23 December 1681	14 December 1683
Enrique Enríquez de Guzmán	14 December 1683	26 January 1688
Capitán General de Caballería Jacinto de Barrios Leal	26 January 1688	1 February 1691
Fernando López de Ursiño	1 February 1691	17 December 1693
Capitán General de Caballería Jacinto de Barrios Leal	17 December 1693	12 November 1695
José de Escals	12 November 1695	26 March 1696
Gen. Gabriel Sánchez de Berrospe	26 March 1696	11 January 1700
Gregorio Carrillo y Escudero	11 January 1700	12 March 1700
Juan Jerónimo Duardo	12 March 1700	4 April 1700
Gregorio Carrillo y Escudero	4 April 1700	5 April 1700
Juan Jerónimo Duardo	5 April 1700	6 April 1700
Gen. Gabriel Sánchez de Berrospe	6 April 1700	30 May 1702
Alonso de Ceballos y Villagutierre	30 May 1702	27 October 1703
José Gergorio Espinoza de los Monteros	29 October 1703	30 August 1706
Gen. Toribio José Cosío y de la Campa (marqués de Torre Campo)	30 August 1706	4 October 1716
Francisco Rodríguez de Rivas	4 October 1716	1 December 1724
Mariscal del Campo Antonio Pedre de Echevers y Subiza	2 December 1724	12 July 1733
Brigadier Pedro de Rivera y Villalón	12 July 1733	16 October 1742
Tomás de Rivera y Santa Cruz	16 October 1742	23 September 1748
José de Araujo y Río	23 September 1748	28 December 1751
Lt. Gen. José Vásquez Prego y Montaos	17 January 1752	24 June 1753
Juan de Velarde y Cienfuegos	25 June 1753	17 October 1754
Mariscal del Campo Alonso de Arcos y Moreno	17 October 1754	27 October 1760
Juan de Velarde y Cienfuegos	28 October 1760	15 June 1761
Mariscal del Campo Alonso Fernández de Heredia	15 June 1761	11 April 1764

Official	Took Office	Left Office
Real Audiencia (oidores)	11 April 1764	14 November 1764
Brigadier Pedro de Salazar Nátera y Mendoza	14 November 1764	5 July 1768
Mariscal del Campo Alonso Fernández de Heredia	5 July 1768	28 January 1769
Juan González Bustillo y Villaseñor	28 January 1769	February 1769
Mariscal del Campo Pedro de Salazar Nátera y Mendoza	February 1769	20 May 1771
Juan González Bustillo y Villaseñor	20 May 1771	12 June 1773
Mariscal del Campo Martín de Mayorga	12 June 1773	4 April 1779
Lt. Gen. Matías de Gálvez (a regent governed while he was on military campaigns, August 1780– September 1781)	4 April 1779	7 March 1783
Brigadier José de Estachería	7 March 1783	3 April 1783
Juan Antonio de Uruñuela (regent)	3 April 1783	31 January 1788
Brigadier José de Estachería	31 January 1788	29 December 1789
Juan Antonio de Uruñuela (regent)	29 December 1789	31 December 1789
Lt. Gen. Bernardo Troncoso Martínez del Rincón	31 December 1789	7 April 1790
Juan Antonio de Uruñuela (regent)	7 April 1790	21 March 1791
Juan José de Villalengua (regent)	21 March 1791	December 1793
Lt. Gen. Bernardo Troncoso Martínez del Rincón	December 1793	25 May 1794
Jefe de Escuadra José Domas y Valle	25 May 1794	18 May 1795
Joaquín de Vasco (oidor)	18 May 1795	9 June 1795
Jefe de Escuadra José Domas y Valle	9 June 1795	12 March 1801
Subinspector of Militias Roque Abarca	12 March 1801	28 July 1801

Official	Took Office	Left Office
Brigadier Antonio González Mollinedo y Saravia	28 July 1801	17 May 1804
Ambrosio Cerdán y Pontero (regent)	4 May 1803	1 June 1804
Subinspector of Militias Roque Abarca	17 May 1804	1 June 1804
Manuel Castillo Negrete (regent)	1 June 1804	October 1804
Capitán General Antonio González Mollinedo y Saravia	October 1804	11 April 1810
José Bernardo Asteguieta y Serraldo (regent)	22 February 1810	?1812
Commandant and Colonel of the Royal Corps of Artillery José de Méndez Quiroga	11 April 1810	21 April 1810
Lt. Gen. Antonio González Mollinedo y Saravia	21 April 1810	14 March 1811
Jefe de Escuadra José Bustamante y Guerra (title became Jefe Político and Jefe Superior in 1812)	14 March 1811	28 March 1818
Lt. Gen. Carlos Urrutia y Montoya (jefe político superior)	28 March 1818	9 March 1821
Subinspector General of the Troops Gabino Gaínza (Jefe Político Superior)	9 March 1821	15 September 1821

SOURCES: Agustín Estrada Monroy, *Hombres, fechas y documentos de la patria,* 119–27; Murdo J. MacLeod, *Spanish Central America: A Socioeconomic History, 1520–1720,* 390–92; *Enciclopedia Universal Ilustrada* 26: 1638.

This appendix has been compiled by relying primarily on Estrada Monroy and comparing his table with MacLeod until 1720. Although there are slight differences in dates and spellings of names, the two sources are in close agreement. Before and after 1720, Estrada Monroy's table was compared to the one in the *Enciclopedia Universal Ilustrada,* which was found to have serious errors and omissions. For example, Gerónimo Garzés Carrillo de Mendoza (1652–54), Lope de Sierra Osorio (1678–81), Tomás de Rivera y Santa Cruz (1742–48), and Matías de Gálvez (1779–83) are all omitted from the *Enciclopedia* list, as are most interim governors and regents. Furthermore, the *Enciclopedia* has erroneous dates for the Pedro de Rivera, José de Araujo y Rio, and Martín de Mayorga administrations and misrenders the name of José Domas as Tomás. Dates for the governors Rodríguez de Quesada and Ramírez de Quiñones have been corrected to reflect information in William L. Sherman, *Forced Native Labor in Sixteenth-Century Central America,* 143 and 408–409 n. 72.

Notes

ABBREVIATIONS

AGCA   Archivo General Centro América, Guatemala City
AGI   Archivo General de Indias, Sevilla, Spain
AGN   Archivo General de la Nación, Mexico City, Mexico
AHN   Archivo Hisórico Nacional, Madrid, Spain
HAHR   *Hispanic American Historical Review*

1. CATASTROPHE, LAND, AMERINDIANS

1. Felipe Cádena, "Breve descripción de la Noble Ciudad de Santiago de los Caballeros de Guatemala y puntual noticia de su lamentable ruina ocasionada de un violento Terremoto, el día veinte y nuebe de Julio del año de 1773. Escrita por el R. P. Lector de Teología Fr. Felipe Cádena, Dr. en la misma facultad en el Rl Universidad de San Carlos, Examinador sindical de este Arzobispado y Secretario de su Provincia de Predicadores, México, Año de 1774," Joaquín García Icazbalceta Collection, No. 232 (201 pages), Nettie Lee Benson Latin American Library, University of Texas at Austin, 39–43. This handwritten document by Father Cádena, completed at the "Establecimiento provisional de la Hermita" (Guatemala City), was dated 10 March 1774. It was acquired by García Icazbalceta in Madrid on 18 January 1853. Father Cádena's eyewitness account of the destruction of Santiago de los Caballeros de Guatemala (today's Antigua) has been published in part in José Antonio Villacorta Calderón, *Historia de la capitanía general de Guatemala,* libro tercero, capítulo 3, pages 428–31. It was also published in full at Mixco, Guatemala, by Antonio Sánchez Cubillas in 1774. These are the only two publications of the document that have been located.

2. Cádena, "Breve descripción," 6.

3. Ibid., 8–10.

4. Ibid., 13–15, 18–24, 26–29.

5. Ibid., 35.

6. Ibid., 36.

7. Ibid., 38.

8. Ibid., 43–51.

9. Ibid., 62–64, 70, 78.

10. Ibid., 172–73.

11. Ibid., 92–98, 102–106.

12. Ibid., 186–87.

13. Eric Wolf, *Sons of the Shaking Earth: The People of Mexico and Guatemala—Their Land, History, and Culture*, 1.

14. Ibid., 21, 34.

15. Robert C. West and John P. Augelli, *Middle America: Its Lands and Peoples*, 38; John Dombrowski et al., *Area Handbook for Guatemala*, 40–41. The *Diccionario Geográfico de Guatemala*, 1:307, states that the elevation of Guatemala City is 1,498.89 meters or 4,946.337 feet.

16. Dombrowski, *Area Handbook for Guatemala*, vii, 39; Guillermo de Zendegui, ed., *Image of Guatemala*, supplement to *Americas* magazine, S-2 and S-3.

17. West and Augelli, *Middle America*, 30.

18. Ibid., 30, 397 (map); Dombrowski, *Area Handbook for Guatemala*, 44–45. Except for Tajumulco Volcano, all elevations have been rounded off to the nearest hundred feet. According to the *Diccionario Geográfico de Guatemala* 2:6, Pacaya Volcano reaches an elevation of 2,552.08 meters or about 8,422 feet.

19. West and Augelli, *Middle America*, 31, 387; Dombrowski, *Area Handbook for Guatemala*, 45, 46; Zendegui, *Image of Guatemala*, S-4.

20. West and Augelli, *Middle America*, 388–89; Dombrowski, *Area Handbook for Guatemala*, 46–47.

21. West and Augelli, *Middle America*, 388; Dombrowski, *Area Handbook for Guatemala*, 43.

22. West and Augelli, *Middle America*, 35, 37–43. According to the *Diccionario Geográfico de Guatemala* 1:307, the average annual rainfall for Guatemala City is 1,250 mm, or about 50 inches.

23. Dombrowski, *Area Handbook for Guatemala*, 46, 48–49; West and Augelli, *Middle America*, 56–58; Zendegui, *Image of Guatemala*, S-4 and S-5.

24. West and Augelli, *Middle America*, 395–99.

25. Murdo J. MacLeod, *Spanish Central America: A Socioeconomic History, 1520–1720*, 229–30; Ralph L. Woodward, *Central America: A Nation Divided*, 2d ed., 23; West and Augelli, *Middle America*, 6 n.3.

26. West and Augelli, *Middle America*, 231–32, establish the limits of Mesoamerica in northern Mexico roughly from present Tampico to Culiacán, with the southern boundary from Honduras to the Nicoya Peninsula of Costa Rica. While all anthropologists and archaeologists may not agree completely with those limits, central and southern Mexico and all of Guatemala lie within the region.

27. Wolf, *Sons of the Shaking Earth*, 96; West and Augelli, *Middle America*, 229–30; MacLeod, *Spanish Central America*, 33.

28. Much has been written on Mayan history, especially by archaeologists and anthropologists. For reliable overviews of Mayan history and civilization, see two books by J. Eric S. Thompson, *The Rise and Fall of Maya Civilization* and *Maya History and Religion;* Michael D. Coe, *The Maya;* Norman Hammond and Gordon R. Willey, eds., *Maya Archaeology and Ethnohistory;* and many other scholarly books and articles in professional journals. Within the past thirty years there also have been numerous contributions to the study of the Mayas in Guatemala. See, for example, Mary W. Helms, *Middle America: A Culture History of Heartland and Frontiers;* Sandra Orellana, *The Tzutujil Mayas: Continuity and Change, 1250–1630;* Robert M. Carmack, *The Quiché Mayas of Utatlán: The Evolution of a Highland Guatemala Kingdom;* Adrián Recinos, *The Annals of the Cakchiqueles;* and essays in Murdo J. MacLeod and Robert Wasserstrom, eds., *Spaniards and Indians in Southeastern Meso-*

america: Essays on the History of Ethnic Relations. Useful in summarizing the pre-Columbian Maya cultures in this chapter have been Wolf, *Sons of the Shaking Earth,* 96–98; MacLeod, *Spanish Central America,* 28–37; West and Augelli, *Middle America,* 229–40; Dombrowski, *Area Handbook for Guatemala,* 10–13; Francis Polo Sifontes, *Historia de Guatemala: Visión de conjunto de su desarrollo político-cultural,* 49–57, 59–65, 67–79; and Dr. Juan Carlos Solórzano, "La conquista de Centroamerica en el contexto de la expansión Europea y el descubrimiento de America," *Avances de investigación,* 25. The most recent and useful publication pertaining to pre-Columbian Middle America is Richard E. W. Adams, *Prehistoric Mesoamerica,* rev. ed. (Norman: University of Oklahoma Press, 1991).

29. Polo Sifontes, *Historia de Guatemala,* 52–54, 71; MacLeod, *Spanish Central America,* 28; Wolf, *Sons of the Shaking Earth,* 96, 98–100.

30. MacLeod, *Spanish Central America,* 28; Polo Sifontes, *Historia de Guatemala,* 63.

31. West and Augelli, *Middle America,* 236; however, Murdo J. MacLeod, "An Outline of Central American Colonial Demographics: Sources, Yields, and Possibilities," in *The Historical Demography of Highland Guatemala,* eds. Robert M. Carmack, John Ealy, and Christopher Lutz, 7, cites a figure of 500,000 to 800,000 for the highland region of today's Guatemala, and perhaps double that if both coasts and the Petén were included.

32. MacLeod, *Spanish Central America,* 33–34; Polo Sifontes, *Historia de Guatemala,* 59–60; Solórzano, "La conquista de Centroamerica," 25. For spelling of the Mayan tribal groups the author has relied upon the *Diccionario Geográfico de Guatemala* 2:415, but variations are common.

33. The best description of the locales occupied by the different Mayan groups or nations, accompanied by a fine map, is in Carmack, *The Quiché Mayas,* 3–6.

34. MacLeod, *Spanish Central America,* 37; Solórzano, "La conquista de Centroamerica," 25.

2. CONTACT, CONQUEST, AND COLONIZATION

1. John E. Kelly, *Pedro de Alvarado, Conquistador,* 129; "Guatemala," *Enciclopedia Universal Ilustrada* (Barcelona: Hijos de Espasa, 1925), 26:1637.

2. Ralph L. Woodward, *Central America,* 31; Hubert H. Bancroft, *History of Central America* 1:652.

3. Kelly, *Pedro de Alvarado,* 3–118; Pedro de Alvarado, *An Account of the Conquest of Guatemala in 1524,* ed. Sedley J. Mackie, 27.

4. Alvarado, *An Account of the Conquest,* 14–15, citing fourth letter of Hernán Cortés to the king, 15 October 1524. Departure early in December 1523 also is indicated by Woodward, *Central America,* 31; F. A. Kirkpatrick, *The Spanish Conquistadores,* 110; and Polo Sifontes, Historia de Guatemala, 99. However, a 13 November 1523 departure date is stated by Domingo Juarros, *A Statistical and Commercial History of the Kingdom of Guatemala in Spanish America . . . ,* trans. J. Baily, 124.

5. Kelly, *Pedro de Alvarado,* 128; Polo Sifontes, *Historia de Guatemala,* 100. Both of these sources are based on Cortés's fourth letter to the king and hence are more reliable than others. John Dombrowski et al., *Area Handbook for Guatemala,* 14, and Juarros, *Statistical and Commercial History,* 124, are also accurate in their summaries of the composition of Alvarado's force. However, Chester L. Jones, *Guatemala: Past*

and Present, 6, errs in numbering the horsemen at 135; and Salvador Rodríguez Becerra, *Encomienda y conquista: los inicios de la colonización en Guatemala,* 3, makes the same mistake. Angel de Altolaguirre y Duvale, *Descubrimiento y conquista de México,* ed. Antonio Ballesteros y Beretta, 341, not only errs in the number of horsemen but also says that there were 390 foot soldiers and that the expedition departed from Mexico City on 4 December 1523. The *Enciclopedia Universal Ilustrada* 26:1637 states that there were 150 horsemen and 3,000 Mexican Indian allies.

6. Kelly, *Pedro de Alvarado,* 133; Rodríguez Becerra, *Encomienda y conquista,* 3–4. Why Kelly states that Alvarado "was not aided by great forces of native allies" (p. 133) is a mystery because Mexican Indians and thousands of Cakchiqueles supplied and fought beside the Spaniards against the Quichés. See, for example, Rodríguez Becerra, *Encomienda y conquista,* 4.

7. Solórzano, *"La conquista de Centroamérica,"* 27; Altolaguirre, *Descubrimiento y conquista,* 344–45.

8. Kelly, *Pedro de Alvarado,* 139, citing letter of Pedro de Alvarado to Hernán Cortés, 11 April 1524.

9. Rodríguez Becerra, *Encomienda y conquista,* 4–5; Solórzano, "La Conquista de Centroamérica," 27. Kelly, *Pedro de Alvarado,* 145, maintains that Alvarado's force was received peacefully by the Tzutujiles.

10. Rodríguez Becerra, *Encomienda y conquista,* 5; Altolaguirre, *Descubrimiento y conquista,* 348.

11. Kelly, *Pedro de Alvarado,* 156.

12. Solórzano, "La conquista de Centroamérica," 27; Kelly, *Pedro de Alvarado,* 149; Juarros, *Statistical and Commercial History,* 125–26; Fray Antonio de Remesal, *Historia general de las indias occidentales, y particular de la gobernación de Chiapa y Guatemala,* 1:21. Remesal erroneously stated that these officials were appointed later in Almolonga, not in Iximché.

13. Kelly, *Pedro de Alvarado,* 157, 159.

14. Bancroft, *History of Central America* 2:79–80, 85; Kelly, *Pedro de Alvarado,* 159–62.

15. Kelly, *Pedro de Alvarado,* 168; Solórzano, "La conquista de Centroamérica," 28.

16. Kelly, *Pedro de Alvarado,* 171–73.

17. Ibid., 173.

18. Ibid., 173, 176n.19; Bancroft, *History of Central America* 2:102; William L. Sherman, "A Conqueror's Wealth: Notes on the Estate of Don Pedro de Alvarado," *The Americas* 26, no. 2 (October 1969): 199.

19. Kelly, *Pedro de Alvarado,* 176–84.

20. Bancroft, *History of Central America* 2:88–95; Rodríguez Becerra, *Encomienda y conquista,* 6; Solórzano, "La conquista de Centroamérica," 28.

21. Juarros, *Statistical and Commercial History,* 125; Remesal, *Historia general* 1:20–21; Woodward, *Central America,* 31; Kelly, *Pedro de Alvarado,* 175; Jones, *Guatemala,* 10.

22. Rodríguez Becerra, *Encomienda y conquista,* 6.

23. Bancroft, *History of Central America* 2:97, 120; Remesal, *Historia general* 1:58; Kelly, *Pedro de Alvarado,* 183. One must always be careful not to confuse vecinos with total inhabitants in early reports.

24. Harry Kelsey, *Juan Rodríguez Cabrillo,* 43, 49–51.

25. Kelly, *Pedro de Alvarado,* 183; Bancroft, *History of Central America* 2:134–35; Remesal, *Historia general* 1:64.

26. Bancroft, *History of Central America* 1:626, and 2:133, 137, 141, 345.

27. Victor Westphall, *Mercedes Reales: Hispanic Land Grants of the Upper Rio Grande Region,* 14, states that the size of a caballería and a peonía were laid down by a royal decree in 1513 (a caballería included a house lot 100 feet by 200 feet and five times as much agricultural land as a peonía, which comprised a lot 50 feet by 100 feet and about 100 acres of agricultural land). Kelsey, *Juan Rodríguez Cabrillo,* 50, says a caballería measured 600 by 300 feet, while a peonía was 300 by 150 feet, or one-half the size of a caballería. Christopher H. Lutz, "Santiago de Guatemala, 1541–1773: The Sociodemographic History of a Spanish Colonial City" (Ph.D. diss., University of Wisconsin, 1976), 124, states that in 1528 lands were apportioned by caballerías, each 600 by 1,000 paces, with peonías about one half that size, and that each caballería amounted to about 105 acres. With such wide varieties of measurement, it is difficult to come to any commonly recognized size for these grants.

28. Bancroft, *History of Central America* 2:120.

29. Sherman, "A Conqueror's Wealth," 200–211.

30. Jones, *Guatemala,* 14.

31. Altolaguirre, *Descubrimiento y conquista,* 442–43.

32. Bancroft, *History of Central America* 2:201.

33. Kelly, *Pedro de Alvarado,* 189–205; Kirkpatrick, *Spanish Conquistadores,* 114–17. Alvarado did not get to Peru, but only as far as Ecuador. There he reached an agreement to withdraw and sell his ships to Diego de Almagro.

34. Kelly, *Pedro de Alvarado,* 204–207; Alvarado, *An Account of the Conquest of Guatemala,* 29; Woodward, *Central America,* 32.

35. Kelly, *Pedro de Alvarado,* 209–17. There is some confusion about the actual day of Alvarado's death. Kelly maintains that he was buried on 30 June 1541 (p. 217), but Mackie in his edition of Alvarado, *Account of the Conquest of Guatemala,* 30–31, says he died on 4 July 1541. The accident on 24 June 1541 at Nochistlán occurred when Baltasar de Montoya's horse lost its footing and rolled down upon Alvarado, who could not flee because of his armor and heavy arms. His chest crushed, bleeding from the mouth, Alvarado was taken to the village of Atenquillo, where he died 4 July 1541. See D. Matías de la Mota Padilla, *Historia de la Conquista de la provincia de la Nueva Galicia,* 65–68, and *Muerte del Pedro de Alvarado,* 14, 36, 39.

36. Kelly, *Pedro de Alvarado,* 218–19; Bancroft, *History of Central America* 2:311–13.

37. Remesal, *Historia general* 1:256–58; Bancroft, *History of Central America* 2:314–16; Kelly, *Pedro de Alvarado,* 220–21; Jones, *Guatemala,* 16. Kirkpatrick, *Spanish Conquistadores,* 119, errs in stating that Doña Beatriz perished in the earthquake of 1542. The number of deaths at Ciudad Vieja, or Almolonga, varies with different sources.

38. Kelly, *Pedro de Alvarado,* 222; Juarros, *Statistical and Commercial History,* 127; Bancroft, *History of Central America* 2:321; Solórzano, "La conquista de Centroamérica," 29. Lutz, "Santiago de Guatemala," 90–92, reviews the two meetings of the cabildo on 27 September and 2 October 1541 with the intervening study of proposed sites by a committee. Interim governors Bishop Marroquín and Licenciado Francisco de la Cueva were present at the 2 October meeting, along with seventy-eight vecinos. Forty-nine approved the move to the valley of Panchoy, while twenty-nine favored reconstructing the capital on the Almolonga site.

39. MacLeod, *Spanish Central America* 44.

40. Rodríguez Becerra, *Encomienda y conquista* 11, 16.
41. Ibid., 28–29.
42. Woodward, *Central America*, 33.

3. GOVERNMENT

1. This statement refutes the observation in Dombrowski, *Area Handbook for Guatemala*, 15, that "the colonial era was virtually a static period in Guatemalan history." Instead the present author has followed the contentions and proofs of, for example, Woodward, *Central America;* MacLeod, *Spanish Central America;* and Miles L. Wortman, *Government and Society in Central America, 1680–1840,* that the nature of Spanish government in the colonial period was ever changing.
2. Kelly, *Pedro de Alvarado,* 173.
3. Agustín Estrada Monroy, *Hombres, fechas y documentos de la patria,* 120–21
4. Remesal, *Historia general* 1:21.
5. "Acta de Fundación de la Ciudad de Santiago de Guatemala en Quinicilapam (Del Valle de Almolonga)," 22 de noviembre de 1527, in Estrada Monroy, *Hombres, fechas y documentos de la patria,* 15–20. There is a contradiction in the names of the first regidores because Jorge de Alvarado also referred to Pedro and Jorge de Acuna and omitted Pedro and Eugenio de Moscoso.
6. Altolaguirre, *Descubrimiento y conquista,* 442–43.
7. Estrada Monroy, *Hombres, fechas y documentos de la patria,* 121.
8. Woodward, *Central America,* 35; Juarros, *Statistical and Commercial History,* 127.
9. The term "kingdom" was applied commonly in Spain and throughout Spanish America to mean a superior or extensive territorial entity within the Spanish empire. Thus there were, for example, the kingdoms of Castile and León and Aragon in Spain along with those of New Spain and Peru, as well as Nueva Vizcaya, in the Indies.
10. Lyle N. McAlister, *Spain and Portugal in the New World, 1492–1700,* 189; Woodward, *Central America,* 36; Carlos Molina Arguello, "Gobernaciones, alcaldías mayores y corregimientos en el Reino de Guatemala," *Anuario de Estudios Americanos* 17 (1960): 108; Juarros, *Statistical and Commercial History,* 127–28.
11. McAlister, *Spain and Portugal,* 78
12. Ibid., 204–205; MacLeod, *Spanish Central America,* 318.
13. McAlister, *Spain and Portugal,* 188, 191.
14. Ibid., 190.
15. Woodward, *Central America,* 36. Juarros, *Statistical and Commercial History,* 128, says that the audiencia moved to Panama City in 1550.
16. José Villacorta Calderón, *Historia de la capitanía general de Guatemala,* 61; Bancroft, *History of Central America* 2:370–71.
17. Woodward, *Central America,* 38; Juarros, *Statistical and Commercial History,* 128.
18. Woodward, *Central America,* 38–39.
19. Juarros, *Statistical and Commercial History,* 127–28.
20. Ralph H. Vigil, *Alonso de Zorita, Royal Judge and Christian Humanist, 1512–1585,* 126–27, 129–30, 147.
21. Lic. Palacios, "Descripción de la Provincia de Guatemala por el oidor," 8 March 1576, [Santiago de Guatemala?], Archivo Histórico Nacional, Diversos Documentos

de Indias, No. 240, Madrid, Spain. The document bears the signature of Palacios, but not his first name. The Archivo Histórico Nacional is hereafter abbreviated as AHN.

22. For a list of these officials, see Estrada Monroy, *Hombres, fechas y documentos de la patria,* 121–24, and MacLeod, *Spanish Central America,* 390–92. The listing of governors in the *Enciclopedia Universal Ilustrada* 26:1638 should be used with caution because of erroneous dates, omissions, and misrendering of some names. See the Appendix for a list of Spanish presidents, captains general, and governors for the colonial period.

23. Villacorta Calderón, *Historia de la Capitanía General de Guatemala,* 62.

24. Estrada Monroy, *Hombres, fechas y documentos de la patria,* 122–23.

25. McAlister, *Spain and Portugal,* 182.

26. Estrada Monroy, *Hombres, fechas y documentos de la patria,* 121.

27. Vigil, *Alonso de Zorita,* 121.

28. Ibid., 124, 127. For a full and authoritative discussion of the reforms, see William L. Sherman, *Forced Native Labor in Sixteenth Century Central America,* especially chapter 8; and Sherman, "Indian Slavery and the Cerrato Reforms," *Hispanic American Historical Review* 51, no. 1 (February 1971): 25–50. The *Hispanic American Historical Review* is hereafter abbreviated as HAHR.

29. Documents pertaining to Lope de Sierra Osorio, Archivo General de Centro América, Guatemala City, specifically numbers A1.23, legajo 4586, folio 65v; A1.23, legajo 4587, folios 23 and 151; A1.23 legajo 4584, folio 278v, appointing an oidor of the Guatemalan audiencia, Lic. Antonio de Navia Bolaños, to take the residencia of Sierra Osorio; and A3.1, expediente 11669, legajo 582, folio 140, pertaining to the pension of the Alvarado heirs. The Archivo General de Centro America is hereafter abbreviated as AGCA. For Lope de Sierra Osorio in northern Mexico, see Oakah L. Jones, Jr., *Nueva Vizcaya: Heartland of the Spanish Frontier,* 3, 87, 103, 270n.38.

30. King Carlos II to Don Enríquez de Guzmán, president of the Audiencia de Guatemala, Madrid, 25 December 1682, AGCA, A1.23, leg. 4587, folio 151.

31. McAlister, *Spain and Portugal,* 187, 424.

32. Molina Arguello, "Gobernaciones, alcaldías mayores y corregimientos en el Reino de Guatemala," 121, 125, 128 (table).

33. Bancroft, *History of Central America* 2:98, observes that the cabildo had eight regidores in 1528.

34. Lutz, "Santiago de Guatemala," 1:66. Lutz's dissertation has been published in Spanish as Christopher H. Lutz, *Historia sociodemográfica de Santiago de Guatemala, 1541–1773* (Antigua, Guat., and South Woodstock, Vt., 1982), and a revised version is forthcoming from the University of Oklahoma Press.

35. McAlister, *Spain and Portugal,* 133, 135. Lutz, "Santiago de Guatemala," 1:67, observes that disputes between the cabildo and the audiencia existed until the eighteenth century when the cabildo lost the struggle. If so, it regained its powers during the independence era.

36. Among the many excellent studies of the Enlightenment in the Spanish Americas, especially in Guatemala, is John Tate Lanning, *The Eighteenth Century Enlightenment in the University of San Carlos de Guatemala.* The introduction of that work provides a good general overview of the principles of the Enlightenment and their transfer from Spain to the Americas. See also Carlos Melendez, *La ilustración en el antiguo reino de Guatemala,* and for Latin America in general, Arthur P. Whitaker, ed., *Latin America and the Enlightenment.* For controversial views concerning Bour-

bon reforms, see, for example, Troy S. Floyd, ed. and trans., *The Bourbon Reformers and Spanish Civilization: Builders or Destroyers?* (Boston: D.C. Heath, 1966).

37. Wortman, *Government and Society in Central America,* 129–130.

38. Woodward, *Central America,* 63.

39. Ibid., 66.

40. "Goathemala. Gobiernos de sus presidentes, de 1734 a 1760," Archivo General de Indias, Sevilla, Spain, Guatemala 448. Hereafter the Archivo General de Indias is abbreviated as AGI.

41. Wilbur E. Meneray, "The Kingdom of Guatemala during the Reign of Charles III, 1759–88," Ph.D. diss., University of North Carolina, 1975, 27.

42. See Appendix and Estrada Monroy, *Hombres, fechas y documentos de la patria,* 1124–27, for lists of these officials.

43. Wortman, *Government and Society in Central America,* 95; Meneray, "Kingdom of Guatemala," 53.

44. Meneray, "Kingdom of Guatemala," 38–41.

45. Ramón A. Salazar, *Historia de veintiún años: la independencia de Guatemala,* 117; "Nota," Guatemala, 22 September 1811, Copia Número 8, AGI, Guatemala 502.

46. The order of the Junta Central de Sevilla on 22 January 1809 recognized governmental errors of the past and proclaimed that all Americans had the right to participate in government. As integral parts of the Spanish monarchy, Spanish territories in America were no longer considered as colonies and their residents were granted national representation as part of the Junta Central Gobernativa. As a result, viceroys and governors were ordered to send representatives of their districts, elected by their ayuntamientos, for the convening of a cortes or legislative body. This order seems to mark the beginning of the ayuntamiento's reemergence as an important, increasingly powerful institution. See Salazar, *Historia de veintiún años,* 117, 119.

47. Woodward, *Central America,* 67; Meneray, "Kingdom of Guatemala," 31–34, 38; Wortman, *Government and Society in Central America,* 149.

48. Wortman, *Government and Society in Central America,* 148; Woodward, *Central America,* 67.

49. Cayetano Alcázar Molina, *Los Virreinatos en el siglo XVIII,* 199–200.

50. Ibid., 202; Ayuntamiento de Guatemala to the king, Guatemala, 14 December 1717, AGI, Guatemala 309. The latter document, signed by Joseph Bernardo Mencos de Coronado and seven others, is a petition to transfer the capital from Ciudad Vieja to the valley of Las Vacas.

51. King Felipe V, royal cedula, Madrid, 22 December 1729, AGCA, A1.23, leg. 4609, fol. 83v.

52. "Testimonio de Poseción de esta Presidenzia," with letter from Pedro de Rivera to Juan Bautista Maturana, Goathemala, 23 February 1734, AGI, Guatemala 229.

53. Guillermo Porras Muñoz, ed., *Diario y derrotero de lo caminado, visto y observado en el discurso de la visita general de precidios, situados en las provincias ynternas de Nueva España, que de orden de su magestad executó D. Pedro de Rivera. . . . ,* 14–21, and Jones, *Nueva Vizcaya,* 124–35. For a full account of this inspection, see Thomas H. Naylor and Charles W. Polzer, eds., *Pedro de Rivera and the Military Regulations for Northern New Spain, 1724–1729.* Porras Muñoz states that Rivera had thirty-four years of service when he became governor and captain general of the Kingdom of Guatemala, but when the king granted him his pension in 1743, it was noted that Rivera had served sixty-three years. Therefore, he must have had fifty-four

years of service before coming to Guatemala. See the king's order to Don Joseph Carvajal y Lancaster, San Yldefonso, 26 August 1743, AGI, Guatemala 448.

54. Pedro de Rivera to Dn. Juan Bentra. de Maturana, Goathema., 26 September 1736, AGI, Guatemala 448.

55. Pedro de Rivera to Your Majesty, Goathemala, 21 June 1737, AGI, Guatemala 231; Rivera to Exmo. Sr.Dn. Joseph Patiño, Goathema., 14 February 1737, AGI, Guatemala 448, Rivera to the king, Goathemala, 15 December 1739, AGI, Guatemala 231; Rivera to Dn. Joseph de la Quintana, Goathemala, 15 September 1740, AGI, Guatemala 232, King to oidores of the Real Audiencia de las Provincias de Guathemala, Aranjuez, 17 April 1742, AGCA, Al.1, expediente 115, legajo 6.

56. Pedro de Rivera to Exmo. Sr.Dn. Joseph the Quintana, Goathemala, 3 November 1740, AGI, Guatemala 448; Rivera to Your Majesty, Goathemala, 21 June 1737, AGI, Guatemala 231; Rivera to Your Majesty, Goathemala, 11 September 1737, AGI, Guatemala 230; Rivera to Your Majesty, Goathemaa., 8 May 1737, AGI, Guatemala 230; Cabildo [of Santiago de Guatemala] to Your Majesty, Goathemala, 27 June 1738, AGI, Guatemala 448.

57. Pedro de Rivera to Marqs. de Torre Nueba, Goatha., 23 November 1737, AGI, Guatemala 448.

58. Pedro de Rivera to Dn. Joseph de la Quintana, Goathemala, 15 September 1740, AGI, Guatemala 232. Spain and Great Britain were at war in the 1740s because of the latter's alleged violations of maritime rights spelled out in the Treaty of Utrecht, English contraband trade with Spanish colonies, England's occupation of Georgia and invasion of Florida, and English allegations that Spaniards had started the so-called War of Jenkins's Ear in 1739, which later merged into the War of the Austrian Succession (King George's War) in Europe and America.

59. Cabildo of Santiago de los Caballeros to Your Majesty, Goathemala, 27 June 1738, AGI, Guatemala 448. Eleven members of the cabildo signed this document.

60. Thomás de Ribera y Sta. Cruz to Señor Don Ferndo. Treviño, Goathemala, 7 November 1743 [?], and letter of audiencia, Guathemala, 24 January 1743, both in AGI, Guatemala 232.

61. Decree, Sn. Yldefonso, 26 August 1743, AGI, Guatemala 448, and AGCA, A3.2, exp. 409, leg.23, fol. 1.

62. Villacorta Calderón, *Historia de la Capitanía General de Guatemala,* 77.

63. Matías de Gálvez to Josef de Gálvez, Nueba Guata., 6 June 1779, and Matías de Gálvez to Josef de Gálvez, Nueva Guatemala, 6 April 1779, both in AGI, Guatemala 451.

64. Matías de Gálvez to Sor. Dn. Martín de Mayorga, Nueva Goatemala, 9 September 1778, AGGC, A2.5, exp. 6692, leg. 299; Matías de Gálvez to José de Gálvez, Omoa, 1 July 1778, AGI, Guatemala 451.

65. Oakah L. Jones, "Matías de Gálvez: Spanish Ally of the American Revolution," unpublished paper delivered at the Phi Alpha Theta Biennial Conference, St. Louis, Missouri, 30 December 1989, is a detailed study of Matías de Gálvez's administration, especially his military campaigns against the British.

66. Matías de Gálvez to Exmo. Señor Don Josef de Gálvez, Nueva Guatemala, 6 May 1779; Matías de Gálvez to Exmo. Sor. Dn. Josef de Gálvez, Nueva Guatemala, 6 June 1779, and His Majesty to the Presidte. de Goatema., San Lorenzo, 11 October, 1779, all in AGI, Guatemala 451.

67. For these campaigns, see Jones, "Matías de Gálvez: Spanish Ally of the Ameri-

can Revolution"; Villacorta Calderón, *Historia de la Capitanía General de Guatemala,* 77, and Troy S. Floyd, *The Ango-Spanish Struggle for Mosquitia.*

68. Cabildo to Your Majesty, Nueva Guatemala de la Asunción, 9 July 1782, AGI, Guatemala 451.

69. Josef Pablo Valiente, Sentencia, Nueva Guatemala de la Asuncíon, 3 December 1783, AGCA, A1.304, exp. 41098, leg. 4760, and [Consejo Real de Indias], Consulta, Madrid, 7 August 1784, AGI, Guatemala 411.

70. Meneray, "The Kingdom of Guatemala," 22, and Alcázar Molina, *Los virreinatos en el siglo XVIII,* 211.

71. Francisco Manuel Ramírez, Contador Mayor, Real Tribunal de Cuentas de Guatemala, Guatemala, 14 February 1783, "Estado de los Empleos Políticos Perpetuos y Temporales que se pagan por las Caxas y Administraciones de este Reyno, con expresión de sueldos, días de su Posesión . . . ," AGCA, A3.1, exp. 18000, leg. 975, año de 1783.

72. Salazar, *Historia de veintiún años,* 13–15.

73. Estrada Monroy, *Hombres, fechas y documentos de la patria,* 126–27; Salazar, *Historia de veintiún años,* 79, 136

74. Villacorta Calderón, *Historia de la capitanía general de Guatemala,* 87–88.

4. THE CHURCH

1. McAlister, *Spain and Portugal,* 59, 74–75, 78.
2. Ibid., 194–96. The quotation appears on page 196.
3. Ibid., 79.
4. Wortman, *Government and Society in Central America,* 41; Mary P. Holleran, *Church and State in Guatemala,* 21, 23.
5. Sandra Orellana, *Tzutujil Mayas,* 112, 195.
6. Kelly, *Pedro de Alvarado,* 129.
7. Villacorta Calderón, *Historia de la Capitanía General,* 221.
8. Orellana, *Tzutujil Mayas,* 195.
9. Villacorta Calderón, *Historia de la Capitanía General,* 224.
10. Woodward, *Central America,* 40. Villacorta Calderón, *Historia de la Capitanía General,* 229, says that the Jesuits did not arrive until 1606.
11. Polo Sifontes, *Historia de Guatemala,* 108–109.
12. Woodward, *Central America,* 40.
13. Villacorta Calderón, *Historia de la Capitanía General,* 224.
14. Woodward, *Central America,* 41; Villacorta Calderón, *Historia de la Capitanía General,* 225.
15. Villacorta Calderón, *Historia de la Capitanía General,* 224.
16. Wortman, *Government and Society in Central America,* 49.
17. For the practice and employment of the policy of *congregaciones,* see Jesús María García Añoveros, *Población y estado socioreligioso de la diócesis de Guatemala en el último tercio del siglo XVIII,* 136–38, and MacLeod, *Spanish Central America,* 121–22. The policy of *congregación* is treated more fully in chapter 5.
18. Lázaro La Madrid, O.F.M., "Bishop Marroquín—Zumárraga's Gift to Central America," *The Americas* 5, no. 3 (January 1949): 333.
19. Ibid., 331, 333, 341; Holleran, *Church and State,* 22.
20. La Madrid, "Bishop Marroquín," 333–38.

21. Ibid., 336; Vigil, *Alonso de Zorita,* 131; William L. Sherman, *Forced Native Labor in Sixteenth Century Central America,* 162–63; William L. Sherman, "Indian Slavery and the Cerrato Reforms," 35.

22. Holleran, *Church and State,* 23; Juarros, *Statistical and Commercial History,* 106. Woodward, *Central America,* 40, states that the first archbishopric was in 1745, while Wortman, *Government and Society in Central America,* 42, maintains that this occurred in 1744.

23. "Relación de los vecinos y encomenderos que hay en la gobernación de Guatemala sacada de un libro que tiene el Presidente Villalobos," AGI, Indiferente General, 1528. Although unsigned and undated, this document can be dated approximately because Doctor Pedro de Villalobos served as president from 1573 to 1578, according to Estrada Monroy, *Hombres, fechas y documentos de la patria,* 122.

24. Orellana, *Tzutujil Mayas,* 197.

25. Wortman, *Government and Society in Central America,* 43.

26. Ibid., 43–45; Orellana, *Tzutujil Mayas,* 208–11. The quotation is on page 211 of the latter source.

27. Orellana, *Tzutujil Mayas,* 215.

28. McAlister, *Spain and Portugal,* 404, 408.

29. Holleran, *Church and State,* 22.

30. Orellana, *Tzutujil Mayas,* 203–204.

31. Wortman, *Government and Society in Central America,* 50, 145–46.

32. García Añoveros, *Población y estado,* 152.

33. Orellana, *Tzutujil Mayas,* 201; Holleran, *Church and State,* 22–23; Wortman, *Government and Society in Central America,* 59–61. Orellana notes that after 1562 the Audiencia, not the Cabildo Eclesiástico, administered the royal funds derived from tribute collections.

34. McAlister, *Spain and Portugal,* 427–28.

35. John Tate Lanning, *The Eighteenth Century Enlightenment in the University of San Carlos de Guatemala,* 81–82; McAlister, *Spain and Portugal,* 428; Villacorta Calderón, *Historia de la Capitanía General,* 237–41. Few autos de fe or inquisitorial trials were conducted, and sentences usually involved jail terms, loss of property, and banishment from the kingdom.

36. McAlister, *Spain and Portugal,* 405, 408.

37. *Diccionario Geográfico de Guatemala* 1:269–70; Stephen F. de Borhegyi, "The Miraculous Shrines of our Lord of Esquipulas in Guatemala and Chimayó, New Mexico," *El Palacio* 60, no. 2 (March 1953): 83–84; Stephen F. de Borhegyi, "The Cult of Our Lord of Esquipulas in Middle America and New Mexico," *El Palacio* 61, no. 12 (December 1954): 388–93. See also Mary C. Smith, "Esquipulas," *Americas,* January 1979, 26–31. In 1961 Pope John XXIII raised the sanctuary of Esquipulas in Guatemala to the rank of "First Basilica of Central America." The worship of Our Lord of Esquipulas was transferred from Guatemala to New Mexico in the early nineteenth century by Don Bernardo de Abeyta, who commissioned wood-carvers to fashion an image of Christ for the small church of the Santuario de Chimayó, a place that has also become famous for its miraculous cures.

38. Woodward, *Central America,* 63; Wortman, *Government and Society in Central America,* 130.

39. Woodward, *Central America,* 63–64.

40. Ibid., 64; Villacorta Calderón, *Historia de la Capitanía General,* 74.

41. Wortman, *Government and Society in Central America,* 133–34.

42. García Añoveros, *Población y estado,* 148; Fr. José Garrigo, Vicario Provincial, to Presidente, Gobor. y Capitan General Dn. Antonio González, Convento de Santo Domingo de Guatemala, 27 May 1803, AGI, Guatemala, 963.

43. Villacorta Calderón, *Historia de la Capitanía General,* 231–33; Woodward, *Central America,* 64; Polo Sifontes, *Historia de Guatemala,* 164.

44. Villacorta Calderón, *Historia de la Capitanía General,* 73.

45. Wortman, *Government and Society in Central America,* 133.

46. King to Consejo de Yndias, Madrid, 3 January 1726, AGI, Guatemala, 962. This order evidently resulted from a memorial of 13 August 1721 addressed by the bishop and Cabildo Ecclesiástico and reporting abuses to the king.

47. Ibid.

48. Fr. José Garrigo to Don Antonio González, Convento de Santo Domingo de Guatemala, 27 May 1803, AGI, Guatemala, 963.

49. Archbishop Pedro [Cortés y Larraz] to the king, Guatemala, 1 December 1773, AGI, Guatemala, 658.

50. Martín de Mayorga, *bando,* Nueva Guatemala de la Asunción, 28 July 1777, AGI, Guatemala, 562.

51. [Martin de Mayorga], Presidente de Guatemala, to Dn. Josef de Gálvez, Nueba Guatemala de la Asunción, 11 September 1777, AGI, Guatemala, 658.

52. García Añoveros, *Población y estado,* 1, 16.

53. Ibid., 10–11, 27.

54. Ibid., 26.

55. Ibid., 27.

56. Ibid., 28.

57. Three basic documents comprised Cortés y Larraz's report: "Testimonio de las respuestas dadas por los curas seculares del Arzobispado de Guatemala en la visita canónica que de sus beneficios hizo D. Pedro Cortés y Larraz del Consejo de Su Majestad, año de 1771"; "Descripción geográfica-moral de la Diócesis de Guatemala, hecho por su Arzobispado, El Ilmo. Sor. Pedro Cortés y Larraz, año de 1771"; and "Expediente de toda la visita que ha hecho en toda su Diócesis, año de 1774"; all in AGI, Guatemala, 948. The archbishop's report also included 118 maps or sketches of the curacies. See AGI, Mapas y Planos, Guatemala, 74–186. See also García Añoveros, *Población y estado,* 1, and his analysis of these reports throughout this work.

58. García Añoveros, *Población y estado,* 29.

59. Ibid., 60.

60. Ibid., 31–32.

61. Ibid., 33–34, 46–47, 54–56.

62. Ibid., 36–39, 43–44. Punishments included incarceration, whipping, and expulsion from the towns (p. 40).

63. Ibid., 57.

64. Ibid., 65, 160–61.

65. Ibid., 72, 162–63.

66. Ibid., 76–80, 82.

67. Ibid., 24–25.

68. Don Juan González Bustillo, Razón particular, 1773, AGI, Guatemala, 658; Juarros, *Statistical and Commercial History,* 113. Bancroft, *History of Central America* 2:718 confuses the number of aisles by stating that there were three naves.

69. González Bustillo, Razón particular, 1773.

70. Author's description from visit to cathedral, June–July 1988.

71. Juarros, *Statistical and Commercial History*, 11–12, 106–107. Holleran, *Church and State*, 49, states that these figures were for 1791.

72. Holleran, *Church and State*, 61.

73. Wortman, *Government and Society in Central America*, 135; "Testimonio del nombramiento hecho el Reverendo Padre, Fr. Franco Viteri, Lista de los religiosos que tiene esta Santa Provincia del Dulcimo Nombre de Jesús de Guatema. con espicificatión de la edad y tiempo de havito hecha en el año de mil ochocientos," AGI, Guatemala, 963.

74. "Nomina de los religiosos que tiene esta Sta Prova del Dulce Nre. de Jesús de Guatemala," 1801, AGI, Guatemala, 963.

75. Villacorta Calderón, *Historia de la Capitanía General*, 221; Salazar, *Historia de veintiún años*, 147–50, 180.

76. José Aycinena to Sor. Dn. José Limanta, Chiclana, 2 November 1813, and unsigned letter, Ysla de León, 15 November 1813, both in AGI, Guatemala, 963.

77. Holleran, *Church and State*, 49–52.

78. García Añoveros, *Población y estado*, 136, 138.

79. Ibid., 155.

80. McAlister, *Spain and Portugal*, 171, 175.

81. García Añoveros, *Población y estado*, 157–60; McAlister, *Spain and Portugal*, 175; Robert Ricard, *The Spiritual Conquest of Mexico: An Essay on the Apostolate and the Evangelizing Methods of the Mendicant Orders in New Spain: 1523–1572*, trans. Lesley Byrd Simpson, 276, 278.

82. Ricard, *Spiritual Conquest of Mexico*, 281.

83. Ibid., 308.

5. SPANISH-INDIAN RELATIONS AND LABOR PRACTICES

1. Murdo J. MacLeod, "An Outline of Central American Colonial Demographics," in Robert M. Carmack et al., eds., *Historical Demography of Highland Guatemala*, 7. West and Augelli, *Middle America*, 236, states that the Amerindian population of Guatemala at Spanish contact may well have been over 1 million.

2. McAlister, *Spain and Portugal*, 153, 154.

3. Ibid., 81.

4. Ibid., 158. See also Lesley Byrd Simpson, trans. and ed., *The Laws of Burgos of 1512–1513: Royal Ordinances for the Good Government and Treatment of the Indians*.

5. McAlister, *Spain and Portugal*, 162.

6. *Recopilacíon de leyes de los reinos de las Indias*, 4 vols., was originally published at Madrid (Ivlian de Paredes, 1681). Tomo 2, libro 6, pertains to Indian relations.

7. McAlister, *Spain and Portugal*, 197, 395, 396.

8. Ibid., 154, quoting Lewis Hanke, *The Spanish Struggle for Justice in the Conquest of America*, 73.

9. See Hanke, *Spanish Struggle for Justice*, 111–32, for the Valladolid dispute of 1550–51.

10. McAlister, *Spain and Portugal*, 159, 177, 391; Sidney D. Markman, "Pueblos de españoles y pueblos de indios en el Reino de Guatemala," *Boletín del Centro de Investigaciones Históricas y Estéticas* (Caracas), no. 12 (November 1971), 76.

11. Lutz, "Santiago de Guatemala," 180–82, 202–204, 220–22, 229–34, 259; Markman, "Pueblos de españoles y pueblos de indios," 82.

12. Markman, "Pueblos de españoles y pueblos de indios, "83–85; McAlister, *Spain and Portugal,* 156.

13. Markman, "Pueblos de españoles y pueblos de indios," 81.

14. Orellana, *Tzutujil Mayas,* 121–23, 131, 226–28; MacLeod, *Spanish Central America,* 122, 125.

15. Wortman, *Government and Society in Central America,* 8.

16. García Añoveros, *Población y estado,* 172–73.

17. Ibid., 174.

18. Ibid., 180.

19. Ibid., 179.

20. Ibid., 182–84.

21. Ibid., 174–75.

22. Ibid., 85–89, 92–93.

23. Woodward, *Central America,* 15–16, 33.

24. Silvio Zavala, *Contribución a la historia de las instituciones coloniales en Guatemala,* 50.

25. Wortman, *Government and Society in Central America,* 172–73.

26. Ibid., 101, 106; Woodward, *Central America,* 289; Bancroft, *History of Central America* 2:696, 700. See also Herbert S. Klein, "Peasant Communities in Revolt: The Tzeltzal Republic of 1712," *Pacific Historical Review* 35 (1966): 247–63.

27. Wortman, *Government and Society in Central America,* 182–83.

28. Ibid., 318n.26.

29. García Añoveros, *Población y estado,* 39, 72.

30. Ibid., 153–54.

31. Ambrosio Cerdán et al., Audiencia de Guatemala, bando, 26 November 1801, Nueva Guatemala, published in *Gazeta de Guatemala,* tomo 6, número 255, 5 April 1802. The *Gazeta de Guatemala* was published weekly in Nueva Guatemala from 1794 to 1812 and was succeeded by the *Gazeta del Gobierno de Guatemala* thereafter.

32. William L. Sherman, *Forced Native Labor in Sixteenth-Century Central America,* 15. Zavala, *Contribución,* 11, states that Indian slavery began with the conquest of Pedro de Alvarado.

33. Sherman, *Forced Native Labor,* 15–19.

34. Ibid., ix.

35. Ibid., 33; Zavala, *Contribución,* 16–17; Woodward, *Central America,* 43; McAlister, *Spain and Portugal,* 155.

36. Sherman, *Forced Native Labor,* 40; Zavala, *Contribución,* 13, 16–17, 19–23.

37. Sherman, *Forced Native Labor,* 36, 67.

38. Ibid., 304–306, 313–14, 317, 321–22.

39. Ibid., 58.

40. Ibid., 69–70, 72–73, 449n. 22.

41. Ibid., 135–36, 147.

42. Ibid., 148–49; Lutz, "Santiago de Guatemala," 146.

43. Sherman, *Forced Native Labor,* 133, 135–36, 147–51, 153, 159–68, 176–77, 181–82, 185; Sherman, "Indian Slavery and the Cerrato Reforms," 25–50; Zavala, *Contribución,* 26, 33, 34, 42.

44. Sherman, *Forced Native Labor,* 82, 328–29.

45. McAlister, *Spain and Portugal*, 157, 159, 160: Lesley Byrd Simpson, *The Encomienda in New Spain: The Beginnings of Spanish Mexico*, xiii; Wortman, *Government and Society in Central America*, 5; MacLeod, *Spanish Central America*, 469; Woodward, *Central America*, 45; Orellana, *Tzutujil Mayas*, 137. McAlister notes that the kings granted encomiendas a second life in 1536, a third one in 1555, and a fourth one in 1629 (pp. 160, 163). The term *encomienda* is derived from the verb *encomendar,* meaning to entrust.

46. McAlister, *Spain and Portugal*, 164; Simpson, *Encomienda in New Spain*, 6; Orellana, *Tzutujil Mayas*, 138–40; Herbert Cerwin, *Bernal Díaz: Historian of the Conquest*, 110, 222. Bernal Díaz del Castillo died in 1584 and was buried in the cathedral of Santiago de Guatemala (Antigua).

47. McAlister, *Spain and Portugal*, xiii, 14; MacLeod, *Spanish Central America*, 111–12; Wortman, *Government and Society in Central America*, 13.

48. Sherman, *Forced Native Labor*, 95.

49. Bancroft, *History of Central America* 2:201.

50. Simpson, *Encomienda in New Spain*, 133.

51. Ibid., app. 4, 230–33; McAlister, *Spain and Portugal*, 162; Woodward, *Central America*, 43.

52. Simpson, *Encomienda in New Spain*, 141.

53. McAlister, *Spain and Portugal*, 162.

54. Simpson, *Encomienda in New Spain*, 154–55.

55. Sherman, *Forced Native Labor,* 85–86, 88.

56. Ibid., 92. For services of the Indians, see also Salvador Rodríguez Becerra, *Encomienda y conquista: los inicios de la colonización en Guatemala,* 57. This is an excellent comprehensive study of encomiendas and repartimientos in Guatemala, especially in the conquest and early colonization periods.

57. Rodríguez Becerra, *Encomienda y conquista,* app. 3, 168–70. The list is based upon documents in the AGI and the AGCA.

58. Orellana, *Tzutujil Mayas,* 141; West and Augelli, *Middle America,* 8; MacLeod, *Spanish Central America,* 292–93, noting that declining numbers of encomienda grants occurred during the seventeenth century.

59. Lesley Byrd Simpson, "A Seventeenth Century Encomienda: Chimaltenango, Guatemala," *The Americas* 15, no. 4 (April 1959): 393–402.

60. Orellana, *Tzutujil Mayas,* 143; Wortman, *Government and Society in Central America,* 101; West and Augelli, *Middle America,* 9. MacLeod, *Spanish Central America,* 449n. 8, states that encomiendas were not abolished until 1787.

61. Orellana, *Tzutujil Mayas,* 157.

62. Rodríguez Becerra, *Encomienda y conquista,* 48, 152.

63. Woodward, *Central America,* 43: MacLeod, *Spanish Central America,* 207. West and Augelli, *Middle America,* 9, call the repartimiento a work-levy system.

64. Rodríguez Becerra, *Encomienda y conquista,* 37.

65. Zavala, *Contribución,* 75.

66. Woodward, *Central America,* 43; MacLeod, *Spanish Central America,* 207–208; Sherman, *Forced Native Labor,* 192.

67. Woodward, *Central America,* 43–44; MacLeod, *Spanish Central America,* 208–209.

68. MacLeod, *Spanish Central America,* 208.

69. Lesley Byrd Simpson, *Studies in the Administration of the Indians of New Spain,* vol. 3, *The Repartimiento System of Native Labor in New Spain and Guatemala,* 45.

70. Woodward, *Central America,* 44.

71. Nicolás Mencos, Guatemala, 26 March 1734, *expediente,* Pueblo de Comalapa, 17 April 1734, and *auto,* Pedro de Rivera, Guatemala, 9 March 1735, all in AGCA, exp. 3987, leg. 223; Simpson, *Repartimiento System,* 96, 100.

72. Simpson, *Repartimiento System,* 100–101.

73. See ibid., 100–16, for a listing and discussion of these petitions for repartimiento Indians and the protests registered.

74. Sololá, 20 October 1773, in Simpson, *Repartimiento System,* 104, 106. The audiencia granted him 155 men for every month except April, when only 100 were authorized.

75. García Añoveros, *Población y estado,* 191.

76. Simpson, *Repartimiento System,* 107–108; Wortman, *Government and Society in Central America,* 161; Zavala, *Contribución,* 85.

77. Sherman, *Forced Native Labor,* 85, 87, 89.

78. McAlister, *Spain and Portugal,* 211; Sherman, *Forced Native Labor,* 211–12.

79. MacLeod, *Spanish Central America,* 192, 290, 296; Wortman, *Government and Society in Central America,* 172–73; Woodward, *Central America,* 44, 76.

80. McAlister, *Spain and Portugal,* 212.

81. MacLeod, *Spanish Central America,* 224–26.

82. Ibid., 226.

83. Ibid., 224, 226.

84. Wortman, *Government and Society in Central America,* 77.

85. Ibid., 174.

86. McAlister, *Spain and Portugal,* 212, 337–38, 359; Lutz, "Santiago de Guatemala," 353.

87. Lutz, "Santiago de Guatemala," 353.

88. McAlister, *Spain and Portugal,* 131. These figures are derived from Angel Rosenblat, *La población indígena y el mestizaje en América, 1492–1950* 1:88.

89. MacLeod, *Spanish Central America,* 298.

90. McAlister, *Spain and Portugal,* 344. Again these figures are derived from Rosenblat, *La población indígena* 1:59.

91. Lutz, "Santiago de Guatemala," 388nn. 2 and 5. The term *piezas de Indias* for black slaves meant "a unit of labor equivalent to a prime young male" rather than an individual slave. Other males and females who did not meet the standard counted as fractional parts. See McAlister, *Spain and Portugal,* 123.

92. McAlister, *Spain and Portugal,* 180, 396–97.

93. Wortman, *Government and Society in Central America,* 74.

94. Ibid., 74–75.

95. Lutz, "Santiago de Guatemala," 354, 356, 357. Perhaps Lutz's figures pertain only to Guatemala, which might make them more reasonable.

96. Patente de navegación, 23 March 1713, AGCA, A1. 23, leg. 4606, f. 90.

97. See AGCA documents, A 1.56, exp. 51270, leg. 5920; A 1.56, exp. 5065, leg. 215; and A 3.16, exp. 26514, leg. 1609.

98. Gaspar Hall to Don Alonso de Arcos y Monroy, Kingston, Jamaica, 24 April 1760, AGCA, A 1.56, exp. 5066, leg. 215.

99. Gerónimo Benedit Hornustinen [?] to President Captain General Dn. Martín de Mayorga, Petén, 8 May 1778, AGCA, A 1.56, exp. 201, leg. 8.

100. Matías de Gálvez, Real Palacio, 3 March 1783, AGCA, A 1.56, exp. 45298, leg. 5359. The map of the house is enclosed with the document.

101. See AGCA, A 1.56, exp. 290, leg. 12.

102. See lists of freed slaves, Omoa, 1808, 1809, 1810, in AGCA, A 1.56.

103. Josef de Gálvez to governor and captain general of Guatemala, San Lorenzo, 4 November 1784, AGCA, A 1.56, exp. 244, leg. 10.

104. Decreto, Real Palacio, 16 March 1785, and Testimonio de la Rl. orn. que se remitan al Consejo las marcas de carimbar para quedar obligada a practicar los Negros, Nueva Guatemala, 25 May 1785, AGCA, A 1.56, exp. 244, leg. 10.

105. Royal cedula, Aranjuez, 31 May 1789, AGCA, A 1.56, exp. 17995, leg. 2376.

106. See, for example, Lázaro Guevera, slave of Don Agustín of Chiquimula, Año de 1806, and other reports of bad treatment to 1818 in AGCA, A 1.56, exp. 3633, leg. 177.

107. See, for example, Don Manuel Jacinto Doblado, royal chaplain and ecclesiastical judge, San Fernando de Omoa, Certification of slaves who died during the year 1796 (four "negros esclavos"), AGCA, A 3.1, exp. 22439, leg. 1331. In addition to the four black slaves who died, the document lists six infants, two female "negras piezas," and nine children, all of whom died during the year, the last nine at birth.

108. Wortman, *Government and Society in Central America,* 308 n. 11.

109. "Domas" [José Domas y Valle], Real Palacio, 19 April 1796, AGCA, A 3.1, exp. 22432, leg. 1330.

110. Antonio González, Comdte. de Omoa, Guatemala, 27 October 1803, and "Relación," 27 October 1803, AGCA, A 1.56, exp. 8278, leg. 396.

111. Lorenzo Ximénez Rubio, Villa de Santísima Trinidad de Sonsonate, 2 March 1809, AGCA, A 1.1, exp. 17995, leg. 2376, f. 236.

112. Padrón de los Ciudadanos y Ladinos del Pueblo de los Esclabos, [1821]?, AGCA, A 1.44, exp. 29145, leg. 3023.

113. García Añoveros, *Población y estado,* 190.

114. Woodward, *Central America,* 79.

6. LAND, TOWNS, AND THE ECONOMY

1. McAlister, *Spain and Portugal,* 355.

2. Woodward, *Central America,* 41.

3. Ibid., 41–42.

4. MacLeod, *Spanish Central America,* 126.

5. Ibid., 124.

6. McAlister, *Spain and Portugal,* 356–58.

7. Ibid., 136–37; MacLeod, *Spanish Central America,* 125. The size of caballerías and peonías varied from one Spanish region in America to another. Cerwin, *Bernal Díaz,* 213, states that a caballería amounted to about 174 acres in New Spain. Lutz, "Santiago de Guatemala," 125, states that a caballería was 600 by 1,000 paces, amounting to 105 acres. Lesley Byrd Simpson, *Many Mexicos,* 86n.1, states that a caballería measured 600 by 300 feet, a peonía 300 by 50 feet, and that Viceroy Antonio de Mendoza fixed a caballería in 1536 at what is about 105.4 acres. The *New World Spanish-English and English-Spanish Dictionary,* Salvatore Ramondino, ed. (New York: New American Library of World Literature, 1968), 97, defines a caballería as a land measure of about 33 acres, but that is far too low. MacLeod, *Spanish Central America,* 468, defines it as 105 acres. George M. McBride, *The Land System of Mexico* (New York: American Geographical Society, 1923), 51, states that a cedula of 18 June

1513 established a standard for land grants in the New World, by which he estimates a caballería to be about 165 acres of arable land and a peonía from 30 to 50 acres. With all those variations considered, the present author has adopted the 105-acre measurement advanced by Simpson, Lutz, and MacLeod.

8. Lutz, "Santiago de Guatemala," 124–26, 145–46.

9. David McCreery, "State Power, Indigenous Communities, and Land in Nineteenth Century Guatemala, 1820–1920," in Carol A. Smith, ed., *Guatemalan Indians and the State; 1540 to 1988,* 98. A *sitio de ganado mayor,* according to McCreery, 114n.6, amounted to 38⅜ "new caballerías" (each slightly less than 112 acres).

10. Ibid., 97–99.

11. Simpson, *Many Mexicos,* 84.

12. Ibid., 82, 84; McAlister, *Spain and Portugal,* 106, 108, 133. The quotation is from McAlister, 133.

13. McAlister, *Spain and Portugal,* 135–37.

14. Ibid., 148.

15. Ibid., 138.

16. Ibid., 139.

17. Ibid., 140–41, 316.

18. Ibid., 141, 147. McAlister uses figures compiled in Juan López de Velasco, *Geografía y descripción universal de las Indias,* ed. Don Marcos Jiménez de Espada, Biblioteca de Autores Españoles, no. 48 (Madrid: Ediciones Atlas, 1971). McAlister cites the erroneous figure of 200 to 300 Spaniards living in Central America in 1570. See Sherman, *Forced Native Labor,* 8, for the correct figures of 2,200 to 2,300.

19. Sherman, *Forced Native Labor,* 6, 8, and Appendix B, citing Antonio Vásquez de Espinosa, *Compendium and Description of the West Indies;* trans. Charles Upson Clark, 204, 216, 226, 229, 231, 233, for 1620 figures.

20. *Diccionario geográfico de Guatemala* 2:75.

21. Lutz, "Santiago de Guatemala," 59; Markman, "Pueblos de Españoles y Pueblos de Indios en al Reino de Guatemala," 78. See also the "Acta de Fundación de la villa de Santiago de Guatemala en Iximché" and its transcription in Estrada Monroy, *Hombres, fechas y documentos de la patria,* 9–13.

22. Markman, "Pueblos de Españoles y Pueblos de Indios," 78.

23. Lutz, "Santiago de Guatemala," 59–61; Markman, "Pueblos de Españoles y Pueblos de Indios," 80.

24. Lutz, "Santiago de Guatemala," 62; Markman, "Pueblos de Españoles y Pueblos de Indios," 80–81.

25. Villacorta Calderón, *Historia de la capitanía general de Guatemala,* 111; Markman, "Pueblos de Españoles y Pueblos de Indios," 81. The king granted San Salvador the status of ciudad in 1545.

26. *Diccionario geográfico de Guatemala* 1:20, 161.

27. Ibid., 1:321.

28. Ibid., 1:143–44, 151

29. Ibid., 2:300, 344. For the founding of Spanish towns, see also Villacorta Calderón, *Historia de la capitanía general de Guatemala,* 90.

30. Markman, "Pueblos de Españoles y Pueblos de Indios," 78.

31. Ibid., 76; Polo Sifontes, *Historia de Guatemala,* 121. A vara is equivalent to about thirty-three inches.

32. Markman, "Pueblos de Españoles y Pueblos de Indios," 76–77.

33. *Diccionario geográfico de Guatemala* 1:309.

34. Ibid.

35. Lutz, "Santiago de Guatemala," 90–97.

36. Ibid., 97–98, 180–82, 202.

37. Ibid., 100, 105, 107.

38. Bancroft, *History of Central America* 2:718. See also Don Juan González de Bustillo, Razón particular, AGI, Guatemala, 658.

39. Oficiales Reales a su majestad, Goatla., 29 October 1717; Presidente Franco. Rodríguez de Rivas, Goathemala, 30 October 1717; "Testimonio de los auttos fechos sobre el fuego que exaló uno de los quatro volances que sircumbalen esta ciudad de Guathemala y terremotos de la noche del día de Señor San Miguel veinte y nueve de septiembre . . . , 1717"; Presidente Franco. Rodríquez de Rivas a su majestad, 10 October 1717; and Francisco Rodríguez de Rivas a su majestad, Guatemala, 5 June 1718. All are in AGI, Guatemala 305. See also "Testimonio de los autos fechos sobre el lastísimo estrago y ruina que padeció la Ciudad de Guatemala, con los terremotos que experimentó la noche de día del Glorioso Arcangel San Miguel," 29 de septiembre del año 1717, AGI, Guatemala 660, and another "Testimonio," año de 1718, AGI, Guatemala 307. See also Juarros, *Statistical and Commercial History,* 152–53, and Villacorta Calderón, *Historia de la capitanía general de Guatemala,* 421, 423–24.

40. Presidente Martín de Mayorga to Your Majesty, La Hermita, 30 June 1774, AGI, Guatemala 661. Emphasis is Mayorga's.

41. "Proyecto que el Presidente y oydores de la Audiencia de Guatemala propone a V.M. segun lo que estima conduzente para la traslación de la Capital de este Reyno asolada," La Hermita, 30 June 1774, AGI, Guatemala 661. This document is signed by Martín de Mayorga and oidores Dn. Juan González Bustillo, Dr. Dn. Basilio Villanaja Benegas, and Manl. Frn. de Villanueva at the Estableciminto Provl. de la Hermita.

42. "Fundamentos que tube el Oydor dn. Eusebio Bentura Beleña para el voto consultativo que dió al Señor Presidente de esta Real Audiencia de Guatemala en 21 de octubre de 1774 sobre . . . la formal traslación de esta capital," AGI, Guatemala 660.

43. Archbishop Pedro to His Majesty, Guatemala, 1 December 1773, AGI, Guatemala 658.

44. Archbishop Pedro to His Majesty, Guatemala, 1 January 1774, AGI, Guatemala 658.

45. Archbishop Pedro to the King, Goathemala, 1 April 1774, AGI, Guatemala 657.

46. Presidente Martín de Mayorga to Your Majesty, Hermita, 5 January 1776, AGI, Guatemala 659. Note that the *Diccionario geográfico de Guatemala,* 1:309, states that the cabildo left for the new city on 29 December 1775.

47. Thomás Ortiz de Landazuri, Ynforme de la Contaduria, Madrid, 13 January 1774, AGI, Guatemala 657.

48. Fiscal [unsigned], Madrid, 14 January 1774, AGI, Guatemala 657.

49. Carlos III, cedula, San Ildefonso, 21 July 1775, enclosed with Dn. Thomás Ortiz de Landazuri to Presidente de Rl. Audiencia y Gobernador y Capitán General de las Provincias de Guatemala, Madrid, 22 July 1775, AGI, Guatemala 662.

50. Bancroft, *History of Central America* 2:724.

51. Polo Sifontes, *Historia de Guatemala,* 150.

52. Ibid.; *Diccionario geográfico de Guatemala* 1:310.

53. *Diccionario geográfico de Guatemala* 1:310; Manual Antonio Arredondo to Presidente Martín de Mayorga, Hermita, 9 February 1775, AGI, Guatemala 660.

54. Presidente Martín de Mayorga to Your Majesty, 5 January 1775, AGI, Guatemala 659.

55. Don Martín de Mayorga, bando, Nueva Guatemala de la Asunción, 28 July 1777, AGI, Guatemala 562.

56. Presidente de Guatemala [Mayorga] to Dn. Josef de Gálvez, Nueva Guatemala de la Asumpción, 11 September 1777, AGI, Guatemala 658.

57. Matías de Gálvez to Exmo. Sor. Dn. Josef de Gálvez, Nueva Guatemala, 6 May 1779; same to same, Nueva Guatemala, 6 June 1779; His Majesty to the Presidte. de Goatema., San Lorenzo, 11 October 1779. All are in AGI, Guatemala 451.

58. *Diccionario geográfico de Guatemala* 1:310.

59. The economy of colonial Guatemala and Central America has been especially well studied in MacLeod, *Spanish Central America;* Wortman, *Government and Society in Central America;* and many useful articles in professional journals and monographs. Woodward, *Central America,* 41, states that "the principal motive for colonization in Central America was economic," but this is perhaps an exaggeration in view of the imperial, religious, prestigious, and personal motives that all appear to be valid.

60. MacLeod, *Spanish Central America,* 148; Wortman, *Government and Society in Central America,* 113–14; Polo Sifontes, *Historia de Guatemala,* 143.

61. McAlister, *Spain and Portugal,* 213–16.

62. MacLeod, *Spanish Central America,* 48

63. Polo Sifontes, *Historia de Guatemala,* 139; Orellana, *Tzutujil Mayas,* 159–61.

64. McAlister, *Spain and Portugal,* 233.

65. Sherman, *Forced Native Labor,* 240–48.

66. MacLeod, *Spanish Central America,* 235, 237–38, 240–42, 244, 246. The quotation is on page 241.

67. Sherman, *Forced Native Labor,* 252.

68. MacLeod, *Spanish Central America,* 178.

69. Ibid., 178–82, 186–87; Sherman, *Forced Native Labor,* 252, 255.

70. Sherman, *Forced Native Labor,* 256–57; MacLeod, *Spanish Central America,* 170–74; Josef Estachería, "Estado en que se manifiesta la abundancia ó escasez que ha havido en las siembas de frutos y crias de ganados en las provincias del Reyno de Goatemala hasta fin de Junio de 1785, el tiempo en que empezaron las aguas . . . , Goatemala," 18 October 1785, AGI, Guatemala 451.

71. Wortman, *Government and Society in Central America,* 242; MacLeod, *Spanish Central America,* 175.

72. Sherman, *Forced Native Labor,* 249–51; MacLeod, *Spanish Central America,* 302–303.

73. Josef Estachería, Estado, AGI, Guatemala 451.

74. Sherman, *Forced Native Labor,* 258.

75. MacLeod, *Spanish Central America,* 127–28.

76. Lutz, "Santiago de Guatemala," 2:570–71.

77. Josef Estachería, Estado, AGI, Guatemala 451.

78. Woodward, *Central America,* 46.

79. Ibid., 46–47. The central market of Santiago de Guatemala, for example, was located on the plaza mayor, according to Lutz, "Santiago de Guatemala," 2:553.

80. McAlister, *Spain and Portugal,* 225–26.

81. For a description of Spanish trade, the fleet system, and taxes, see McAlister, *Spain and Portugal,* 233–34, 243–44, and 363.

82. Ibid., 236.

83. MacLeod, *Spanish Central America,* 155, 157, 158.

84. Ibid., 170.

85. Ibid., 268.

86. Ibid., 255, 281, 283. MacLeod errs on page 281 when he states that "Central America did not obtain a mint of its own until 1774." The first mint clearly was established at Santiago de Guatemala in 1733–34. See Woodward, *Central America,* 66, and Wortman, *Government and Society in Central America,* 114–15, as well as documents relating to its foundation in the AGI.

87. Sherman, *Forced Native Labor,* 111.

88. Ibid., 113–14.

89. Ibid., 118.

90. Ibid., 120.

91. MacLeod, *Spanish Central America,* xiii, 374–75. MacLeod discusses and expands on his periodization at various places throughout his book.

92. Woodward, *Central America,* 63, 65.

93. Juarros, *Statistical and Commercial History,* 139–40; Wortman, *Government and Society in Central America,* 114–15. The figures for the mint's output are from Wortman's table on page 115.

94. Wortman, *Government and Society in Central America,* 143–45; Woodward, *Central America,* 73.

95. Wortman, *Government and Society in Central America,* 141–42.

96. Woodward, *Central America,* 65; Wortman, *Government and Society in Central America,* 118–19.

97. Woodward, *Central America,* 78–69; Wortman, *Government and Society in Central America,* 167.

98. Wortman, *Government and Society in Central America,* 122–24, 161–62; Woodward, *Central America,* 74–75

99. Wortman, *Government and Society in Central America,* 130.

100. Troy S. Floyd, "The Guatemalan Merchants, the Government, and the Provincianos, 1750–1800," *Hispanic American Historical Review* 46, no. 1 (February 1961): 99, 109.

101. Wortman, *Government and Society in Central America,* 149, 151–52, 155.

102. Ibid., 113.

103. Ibid., 146.

104. Archbishop Pedro to the King, Guatemala, 1 November 1774, AGI, Guatemala 657, giving thanks for the king's cedula of 16 June 1774.

105. Josef Estachería to Exmo. Señor Dn. Anto. Parlier, Goatemala, 28 October 1788, AGI, Guatemala 564. The report is signed by Juan Manuel Ramírez, Tribunal y Contaduria Mayor de Cuentas, on 29 July 1788.

106. Floyd, "Guatemalan Merchants," 109.

107. Wortman, *Government and Society in Central America,* 162. For an example of the food shortages in Nueva Guatemala causing suffering, particularly among Indian workers and residents, see "Testimonio del pedimiento del Sor. Fiscal, Dr. Don Francisco Saabedra y Carbaxal," 1776, AGI, Guatemala 658.

108. Woodward, *Central America,* 81–82; Wortman, *Government and Society in Central America,* 197; Juarros, *Statistical and Commercial History,* 143–44; Louis E. Bumgartner, *José del Valle of Central America,* 20, 23, 25. Woodward, *Central Amer-*

ica, 291, states that the royal order to suppress the society was issued in 1799, but Juarros clearly states that it was issued on 14 July 1800.

109. Wortman, *Government and Society in Central America,* 199.

110. Woodward, *Central America,* 73.

111. Wortman, *Government and Society in Central America,* 157.

112. Ibid., 184–89, 191, 193. The quotation is from p. 193.

7. POPULATION, SOCIETY, AND CULTURE

1. McAlister, *Spain and Portugal,* 108.

2. MacLeod, "Outline of Central American Colonial Demographics," in *The Historical Demography of Highland Guatemala,* ed. Robert M. Carmack et al., 7.

3. McAlister, *Spain and Portugal,* 24, 181, 391–97, 398, 422, 452. Although McAlister's observations are for Spanish America in general, they are applicable in particular to Guatemala.

4. Lutz, "Santiago de Guatemala," 2:516–17; Bancroft, *History of Central America* 2:97; Kelly, *Pedro de Alvarado,* 183; Kelsey, *Juan Rodríguez Cabrillo,* 43, 49–51. See chap. 2 for the establishment of this town.

5. Lutz, "Santiago de Guatemala," 2:516–17.

6. Van Oss, "La población de América Central hacia 1800," *Anales de la Academia de Geografía e Historia de Guatemala,* 291. Dr. Van Oss died in 1984 at age thirty-six, only two years after receiving his Ph.D. from the University of Texas.

7. Ibid., 291–92.

8. García Añoveros, *Población y estado,* 16.

9. Woodward, *Central America,* 79.

10. García Añoveros, *Población y estado,* 16.

11. Ibid., 22–25. By 1800 the ladino population had not reached 20 percent of the total, according to García Añoveros, *Población y estado,* 135.

12. Woodward, *Central America,* 79.

13. Consejo de las Indias to the King, Madrid, 11 May 1778, AGI, Guatemala 410.

14. La Real Audiencia de Guatemala to the King, Nueva Guatemala, 6 December 1778, AGI, Guatemala 560, enclosing the tabular "Estado que manifiesta el número de Provincias que comprende el Reyno de Guatemala . . . numeración de tributarios de ellas, sus pueblos, tributarios, naborias, leguas que andubieron, meses y dias que gastaron todo con el arreglo a los padrones origins."

15. Wortman, *Government and Society in Central America,* 3.

16. Lutz, "Santiago de Guatemala," 1:229–34, 241.

17. Ibid., 1:319–20.

18. García Añoveros, *Población y estado,* 16.

19. Ibid., 18.

20. Ibid., 22–24.

21. Ibid., 24–25.

22. Ibid., 139–41.

23. Ibid., 39–44.

24. Ibid., 186.

25. Certification of the *padrón* done on order of the superior government, La Hermita, 7 September 1776, AGI, Guatemala 658.

26. MacLeod, *Spanish Central America,* pp. 227–29.

27. Francisco de Paula García Peláez, *Memorias para la historia del Antiguo Reyno de Guatemala* 1:202. The original version of this work was published in 1851–52. Garcia Peláez was archbishop of Guatemala.

28. MacLeod, *Spanish Central America,* 133.

29. Ibid., 138. Orellana, *Tzutujil Mayas,* 167, 170, 179, 232, observes that the Tzutujil caciques and other leaders continued to govern their people and were rewarded with the title of "don" as well as the rights to bear arms, ride horses, and have a coat of arms. Thus, according to her, their social structure persisted with modifications, permitting them to maintain their cultural identity.

30. García Añoveros, *Población y estado,* 190.

31. Wortman, *Government and Society in Central America,* 168–71; Audiencia de Guatemala, "Cuentas dadas por D. Bernardo [H]erbella, comisionado para la colectación y embarque de familias probladores destinadas a la costa de los Mosquitoes, Año de 1787," AGI, Guatemala 828. The document does not state when the colonists sailed from La Coruña or when they reached Trujillo.

32. Wortman, *Government and Society in Central America,* 171; Order of the King to Viceroy of Santa Fe, Aranjuez, 28 June 1791, AGI, Guatemala 422.

33. Lutz, "Santiago de Guatemala," 2:602.

34. McAlister, *Spain and Portugal,* 181, 398, 418–22.

35. Polo Sifontes, *Historia de Guatemala,* 155.

36. John Tate Lanning, *The Eighteenth Century Enlightenment in the University of San Carlos de Guatemala,* 5n.2. The language problems in Guatemala involved the teaching of Castilian to the Indians and the study by Spanish-speakers of the Cakchiquel, Quiché, Tzutujil, and Nahuatl tongues (the last sometimes called Pipil).

37. Lázaro La Madrid, "Bishop Marroquín—Zumárraga's Gift to Central America," *The Americas,* 338.

38. Polo Sifontes, *Historia de Guatemala,* 156; Wortman, *Government and Society in Central America,* 51.

39. Unsigned report of the Audiencia de Guatemala to the King, Guatemala, 12 May 1696, University of Texas, Nettie Lee Benson Latin American Library, Genaro García Collection, GC19–10.

40. García Añoveros, *Población y estado,* 76–82.

41. Ibid., 166–69.

42. Endorsed document by Captain General José de Bustamante y Guerra, 1812, AGCA, B1.12, exp. 79.405, leg. 3477, fol. 209 (misnumbered in the fichero as 109).

43. García Añoveros, *Población y estado,* 170–71.

44. Ramón A. Salazar, *Historia de veintiún años,* 38.

45. Juarros, *Statistical and Commercial History,* 131–32; Polo Sifontes, *Historia de Guatemala,* 156.

46. Horacio Cabezas, "Creación de la Universidad de San Carlos de Guatemala y consolidación de los sístemas de explotación nacional," *Revista de Historia de América,* 161; José Mata Gavidia, *Fundación de la universidad en Guatemala, 1548–1688,* 53.

47. Juarros, *Statistical and Commercial History,* 132–34; Mata Gavidia, *Fundación de la universidad en Guatemala,* 53–54, 61–62, 69.

48. Presidents Dn. San. Albarez to Your Majesty, Guatemala, 5 March 1667, AGI, Guatemala 673.

49. Don Pedro de Barceno, Secretario de la Real Universidad de San Carlos, Certi-

fication, Santiago de los Caballeros de Guatemala, 27 November 1677, AGI, Guatemala 373; unsigned expediente, AGI, Guatemala 136; Mata Gavidia, *Fundación de la
universidad en Guatemala,* 107. All those sources give the correct date for the university's founding or authorization as 31 January 1676. Juarros, *Statistical and Commercial History,* 134, errs in giving the date of the decree as 5 January 1676.
  50. Mata Gavidia, *Fundación de la universidad en Guatemala,* 205, 220.
  51. Ibid., 110–11; Lanning, *Eighteenth Century Enlightenment in the University of
San Carlos,* 9.
  52. Mata Gavidia, *Fundación de la universidad en Guatemala,* 123–25; Don Pedro
de Barceno, Secretario de la Real Universidad de San Carlos, Certification, Santiago
de los Caballeros de Guatemala, 27 November 1677, AGI, Guatemala 373.
  53. Mata Gavidia, *Fundación de la universidad en Guatemala,* 209; Don Pedro de
Barcena, Certification, AGI, Guatemala 373; unsigned document (evidently from
oidor Francisco de Sarasa to the king), 17 May 1681, AGI, Guatemala 136. Polo
Sifontes, *Historia de Guatemala,* 156, states that Crespo y Suárez himself donated
20,000 pesos, but the document in the AGI, Guatemala 136, clearly states that his
executors contributed 3,000 pesos.
  54. Mata Gavidia, *Fundación de la universidad en Guatemala,* 225.
  55. Pedro de Barceno, Certification, 27 November 1677, AGI, Guatemala 373.
  56. Mata Gavidia, *Fundación de la universidad en Guatemala,* 174, 178–79.
  57. Oidor Don Franco. de Sarasa to His Majesty, Guatemala, 17 May 1681, AGI,
Guatemala 136.
  58. Ibid.
  59. Mata Gavidia, *Fundación de la universidad en Guatemala,* 196, 206.
  60. Lanning, *Eighteenth Century Enlightenment in the University of San Carlos,*
356.
  61. Mata Gavidia, *Fundación de la universidad en Guatemala,* 225; Juarros, *Statistical
and Commercial History,* 137; *Constituciones de la Real Universidad de San Carlos de
Guatemala aprobadas por la magestad del señor rey Don Carlos II,* Año de MDCLXXXVI
(Madrid: Julian de Paredes, 1686), AGI, Guatemala 373. This is a printed document of
168 pages, not numbered.
  62. *Constituciones de la Real Universidad de San Carlos de Guatemala,* various
pages. This code is also published in Mata Gavidia, *Fundación de la universidad en
Guatemala,* 235–311.
  63. Lanning, *Eighteenth Century Enlightenment in the University of San Carlos,* 51,
53–72, 229–31, 354–56,
  64. Woodward, *Central America,* 82.
  65. Ibid.
  66. Arturo Taracena Arriola, *La expedición científica al reino de Guatemala (1795–
1802): José Mariano Moziño, un ilustrado americano,* 1, 6–7, 35–37, 103; Iris H. W.
Engstrand, *Spanish Scientists in the New World: The Eighteenth Century Expeditions,*
153–55, 157–58. For a thorough treatment of José Mariano Moziño, see Iris H. W.
Engstrand, "Mexico's Pioneer Naturalist and the Spanish Enlightenment," *The Historian* 53, no. 1 (Autumn 1990): 17–32, which on page 29 traces Moziño's route to Nueva
Guatemala. Engstrand notes that he analyzed the drinking water in the capital, and
observes that he wrote a treatise on the cultivation and benefits of indigo (*Tratado del
Xiquilite y Añil de Guatemala,* published in Guatemala in 1799).
  67. Woodward, *Central America,* 62. The first printing press was brought to San-

tiago de Guatemala by Fray Payo Enríquez de Ribera, bishop of Guatemala, who also brought José de Pineda de Ibarra as its printer.

68. Ignacio Beteta, solicitation for license, 1794, AGCA, A1.58.2, exp. 17157, leg. 2312.

69. Ignacio Beteta, request for documents, 1797, AGCA, 1.58, exp. 45314–5, leg. 5361.

70. Files of the *Gazeta de Guatemala* and the *Gazeta del Gobierno de Guatemala* may be found, though not always complete, in the AGCA. See also the Edward E. Ayer Collection, Newberry Library, Chicago, Illinois, for examples.

71. Herbert Cerwin, *Bernal Díaz: Historian of the Conquest,* 110, 113, 156, 170, 192, 195, 220.

72. Polo Sifontes, *Historia de Guatemala,* 157–58.

73. J. Joaquín Pardo, Pedro Zamora Castellanos, and Luis Luján Muñoz, *Guía de Antigua, Guatemala,* 3d. ed., 271, 272.

74. Polo Sifontes, *Historia de Guatemala,* 158; Pardo et al., *Guía de Antigua,* 272, 274.

75. Polo Sifontes, *Historia de Guatemala,* 158; Pardo et al., *Guía de Antigua,* 266, 276.

76. Pardo, Zamora Castellanos, and Luján Muñoz, *Guía de Antigua,* 269, 275, 277–78.

77. Polo Sifontes, *Historia de Guatemala,* 158; Pardo et al., *Guía de Antigua,* 273.

8. DISASTERS AND DEFENSE

1. Juarros, *Statistical and Commercial History,* 145.

2. Ibid., 145–46.

3. Wolf, *Sons of the Shaking Earth,* 1, describes the people of Guatemala and Mexico as those who "live in the mouth of the volcano."

4. D. G. A. Whitten and J. R. V. Brooks, *The Penguin Dictionary of Geology,* 142.

5. Felipe Cádena, "Breve descripción," 39–43.

6. Juarros, *Statistical and Commercial History,* 146; Villacorta Calderón, *Historia de la capitanía general de Guatemala,* 418.

7. Juarros, *Statistical and Commercial History,* 148; Pardo et al., *Guía de Antigua,* 18–19, 87; Don Juan González Bustillo, "Razón puntual . . . ," AGI, Guatemala, 658, p. 1.

8. Villacorta Calderón, *Historia de la capitanía general de Guatemala,* 419; Juarros, *Statistical and Commercial History,* 148–49; González Bustillo, "Razón puntual," AGI, Guatemala, 658, p. 2.

9. Villacorta Calderón, *Historia de la capitanía general de Guatemala,* 419–20; Pardo et al., *Guía de Antigua,* 20–21.

10. Oficiales Reales to your majesty, Goatla., 29 October 1717, AGI, Guatemala, 305; Presidente Franco. R[odríguez] de Rivas to Dn. Andrés de Elecorobarrutia, Goathemala, 30 October 1717, AGI, Guatemala, 305; Presidente Franco Rodríguez de Rivas to the king, Goathemala, 10 October 1717, AGI, Guatemala, 305; "Testimonio de los auttos fechos sobre el fuego que exaló uno de los quatro volcanes que sircumbalen esta Ciudad de Guathemala y terremotos de la noche del día de señor San Miguel veinte y nueve de septiembre . . . , 1717," AGI, Guatemala, 305; "Testimonio de los autos fechos sobre el lastísimo estrago y ruina que padeció la Ciudad de Guathemala, con los terremotos que experimentó la noche del día del Glorioso Arcangel San

Miguel, 29 de Septiembre del año de 1717," AGI, Guatemala, 660; "Extracto ó relación," printed doc. 1 of cuaderno, 1774, AGI, Guatemala, 658. For the earthquake of San Miguel, see also Juarros, *Statistical and Commercial History,* 152–53, and Villacorta Calderón, *Historia de la capitanía general de Guatemala,* 421, 423–24.

11. Presidente Franco. R[odríguez] de Rivas to Dn. Andrés de Elecorobarrutia, Goathemala, 30 October 1717, AGI, Guatemala, 305.

12. "Testimonio sobre el lastísimo estrago y ruina que padeció la Ciudad de Guatemala . . . , Año de 1718," enclosed with a letter of the president, 16 April 1718, AGI, Guatemala, 307. The report shows estimates for the repair of the cathedral at 10,000 pesos, the church and convent of Santo Domingo at 28,000 pesos, the church of San Francisco with its chapel of San Antonio at 46,000 pesos, the church and convent of La Merced at 80,000 pesos, the church and convent of San Agustín at 38,000 pesos, the church and school of the Compañia de Jesus (the Jesuits) at 11,000 to 12,000 pesos, and the church, convent, and hospital of San Juan de Dios at 6,000 pesos. It also is evident that the church of San Pedro also had damage to its hospital. Only 10,750 pesos were estimated for the repairs of the cabildo, jail, assessor's home, four meat markets, office of the slaughterhouse, and waterworks—all city facilities. Repair of the royal buildings was estimated at 2,000 pesos in Rodríguez de Rivas's letter to Don Andrés Elecorobarrutia, Goathemala, 30 October 1717, AGI, Guatemala, 305.

13. "Testimonio de los autos fechos . . . ," AGI, Guatemala, 660.

14. "Extracto ó relación," printed doc. 1 of cuaderno, 1774, AGI, Guatemala, 658; Francisco Rodríguez de Rivas to the king, Guatemala, 5 June 1718, AGI, Guatemala, 305.

15. Copy of cedula, San Lorenzo, 7 July 1720, in "Testimonio de los auttos fhos. en virtud de Real Cédula sobre el felis estado que[h]oy goza esta Ziudad en la redificación de sus casas y templos," AGI, Guatemala, 309.

16. González Bustillo, "Razón puntual," AGI, Guatemala, 658, pp. 6–7, 11; Dn. Joseph de Araujo y Río to Marqués de Ensenada, Goathemala, 24 March 1751, AGI, Guatemala, 448; Pardo, et al., *Guía de Antigua,* 35.

17. Felipe Cádena, "Breve descripción," 6; Juarros, *Statistical and Commercial History,* 154; Villacorta Calderón, *Historia de la capitanía general de Guatemala,* 429; González Bustillo, "Extracto ó relación," AGI, Guatemala, 658.

18. González Bustillo, "Extracto ó relación," AGI, Guatemala, 658, p. 12.

19. Ibid., p. 13.

20. Ibid.; Felipe Cádena, "Breve descripción," 38; Martín de Mayorga and Bishop Pedro to the king, Guatemala, 2 August 1773, AGI, Guatemala, 661; Villacorta Calderón, *Historia de la capitanía general de Guatemala,* 429.

21. Felipe Cádena, "Breve descripción," 38.

22. González Bustillo, "Extracto ó relación," AGI, Guatemala, 658, p. 14.

23. Felipe Cádena, "Breve descripción," 39–43, 87–90.

24. Ibid., 62.

25. González Bustillo, "Extracto ó relación," AGI, Guatemala, 658, pp. 15–16.

26. Ibid., p.16.

27. Ibid., p. 17; Presidente, Arzobispo, Ministerios y Cabildo (president Martín de Mayorga, Archbishop Pedro, Don Juan González Bustillo, and thirteen others) to the king, Guatemala, 2 August 1773, AGI, Guatemala, 657; Felipe Cádena, "Breve descripción," 63, 70.

28. Presidente, Arzobispo, Ministerios y cabildo to the king, Guatemala, 2 August

1773, AGI, Guatemala, 657; Martín de Mayorga and Archbishop Pedro to the King, Guatemala, 2 August 1773, AGI, Guatemala, 661.

29. Martín de Mayorga and Archbishop Pedro to the king, Guatemala, 2 August 1773, AGI, Guatemala, 661; González Bustillo, "Extracto ó relación," AGI, Guatemala, 658, p. 19.

30. González Bustillo, "Extracto ó relación," AGI, Guatemala, 658, p. 24; Felipe Cádena, "Breve descripción," 172–73.

31. Juan González Bustillo, "Razón particular de los templos, casas de communidades y edificios públicas, y por mayor número de los vecinos de la capital de Guatemala, y del deplorable estado a que se hallan reducidos por los terremotos de la tarde del veinte y nueve de julio, trece y catorce de diciembre del año próximo pasado de setenta y tres, [printed in] establecimiento provisional de la Hermita, Año de 1774," AGI, Guatemala, 658.

32. Felipe Cádena, "Breve descripción," 94–98, 102–104.

33. Ibid., 105–106.

34. Archbishop Pedro to the king, Goathemala, 1 April 1774, AGI, Guatemala, 657.

35. Villacorta Calderón, *Historia de la capitanía general de Guatemala*, 431; "Fundamentos que tubo el oidor dn. Eusebio Bentura Beleña para el voto consultativo que dió al Señor Presidente de esta Real Audiencia de Guatemala, en 21 de octubre de 1774 sobre . . . la formal traslación de esta Capital," AGI, Guatemala, 660; Presidente Martín de Mayorga, Dn. Juan González Bustillo, Manl. Frz. de Villanueva, and Basilio Villarrasa, La Hermita, 30 June 1774, AGI, Guatemala, 661.

36. Unsigned opinion of fiscal, Madrid, 15 January 1774, AGI, Guatemala, 657; copy of king's cedula, San Yldefonso, 21 July 1775, transmitted with letter from Dn. Thomás Ortiz de Landazuri to president of the royal audiencia and governor and captain general of the provinces of Guatemala, Madrid, 22 July 1775, AGI, Guatemala, 662.

37. Villacorta Calderón, *Historia de la capitanía general de Guatemala*, 439.

38. Presidente de Goatha. to Sor. Bo. Fr. Julián de Arriaga, Hermita, 31 July 1775, AGI, Guatemala, 450. In a second letter to Arriaga on 31 August 1775, President Mayorga explained that the mouths of the volcano continued to emit "considerable" fire and the reverberations of the volcano were frequent. Although the river of fiery molten lava neither diminished nor grew, according to Mayorga, the copious dust and the belching of rock and sand that rained on the pueblo of Amatitán obliged the people there to flee. See also "Testimonio de los autos . . . ," La Hermita, 3 July 1775, AGI, Guatemala, 662. Two sketches of this eruption of Pacaya were drawn by the lieutenant of engineers Don Joseph de Alexandre, who observed it from a nearby hill. These sketches are in AGI, Mapas y Planos, Guatemala, 219bis and 315.

39. José de Bustamante y Guerra to Alcalde Mayor Into. of Totonicapán, Guatemala, 3 August 1816, AGCA, 1.21, exp. 56, 670, leg. 6118.

40. Juarros, *Statistical and Commercial History*, 146–47.

41. Ibid., 147.

42. Martín de Mayorga to Josef de Gálvez, Hermita, 4 July 1776, and reply to Presidente de Guatemala, Madrid, 20 December 1776, both in AGI, Guatemala, 450.

43. Testimonio del pedimento del Sor. Fiscal, Expediente No. 16, and certification of escribano, 10 September 1776, AGI, Guatemala, 658.

44. José de Bustamante to Señores de la Real Audiencia, Real Palacio, 10 July 1811, and Bustamante to Real Audiencia, Real Palacio, 26 August 1811, both in AGCA, A 1.21.4, exp. 7796, leg. 377.

45. Don Joseph de Araujo y Río to the king, Santiago de Guatemala, 2 December 1748, in "Testimonio del autto proveido por este Supor. Govierno en que se prohive el traer de armas corttas, Año de 1749," and Araujo y Río to the King, Guatemala, 19 April 1749, both in AGI, Guatemala, 448.

46. "Testimonio . . . que se da cuenta a S.M. del número de causas despachados en todo el año próximo pasado de 1787 en esta Real Audiencia," AGI, Guatemala, 575. Another *testimonio* of 54 cases—24 in Nueva Guatemala, 9 in Chiquimula, 5 in Sonsonate, 1 in León, 3 in Quezaltenango, 2 in Suchitepéques, 1 in Tuxtla, and 9 in Ciudad Real—appears in the same source.

47. Audiencia de Guatemala, 2 March 1789, AGI, Guatemala, 576.

48. Juarros, *Statistical and Commercial History,* 148, 151.

49. Wortman, *Government and Society in Central America,* 181–82.

50. [Jose de] Bustamante to Sres. de la Junta de Sanidad de esta Capital, Real Palacio, 22 June 1814, AGCA, A 1.4–6, exp. 31,029, leg. 4,027. No copies of the instructions are found with this letter.

51. Juarros, *Statistical and Commercial History,* 153.

52. Wortman, *Government and Society in Central America,* 181.

53. Juarros, *Statistical and Commercial History,* 158.

54. Juan Obispo de Guatemala to the king, Guatemala, 11 January 1731, enclosing "Testimonio de los auttos fechos por el Illmo. Sr. obispo de este obispado de Guathemala . . . a averiguar el estado de el Hospital e Yglesia de Sn Pedro," AGI, Guatemala, 309.

55. Lanning, *Eighteenth Century Enlightenment,* 222, 244–45.

56. Ibid., 342.

57. Ibid., 245.

58. Michael M. Smith, *The "Real Expedición Marítima de la Vacuna" in New Spain and Guatemala,* 15–16, 20. For a study of the entire expedition, see Gonzalo Díaz de Iraola, *La vuelta al mundo de la expedición de la vacuna.* See also AGI, Indiferente General, 1558.

59. José Felipe Flores, report, 28 February 1803, AGI, Indiferente General, 1558; Lanning, *Eighteenth Century Enlightenment,* 250–51; Smith, *Real Expedición Marítima,* 13, 50.

60. Smith, *Real Expedición Marítima,* 151–52.

61. Ibid., 153. On Doctor Esparragosa's activities in connection with the administration of the vaccine, sometimes in his own home, as well as in the barrios, the plaza, and Indian villages, see Manuel Vela, secretary of the Junta Central de Vacuna of the Reyno de Guatemala, Nueva Guatemala, 15 November 1806, AGI, Indiferente General, 1558A.

62. Smith, *Real Expedición Marítima,* 54–56.

63. Ibid., 56.

64. *Gazeta de Guatemala,* tomo IX, no. 430, 31 March 1806, AGI, Indiferente General, 1558. The totals of 1,562 for Nueva Guatemala and 44,082 for it and the provinces shown in the issue of the *Gazeta* are incorrect, and therefore corrected totals have been computed by the author.

65. José de Bustamante y Guerra to ayuntamiento of this capital, Real Palacio, 16 February 1815, AGCA, A 1.4–7, exp. 31,034, leg. 4,027.

66. Wortman, *Government and Society in Central America,* 182.

67. Lanning, *Eighteenth Century Enlightenment,* 207–303, provides a full discussion and analysis of these improvements and their effects.

68. For the activities of the English, French, and Dutch in the Caribbean and along the coasts of Central America, two of the best works are Arthur P. Newton, *The European Nations in the West Indies, 1493–1688,* 2d ed., and John Exquemeling, *Bucaniers of America or a True Account of the Most Remarkable Assaults Committed of Late Years upon the Coasts of the West Indies by the Bucaniers of Jamaica and Tortuga, both English and French* (London: Printed for William Crooke, at the Green Dragon, without Templebar, 1684).

69. Mariano Rodríguez del Valle, *El Castillo de San Felipe del Golfo Dulce,* 3–5. Manuel Rubio Sánchez, *Historia del Ejército de Guatemala: Siglo XVI—Antecedentes,* 125–26, states that the construction of this tower occurred in 1586.

70. Rodríguez del Valle, *Castillo de San Felipe,* 3–5, 14–17, 20–27, 40–43; however, note the discrepancy between the author's statements that the Dutch attacked on 27 April 1684 (p. 41) and that they left on 5 March 1684 (p. 43). Perhaps there were two attacks on Fort San Felipe.

71. Ibid., 49–54.

72. Ibid., 54, 56.

73. Ibid., 62–64.

74. Ibid., 54, 66–68, 74, 78. Díez de Navarro's drawings of the fortress of San Felipe are in AGI, Mapas y Planos, Guatemala, 195 and 196.

75. Woodward, *Central America,* 63–65, 67. For this rivalry, see Troy S. Floyd, *The Anglo-Spanish Struggle for Mosquitía.*

76. Wortman, *Government and Society in Central America,* 154; Rodríguez del Valle, *Castillo de San Felipe,* 53; Manuel Rubio Sánchez, *Historia de la fortaleza y puerto de San Fernando de Omoa,* 7–9.

77. Rubio Sánchez, *Historia de la fortaleza de Omoa,* 14–19.

78. Ibid., 20, 23, 25, 28, 95.

79. Ibid., 108. These expenses included 39,515 pesos and 5½ reales for salaries, 995,806 pesos and 5 reales in remitted cash, 435,718 pesos and 3½ reales for provisions and freight, 55,760 pesos for purchasing Negroes, and 125,993 pesos and 1½ reales for various tools, other freight, and minor expenses.

80. Ibid., 108, 114, 124.

81. Dn. Alonso de Arcos y Moreno, Presidente de Guatemala, to Dn. Julián de Arriaga, Guatemala, 17 February 1755, AGI, Guatemala, 871.

82. *Arreglamento y método que se deberá observar por todas las Milicias del Reyno de Guatemala dispuesto por su Presidente . . . Don Alonso Arcos y Moreno* (Guatemala?: Impreso por Sebastián de Arebalo, Año de 1755), AGI, Guatemala, 871. This is a printed pamphlet of 28 unnumbered pages.

83. Ibid.

84. "Estado General de las Milicias, Ynfantería y Caballería que contiene toda la Dominación de Guatemala, arreglado por su Presidente Mariscal del Campo Dn Alonso de Arcos y Moreno [signed "Arcos"]," Guatemala, 20 August 1756, AGI, Guatemala, 871.

85. Alonso de Arcos y Moreno to Exmo. Sor. Bo. F. Dn. Julián de Arriaga, Guatemala, 26 April 1757, AGI, Guatemala, 871.

86. [Don Julián de Arriaga] to Dn. Pedro de Salazar, Madrid, 11 December 1764, AGI, Guatemala, 871.

87. Pedro de Salazar to Dn. Julián de Arriaga, "Estado General que representa la fuerza de hombres que contienen las milicias de Ynfantería y Cavalla. del Reyno de

Guathemala, Guathemala, 1 December 1767," and Alexandro O'Reilly to Dn. Julián de Arriaga, Madrid, 23 April 1768, both in AGI, Guatemala, 871. Salazar also reported detailed figures concerning the number of companies and militiamen for each jurisdiction of the kingdom. O'Reilly is the same person who brought military and administrative reforms to Cuba and Louisiana in the 1760s.

88. Matías de Gálvez to José de Gálvez, Omoa, 1 July 1778, AGI, Guatemala, 451; Matías de Gálvez to Sor. Dn. Martín de Mayorga, Nueva Guatemala, 9 September 1778, AGCA, A 2.5, exp. 6,692, leg. 299.

89. Bancroft, *History of Central America* 2:727.

90. "Don Joseph de Gálvez, Reglamento del haber mensual que deberan gozar los Oficiales y demás Individuos del Batallón de Infantería de Goatemala," Aranjuez, 8 May 1777, AGI, Guatemala, 451. This is a five-page printed document.

91. Bancroft, *History of Central America* 2:727.

92. Matías de Gálvez to José de Gálvez, Omoa, 1 July 1778, AGI, Guatemala, 451; Oakah L. Jones, "Matías de Gálvez: Spanish Ally of the American Revolution," unpublished paper delivered at the biennial convention of Phi Alpha Theta, St. Louis, Mo., 30 December 1989, 3. This paper described Gálvez's inspections, military preparations, and campaigns, based upon the following documents in the AGI and AGCA in addition to the above cited letter of 1 July 1778: Matías de Gálvez to Sor. Dn. Martín de Mayorga, Nueva Goatemala, 9 September 1778, AGCA, A 2.5, exp. 6692, leg. 299; Matías de Gálvez to Josef de Gálvez, Nueba Goata., 6 June 1779, and same to same, Nueva Guatemala, 6 April 1779, both in AGI, Guatemala, 451; Matías de Gálvez to Josef de Gálvez, Nueva Guatemala, 19 January 1781, AGI, Guatemala, 465; Matías de Gálvez, Diario general de los subcesos ocurridos en las expediciones de mar y tierra dirigidas por el Mariscal del Campo el Sor. Dn. Matías de Gálvez, Truxillo, 18 April 1782, and Matías de Gálvez to Joseph de Gálvez, Puerto de Truxillo, 20 April 1782, both in AGI, Guatemala, 466; and muster rolls and reports of battalions, AGCA, A3.1, exp. 17996, leg. 972, folios 94 and 465. See also, Floyd, *Anglo-Spanish Struggle for Mosquitía,* 139-62, for a general discussion of these campaigns against the British.

93. Jones, "Matías de Gálvez," 5; Rubio Sánchez, *Historia de la fortaleza de Omoa,* 130; Matías de Gálvez to Josef de Gálvez, Nueba Goata., 6 June 1779, and same to same, Nueva Guatemala, 6 April 1779, both in ACI, Guatemala, 451.

94. Jones, "Matías de Gálvez," 6; Rubio Sánchez, *Historia de la fortaleza de Omoa,* 131-32; Floyd, *Anglo-Spanish Struggle for Mosquitía,* 131, 139-40.

95. Matías de Gálvez to Josef de Gálvez, Nueva Guatemala, 19 January 1781, AGI, Guatemala, 465; Jones, "Matías de Gálvez," 6-8; Floyd, *Anglo-Spanish Struggle for Mosquitía,* 151-52.

96. Jones, "Matías de Gálvez," 8-11; Floyd, *Anglo-Spanish Struggle for Mosquitía,* 153-56; Rubio Sánchez, *Historia de la fortaleza de Omoa,* 139, 144-49; Matías de Gálvez, "Ordenanza provisional para las milicias del Reyno de Goatemala," Nueva Guatemala, 28 June 1782, AGCA, A 1.23, leg. 1541; Matías de Gálvez to Josef de Gálvez, Nueva Guatemala, 29 August 1782, AGI, Guatemala, 466.

97. Matías de Gálvez, "Diario general de los subcesos ocurridos en las expediciones de mar y tierra dirigidas por el Mariscal del Campo el Sor Dn Matías de Gálvez, Truxillo," 18 April 1782, and Matías de Gálvez to Joseph de Gálvez, Puerto de Truxillo, 20 April 1782, both in AGI, Guatemala, 466.

98. Floyd, *Anglo-Spanish Struggle for Mosquitía,* 157-62.

99. Rubio Sánchez, *Historia de la fortaleza de Omoa,* 149; Jones, "Matías de Gálvez," 12.

100. Josef Estachería, "Estado que manifiesta el Armamento y fornitura que existe en este Reyno . . . ," Guatemala, 14 March 1785, enclosed with letter from Estachería to Joseph de Gálvez, Guatemala, 14 March 1785, AGI, Guatemala, 466.

9. INSTABILITY AND INDEPENDENCE

1. Woodward, *Central America,* 73.

2. Ibid., 80–81.

3. Ibid., 81–82, Lanning, *Eighteenth Century Enlightenment,* 321; Wortman, *Government and Society in Central America,* 218–19; Dombrowski et al., *Area Handbook for Guatemala,* 22–23.

4. Louis E. Bumgartner, *José del Valle of Central America,* 5, 6, 9, 14, 16, 17, 19, 22–32, 54, 69, 86, 99, 107, 145–46; Polo Sifontes, *Historia de Guatemala,* 169; "José Cecilio del Valle," anonymous pamphlet (Washington, D.C.: General Secretariat of the Organization of American States, [1977]).

5. Woodward, *Central America,* 68.

6. Ramón A. Salazar, *Historia de veintiún años,* 75, 77.

7. Ibid., 79.

8. Ibid., 79–80; Woodward, *Central America,* 291; Wortman, *Government and Society in Central America,* 199–200.

9. *Gazeta de Guatemala* 10, no. 3 (2 December 1808).

10. Bumgartner, *José del Valle,* 54–56; Salazar, *Historia de veintiún años,* 113.

11. Bumgartner, *José del Valle,* 57, 59; Salazar, *Historia de veintiún años,* 117.

12. Bumgartner, *José del Valle,* 59; Salazar, *Historia de veintiún años,* 119.

13. Bumgartner, *José del Valle,* 60–61; Salazar, *Historia de veintiún años,* 119, 123.

14. Bumgartner, *José del Valle,* 61; Salazar, *Historia de veintiún años,* 119, 129–32; "Instrucciones para la constitución fundamental de la Monarquia Española y su gobierno que ha de tratarse en las próximas Cortes Generales de la Nación," given by the ayuntamiento of "La. M. N. y L. [Very Noble and Loyal] Ciudad de Guatemala a su diputado el Sr. Dr. D. Antonio de Larrazábal," Written by José María Peinado ([Cádiz]: Imprenta de la Junta Superior, 1811), printed pamphlet of 65 pages in AGI, Guatemala, 502.

15. Salazar, *Historia de veintiún años,* 133–35. González took charge thereafter of the royal army in southern and western New Spain, where he was captured by the forces of José María Morelos and shot on 25 November 1812.

16. Ibid., 136, 138, 151; Franco. de Egrica? to Secretario de Estado y del Despacho de Gracias y Justa., Ysla de León, 21 March 1810, AGI, Guatemala, 502; Consejo Supremo to Señor Capitán General de Guatemala, Ysla de León, 21 March 1810, AGCA, A 3.2, exp. 506, leg. 27. For Bustamante's service with Malaspina, see Donald C. Cutter, *Malaspina in California,* 4, and biographical note in Engstrand, *Spanish Scientists in the New World,* 45, 107n.56.

17. Salazar, *Historia de veintiún años,* 138.

18. José de Bustamante to Sres. Regidores y Alcaldes de la M. N. y L. Ciud. de Guatemala, Xalapa [Mexico], 16 July 1810, AGCA, B 1.14, exp. 583, leg. 20, and Bustamante to Ayuntamiento of this city, AGCA, B 1.14, exp. 8448, leg. 496.

19. Salazar, *Historia de veintiún años,* 140, 146, 147–50.

20. Ibid., 152, 154, 155; *Gazeta de Guatemala* 16 no. 250 (12 December 1811).

21. José de Bustamante, Reglamento, Real Palacio de Guatemala, 16 January 1812, AGCA, B 1.5, exp. 290, leg. 7.

22. Ibid.

23. Salazar, *Historia de veintiún años,* 160; Polo Sifontes, *Historia de Guatemala,* 167.

24. Salazar, *Historia de veintiún años,* 160.

25. Ibid., 161–62, 164.

26. José de Bustamante, Real Palacio de Guatemala, 10 April 1812, AGCA, B 1.8, exp. 2249, leg. 76.

27. Wortman, *Government and Society in Central America,* 205–206, 209.

28. "Actas Capitulares," 1812–13, Guatemala, 3 January 1813, AGCA, A 1.2, exp. 15739, leg. 2190, f. 19.

29. Wortman, *Government and Society in Central America,* 207–10.

30. Salazar, *Historia de veintiún años,* 175–77; Wortman, *Government and Society in Central America,* 206–207; Woodward, *Central America,* 85.

31. Salazar, *Historia de veintiún años,* 178–80.

32. Don José Barrundia to the king, Teapa, 9 November 1817, AGI, Guatemala, 502.

33. Tomás Ruiz to the king, Nueva Guatemala, 15 January 1818, AGI, Guatemala, 502.

34. Salazar, *Historia de veintiún años,* 181; José de Bustamante to Secretario del Estado y del Despacho de Gracia y Justicia, Guatemala, 3 September 1814, AGI, Guatemala, 502.

35. Bustamante to Secretario del Estado, Guatemala, 3 September 1814, AGI, Guatemala, 502; José Matías Delgado, Rector [of the university] and fifteen others to the king, Nueva Guatemala, 3 September 1814, AGI, Guatemala, 502.

36. José de Bustamante to the king, Guatemala, 18 September 1814, AGI, Guatemala, 502.

37. Woodward, *Central America,* 85–86.

38. José de Bustamante to Sres. Ministros de la Rl. Audiencia, Real Palacio, 22 December 1815, AGCA, B 1.9, exp. 2267, leg. 76; José de Bustamante to Secretario del Estado y del Despo. Universal de Indias, Guatemala, 3 January 1816, AGI, Guatemala, 502.

39. José de Bustamante, Manifiesto, Guatemala, 18 March 1815, and Bustamante to Secreto. de Estado y del Despacho Universal de Indias, Guatemala, 18 March 1815, both in AGI, Guatemala, 502.

40. José de Bustamante to Sres. Ministros de la Audiencia, Real Palacio, 16 October 1816, and dispatch to Sr. Regente de la Audiencia de Guatemala, Madrid, 14 November 1817, both in AGCA, A 1.39.2, exp. 53647, leg. 6056.

41. Wortman, *Government and Society in Central America,* 211.

42. El Consejo Pleno de Yndias, 28 February 1817, AGI, Guatemala, 502. Earlier in 1814 the regency in Spain had removed Bustamante from office and ordered him back to Spain for health reasons, but the restoration of King Fernando VII had overturned that act. See José de Bustamante to Sres. Rector y Claustro de la Rl. Universidad de Sn. Carlos, Real Palacio, 18 March 1814, AGCA, A .325, exp. 13305, leg. 1963.

43. El Consejo Pleno de Yndias, 12 August 1817, AGI, Guatemala, 502.

44. Ibid.

45. Unsigned to Sor. Pres. del Consejo de Yndias, Palacio, 12 July 1818, AGI,

Guatemala, 502; petition of ayuntamiento, Guatemala, 13 November 1817, AGCA, A 1.30–4; exp. 22002, leg. 2639, ano de 1817.

46. José García Zelaya to Exmo. Señor [probably Urrutia], n.d., n.p. Signed on back by Felipe de Alvarado, Palacio, 25 April 1818, AGCA, A 1.30–4, exp. 4376, leg. 38.

47. Salazar, *Historia de veintiún años*, 201.

48. José de Bustamante to Exmo. Sor. Dn. Carlos de Urrutia, Guatemala, 31 March 1818, AGCA, A 1.2, exp. 1130, leg. 44. Evidently King Fernando had originally decided in June 1817 to have Bustamante's residencia conducted. See the king to Captain General of the Kingdom of Guatemala, Palace, 13 June 1817, in this same AGCA reference.

49. Presidente del Consejo de Indias, 2 September 1818, AGI, Guatemala, 502.

50. Franco. de Paula y Vilches to Presidente Dn. Carlos de Urrutia, Guatemala, 27 April 1819, AGCA, A 1.30.4, exp. 923, leg. 31, f. 8.

51. Ibid.; "Testimonio del memorial afurtado," beginning with Franco. de Paula y Vilches to the king, Guatemala, 16 October 1820, AGCA, A 1.30–4, exp. 11581, leg. 1739.

52. Franco. de Paula y Vilches to the king, Guatemala, 16 October 1820.

53. Salas de Justicia del Cono. de Yndias to Don José de Bustamante, Madrid, 27 November 1819, AGI, Guatemala, 502; Wortman, *Government and Society in Central America*, 211; José Surciria Ruiz to Secreto. del Despacho de Gracia y Justa., Madrid, 10 January 1821, AGI, Guatemala, 502.

54. Wortman, *Government and Society in Central America*, 211.

55. Woodward, *Central America*, 86–87.

56. Salazar, *Historia de veintiún años*, 202.

57. Wortman, *Government and Society in Central America*, 218–20; Polo Sifontes, *Historia de Guatemala*, 169. Salazar, *Historia de veintiún años*, 209, explains that the term *gazistas* was applied to those who were prudish *(gaz)* and that *cacos* were thieves.

58. Salazar, *Historia de veintiún años*, 215.

59. Ibid., 215–16.

60. Wortman, *Government and Society in Central America*, 220–21; Woodward, *Central America*, 87–88.

61. Wortman, *Government and Society in Central America*, 222–26.

62. Woodward, *Central America*, 87–89; Salazar, *Historia de veintiún años*, 208, 220–21; Bumgartner, *José del Valle*, 106–107. However, note that Bumgartner states that the central issue was not independence but a rivalry for positions of influence and prestige.

63. Salazar, *Historia de veintiún años*, 221, 222.

64. Bumgartner, *José del Valle*, 144.

65. Woodward, *Central America*, 89; Salazar, *Historia de veintiún años*, 223; Bumgartner, *José del Valle*, 145–46.

66. See the handwritten act of 15 September 1821, Gaínza's proclamation, and the printed act of 16 September in Estrada Monroy, *Hombres, fechas y documentos de la patria*, illustrations 31–51. The author of the present study also examined the original document in the display case at the Archivo General Centro América in Guatemala City. Both the handwritten and printed versions are published in Ministerio de Educación, *Documentos Fundamentales de la Independencia de Guatemala*, 7–19.

67. See the preceding note for citations of the Act of Independence.

Glossary of Spanish Terms

Achiote. Red or yellow vegetable dye produced from round husks of red grains grown on a plant with heart-shaped leaves. Mixed with chocolate to give it brick color.

Adelantado. An advance agent in conquering and settling a region, usually a frontier; a leader of an expedition.

Aguardiente. Brandy or another strong alcoholic drink locally produced.

Alcabala. Sales tax.

Alcalde mayor. A district official, high justice, and administrator.

Alcalde ordinario. A municipal magistrate elected yearly by the cabildo.

Alcaldía mayor. District administered by an alcalde.

Alférez. Sublieutenant; also, the royal herald or standard bearer.

Alguacil mayor. Chief constable or police officer, usually attached to a cabildo.

Almojarifazgo. A customs duty on exports and imports.

Altiplano. Highland region of Guatemala.

Amanecebamiento. Indian practice of living with unmarried partners.

Añil. Indigo.

Antigua. Santiago de Guatemala in the valley of Panchoy.

Arriero. Mule driver or muleskinner.

Arroba. Measure of weight amounting to about twenty-five pounds.

Asadón. Two-sided hoe (metal).

Asentista. Holder of a contract to import black slaves.

Asiento. Slave contract with an individual.

Audiencia. A body of justices or a court to administer a geographical region in America, such as Guatemala or all of colonial Central America. Composed of a president and *oidores,* or judges. Had administrative, legislative, and judicial functions.

Avería. Duty for expenses of the fleets.

Ayuntamiento. Municipal or town council. *See also* Cabildo.

Bachillerato. Bachelor's degree.

Bahía. Bay.

Bando. Decree or order.

Barrio. Suburb or district of a city; a quarter.

Beata. Pious woman.

Beaterio. A house or residence of pious women, but not a nunnery or convent.

Boca costa. The piedmont or foothills between the Guatemalan highlands and the Pacific Coast.

Bozales. Black slaves, usually males.

Caballería. A measure of land allocated to a nobleman or mounted Spaniard. It amounted to about 105 acres, but estimates vary.

Cabildo. Town or municipal council; also the building where it meets. *See also* Ayuntamiento.

Cabildo abierto. An open meeting of the town council where members of the cabildo are supplemented by principal officials and townspeople.

Cabildo Eclesiástico. Church Council, or cathedral chapter.

Cacique. An Indian leader or headman of a tribe, nation, or town.

Caco. One who favors free trade and Creole government. An early liberal.

Caja de comunidad. Community treasury or fund.

Capitanía general. Captaincy general, or military jurisdiction.

Capitulación. Contract between the king and an individual or group, delineating requirements, privileges, and responsibilities.

Carga. A load of produce.

Carreta. Two-wheeled cart.

Carro. Large wagon.

Casa de Moneda. Royal mint.

Casa real. Royal palace.

Castas. Persons of mixed racial heritage.

Castillo. Fortress or castle.

Cédula. A royal decree.

Chicha. A corn liquor with a strong odor.

Ciudad. City or major community.

Ciudad Vieja. The old city, a term used to describe Santiago de Guatemala at Almolonga.

Cochinilla. Cochineal.

Cofradía. A lay brotherhood.

Colegio. School or college.

Comandante inspector. Commandant inspector of military forces and provisions.

Composición. A payment made to regularize a possession; a fee paid to legalize a possession, such as a *composición de tierra* to provide a legal claim to land already occupied.

Comunidad. Community.

Congregación. An Indian town created by Spanish authorities.

Consejo Real de Indias. Royal Council of the Indies in Spain.

Constituciones. A code of laws or a constitution, such as that regulating the University of San Carlos.

Consulado. Merchant guild.

Contador general. Auditor general or controller.

Convento. A convent for priests or nuns.

Corregidor. A district official.

Corregimiento. District governed by a corregidor.

Cortes. Spanish parliament or legislature.

Criollo. A Creole, or a Spaniard born in America.

Cuadrilla. Slave gang or work force.

Cura. A parish priest; a religious of the secular clergy.

Cursante. A student or scholar.

Diezmo. The tithe collected from each person (one-tenth of earnings or products) by the church.

Diputación. Deputation or administrative body, such as the Diputación Provincial, or Provincial Deputation, after 1812.

Doctrinas. Parishes; also religious centers for Christianized Indians.

Donativo. Donation or contribution.

Ejido. Property belonging to a town and its residents with land held in common.

Encomendero. Holder or grantee of an encomienda.

Encomienda. Grant of Indians for labor and tribute to a Spaniard in return for service rendered to the crown.

Encomienda eclesiástica. Grant of Indians for labor and tribute to the Catholic Church.

Escribano. Scribe or public notary.

Español. Technically, a Spaniard, but often extended to include those born in America who were supposedly Creoles.

Expediente. A dossier on a particular subject.

Fanega. Measure of weight amounting to 116 pounds, but varying.

Fiel ejecutor. Inspector of weights, measures, and prices.

Fiscal. An attorney for the Crown or any administrative agency; also (cf. Gage), an Indian officer in a town, who had to be able to read and write and who carried a staff with a little silver cross on the top and gathered the people of the village to Mass.

Flota. A Spanish fleet between Spain and New Spain.

Forastero. A foreigner.

Frontera. Frontier.

Frontera septentrional. Northernmost frontier.

Fuero. Privilege.

Fuero eclesiástico. Body of privileges granted to the church by the Crown, or
    assumed by the church.

Fuero militar. Body of privileges granted to members of the military profession.

Fusilero. Rifleman or musketeer.

Galeones. Galleons, or the Spanish fleet between Spain and South America or
    Panama.

Ganado. Livestock.

Ganado mayor. Large livestock such as cattle, oxen, horses, or mules.

Ganado menor. Small livestock such as sheep or goats.

Gazista. One who favored conservative government and protectionist trade
    policies; an early-day conservative.

Gente de razón. Civilized people.

Gobernación. Governancy.

Gobierno. Governmental jurisdiction.

Golpe de estado. A coup d'état or change of government.

Granadero. Grenadier or artilleryman.

Guatemaltecos. Guatemalans.

Hacendado. Owner of an hacienda.

Hacienda. Private rural landed estate.

Hermita. Hermitage or small chapel (sometimes rendered "ermita").

Hidalgo. Member of the lesser nobility or upper class.

Iluminación. Lighting, illumination; often used for fireworks.

Indio. Indian.

Indios bárbaros. Wild or uncivilized Indians.

Intendencia. An intendancy, or district government, created by the Bourbons
    in Central America after 1786, but not for Guatemala.

Invierno. Winter or rainy season.

Jacal. A hut or temporary primitive structure used as a residence.

Jefe político. Political chief or ruler.

Jefe superior. Supreme political chief or ruler.

Juego de cacao. A gambling game using cacao beans.

Juez. Judge, justice, or magistrate.

Juez del repartidor. Officer who makes repartimientos, or assignments, of
    Indians, usually for work details.

Junta. A meeting, temporary governing body, or board.

Junta Consultativa. The meeting in Guatemala on 15 September 1821 to
    decide on independence and adopt the Declaration of Independence.

Junta de guerra. War council.

Junta universitaria. University governing board such as that for University of San Carlos.

Justicia mayor. Principal justice or magistrate.

Ladino, -na. A person of mixed racial ancestry; a non-Indian of Guatemala, where the term *ladino* is similar to *mestizo* elsewhere in colonial Latin America.

Latifundia, plur. The system of large-scale private land ownership.

Legajo. A bundle of documents.

Licencia. License.

Licenciado. One who holds a master's degree, such as a lawyer or other intellectual graduated from a university.

Limosnas. Alms or offerings.

Limpieza de sangre. Purity of blood.

Llano. Plain.

Maestro. A master of a trade or a teacher.

Manzana. Town block.

Mayordomo. Manager, headman, boss, foreman, overseer; also the head of a *cofradía* or the overseer of an hacienda.

Merced. A grant or gift of something.

Merced real de tierra. A grant of land to a private individual or a corporation by the Crown or its designated authority.

Mestizaje. The process of mixing people of different races.

Mestizo. A person of mixed racial ancestry. *See* Ladino.

Milpa. Maize field or cultivated rural property.

Monja blanca. The white nun flower of Verapaz; national flower of Guatemala.

Mulato. A person of European and black racial mixture.

Municipio. Municipality.

Naboríos. "Free" Indian workers or servants, usually employed on haciendas.

Negro. A person of black African heritage.

Negros Caribes. Black Caribs, persons imported to Guatemala by the English in the eighteenth century and settled in separate communities.

Nortes. Northers, strong wind storms from the north.

Novena. Special worship and prayers over a period of nine days, usually for divine guidance or intervention. Also, a portion of one-ninth.

Obraje. A dye work or workshop, a factory, or a textile mill

Oidor. Judge or justice, member of the audiencia.

Padrón. Census.

Paisano. Countryman, everyday person.

Pardo. A person of black and European racial mixture, or simply someone of color.

Partido. Subdivision within a governancy.

Patronato real. Royal patronage over the temporal church granted by the pope to the monarchs of Castile.

Peninsulares. Spaniards born in Spain.

Peonaje. The system of debt peonage.

Peonía. A measure of land, about one-fifth the size of a *caballería,* allotted to foot soldiers and settlers not of the upper class or lesser nobility.

Personalismo. Individual or personal rule without regard to law or principle.

Peso. Spanish colonial coin worth eight reales.

Piezas de Indias. Spanish term to describe black slaves from Africa. A unit of labor equivalent to that of a prime young black male.

Piragua. A pirogue, or small vessel.

Plaza mayor. Main or principal plaza in a town or city; sometimes called the *plaza principal* or *plaza de armas.*

Población. A small town without a charter; a settlement.

Poblador. A settler or colonizer; *primeros pobladores* are first or original settlers.

Portales. Portals or an arcade.

Primeras letras. Fundamental subjects taught in school or by individual teachers—reading, writing, arithmetic.

Principales. Indian headmen or chiefs.

Procurador. Procurator or attorney.

Protomédico. Doctor who examines physicians, surgeons, bleeders, and druggists to determine their qualifications to practice.

Provincia. Province.

Provinciano. One who lives in a province, usually one who lives outside the capital or towns.

Pueblo. A town or people.

Pueblos de indios. Towns of Indians.

Pueblos de españoles. Towns of Spaniards and/or mixed races.

Quetzal. Colorful long-tailed bird of highland Guatemala; also the national currency of the Republic of Guatemala. Symbol of freedom and liberty.

Quintal. Measurement or about one hundred pounds.

Quinto real. The royal fifth, a tax on all slaves sold and minerals produced.

Ranchería. Small outlying rural settlement; also, a temporary camp.

Rancho. Small privately owned landholding or a farm.

Real. Adj., royal. Also, a coin valued at one-eighth of a peso.

Real de minas. Mining district.

Regidor. Alderman of a cabildo or ayuntamiento.

Reino. Kingdom (also rendered as "reyno").

Repartimiento. A division of something; a division of Indians *(repartimiento de indios)*or of lands *(repartimiento de tierra);*a quota system for Indian labor.

República. Republic.

República de españoles. Republic of Spaniards.

República de indios. Republic of Indians.

Residencia. An end-of-term inspection or investigation by a royally appointed official.

Río. River.

Sacristán. Sexton of a church. Cares for the vestry and altars for the Mass.

Sangrador. Bloodletter.

Santos. Religious images of two types: *retablos* (flat painted renditions of religious figures) and *bultos* (statues carved in the round of religious figures).

Sarampión. Measles.

Sierra. Mountain range.

Síndico. Attorney.

Sínodo. Financial remuneration paid annually by the king to each religious person.

Sitio. One square league of land for a townsite.

Solar. Town lot.

Subdelegado. Subdelegate or district administrator subordinate to an intendant.

Suerte. Agricultural plot within a township.

Tameme. Indian carrier or burden bearer.

Tepec. Aztec/Nahuatl for place on a mountain or hill.

Tertulia. Social gathering or meeting.

Tierra. Land.

Tierra caliente. Hot, humid land or zone.

Tierra fría. Cold land or zone.

Tierra templada. Temperate land or zone.

Tierras realengas. Royal lands.

Tostón. One-half of a peso, or four reales.

Trapiche. Sugar mill where cane is ground.

Traza. Plan or drawing of a town.

Tribunal. Tribunal or court. *Tribunal de fidelidad* is a loyalty court.

Tropa veterana. Veteran troop; soldiers of the royal army.

Vaquero. One who works livestock, usually cattle; a cowhand or cowboy.

Vara. Measure of length about thirty-three inches.

Vecino. Principal town resident or head of household recognized by authorities; freeholding citizen of a town.

Verano. Summer or dry season.

Vicepatronato. Right of civil authorities over the church's temporal affairs, delegated to them by the king.

Villa. Chartered town with specific rights and privileges granted by the king.

Viruelas. Smallpox.

Visita. A tour of inspection or investigation by religious or civil administrators.

Visitador. Royal inspector.

Volcán. Volcano

Xiquilite. Indian name for indigo; *see* Añil.

Zambo. A person of Indian and Negro ancestry; also rendered "sambo."

Bibliography

IN RESEARCHING THIS HISTORY, the emphasis has been on primary materials such as unpublished manuscripts in repositories in Spain, Guatemala, and the United States. Published documents, other primary sources, and secondary works have also been consulted to supplement investigation of manuscripts. Although many of the manuscripts are correspondence between Spain and Guatemala by Spanish officials, some valuable unpublished reports add greatly to understanding political, economic, social, and international developments in the province and kingdom of Guatemala. Some of these are Father Felipe de Cádena's eyewitness description, and that of the oidor and former interim governor González de Bustillo, about the disastrous earthquake of 29 July 1773; Matías de Gálvez's reports of campaigns against the British; Mariscal del Campo Alonso de Arcos y Moreno's efforts to organize and standardize militias in the mid-1750s; Archbishop Pedro Cortés y Larraz's "Descripción" of his visit to the Guatemalan villages between 1768 and 1770; and the Constituciones de la Real Universidad de San Carlos de Guatemala, approved in 1686 but drawn up in 1681 by the rector of the university and oidor of the Audiencia de Guatemala, Francisco de Sarasa.

Among the principal sources of manuscript material are the following archives and repositories:

Austin, Texas. Nettie Lee Benson Latin American Library, University of Texas, Special Collections.
Bloomington, Indiana. Lilly Library, Indiana University. Mendel Collection.
Chicago, Illinois. Newberry Library, Edward E. Ayer Collection.
Guatemala City, Guatemala. Archivo General de Centro América.
Madrid, Spain. Archivo Histórico Nacional.
Mexico City, Mexico. Archivo General de la Nación.
Seville, Spain. Archivo General de Indias. Ramos of Audiencia de Guatemala, Mapas y Planos, and others.

In addition to those major collections, two other important agencies have considerable collections, especially of published materials, dealing with colonial Guatemala:

Antigua, Guatemala, and South Woodstock, Vermont. Centro de Investigaciones Regionales de Mesoamérica (CIRMA). This private, nonprofit Guatemalan institute has published a scholarly compilation of essays in English and Spanish entitled *Mesoamérica* since 1980.

Guatemala City, Guatemala. Academía de Geografía e Historia de Guatemala (known before 7 August 1979) as the Sociedad de Geografía e Historia de Guatemala). Its important series of monographs pertaining to Guatemalan history and geography, Anales de la Academia de Geografía e Historia, runs from 1924 to the present. Some of the publications are cited hereafter by author and title.

REFERENCES, GUIDES, AND FINDING AIDS

Anales de la Academia de Geografía e Historia. Número extraordinario, tomo 49 (1980). An index for the first 50 volumes from 1924 to 1977.

Catalog of the Latin American Collection, University of Texas Library, Austin, Texas. 31 vols. Boston, 1969, and 3 supplements to 1975.

Diccionario Geográfico de Guatemala. 2 vols. Guatemala, C.A.: Dirreción General de Cartografía, Talleres de la Tipografía Nacional de Guatemala, 1961–62.

Estrada Monroy, Agustín. *Datos para la historia de la iglesia en Guatemala.* Serie Biblioteca Goathemala, vols. 26, 27, 30. Guatemala City: Academia de Geografía e Historia, 1972, 1974, 1979.

———. *Hombres, fechas y documentos de la patria.* Guatemala City: Editorial José de Pineda Ibarra, 1977.

Grieb, Kenneth J., ed. *Research Guide to Central America and the Caribbean.* Madison: University of Wisconsin Press, 1985.

"Guatemala." *Enciclopedia Universal Ilustrada* 26:1610–51. Barcelona, Spain: Hijos de J. Espasa, 1925.

Luján Muñoz, Jorge. *Guía del Archivo General de Centro América.* Guatemala City: Archivo General de Centro América y Ministerio de Educación, 1982.

Lutz, Cristóbal H., and Stephen Webre. "El Archivo General de Centro América." *Mesoamérica* 1 (1980): 274–85.

———. "The Archivo General de Centro América." In Kenneth J. Grieb, ed., *Research Guide to Central America and the Caribbean,* 105–110.

Markman, Sidney. *Colonial Central America: A Bibliography.* Tempe, Ariz.: Arizona State University, Center for Latin American Studies, 1977.

Moore, Richard E. *Historical Dictionary of Guatemala*. Rev. ed. Metuchen, N.J.: Scarecrow Press, 1973.

————. *A Checklist of Manuscripts in the Edward E. Ayer Collection*. Compiled by Ruth L. Butler. Chicago: Newberry Library, 1937.

Newberry Library. *Dictionary Catalog of the Edward E. Ayer Collection*. 16 vols. Boston: G. K. Hall Co., 1961.

Sánchez Belda, Luis. *Guía del Archivo Histórico Nacional*. Valencia, Spain: Tipografía Moderna, 1958.

Torres Lanzas, Pedro. *Relación descriptiva de los mapas, planos, etc., de la Audiencia y Capitanía General de Guatemala (Guatemala, San Salvador, Honduras, Nicaragua y Costa Rica) existentes en el Archivo General de Indias*. Madrid: Tipografía de la Revista de Archivos, Bibliotecas y Museos, 1903.

Woodward, Ralph L., Jr. "The Historiography of Modern Central America since 1960." *Hispanic American Historical Review* 67, no. 3 (August 1987): 461–96.

PUBLISHED DOCUMENTS AND PRIMARY SOURCES

Alvarado, Pedro de. *An Account of the Conquest of Guatemala in 1524*. Edited by Sedley J. Mackie. New York: Cortés Society, 1924; Kraus Reprint, 1969.

————. *Relación hecha por Pedro de Alvarado a Hernando Cortés, en que se refieren las guerras y batallas para pacificar las provincias del antiguo reino de Goathemala*. México: José Porrúa e Hijos, 1954.

Colección de documentos inéditos relativos al déscubrimiento, conquista y organización de las antiguas posesiones españolas de América y Oceanía, sacadas de los archivos del reino y muy especial de las Indias. 42 vols. Madrid, 1864–84.

Colección de documentos inéditos relativos al déscubrimiento, conquista y organización de las antiguas posesiones españolas de Ultramar. 25 vols. Madrid, 1885–1932.

Cortés y Larraz, Pedro. *Descripción Geográfico-Moral de la Diócesis de Goathemala hecha por su arzobispo el Ilmo. Sor. Don Pedro Cortés y Larraz del Consejo de S.M. . . .* Edited by Adrián Recinos. 2 vols. Guatemala City: Tipografía Nacional, 1958.

Díaz del Castillo, Bernal. *Verdadera y notable relación del descubrimiento y conquista de la Nueva España y Guatemala*. Guatemala City: Tipografía Nacional, 1934.

Gage, Thomas D. *Travels in the New World*. Edited by J. Eric S. Thompson, Norman: University of Oklahoma Press, 1958.

Gazeta de Guatemala, 1794–1812.

Gazeta del Gobierno de Guatemala, 1812–1821.

Ministerio de Educación. *Documentos Fundamentales de la Independencia de Guatemala.* Guatemala City: Editorial José de Pineda Ibarra, 1967.

Muerte de Pedro de Alvarado: Cartas de relación de Alvarado a Hernán Cortés, cartas antiguas de Goathemala. Biblioteca de Cultura Popular, vol. 4. Guatemala: Ministerio de Educación Pública, n.d.

Porras Muñoz, Guillermo, ed. *Diario y derrotero de lo caminado, visto y obcervado en el discurso de la visita general de precidios, situados en las provincias ynternas de Nueva España, que le orden de su magestad executó D. Pedro de Rivera. . . .* México, D.F.: B. Costa-Amic, 1945.

Recinos, Adrián, ed. *The Annals of the Cakchiquels.* Translated by Delia Goetz. Norman: University of Oklahoma Press, 1967.

Recopilación de leyes de los reinos de las Indias. 4 vols. 1681. Madrid: Ediciones Cultura Hispanica, 1973.

Simpson, Lesley Byrd, trans. and ed. *The Laws of Burgos of 1512–1513: Royal Ordinances for the Good Government and Treatment of the Indians.* San Francisco: John Howell Books, 1960.

Stevens, Henry, and F. W. Lucas, trans. and eds. *The New Laws of the Indies for the Good Treatment and Preservation of the Indians.* London, 1892.

GENERAL WORKS

Bancroft, Hubert H. *History of Central America.* 3 vols. Vols. 6–8 of *The Works of Hubert Howe Bancroft.* San Francisco: A. L. Bancroft Co., 1882, History Co., 1887.

Chinchilla Aguilar, Ernesto. *Historia de Centroamérica.* 3 vols. Guatemala City, 1974–77.

Dombrowski, John, Elinor C. Betters, Howard I. Blutstein, et al. *Area Handbook for Guatemala.* Washington, D.C.: U.S. Government Printing Office, 1970.

Fuentes y Guzmán, Francisco Antonio de. *Historia de Guatemala o recordación Florida, escrito en el siglo XVII por el capitán D. Francisco Antonio de Fuentes y Guzmán.* Edited by D. Justo Zaragoza. 2 vols. Madrid: Luis Navarro, 1882.

————. *Recordación Florida. Discurso historial y demostración natural, material, militar y política del Reyno de Guatemala escribela el Cronista del mismo Reyno Capitán D. Francisco Antonio de Fuentes y Guzmán.* Biblioteca Goathemala, tomos 6–8. Guatemala City: Tipografía Nacional and Sociedad de Geografía e Historia de Guatemala, 1932.

Garcia Peláez, Francisco de Paula. *Memorias para la historia del Antiguo Reyno de Guatemala.* 3d ed. 3 vols. Guatemala City: Biblioteca "Goathemala" de la Socieded de Geografía e Historia de Guatemala, 1968–71.

Gavarrete Escobar, Juan. *Anales para la historia de Guatemala (1497–1811)*. Guatemala City: Editorial José de Pineda Ibarra, 1980.

Jensen, Amy E. *Guatemala: A Historical Survey.* New York: Exposition Press, 1955.

Jones, Chester L. *Guatemala, Past and Present.* 1940. Reprint. New York: Russell and Russell, 1966.

Juarros, Domingo. *Compendio de la historia de la ciudad de Guatemala.* 3d ed. 2 vols. Guatemala City: Tipografía Nacional, 1936 and 1937.

————. *A Statistical and Commercial History of the Kingdom of Guatemala in Spanish America. . . .* Translated by J. Baily. London: J. Hearne, 1823.

MacLeod, Murdo J. *Spanish Central America: A Socioeconomic History, 1520–1720.* Berkeley and Los Angeles: University of California Press, 1973.

Marroquín Rojas, Clemente. *Historia de Guatemala.* Guatemala City: Tipografía Nacional, 1971.

Mota Padilla, D. Matías de la. *Historia de la Conquista de la Provincia de la Nueva Galicia.* México: Sociedad Mexicana de Geografía y Estadística, Imprenta del Gobierno, 1870.

Polo Sifontes, Francis. *Historia de Guatemala: visión de conjunto de su desarrollo Político-cultural.* León, Spain: Editorial Evergraficas, 1988.

Remesal, Antonio de. *Historia general de las indias occidentales, y particular de la gobernación de Chiapa y Guatemala.* 2 vols. Edited by P. Carmelo Sáenz de Santa María. Madrid: Atlas, 1964–66.

Vásquez, Fray Francisco. *Crónica de la Provincia del Santísmo Nombre de Jesús de Guatemala.* 2d. ed. Guatemala City: Academia de Geografía e Historia, 1944.

Vásquez de Espinosa, Antonio. *Compendium and Description of the West Indies.* Translated by Charles Upsom Clark. Washington, D.C.: Smithsonian Institution, 1942.

Villacorta Calderón, José Antonio. *Historia de la capitanía general de Guatemala.* Guatemala City: Tipografía Nacional, 1942.

Woodward, Ralph L., Jr. *Central America: A Nation Divided.* 2d ed. New York and Oxford: Oxford University Press, 1985.

Wortman, Miles L. *Government and Society in Central America, 1680–1840.* New York: Columbia University Press, 1982.

Ximenes, Fray Francisco. *Historia de la Provincia de San Vicente de Chiapa y Guatemala de la Orden de Predicadores.* 2 vols. Guatemala City: Serie Biblioteca Goathemala, 1930–31.

BOOKS

Adams, Richard E. W. *Prehistoric Mesoamerica.* Rev. ed. Norman and London: University of Oklahoma Press, 1991.

Alcaide, Elis Luque. *La Sociedad Económica de Amigos del País* Guatemala. Seville: Escuela de Estudios Hispano-Americanos, 1962.

Alcazar Molina, Cayetano. *Los virreinatos en el siglo XVIII.* Tomo 13, *Historia de América y de los Pueblos Americanos,* ed. Antonio Ballesteros y Beretta. Barcelona and Buenos Aires: Salvat Editores, 1945.

Altolaguirre y Duvale, Angel de. *Descrubrimiento y conquista de México.* Tomo 7, *Historia de América y de los Pueblos Americanos,*ed. Antonio Ballesteros y Beretta. Barcelona and Madrid: Salvat Editores, 1954.

Annis, Verne I. *La arquitectura de la Antigua Guatemala, 1543–1773.* Bilingual ed. Guatemala City: Universidad de San Carlos, Editorial Universitaria, 1968.

Bumgartner, Louis E. *José del Valle of Central America.* Durham, N.C.: Duke University Press, 1963.

Carmack, Robert M. *The Quiché Mayas of Utatlán: The Evolution of a Highland Guatemala Kingdom.* Norman: University of Oklahoma Press, 1981.

Carmack, Robert M., John Early, and Christopher Lutz, eds. *The Historical Demography of Highland Guatemala.* Albany, N.Y.: Institute for Mesoamerican Studies, 1982.

Cerwin, Herbert. *Bernal Díaz: Historian of the Conquest.* Norman: University of Oklahoma Press, 1963.

Chinchilla Aguilar, Ernesto. *El ayuntamiento colonial de la ciudad de Guatemala.* Guatemala City: Editorial Universitaria, Universidad de San Carlos de Guatemala, 1961.

Coe, Michael D. *The Maya.* New York: Frederick A. Praeger, 1967.

Cook, Noble D., and W. George Lovell, eds. *"Secret Judgments of God" : Old World Disease in Colonial Spanish America.* Norman and London: University of Oklahoma Press, 1991.

Cutter, Donald C. *Malaspina in California.* San Francisco: John Howell Books, 1960.

Díaz de Iraola, Gonzalo. *La vuelta al mundo de la expedición de la vacuna.* Anuario de Estudios Americanos. Seville: Escuela de Estudios Hispano-Americanos, 1948.

Engstrand, Iris H. W. *Spanish Scientists in the New World: The Eighteenth Century Expeditions.* Seattle and London: University of Washington Press, 1981.

Floyd, Troy S., ed. and trans. *The Bourbon Reformers and Spanish Civilization: Builders or Destroyers?* Boston: D. C. Heath, 1966.

————. *The Anglo-Spanish Struggle for Mosquitía.* Albuquerque: University of New Mexico Press, 1967.

Foster, George M. *Culture and Conquest: America's Spanish Heritage.* Chicago: Quadrangle Books, 1960.

García Añoveros, Jesús María. *Población y estado sociorreligioso de la diócesis de Guatemala en el último tercio del siglo XVIII.* Guatemala City: Editorial Universitaria, Universidad de San Carlos de Guatemala, 1987.

Guillemin, Jorge F. *Iximché, Capital del Antiguo Reino Cakchiquel.* Guatemala City: Instituto de Antropología e Historia, 1965.

Hammond, Norman, and Gordon R. Willey, eds. *Maya Archeology and Ethnohistory.* Austin and London: University of Texas Press, 1979.

Hanke, Lewis. *The Spanish Struggle for Justice in the Conquest of America.* Boston: Little, Brown, 1965.

Helms, Mary W. *Middle America: A Culture History of Heartland and Frontiers.* Englewood Cliffs, N.J.: Prentice-Hall, 1975.

Holleran, Mary P. *Church and State in Guatemala.* New York: Columbia University Press, 1949.

Hoffman, Paul E. *The Spanish Crown and the Defense of the Caribbean, 1535–1585: Precedent, Patrimonialism, and Royal Parsimony.* Baton Rouge: Louisiana State University Press, 1980.

Jones, Oakah L., Jr. *Nueva Vizcaya: Heartland of the Spanish Frontier.* Albuquerque: University of New Mexico Press, 1988.

Kelly, John E. *Pedro de Alvarado, Conquistador.* 1932. Reprint. Port Washington, N.Y.: Kennikat Press, 1971.

Kelsey, Harry. *Juan Rodríguez Cabrillo.* San Marino, Calif.: Huntington Library, 1986.

Kirkpatrick, F. A. *The Spanish Conquistadores.* 1934. Cleveland and New York: World Publishing Co., 1967.

Lanning, John Tate. *The University in the Kingdom of Guatemala.* Ithaca, N.Y.: Cornell University Press, 1955.

————. *The Eighteenth Century Enlightenment in the University of San Carlos de Guatemala.* Ithaca, N.Y.: Cornell University Press, 1956.

Lovell, W. George. *Conquest and Survival in Colonial Guatemala: A Historical Geography of the Cuchumatan Highlands, 1500–1821.* Kingston and Montreal: McGill-Queens University Press, 1985.

Luján Muñoz, Luis. *José de Pineda Ibarra y la primera imprenta en Guatemala.* Guatemala City: Editorial José de Pineda Ibarra, 1977.

Lutz, Christopher H. *Historia sociodemográfica de Santiago de Guatemala, 1541–1773.* Antigua, Guatemala, and South Woodstock, Vt.: Centro de Investigaciones Regionales de Mesoamérica, 1982.

McAlister, Lyle N. *Spain and Portugal in the New World, 1492–1700*. Minneapolis: University of Minnesota Press, 1984.

MacLeod, Murdo J., and Robert Wasserstrom, eds. *Spaniards and Indians in Southeastern Mesoamerica: Essays on the History of Ethnic Relations*. Lincoln: University of Nebraska Press, 1983.

Martínez, Peláez, Severo. *La patria del criollo: ensayo de interpretación de la realidad guatemalteca*. Guatemala City, 1971.

Mata Gavidia, José. *Fundación de la universidad en Guatemala, 1548–1688*. Guatemala City; Editorial Universitaria, 1954.

Medina, José Toribio. *La imprenta en Guatemala (1660–1821)*. 2d ed. 2 vols. Guatemala City: Tipografía Nacional, 1960.

Melendez Chaverri, Carlos. *La ilustración en el antiguo reino de Guatemala*. San José, Costa Rica: Editorial Universitaria Centroamericana, 1974.

Mencos Franco, Agustín, *Literatura guatemalteca en el período de la colonia*. Guatemala, C.A.: Tipografía Nacional, 1937.

Morales Padrón, Francisco. *Pedro de Alvarado*. Madrid: Publicaciones Españoles, 1955.

Naylor, Thomas H., and Charles W. Polzer, eds.*Pedro de Rivera and the Military Regulations for Northern New Spain, 1724–1729*. Tucson: University of Arizona Press, 1988.

Newton, Arthur P. *The European Nations in the West Indies, 1493–1688*. 2d ed. New York: Barnes and Noble, 1967.

Orellana, Sandra. *The Tzutujil Mayas: Continuity and Change, 1250–1630*. Norman: University of Oklahoma Press, 1984.

Pardo, J. Joaquín, Pedro Zamora Castellanos, and Luis Luján Muñoz, *Guía de Antigua, Guatemala*. 3d ed. Guatemala City: Editorial José de Pineda Ibarra, 1969.

Paz Solórzano, Juan. *Historia del Santo Cristo de Esquipulas*. Guatemala, 1949.

Pérez Bustamente, Ciriaco. *Los virreinatos en los siglos XVI y XVII*. Tomo 12, *Historia de América y de los Pueblos Americanos*, ed. Antonio Ballesteros y Beretta. Barcelona y Madrid: Salvat, 1954.

Recinos, Adrián. *Pedro de Alvarado, conquistador de México y Guatemala*. México, D.F.: Fondo de Cultura Económica, 1952.

Ricard, Robert. *The Spiritual Conquest of Mexico: An Essay on the Apostolate and the Evangelizing Methods of the Mendicant Orders in New Spain, 1523–1572*. Translated by Lesley Byrd Simpson. Berkeley and Los Angeles: University of California Press, 1966.

Rodríguez, Mario. *The Cádiz Experiment in Central America, 1808–1826*. Berkeley: University of California Press, 1978.

Rodríguez Becerra, Salvador. *Encomienda y conquista: los inicios de la colonización en Guatemala.* Seville: Universidad, 1977.

Rodríguez del Valle, Mariana. *El castillo de San Felipe del Golfo Dulce.* Seville: Escuela de Estudios Hispano-Americanos, 1960.

Rosenblat, Angel. *La población indígena y el mestizaje en América, 1492–1950.* 2 vols. Buenos Aires: Editorial Nova, 1954.

Rubio Sánchez, Manuel. *Historia del edificio del ayuntamiento de la ciudad de Antigua, Guatemala.* Guatemala City: Academia de Geografía e Historia de Guatemala, 1953.

————. *Historia de la Sociedad Económica de Amigos del País.* Guatemala City, n.d.

————. *Comercio terrestre de y entre las provincias de Centroamerica.* Guatemala City: Editorial del Ejército, 1973.

————. *Gabino Gaínza.* Guatemala City: Cenaltex, Ministerio de la Educación, 1985.

————. *Historia de la fortaleza y puerto de San Fernando de Omoa.* Vol. 1. Guatemala City: Negociado de Historia, Departamento de Información y Divulgación del Ejército, 1987.

————. *Historia de la Ejército de Guatemala: Siglo XVI—Antecedentes.* Vol. 1. Guatemala City: Negociado de Historia del Departamento de Información y Divulgación del Ejército, 1987.

Sáenz de Santamaría, Carmelo. *El licenciado Don Francisco Marroquín, primer obispo de Guatemala (1499–1563): su vida, sus escritos.* Madrid: Ediciones Cultura Hispánica, 1964.

————. *El siglo XVII en el reino de Guatemala a través de su cronista don Francisco Antonio de Fuentes y Guzmán.* Seville: Escuela de Estudios Hispano-Americanos, 1971.

Salazar, Ramón A. *Historia de veintiún años: la independencia de Guatemala.* Guatemala City: Tipografía Nacional, 1928. 2d ed. by Ministerio de Educación Pública, 1956.

Samayoa Guevara, Hector Humberto. *Implantación del regimen de intendencias en el Reino de Guatemala.* Guatemala City: Instituto de Antropología e Historia, Editorial del Ministerio de Educación Pública José de Pineda Ibarra, 1960.

Sauer, Carl O. *The Early Spanish Main.* Berkeley and Los Angeles: University of California Press, 1966.

Sherman, William L. *Forced Native Labor in Sixteenth Century Central America.* Lincoln: University of Nebraska Press, 1979.

Silvert, Kalman H. *A Study in Government: Guatemala.* Middle American Research Institute Publication no. 21. New Orleans: Tulane University, 1954.

Simpson, Lesley Byrd. *Studies in the Administration of the Indians of New Spain.* Vol. 3, *The Repartimiento System of Native Labor in New Spain and Guatemala.* Berkeley: University of California Press, 1938.

———. *The Encomienda in New Spain: The Beginnings of Spanish Mexico.* Berkeley and Los Angeles: University of California Press, 1950.

———. *Many Mexicos.* 3d ed. Berkeley and Los Angles: University of California Press, 1959.

Smith, Carol A., ed. *Guatemalan Indians and the State, 1540 to 1988.* Austin: University of Texas Press, 1990.

Smith, Michael M. *The "Real Expedición Marítima de la Vacuna" in New Spain and Guatemala.* Philadelphia, Pa.: American Philosophical Society, 1974.

Solano, Francisco de. *Tierra y sociedad en el Reino de Guatemala.* Guatemala City: Editorial Universitaria, 1977.

Stoll, Otto. *Etnografía de Guatemala. Seminario de Integración Social Guatemalteca.* Guatemala City: Ministerio de Educación Pública, 1958.

Szecsy, Janos de. *Santiago de los Caballeros de Guatemala en Almolonga.* Guatemala City: Instituto de Antropología e Historia, 1953.

Taracena Arriola, Arturo. *La expedición científica al Reino de Guatemala (1795–1802): José Mariano Moziño, un ilustrado americano.* Guatemala City: Universidad de San Carlos de Guatemala, 1978.

Thompson, J. Eric S. *The Rise and Fall of Maya Civilization.* 2d ed. Norman: University of Oklahoma Press, 1966.

———. *Maya History and Religion.* University of Oklahoma Press, 1970.

Van Oss, C. Adriaan. *Catholic Colonialism: A Parish History of Guatemala, 1524–1821.* Cambridge, Eng.: Cambridge University Press, 1986.

Vigil, Ralph H. *Alonso de Zorita: Royal Judge and Christian Humanist, 1512–1585.* Norman and London: University of Oklahoma Press, 1987.

Villacorta Calderón, José Antonio. *Prehistoria e historia antigua de Guatemala.* Guatemala City: Tipografía Nacional, 1938.

West, Robert C., and John P. Augelli. *Middle America: Its Lands and Peoples.* Englewood Cliffs, N.J.: Prentice-Hall, 1966.

Westphall, Victor. *Mercedes Reales: Hispano Land Grants of the Upper Río Grande Region.* Albuquerque: University of New Mexico Press, 1983.

Whetten, Nathan L. *Guatemala, the Land and the People.* New Haven, Conn.: Yale University Press, 1961.

Whitaker, Arthur P., ed. *Latin America and the Enlightenment.* New York: D. Appleton-Century, 1942.

Whitten, D. G. A., and J. R. V. Brooks. *The Penguin Dictionary of Geology.* Harmondsworth, Middlesex, Eng.: Penguin Books, 1972.

Wolf, Eric. *Sons of the Shaking Earth: The People of Mexico and Guatemala—*

Their Land, History, and Culture. Chicago: University of Chicago Press, 1959.

Woodward, Ralph L., Jr. *Class Privilege and Economic Development: The Consulado de Comercio of Guatemala, 1793–1871.* Chapel Hill: University of North Carolina Press, 1966.

Zavala, Silvio. *Contribución a la historia de las instituciones coloniales en Guatemala.* México, D.F.: Colegio de México, 1945; Guatemala City: Universidad de San Carlos de Guatemala, 1967.

Zendegui, Guillermo de, ed. *Image of Guatemala.* Supplement to Americas Magazine. Washington, D.C.: General Secretariat of the Organization of American States, November-December 1972.

ARTICLES AND CHAPTERS

Araña, Tomás de. "Relación de los estragos y ruinas que ha de padecido la ciudad de Santiago de Guatemala, por los terremotos y fuego de sus volcanes, en este año de 1717." *Anales de la Sociedad de Geografía e Historia de Guatemala* 17 (1941): 148–60, 232–43.

Borhegyi, Stephen F. "The Miraculous Shrines of Our Lord of Esquipulas in Guatemala and Chimayó, New Mexico." *El Palacio* 60, no. 3 (March 1953): 83–111.

———. "The Cult of Our Lord of Esquipulas in Middle America and New Mexico." *El Palacio* 61, no. 12 (December 1954): 387–401.

———. "Settlement Patterns of the Guatemalan Highlands." In *Handbook of Middle American Indians,* vol. 2, pt. 1, 59–75 Austin: University of Texas Press, 1965.

Broussard, Ray F. "Bautista Antonelli: Architect of Caribbean Defense." *Historian* 50, no. 4 (August 1988): 507–520.

Brown, Vera L. "Contraband Trade: A Factor in the Decline of Spain's Empire in America." *Hispanic American Historical Review* 8, no. 2 (May 1928).

Cabezas, Horacio. "Creación de la Universidad de San Carlos de Guatemala y consolidación de los sistemas de explotación colonial." *Revista de Historia de América* 88 (July-December 1979): 155–65.

Engstrand, Iris H. W. "Mexico's Pioneer Naturalist and the Spanish Enlightenment." *Historian* 53, no. 1 (Autumn 1990): 17–32.

Estrada Monroy, Agustín. "Los primeros españoles que llegaron a Guatemala." *Anales de la Sociedad de Geografía e Historia de Guatemala* 41 (1968): 565–68.

Floyd, Troy S. "The Guatemalan Merchants, the Government, and the Provincianos, 1750–1800." *Hispanic American Historical Review* 41, no. 1 (February 1961): 90–110.

Klein, Herbert S. "Peasant Communities in Revolt: The Tzeltzal Republic of 1712." *Pacific Historical Review* 35 (1966): 247–63.

La Madrid, Lázaro. "Bishop Marroquín—Zumárraga's Gift to Central America." *The Americas* 5, no. 3 (January 1949): 331–41.

Lockhart, James. "Encomienda and Hacienda: The Evolution of the Great Estate in the Spanish Indies." *Hispanic American Historical Review* 49, no. 3 (August 1969): 411–29.

Lovell, W. George. "Disease and Depopulation in Early Colonial Guatemala." Chap. 2 in *"Secret Judgments of God": Old World Disease in Colonial Spanish America,* ed. Noble D. Cook and W. George Lovell. Norman and London: University of Oklahoma Press, 1991.

MacLeod, Murdo J. "Colonial Central America." In *The Caribbean: the Central American Area,* ed. Curtis P. Wilgus. Gainesville: University of Florida Press, 1961.

Markman, Sidney D. "Pueblos de españoles y pueblos de indios en el Reino de Guatemala." *Boletín del Centro de Investigaciones Históricas y Estéticas* (Caracas), no. 12 (November 1971), 76–97.

Molina Arguello, Carlos. "Gobernaciones, alcaldías mayores, y corregimientos en el Reino de Guatemala." *Anuario de Estudios Americanos* (Seville: Escuela de Estudios Hispano-Americanos), 17(1960): 105–32.

Pineda, Juan de. "Relación Pineda: Descripción de la Provincia de Guatemala (1594)." *Anales de la Sociedad de Geografía e Historia de Guatemala* 1 (1925): 327–63.

Sáenz de Santamaría, Gonzalo. "La conquista espiritual del reino de Guatemala." *Anuario de Estudios Americanos* (Seville: Escuela de Estudios Hispano-Americanos), 27 (1970): 61–108.

Sherman, William L. "A Conqueror's Wealth: Notes on the Estate of Don Pedro de Alvarado." *The Americas* 26, no. 2 (October 1969): 199–213.

———. "Indian Slavery and the Cerrato Reforms." *Hispanic American Historical Review* 51, no. 1 (February 1971): 25–50.

Simpson, Lesley Byrd. "A Seventeenth Century Encomienda: Chimaltenango, Guatemala." *The Americas* 15, no. 4 (April, 1959): 393–402.

Smith, Mary C. "Esquipulas." *Americas,* January 1979; 26–31.

Smith, Robert S. "Origins of the Consulado de Guatemala." *Hispanic American Historical Review* 26, no. 2 (May 1946):150–61.

———."Forced Labor in the Guatemalan Indigo Works." *Hispanic American Historical Review* 36, no. 3 (August 1956): 319–28.

————. "Indigo Production and the Trade in Colonial Guatemala." *Hispanic American Historical Review* 39, no. 2 (May 1959):181–211.

Solano Pérez-Lila, Francisco de. "La poblacíon indígena de Guatemala (1492–1800)." *Anuario de Estudios Americanos* (Seville: Escuela de Estudios Hispano-Americanos), 26 (1969): 279–355.

Solórzano, Juan Carlos. "La conquista de Centroamerica y el descrubrimiento de América." *Avances de investigación* (San Jose: Centro de Investigaciones Históricas, Universidad de Costa Rica), no. 30 (1987).

Van Oss, Adriaan Cornelis. "La población de América Central hacia 1800." *Anales de la Academia de Geografía e Historia de Guatemala* 55 (1981): 291–311.

Woodward, Ralph L., Jr. "The Guatemalan Merchants and National Defense, 1810." *Hispanic American Historical Review* 45, no. 2 (May 1965):452–62.

————. "Economic and Social Origins of the Guatemalan Political Parties (1773–1823)." *Hispanic American Historical Review* 45, no. 4 (November 1965): 544–66.

Woodward, Ralph L., Jr. "The Economy of Central America at the Close of the Colonial Period." *Estudios del Reino de Guatemala,* ed. Duncan Kinkead, 117–34. Seville: Escuela de Estudios Hispano-Americanos, 1985.

Wortman, Miles L. "Bourbon Reforms in Central America, 1750–1786." *The Americas* 32 (October 1975): 222–38.

DISSERTATIONS, THESES, UNPUBLISHED PAPERS

Jones, Oakah L. "Matías de Gálvez: Spanish Ally of the American Revolution." Paper delivered at biennial convention of Phi Alpha Theta, 30 December 1989, St. Louis, Mo.

Lutz, Christopher H. "Santiago de Guatemala, 1541–1773: The Sociodemographic History of a Spanish-American Colonial City." Ph.D. diss.; University of Wisconsin—Madison, 1976.

Meneray, Wilbur E. "The Kingdom of Guatemala during the Reign of Charles III, 1759–1788." Ph.D. diss. University of North Carolina, 1975.

Sherman, William L. "Indian Slavery in Spanish Guatemala, 1524–1550." Ph.D. diss., University of New Mexico, 1967.

Webre, Stephen A. "The Social and Economic Bases of Cabildo Membership in Seventeenth Century Santiago de Guatemala." Ph.D. diss., Tulane University, 1980.

Index

331